NORTON ANTHOLOGY OF
WESTERN MUSIC

Volume 1: Ancient to Baroque

SEVENTH EDITION

NORTON ANTHOLOGY OF
WESTERN MUSIC

Volume 1: Ancient to Baroque

SEVENTH EDITION

Edited by

J. PETER BURKHOLDER

and

CLAUDE V. PALISCA

W. W. NORTON & COMPANY
NEW YORK · LONDON

W. W. Norton & Company has been independent since its founding in 1923, when William Warder Norton and Mary D. Herter Norton first published lectures delivered at the People's Institute, the adult education division of New York City's Cooper Union. The firm soon expanded its program beyond the Institute, publishing books by celebrated academics from America and abroad. By mid-century, the two major pillars of Norton's publishing program—trade books and college texts— were firmly established. In the 1950s, the Norton family transferred control of the company to its employees, and today—with a staff of four hundred and a comparable number of trade, college, and professional titles published each year—W. W. Norton & Company stands as the largest and oldest publishing house owned wholly by its employees.

Director of Production, College: Jane Searle

Composition: David Botwinik

Manufacturing: Quad Graphics, Taunton, Massachussetts

ISBN 978-0-393-92161-8 (pbk.)

W. W. Norton & Company, Inc., 500 Fifth Avenue, New York, N.Y. 10110
wwnorton.com

W. W. Norton & Company Ltd., 15 Carlisle Street, London W1D 3BS

6 7 8 9 0

CONTENTS

THE RENAISSANCE

THE SEVENTEENTH CENTURY

MAKING CONNECTIONS:
How to Use This Anthology

The *Norton Anthology of Western Music* (NAWM) is a companion to *A History of Western Music*, Ninth Edition (HWM), and *Concise History of Western Music*, Fifth Edition (CHWM). It is also designed to stand by itself as a collection representing the most significant traditions, trends, genres, national schools, innovations, and historical developments in the history of music in Europe and the Americas.

The editions of the scores are the best available for which permission could be secured, including several editions especially prepared for NAWM. Where no publication or editor is cited, Claude V. Palisca or I have edited the music from the original source. All foreign-language texts are accompanied by English translations either in the score or immediately following it. Texts that follow the score are arranged to show their poetic form and feature translations by one or both coeditors, except where another translator is credited. Most translations are literal to a fault, corresponding to the original line by line, often word for word, to facilitate understanding of the ways the composer has set the text.

Each selection is followed by a detailed commentary, separate from the discussion of the piece in HWM or CHWM, that describes the piece's origins, points out its important features and stylistic traits, and addresses issues of performance practice, including any unusual aspects of notation.

Recordings

An anthology of musical scores is greatly enhanced by recordings. Excellent, authoritative recorded performances of all the items in NAWM are included on the *Norton Recorded Anthology of Western Music*. These recordings are available in a variety of formats, including a three-volume set of mp3 discs, corresponding to the three volumes of NAWM, and a Concise mp3 disc including 109 works that are featured in CHWM (indicated in NAWM by the icon concise). All of these recordings are also available online as part of Total Access, a suite of media resources that comes with every new copy of HWM and CHWM. In addition to recordings, Total Access includes listening quizzes for every item in NAWM and stunning Metropolitan Opera videos of a dozen of the operatic scenes in this anthology, from Gluck's *Orfeo ed Euridice* (NAWM 110) to John Adams's *Doctor Atomic* (219). The availability of a Metropolitan Opera video is indicated by a ▶ symbol at the end of a commentary.

Many of the recordings that accompany this anthology are new to this edition. The recordings feature some of the best performers and ensembles working today, alongside classic recordings from earlier generations. For music composed prior to 1780, the performers on the recordings use period instruments and seek to reflect the performance practice of the time, to the extent that we understand it today.

The recordings also include performances with period instruments for several works composed during the late eighteenth and nineteenth centuries, including symphonies by Haydn, Mozart, Beethoven, Berlioz, and Schumann and vocal works by Mendelssohn and Stephen Foster. The ragtime and jazz recordings all feature the original artists, and several of the twentieth- and twenty-first-century pieces appear in performances by the composer or by the performers for whom they were written. In many periods and genres, musicians were expected to improvise, embellish, or otherwise alter the written music, as evident in many of the performances on the accompanying recordings. When these or other discrepancies occur between score and recording, we have provided an explanation in the commentary.

To make it easier to coordinate listening with the study of the scores, timings have been added to the scores at major sections, themes, and other events in the music, especially those pointed out in the commentaries. Timings have also been added to texts and translations for many of the vocal works with multiple stanzas, repetitive forms, or long texts, to make it easier to listen while following the words rather than the score.

Why These Pieces?

We have aimed to include outstanding works that represent their makers, genres, and times. Only a small fraction of the music worthy of attention could be included, making it important for us to choose pieces that could accomplish several purposes at once. Knowing the thinking behind our choices will help students and teachers make the best use of this collection. The rest of this preface explains several of the themes that determined our selections.

Placing Music in Historical Context

The title *Norton Anthology of Western Music* needs one important qualifier: this is a historical anthology of the Western musical tradition. Rather than serve up great works to be studied in splendid isolation, this anthology seeks to place each piece in a historical context, relating it to the society from which it came and to other music that the composer used as model or inspiration. Studying music in its contexts can illuminate the choices composers made, the values of the society they lived in, and the meanings of the pieces themselves. Just as composers did not create in a musical void, standing aloof from their predecessors and contemporaries, so the historically oriented listener must have access to the primary material in order to establish connections. This anthology invites students and teachers to make such connections.

Breadth and Depth of Repertoire

Making connections depends on having a wide range of examples. The repertoire in this edition of NAWM is broader and more diverse than ever before.

Among the thirty-nine new additions, excerpts from J. S. Bach's *Well-Tempered Clavier* and *St. Matthew Passion* (NAWM 102 and 104), a complete string quartet and symphony by Haydn (118 and 119), the first movement of Mendelssohn's Violin Concerto (139), and choral works by Schubert (141) and Bruckner (157) enhance the already extensive coverage of major composers from the eighteenth and nineteenth centuries. The twentieth century is represented by over fifty selections, including new works by Strauss, Ravel, Weill, Villa-Lobos, Revueltas, Varèse, and Bernstein. For the first time, music from the twenty-first century is featured, with pieces by Saariaho, Golijov, Carter, Adams, and Higdon (216–220), each of which simultaneously extends a trend of the late twentieth century and harks back to music of an earlier era. Coverage of early music is expanded with motets by Petrus de Cruce (23), Vitry (25), and Gombert (50); secular songs by Machaut (27), Landini (31), Josquin (42), and Cara (55); an anthem by Tallis (48); a divertissement by Lully (85b); and instrumental pieces by Holborne (67), Byrd (69), Couperin (97c), and Telemann (99).

Women composers are represented across the centuries—in the twelfth century by Hildegard of Bingen (7) and Comtessa de Dia (9); in the seventeenth by Barbara Strozzi (77) and Elisabeth-Claude Jacquet de la Guerre (88); in the nineteenth by Fanny Mendelssohn Hensel (133), Clara Schumann (142), and Amy Beach (162); in the twentieth by Bessie Smith (182), Ruth Crawford Seeger (194), and Sofia Gubaidulina (213); and in the twenty-first by Kaija Saariaho (216) and Jennifer Higdon (220).

Music of Spain and Latin America is well represented, with a medieval cantiga (12), a Renaissance motet and mass (52a and b), a secular villancico (54), works for vihuela (68a and b), a South American Christmas villancico (91), the first opera composed and staged in the New World (90), a chamber aria by Brazil's Heitor Villa-Lobos (190), a symphonic homage by Mexico's Silvestre Revueltas (191), and a Passion by Argentine composer Osvaldo Golijov (217). The African American traditions of ragtime, blues, and jazz are included, with a Joplin rag (164), Bessie Smith's *Back Water Blues* (182), Louis Armstrong's rendition of *West End Blues* (183), Duke Ellington's *Cotton Tail* (184), and Charlie Parker and Dizzy Gillespie's *Anthropology* (197). Also here are classics of band literature, from Sousa (163) to Persichetti (199). The coverage of American and East European music is extensive, including works by sixteen composers from Eastern Europe and twenty-nine working in the United States.

Breadth of repertoire is matched by depth. Several composers are represented by more than one work to permit comparison of early and later styles (for example, Du Fay, Monteverdi, Beethoven, Schubert, Schoenberg, Stravinsky, Varèse, Cage, and Adams) and to show distinct approaches by a single composer to diverse genres (for example, Adam de la Halle, Machaut, Du Fay, Josquin, Byrd, Lassus, Bach, Handel, Pergolesi, Haydn, Mozart, Beethoven, Schubert, Schumann, Mendelssohn, and Brahms). Instead of relying solely on excerpts to give a taste of multimovement genres, NAWM includes complete examples of a Gregorian chant Mass, Baroque keyboard suite, Corelli trio sonata, Vivaldi concerto, Bach cantata, and Haydn string quartet and symphony to show how such works are constructed and what types of movements they contain. In the same spirit, complete scenes from operas by Monteverdi, Rameau, Handel, Mozart, Rossini, Meyerbeer, Weber, Verdi, Berg, Saariaho, and Adams demonstrate how differently these composers construct a scene.

Styles and Genres

Perhaps the primary role of a historical anthology is to present examples of the most important styles and genres in music history and to trace their development through time. The generally chronological organization of NAWM follows the order in which these selections are discussed in HWM. Volume 1 highlights changes in both style and genre from ancient Greece (1–2), medieval monophony (3–13), and early polyphony (14–24) through the fourteenth century (25–32); the first, middle, and later generations of Renaissance composers (33–38, 39–45, and 46–70); and the early, middle, and late Baroque period (71–84, 85–95, and 96–106). Volume 2 includes the Classic era (107–124) and the first and second halves of the nineteenth century (125–148 and 149–163). Volume 3 focuses on the twentieth century, divided by World War II (164–196 and 197–215), and the twenty-first century (216–220).

Genres, styles, conventions, and forms develop only because composers pick up ideas from each other and replicate or build on them in their own music, a process that can be observed again and again through the pieces in this anthology. The monophonic songs of the troubadours in southern France (8–9) inspired those of the trouvères in the north (10), Minnesinger in Germany (11), and cantiga composers in Spain (12). Later generations of poet-musicians, active in the fourteenth century, wrote polyphonic secular songs and codified standard forms for them, notably the French virelai (27 and 39), rondeau (28 and 35), and ballade (29 and 36) and the Italian madrigal, caccia, and ballata (30–32). In the Renaissance, new forms and styles of secular song emerged with the Spanish villancico (54), German Lied (41), Italian frottola and madrigal (55–59 and 71–72), and new types of song in French (42–43 and 60–62) and in English (63–65). In the nineteenth century, the song for voice and piano became the mainstay of home music-making, exemplified by the Lieder of Schubert and Schumann (128–130) and the parlor songs of Stephen Foster (131), but then splintered into two different traditions: art songs, like those of Fauré (159) and Ives (180), and popular songs, like those by Gershwin, Smith, and Oliver (181–183). Outgrowths of the art song include the orchestral song, such as Mahler's *Kindertotenlieder* (165), and the song for voice and chamber ensemble, as in Boulez's *Le marteau sans maître* (202).

Similar paths can be traced in religious music from Gregorian chant (3–5) to the modern style of Pärt (215); in Passions from J. S. Bach (104) to Golijov (217); and in opera from its creation in Italy (73–75) through its diffusion to other lands (76, 85, 89, and 90) and the many changes in style throughout the eighteenth (93, 98, 105, 107–110, and 124), nineteenth (145–154), twentieth (166, 174, 186, and 200), and twenty-first centuries (216 and 219). Exploring and explaining changes in these and other genres is a central theme of this anthology and of HWM and CHWM.

Musicians frequently use an old word to mean new things, so that the very nature of a genre may change. Through this anthology, the listener can follow the motet as it changes from a work that adds text to existing music (21a) to a new work based on chant (21c). It then acquires greater rhythmic diversity among the voices (22 and 23) and rich rhythmic patterning in the lowest voice (22), leading to the isorhythmic motets of Vitry (25). Next, the motet is redefined as a newly composed Latin sacred work with equal voices in works by Dunstable (34), Josquin (44), Gombert (50), Victoria (52a), and Lassus (53). Finally, the meaning of *motet* is broadened in the seventeenth century to embrace sacred works with instrumental accompaniment for any number of voices from one (79) to many (78 and 86). Even more surprising is the change in meaning of *concerto*, which in the early seventeenth century designated a work for voices and instruments, such as Schütz's sacred concertos (81), but came to mean a piece for one or more solo instruments with orchestra. The latter type is represented here by a Vivaldi violin concerto (96), illustrating the genre's first maturity in the late Baroque; piano concerto movements from the Classic era by J. C. Bach (117) and Mozart (122), showing the latter's debt to the former; Mendelssohn's Violin Concerto (139), representing the Romantic concerto; and Schnittke's Concerto Grosso No. 1 (214), a postmodern reinterpretation of a Baroque genre.

Similar chains of development can be seen in instrumental music. Dance music in the Middle Ages (13) and Renaissance (66–67) led to stylized dances of many types: songs in the form of dances, such as Dowland's *Flow, my tears* (65); independent pieces for keyboard or lute, including those by Gaultier (87), Chopin (134), and Dvořák (161); keyboard dance suites in the Baroque period, such as those by Jacquet de la Guerre (88) and François Couperin (97), a genre revived in the modern era by Ravel (168), Schoenberg (173), and others; and dance movements in other works, including Corelli's trio sonatas (94d) and symphonies from Haydn (119c) to Shostakovich (189). Ballets or dance episodes appear in operas, as in the scenes included here from Lully's *Armide* (85b), Gluck's *Orfeo ed Euridice* (110), and Berg's *Wozzeck* (174b). Stravinsky's *Rite of Spring* (176) and Copland's *Appalachian Spring* (195), known today primarily as orchestral works, were originally composed as dance music for ballets, as was Milhaud's *La création du monde* (185). More generally, dance rhythms infect many vocal and instrumental works, including the air in minuet rhythm from Lully's opera *Armide* (85c); Araujo's *Los coflades de la estleya* (91) and Torrejón y Velasco's *La púrpura de la rosa* (90), both full of Spanish dance rhythms; the aria in gigue rhythm in Scarlatti's cantata *Clori vezzosa, e bella* (92b); the sarabande-influenced aria from Handel's opera *Giulio Cesare* (105b); the waltzes in Schumann's *Carnaval* (132); Gottschalk's *Souvenir de Porto Rico* (137), suffused with rhythms from Latin American dances; and the seguidilla from Bizet's *Carmen* (152).

The canzonas of Gabrieli (70) and others established a tradition of extended instrumental works in several sections with contrasting meters, tempos, and moods, leading to the sonatas of Marini (84) and the multimovement sonatas of Corelli (94) and later composers. Out of this tradition grew the chamber music of Telemann (99); the string quartet, represented here by Haydn (118), Beethoven (127), Ruth Crawford Seeger (194), and George Crumb (205); string quintets, including Schubert's (141); and chamber works with piano, such as Clara Schumann's Piano Trio (142) and piano quintets by Brahms (156) and Amy Beach (162). The symphony grew from its Italian beginnings, represented by Sammartini (115), to become the major instrumental genre of the late eighteenth and nineteenth centuries, dominated by Austrian and German composers such as Stamitz (116), Haydn (119), Mozart (123), and Beethoven (126). Symphonists after Beethoven reinterpreted the tradition in varying ways, including Berlioz's programmatic *Symphonie fantastique* (138), reconceptions of form in Schumann's Fourth Symphony (140) and Tchaikovsky's *Pathétique* Symphony (160), and Brahms's embrace of the past in his Fourth Symphony (155).

The symphony was a continuing presence in the twentieth century, represented here by Webern (175), Stravinsky (177), Hindemith (187), Shostakovich (189), Still (196), and Persichetti (199).

Descriptive instrumental passages in opera, like Rameau's picture of a stormy sea in *Hippolyte et Aricie* (98), inspired composers to write instrumental music intended to convey a mood, character, scene, or story, as in the character pieces of Couperin (97), Schumann (132), Liszt (136), Gottschalk (137), Scriabin (170), Satie (171), and Cowell (193) and the orchestral tone poems and descriptive pieces by Strauss (158), Debussy (167), Penderecki (208), Adams (211), and Higdon (220).

As suggested by these descriptions, almost every genre has roots in an earlier one. Here is where the evolutionary metaphor so often applied to music history seems most applicable, tracing lines of development both within and among genres. This anthology provides ample material for making these connections.

Techniques

In addition to genres, composers often learn techniques from their contemporaries or predecessors and extend them in new ways. Compositional practices that start in one genre or tradition often cross boundaries over time. To give just one example, imitative counterpoint, developed in the medieval canon (24) and caccia (31), became a structural principle in Renaissance vocal music from the late fifteenth century through the early seventeenth century, illustrated by Busnoys's chanson *Je ne puis vivre* (39), Josquin's motet *Ave Maria . . . virgo serena* (44), and Weelkes's madrigal *As Vesta was* (64). The technique was brought into instrumental music through the canzona (70) and ricercare (83), and the latter developed into the fugue (95, 100, and 102). Fugal passages occur in many genres, from oratorios (106c and 143) to symphonies (123, 126, and 138), and imitation remains a device learned by every student of Western music.

Forms morph into new forms or combine with others. Binary form, invented for dance music (66a, 87, and 88), was used for abstract sonata movements by Corelli (94d), Domenico Scarlatti (113), and others and developed into sonata form as used in piano sonatas (114, 121, and 125), chamber works (118a, 141, 156, and 162), and symphonies (115, 116, 119a, 123, 126, and 140). A small binary form could also be expanded by serving as the theme for a movement in rondo form, as in the finales of Haydn's *Joke* String Quartet (118d) and Symphony No. 88 in G Major (119d). The elements of sonata form could in turn be combined with ritornello form in a concerto first movement (117 and 122) or with rondo form in a sonata-rondo, used often for finales (127b).

Styles also cross genres and traditions. Vocal music served as the basis for early instrumental works, like the intabulations and variations of Narváez (68). Moreover, the styles and gestures of vocal music have been imitated by instrumental composers again and again, including recitative and vocal monody in Marini's violin sonata (84), singing styles in piano sonatas by C. P. E. Bach (114) and Mozart (121), and bel canto operatic style in Chopin's nocturnes (135). Musicians cannot afford to know only the literature for their own instrument, because composers are constantly borrowing ideas from other repertoires, and performers need to know how to reflect these allusions to other styles in their performances.

Several selections document the influence of vernacular and traditional music on art music. Medieval English singers improvised polyphony with parallel thirds and sixths, which entered notated music in the thirteenth-century *Sumer is icumen in* (24), fifteenth-century carols (33), and the works of English composer John Dunstable (34) and exercised a profound influence on Continental composers such as Binchois (35) and Du Fay (37 and 38). Debussy adapted the texture and melodic idiom of Asian music to his own orchestral conception in *Nuages* (167). Satie borrowed from Parisian café music in *Embryons desséchés* (171). Stravinsky simulated Russian folk polyphony in *The Rite of Spring* (176). Bartók borrowed elements of Hungarian peasant song in *Staccato and Legato* (178) and Serbo-Croatian song and Bulgarian dance styles in his *Music for Strings, Percussion and Celesta* (179). Milhaud's *La création du monde* (185) and Weill's *Die Dreigroschenoper* (186) draw on jazz and blues, and Still's *Afro-American Symphony* (196) incorporates the twelve-bar blues, the African American spiritual, and instrumental sounds from jazz. Sheng makes the cellist imitate the sounds and playing styles of Chinese instruments in his *Seven Tunes Heard in China* (209), and Villa-Lobos, Revueltas, and Golijov combine styles and rhythms from Latin America with European genres and techniques. Influences also go the other way; Foster's *Jeanie with the Light Brown Hair* (131) includes a brief cadenza, an idea borrowed from opera, and "Cool" from Bernstein's Broadway musical *West Side Story* (198) mixes fugue and twelve-tone technique with elements of pop, bebop, and cool jazz styles.

Twentieth-century composers have introduced a constant stream of innovations, and this anthology includes a number of pioneering works. Notable are Schoenberg's *Pierrot lunaire* (172), his most famous atonal piece and the first to use Sprechstimme; his Piano Suite (173), the first complete twelve-tone work; Webern's Symphony (175), a model of *Klangfarbenmelodie* and pointillism; Stravinsky's *Rite of Spring* (176), whose propulsive rhythm and block construction influenced so many later composers; Varèse's *Hyperprism* (192) and *Poème électronique* (206), which reconceive music as sound masses moving through space; Cowell's *The Banshee* (193), based on new sounds produced by playing directly on the strings of a piano; Ruth Crawford Seeger's *String Quartet 1931* (194), whose novel approach to counterpoint made it a classic of the American experimentalist tradition; Cage's *Sonatas and Interludes* (203) for prepared piano and *Music of Changes* (204), one of the first pieces composed using chance operations; Boulez's *Le marteau sans maître* (202), which extends serialism to duration and dynamics; Crumb's *Black Angels* (205), full of new sounds from an electrified string quartet; Babbitt's *Philomel* (207), an early example of combining a live singer with electronic music on tape; Penderecki's *Threnody* (208), which produces novel clusters of sound from a string orchestra; Adams's *Short Ride in a Fast Machine* (211), which applies minimalist techniques to create a gradually changing canvas of sound; and Ligeti's *Vertige* (212), an exercise in micropolyphony.

Learning from History

Besides learning from their contemporaries and immediate predecessors, many composers have reached back across the centuries to revive old methods or genres, often producing something remarkably new in the process. Inspired by the ancient Greek idea of suiting music to the rhythm and mood of the words, illustrated here by the *Epitaph of Seikilos* (1), Renaissance composers sought to capture the accents and feelings of the text, evident in motets by Josquin (44) and Lassus (53), in the new genre of the madrigal (56–59, 64, and 71–72), and in the *musique mesurée* of Le Jeune (62). Among the tools Renaissance composers borrowed from ancient Greek music and music theory was chromaticism, found in Euripides' *Orestes* (2); after madrigal composers like Rore (57), Marenzio (58), and Gesualdo (59) used it as an expressive device, it became a common feature in instrumental music as well, such as in Frescobaldi's chromatic ricercare (83), and later composers from Bach (100–101) to Wagner (149) made it an increasingly central part of the musical language. In a classic example of creating something really new by reaching into the distant past, the attempt to revive the principles of ancient Greek tragedy led to the invention of opera and recitative in Peri's *Euridice* (73).

Romantic and modern composers have often sought to revive the spirit of earlier music. Recollections of Baroque music include Beethoven's fugue in his String Quartet in C♯ Minor (127a), Brahms's chaconne in the finale of his Fourth Symphony (155), Schoenberg's passacaglia in *Nacht* from *Pierrot lunaire* (172a), and evocations of J. S. Bach's music by Villa-Lobos (190), Sheng (209), and Golijov (217). Bruckner's *Virga Jesse* (157) combines elements of Renaissance motet style with Romantic harmony. Webern's twelve-tone Symphony (175) contains elaborate canons modeled on those of the Renaissance, and Reich's *Tehillim* (210) reconciles canons with minimalist procedures. Messiaen borrowed the isorhythmic techniques of Vitry (25) and Machaut (26a) in his *Quartet for the End of Time* (201), and Saariaho's *L'amour de loin* (216) evokes the lament of a medieval troubadour in the modernist style of spectral music.

Reworkings

In addition to drawing on general styles, genres, and techniques, composers have often reworked particular compositions, a process that can be traced through numerous examples in this anthology. In one notable case, a single chant gave rise to a chain of polyphonic accretions. *Viderunt omnes* (3d) was elaborated by Leoninus and colleagues in an organum for two voices (17), which in turn was refreshed by his successors with new clausulae (18) that substituted for certain passages in the original setting. His younger colleague Perotinus composed a four-voice organum on the same chant (19). Meanwhile, anonymous musicians fitted words to the upper parts of some of the clausulae, creating the new genre of the motet (21a). Later composers borrowed the tenor line of a clausula (21b) or a passage from the original *Viderunt omnes* chant (21c and 22) and added new voices to create ever more elaborate motets.

NAWM contains many other instances in which composers reworked existing music into new pieces, a recurring thread in music history. Anonymous medieval church musicians added monophonic tropes (6) to the chant *Puer natus* (3a) and developed early types of polyphony that add other voices to a chant (14–15). Machaut based the Kyrie of his *La Messe de Nostre Dame* (26a) on the chant *Kyrie Cunctipotens Genitor* (3b) and the Gloria (26b) on a chant Gloria (a variant of 3c). Many Renaissance composers wrote masses that rework existing models using a fascinating variety of methods, including Du Fay's cantus-firmus mass based on his own polyphonic ballade *Se la face ay pale* (38a and b), Josquin's paraphrase mass on the chant hymn *Pange lingua* (45), and Victoria's imitation mass on his own motet *O magnum mysterium* (52a and b). Du Fay elaborated a Gregorian hymn in fauxbourdon style (37), and Luther recast another chant hymn (46a) as a Reformation chorale (46b), later used by J. S. Bach as the basis for a cantata (103). Luther's chorale *Ein feste Burg* (46c) was set in four parts by Johann Walter (46d), one of over a hundred reworkings of that famous tune. J. S. Bach's setting of *Durch Adams Fall* (101) exemplifies an entire genre of chorale preludes for organ, and his *St. Matthew Passion* includes a chorale (104e) whose tune was taken from a secular Renaissance song set by Isaac (41).

Such elaborations of existing material are not confined to religious music. Narváez's *Cancion Milles regres* (68a) is a reworking for vihuela of Josquin's chanson *Mille regretz* (43), and Byrd's *John come kiss me now* (69) offers sixteen variations for keyboard of a popular song of his day. Gottschalk's *Souvenir de Porto Rico* (137) uses a melody of Puerto Rican street musicians. Berlioz's *Symphonie fantastique* (138) and Crumb's *Black Angels* (205) both borrow phrases from the Gregorian chant *Dies irae*. Luther's *Ein feste Burg* (46c) makes a dramatic appearance in Meyerbeer's opera *Les Huguenots* (147) as a symbol of the Reformation. Puccini borrowed two Japanese songs to depict his title character in *Madama Butterfly* (151), and identified her American husband with *The Star-Spangled Banner*. The Coronation scene from Musorgsky's *Boris Godunov* (153) incorporates a Russian folk song, and Stravinsky's *Rite of Spring* (176) uses several. The repeating bass figure in the chaconne finale of Brahms's Fourth Symphony (155) is adapted from a chaconne movement of a Bach cantata. The theme of the finale of Beach's Piano Quintet (162) is modeled on a theme from Brahms's Piano Quintet (156). Ives's *General William Booth Enters into Heaven* (180) is based on a hymn tune and quotes a drum pattern and a minstrel show song. Both Ellington's *Cotton Tail* (184) and Parker and Gillespie's *Anthropology* (197) borrow the harmonic progression from the chorus of Gershwin's song *I Got Rhythm* (181). Copland's *Appalachian Spring* (195) includes variations on a Shaker hymn, and the first movement of Sheng's *Seven Tunes Heard in China* (209) varies the melody of a Chinese song.

Improvisation

Improvisation has been part of the Western tradition since ancient times. Every type of medieval organum (14–19) was an improvisatory practice before it was a written one. Singers and instrumentalists from the Renaissance to the early nineteenth century often improvised ornaments and embellishments to decorate the written music, as represented on many of the recordings that accompany this anthology. Lutenists and keyboard players demonstrated their skill through elaborate improvisations, exploring a mode or introducing another work; from these developed the written tradition of the toccata and prelude, represented by examples from Frescobaldi (82), Jacquet de la Guerre (88a), Buxtehude (95), and J. S. Bach (100a and 102a). Part of the individuality of the keyboard music of C. P. E. Bach (114), Schumann (132), Hensel (133), Chopin (135), Liszt (136), Rachmaninoff (169), and Scriabin (170) derives from textures or passages that sound improvisatory, however carefully calculated they may be. The invention of sound recording has made possible the preservation of improvisations them-selves, which are a fundamental part of the blues and jazz tradition, represented here in the recordings of Scott Joplin and Jelly Roll Morton playing Joplin's *Maple Leaf Rag* (164a and b), Bessie Smith's blues (182), Louis Armstrong's performance on King Oliver's *West End Blues* (183b), Ben Webster's solo in Ellington's *Cotton Tail* (184), and Charlie Parker's solo in *Anthropology* (197).

Reception

Certain pieces won a place in this anthology because contemporary critics or the composers themselves singled them out. A legend developed that when some Catholic leaders sought to ban polyphonic music from church services, Palestrina saved it by composing his *Pope Marcellus Mass* (51). Giovanni Maria Artusi attacked Monteverdi's *Cruda Amarilli* (71) in his 1600 treatise, provoking a spirited and now famous defense from Monteverdi. Caccini wrote that *Vedrò 'l mio sol* (72) was one of his pioneering attempts to write a new type of solo song. Cesti's *Intorno all'idol mio* (76b) was one of the most frequently cited arias of the mid-seventeenth century. Athanasius Kircher praised the final scene of Carissimi's *Jephte* (80) as a triumph of the powers of musical expression. Jean-Jacques Rousseau roundly criticized and Jean le Rond d'Alembert carefully analyzed Lully's monologue in *Armide, Enfin il est en ma puissance* (85c). Pergolesi's *La serva padrona* (107) was a hit with the public in Italy and provoked a battle between critics in France, and his *Stabat mater* (111) was one of the most widely praised and performed works of religious music from its time. The opening chorus of Haydn's *The Creation* (120) was hailed as the height of the sublime in music. The first movement of Beethoven's *Eroica* Symphony (126) and Stravinsky's *The Rite of Spring* (176) were both objects of critical uproars after their premieres. Britten's *Peter Grimes* (200) was the first English opera to win international acclaim in over two centuries, and Higdon's *blue cathedral* (220) has been one of the most frequently performed new pieces of orchestral music in the past twenty-five years. The reactions to these compositions are exemplars of "reception history," a field that has attracted considerable attention among teachers and historians.

Relation to Politics

Finally, musical influences are not the only connections that can be made among these pieces. For example, many grew out of a specific political context, and studying the ways those links are reflected in the music can be illuminating. Walther von der Vogelweide's *Palästinalied* (11) is a crusade song, celebrating the Christian warriors from Western Europe who sought to wrest the Holy Land from the Muslims. *Fole acostumance/Dominus* (21b) attacks hypocrisy and deception in the church and in French politics. Du Fay's *Resvellies vous* (36) and Peri's *Euridice* (73) were both written for aristocratic weddings, and many other works in NAWM were composed for royal or aristocratic patrons. Indeed, Lully's operas and church music (85–86) were part of a political program to glorify King Louis XIV of France and centralize his power through the arts. Gay's *The Beggar's Opera* (109) spoofed social norms by taking a criminal as its hero. Beethoven originally dedicated his *Eroica* Symphony (126) to Napoleon, whom he saw as the embodiment of republican ideals, then tore up the dedication when Napoleon named himself emperor. Political commentary is a recurrent theme in twentieth-century music, including Berg's appeal for better treatment of the poor in *Wozzeck* (174), Weill's satire of social class structure in *Die Dreigroschenoper* (186), Britten's condemnation of social ostracism in *Peter Grimes* (200), Crumb's reflections on the Vietnam War in *Black Angels* (205), and Penderecki's memorial for the first victims of nuclear war (208). Sometimes the role of politics is unclear, even if inescapable; musicians and critics are still trying to puzzle out the intended meanings of Hindemith's *Symphony Mathis der Maler* (187) written in Germany during the Nazi era, and Shostakovich's Fifth Symphony (189), composed in the Soviet Union during the height of Stalin's repression.

Your Turn

All of these and many other potential connections can be made through the works in this anthology. But they remain unrealized until you, the reader, make them real for yourself. We invite you to study each piece for what it shares with others as well as for its own distinctive qualities. You will encounter much that is unfamiliar, perhaps including pieces you will grow to love and others that may never suit your tastes. At the end, the goal is to understand as much as possible about why those who created this music made the choices they did, and how each piece represents a genre, style, trend, and time that played an important role in our long and ever-changing tradition of Western music.

—*J. Peter Burkholder*
February 2014

ACKNOWLEDGMENTS

The creative efforts of many people are represented in these pages. W. W. Norton and I appreciate the individuals and publishers cited in the source notes who granted permission to reprint or adapt material under copyright. I am especially grateful to John Hajdu Heyer for his edition of Lully's *Te Deum*, to Edward H. Roesner for his edition of *Viderunt omnes* by Leoninus and colleagues, and to Rebecca A. Baltzer for her editions of *Factum est salutare/Dominus* and *Fole acostumance/Dominus* and her editorial revisions of Adam de la Halle's *De ma dame vient/Dieus, comment porroie/Omnes*, which were prepared specifically for NAWM. Thomas J. Mathiesen kindly provided phonetic transliterations of the Greek poetry and new engravings of the music for NAWM 1 and 2. David Botwinik contributed the beautiful layout and elegantly typeset several items that were not reproduced from existing editions. Laura Dallman typeset the first movement of Persichetti's *Symphony for Band* (NAWM 199), and Nathan Landes scanned several new selections. Daniel T. Rogers researched the background to each of the works added to this edition. I had assistance in writing several of the commentaries on new items, from Laura Dallman (NAWM 67, 69, 168, 186, 190, 191, 199, and 220), Harry Haskell (157, 159, and 216–218), Nathan Landes (206), and Amanda Sewell (219). Katherine Baber offered ideas for the commentary on *West Side Story* (198). Lewis Lockwood and Alan Gosman generously provided portions of their edition of Beethoven's *Eroica* sketchbook prior to publication (126). Daniel R. Melamed provided helpful editorial comments on commentaries for the new Telemann and Bach items (99, 102, and 104) and drafted some of the text for the last, on *Erbarme dich*. Giuliano Di Bacco and Michael Long helped with Italian and Latin translations for new medieval items (25 and 31). I am deeply indebted to all of them for their assistance.

Members of the Editorial Advisory Board for HWM—Michael Alan Anderson, Arved Ashby, Gregory Barnett, James A. Borders, Mauro Calcagno, Drew Edward Davies, Andrew Dell'Antonio, Charles Dill, Don Fader, Andrew Flory, Rebecca L. Gerber, Jonathan Gibson, Robert O. Gjerdingen, David Grayson, Helen M. Greenwald, James Grier, Karen Henson, D. Kern Holoman, Steven Johnson, Lewis Lockwood, Michael P. Long, Melanie Lowe, Rebecca Maloy, Michael Marissen, Mary Sue Morrow, Margaret Notley, Gretchen Peters, Heather Platt, Hilary Poriss, John Rice, Margaret Rorke, Jesse Rosenberg, Stephanie P. Schlagel, Carl B. Schmidt, W. Anthony Sheppard, Christopher J. Smith, Larry Starr, Pamela F. Starr, Russell Stinson, Susan Youens, Charles Youmans, and Laurel Zeiss—made very helpful suggestions, from choice of repertoire to details in the commentaries. Bryan Christian, Barbara Russano Hanning, Ralph Locke,

Massimo Ossi, William F. Prizer, Kristen Strandberg, Michael Strasser, Charles Whitman, Natalie Williams, and many other colleagues, students, and friends offered ideas and useful corrections. Over three hundred instructors provided extensive feedback about the previous edition and suggestions for changes. Their help has made this a much better anthology, and I am very grateful.

Assembling the recordings was an especially complex task. I began with an initial list, matching editions to recordings wherever possible. Roger Hickman found other high-quality recordings. He also worked with Ronnie Thomas from Naxos to ensure that the mastering of each recording was precise. Randall Foster, licensing director of Naxos, oversaw the production of the recordings and, with the assistance of his staff, negotiated a license for each track—a laborious and complicated effort. Their enthusiastic work brought the recordings to fruition, and I greatly appreciate their contributions.

In addition, I remain indebted to the many people who assisted in preparing the previous editions, especially John Anderies, Rika Asai, Katherine Baber, David N. Baker, Nicole Baker, Jonathan Bellman, Jane A. Bernstein, Geoffrey Block, Ira L. Braus, Michael Broyles, Anna Maria Busse Berger, Catherine J. Cole, Vincent Corrigan, Felix O. Cox, Richard Crawford, Stephen A. Crist, Drew Edward Davies, Luis Dávila, Andrew Dell'Antonio, Charles Dill, Matthew Dirst, Cathy Ann Elias, Paul Elliott, Margot Fassler, Kristine Forney, James Franklin, Jonathan Gibson, Jonathan Glixon, Halina Goldberg, Robert A. Green, James Grier, Bruce Gustafson, Barbara Russano Hanning, Kunio Hara, Stephen E. Hefling, Jan Herlinger, Roger Hickman, Robert Hopkins, Steven Huebner, David R. Hurley, Steven Johnson, Jeffrey Kallberg, William Kinderman, Gesa Kordes, Dennis Leclaire, Luiz Fernando Lopes, Melanie Lowe, Kathryn Lowerre, Claudia Macdonald, Jeffrey Magee, Roberta Montemorra Marvin, Alan Matheson, Thomas J. Mathiesen, Daniel Melamed, Alison Mero, David Metzer, Felicia Miyakawa, Kevin N. Moll, Margaret Murata, Russell E. Murray, Jessie Ann Owens, Heather Platt, William F. Prizer, Brent C. Reidy, Samuel Rosenberg, Ann Shaffer, Alexander Silbiger, Jeremy L. Smith, Rex Sprouse, Pamela F. Starr, Derek Stauff, Scott Stewart, Kristen Strandberg, R. Larry Todd, Patrick Warfield, Stephen A. Willier, Travis Yeager, Christopher Young, and Neal Zaslow. Their contributions continue to enhance this new edition.

It has been a pleasure to work with the staff at W. W. Norton. Justin Hoffman oversaw and coordinated the entire NAWM project, facilitated communication between all of the project's contributors, offered encouragement, and made the schedule work when I fell behind. Courtney Hirschey copyedited the entire manuscript and suggested numerous improvements. Kathleen Karcher contacted rights holders and secured permissions for the works in the anthology. Barbara Curialle proofread, making further refinements to the text, and Pamela Lawson project edited, cheerfully tolerating my last minute revisions. Nicole Schilder scanned scores for new selections, and Jane Searle oversaw production of both NAWM and HWM. Maribeth Anderson Payne, music editor, has been a constant source of ideas and enthusiasm for NAWM as well as HWM, and her careful scrutiny of the commentaries helped make them clearer and more accurate. I cannot thank them all enough for their skill, dedication, care, and counsel.

Thanks finally but most of all to my family, especially my parents Donald and Jean Burkholder, who introduced me to the love of music; Bill, Joanne, and Sylvie Burkholder, whose enthusiasm renewed my own; and P. Douglas McKinney, whose patient support and encouragement have sustained me through three editions over more than a dozen years. My father passed away as I was preparing this edition. He never learned to play an instrument but loved to listen to music, especially the classics from Bach through Bartók. During my more than thirty years as a music historian, knowing he would read and share with others everything I wrote about music, I have always written with him in mind, trying to make my writing clear and accessible not only to scholars and students but to him and all lovers of music. It is a habit too ingrained to break. I miss him, but his spirit is still with me and on every page of this anthology.

—*J. Peter Burkholder*
February 2014

PITCH DESIGNATIONS

In this anthology, a note referred to without regard to its octave register is designated by a capital letter (A). A note in a particular octave is designated in italics, using the following system:

C to B

c to b

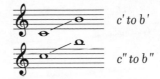

c′ to b′

c″ to b″

In this anthology, a unit refers to an orchestral system in which a low-register C is designated by a capital letter C (...). Notes in particular octaves are represented in relation to this by the following table:

Epitaph of Seikilos

Song (epigram)

FIRST CENTURY C.E.

Hoson zis phenou
miden holos su lupou
pros oligon esti to zin
to telos ho chronos apeti.

As long as you live, be lighthearted.
Let nothing trouble you.
Life is only too short,
and time takes its toll.

The *Epitaph of Seikilos* is a brief song inscribed on a tombstone dating from the first century c.e. (Common Era, equivalent to A.D.). Originally erected in southwestern Turkey, near the modern city of Aydin, the round stone column (shown in Figure 1.10 in HWM, p,18) is now in the National Museum in Copenhagen. The opening lines of the inscription make clear the purpose of the stone:

> I am a tombstone, an icon. Seikilos placed me here as an everlasting sign of deathless remembrance.

The poem that follows is an *epigram*, a short verse that makes a pointed remark, often by wittily juxtaposing contrasting ideas. Here we are encouraged to be cheerful, not in spite of death and the ravages of time but, ironically, because of them. The ethos of the epigram is one of moderation between extremes. The inscription ends with two lines whose meaning is uncertain but which appear to ascribe the poem and perhaps the music to Seikilos.

Above the words of the epigram are letters and other symbols representing pitches in Greek notation. Above these symbols are signs indicating durations. The score included here shows the original notation above the modern transcription with the Greek text and a phonetic transliteration.

The clear rhythmic notation has made this song of particular interest to historians. The notes without rhythmic markings above the alphabetical signs are worth one unit of duration (*protos chronos*), rendered in the transcription as an eighth note. The horizontal dash (—) indicates a *diseme*, worth two units, and the horizontal dash with an upward stroke to the right is a *triseme*, worth three. Note that the duration indicated is that of the syllable, not of the pitch, so that a *diseme* may include two pitches (as in the second line) and the *triseme* one, two, or three (as at the end of each line).

It is possible to transcribe the piece into modern notation using tables given by Alypius in his *Introductio musica*, probably compiled in the late fourth or fifth century c.e. Alypius presented the letter notations for fifteen *tonoi*, each of which places the sequence of intervals in the Greater Perfect System in a specific range (see HWM, p. 16). There are two sets of letters for each tonos—one for vocal pitches and the other for instruments. The *Epitaph of Seikilos* uses the vocal notes of the diatonic Iastian tonos, conventionally transcribed as the two-octave scale from *B* to *b'* with two sharps:

The music reflects the text in several important ways. Most obvious, the four lines of poetry are set to four distinct musical phrases, each the same length (twelve units of time) and each closing with a triseme preceded by another long duration. The Greek language had long and short syllables; all the long syllables in the epitaph are set to long durations, so that the music follows the rhythms of the text. Each phrase begins with a rising gesture up to *e'* and then falls to a cadence, paralleling the inflections of speech. The gradual descent through an octave in the final phrase creates a strong sense of closure.

The Iastian tonos is consistent with the moderate ethos of the epigram, balanced between two extremes. In Alypius's arrangement of the fifteen tonoi, the Iastian is number 7, intermediate between the lowest, Hypodorian, and the highest, Hyperlydian. The use of the diatonic genus is also appropriate for an ethos of moderation because it avoids the more extreme emotions associated with the chromatic and enharmonic genera.

The melody is restricted to the central octave from *e* to *e'*. The octave species is the one called Phrygian by Cleonides, with a succession of whole and half steps equivalent to the octave from D to D on the white keys of a piano. The high and low notes receive special emphasis—*e'* as the topmost pitch in all four phrases and *e* as the last note in the piece. The notes *a* and *c♯'* are also prominent as the most frequent notes (each occurs eight times) and the notes used to begin phrases. Today and perhaps also then, the major thirds that begin or end the last three phrases would be perceived as bright, as would the rising fifth at the opening. These bright intervals cast the message of the poem in a somewhat optimistic light.

This melody is interesting also because it conforms closely to Greek theoretical writings on melody. It uses patterns described by theorists such as Cleonides and Aristides Quintilianus: repeating notes, as in the first and fourth phrases; moving up or down the scale, as in the second phrase; and repeating the same interval succession a step lower or higher, as at the end of the third phrase (*c♯'–a, b–g*) and the beginning of the fourth (*a–c♯', b–d'*). Subtle melodic resemblances link each phrase to the next. For example, the last four notes of the first phrase are echoed at the beginning of the second; the second and third phrases end with the same three notes and rhythms; and the third and fourth phrases begin with similar contours. Like the poem, the music is more complex and intriguing than it may appear at first hearing.

Although there is no indication of an accompaniment, a singer would likely have accompanied himself or herself on a lyre or other plucked string instrument, perhaps playing the melody in unison with the voice or sounding the *a*, *e*, or other prominent notes. On the accompanying recording, the melody is first played on the lyre, then sung in unison with the lyre. Poetry that was accompanied by a lyre (or by another plucked string instrument) was known as *lyric poetry*, which in later centuries became a term for relatively brief poems in regular meter that express a feeling or personal viewpoint, as this poem does.

Euripides (CA. 485–CA. 406 B.C.E.)

Orestes: Stasimon chorus

Greek tragedy

408 B.C.E.

κατολοφ]ύ - ρο - μαι   ἰ   μα - τέ - ρος   [αἷμα σᾶς
ka-to-lo-phi - ro - me   ma - te - ros   hema sas

ὅ σ' ἀναβα]κ - χεύ - ει   ἰ   ὁ   μέ - γας   [ὄλβος οὐ
hos' a-na-bak - cheu - i   ho   me - gas   hol-bos ou

μόνιμο]ς   ἐμ   βρο - τοῖς   ἰ   ἀ - νὰ [δὲ λαῖφος ὥς
monimos   em   bro - tis   a - na   de lephos hos

τι]ς ἀ - κά - του   θο - ᾶς   τι - νά[-ξας δαίμων
tis a - ka - tou   tho - as   ti - na -xas de - mon

κατ - έκ - λυ - σεν   δ[εινῶν
kat - ek - li - sen   di - non

πόνω]ν   ω - ὡς πόντ[ου
po - non   ho - os   pontou

[text uncertain]

Vienna, Österreichische Nationalbibliothek, Papyrus G2315 (for photograph, see HWM, p. 19, Figure 1.11).
Transcription of fragment from Thomas J. Mathiesen, *Apollo's Lyre: Greek Music and Music Theory in Antiquity and the Middle Ages* (Lincoln: University of Nebraska Press, 1999), 117–18. Reprinted by permission of the University of Nebraska Press. © 1999 by the University of Nebraska Press. For a detailed analysis, see ibid., pp. 117–20. Phonetic transliteration by Thomas J. Mathiesen. © 2001 by Thomas J. Mathiesen. Used by permission.

katolophirome   materos hema sas
hos' anabakcheui   ho megas holbos ou
monimos em brotis   ana de lephos hos
tis akatou thoas   tinaxas demon
kateklisen   dinon
ponon   hoos pontou

You wild goddesses who dart across the
skies seeking vengeance for murder, we
implore you to free Agamemnon's son
from his aging fury. We grieve for this boy.
Happiness is brief among mortals. Sorrow
and anguish sweep down on it like a swift
gust of wind on a sloop, and it sinks under
the tossing seas.

A small scrap of papyrus dating from the third century B.C.E. (shown in Figure 1.11 in HWM, p. 19) contains seven lines of a chorus from *Orestes* by the great Greek playwright Euripides, with musical notation above the words. The tragedy has been dated 408 B.C.E. It seems likely that the music was composed by Euripides himself, who was renowned for his musical settings, but we cannot be certain. This fragment of Greek music is centuries older than the *Epitaph of Seikilos* (NAWM 1) but is presented second here because it poses greater difficulties in reading and reconstructing the music.

Only the center of each line of text and music survives on the papyrus. The missing words can be restored from other copies of the play and are printed in brackets in this transcription. However, this papyrus is the only extant source for the music, and many of the notes are missing. Any performance of the piece must be a reconstruction, conjecturing what the absent notes might have been. The recordings that accompany this anthology include two very different reconstructions, both based on the assumption that the missing segments of melody probably resembled the notes set to parallel portions of other lines of the text.

In a Greek tragedy, the chorus plays an important role, witnessing and commenting on the events of the drama. This song is a *stasimon*, an ode the chorus sings while standing still in their place in the *orchestra*, a semicircular rim between the stage and the benches of the spectators. In this stasimon, the women of Argos implore the gods to have mercy on Orestes, who murdered his mother Clytemnestra six days before the play begins. He had plotted with his sister Electra to punish their mother for infidelity to their father, Agamemnon. The chorus begs that Orestes be released from the madness that has overwhelmed him since the murder.

The dochmiac rhythm—six syllables in the pattern short-short-short long-short-long—suffuses the poetry and predominates in the music. The dochmiac rhythm was often used in Greek tragedy for passages of intense agitation and grief, so it is perfectly suited to this moment in the play.

Contemporary descriptions of Euripides' music noted that he had a complex, somewhat disjunct melodic style in which the pitch contour and rhythm sometimes departed from the natural contour and rhythm of the text. This characterization fits this melody, which jumps back and forth between a lower and a higher range and includes some rhythmic symbols that modify the textual rhythm.

Plutarch credited Euripides with helping to introduce the chromatic genus into tragedy, and that is also apparent in this melody. The notation indicates a mixture of the diatonic and the chromatic (or possibly the enharmonic) genera. The vocal melody moves in the range g to g', combining diatonic tetrachords on e–f–g–a and e'–f'–g'–a' with a chromatic tetrachord on a–$b\flat$–$b\natural$–d'. This combination exemplifies both Euripides' fondness for chromaticism and his preference for complexity, which tend to confirm him as the composer. Moreover, the chromaticism combines with the dochmaic rhythm to convey the anguish of the chorus at this moment in the drama.

As noted above, it is possible to read the notation as indicating the enharmonic genus (which uses quarter tones) rather than the chromatic. The transcription shown here and the first of the two performances on the recordings render the small intervals as chromatic; the second performance renders them as enharmonic (the notes shown here as $B\flat$ are lowered a quarter tone, and B is lowered to $B\flat$), producing quite a different effect. The chromatic performance is sung by a unison male chorus. In the enharmonic performance, a female singer (a soloist standing in for the chorus) is accompanied by an aulos (the double-reed instrument of the Greeks) playing in unison with the voice but also holding drones against it. Auloi were used to accompany Greek tragedy, but their precise function is unclear.

Certain musical symbols in this setting are not associated with syllables of text. The transcription and the chromatic performance on the recordings interpret these as notes for instruments, which had their own letter notation. The sign transcribed here as high g' may simply indicate a break between lines of text and is omitted in the enharmonic performance. But the $f\sharp$–b figure in lines 5 and 6 is clearly intended for instruments, read as an interjection between lines in the chromatic performance and as a change of drone in the enharmonic.

Mass for Christmas Day

Gregorian chant Mass

3

Christmas (from "Christ-Mass"), known more formally as the feast of the Nativity of Our Lord, celebrates the birth of Jesus. It is one of the most important days in the entire Christian church year, second only to Easter. To mark its great significance, there are three Masses: the first at midnight, as part of the vigil that precedes the holy day itself; the second at dawn; and the third mid-morning, at the usual time for Mass (after the Office service Terce, sung around 9 A.M.). This is the third. Later that day, at sunset, the Vespers service excerpted in NAWM 4 is celebrated.

A Gregorian chant Mass includes a variety of elements—some sung, some in-toned, and some spoken. Included here are only the portions of the Mass for Christmas Day that are sung by the choir. Some of these, the Proper chants (Introit, Gradual, Alleluia, Offertory, and Communion), have texts and melodies that are unique to this day in the church calendar. The others, the Ordinary chants (Kyrie, Gloria, Credo, Sanctus, Agnus Dei, and Ite, missa est), have texts that are sung in all or most Masses, but each Ordinary text has many musical settings. Beginning in the thirteenth century, Ordinary chants were organized into cycles with one mu-sical setting for each text in the Ordinary except the Credo. The edition included here is from the *Liber usualis*, a book of prayers, lessons, and chants for the Roman Catholic services of the Mass and the Office that was first issued in 1896 by the Benedictine monks of Solesmes, France. This cycle is numbered IV in the *Liber usualis*, and the Credo—one of the oldest—is numbered I.

The various elements of the Mass were added at different times, so each has its own history. Neither the chants of the Proper for a given day nor the Ordinary cycle shows any consistency of age or of mode. However, as is true for most feast days, the Proper chants in this Mass are much older than the Ordinary melodies, and the two groups differ somewhat in style. All the Proper chants are derived from psalm-singing. They tend to include passages of decorated recitation, centering around a single note with embellishing gestures (for example, see the Introit at "et vocabitur nomen ejus," the Gradual at "omnes fines terrae," and the Alleluia at "sanctificatus illuxit"). They also tend to draw on a fund of melodic motives com-mon to chants in the same mode, a sign of their oral composition and transmission for centuries before the invention of notation. The Ordinary chants, in contrast, are more individual melodies, with distinctive motives, frequent stepwise mo-tion, and little recitation. The Kyrie, Gloria, Sanctus, and Agnus Dei included here

Kyrie, Gloria, Sanctus, Agnus Dei, and Ite, missa est from Mass IV, *Liber usualis* (Tournai: Desclée, 1961), 25–28. Credo I from ibid., 64–66. Proper chants from ibid., 408–10. *Gloria Patri* (Lesser Doxology) from ibid., 15–16. Reprinted by permission of St. Bonaventure Publications. English translations for the Proper from *The Saint Andrew Daily Missal*, ed. Dom Gaspar Lefebvre, O.S.B. (St. Paul: E. M Lohmann Co., 1940), 38–40. Translations for the Ordinary adapted from ibid., 519–20, 523–25, 534, and 546. Reprinted by permission.

were all composed after the system of eight modes was established in the ninth and tenth centuries, and as a result each conforms closely to its mode, signaling it unambiguously in virtually every phrase (unlike the Credo, which is apparently much older).

INSTRUCTIONS FOR READING SOLESMES CHANT NOTATION

The official Vatican editions of Gregorian chant, prepared by monks at the Benedictine Abbey of Solesmes, use a modernized chant notation based on late medieval forms. The staff has four lines rather than five but follows the familiar principle of alternating lines and spaces for the steps of the scale. A clef designates one line as either middle C (♭) or the F a fifth below it (♯); these clefs locate the half-steps E–F and B–C, important for the medieval singer. These are not absolute but relative pitches; singers may perform the chants in any comfortable range (although in the accompanying recording, most chants are performed at written pitch). Flat signs are valid only until a new word begins or a vertical division line appears.

The notes are indicated by *neumes*, which may contain one or more notes. The basic note shape is square (■) rather than round, reflecting the flat quills of medieval copyists. Notes are assumed to have equal durations, with exceptions as specified below. Notes are read from left to right as in standard notation, except when two notes are stacked vertically (▮), in which case the lower note is sung first. Successive notes on the same pitch and syllable are sung as though tied or slightly pulsed. Diamond-shaped notes (♦) are used in descending patterns to save space but have the same duration as square notes. Small notes, called *liquescent neumes* (♪), signify closing the mouth or tongue on a voiced consonant such as "n" or "m" at the end of a syllable. A diagonal stroke of the pen, found in *oblique neumes* (◥), indicates two notes—the pitches on which the stroke

begins and ends. A wavy line used in some ascending figures, called a *quilisma* (∿), may have signified an ornament; in Solesmes performing style, it is sung normally, but the preceding note is slightly lengthened. The symbol (♪) at the end of each staff is a *custos* (guard), a guide to lead the reader to the first note on the following line.

The Solesmes editors added interpretive signs, which do not necessarily reflect how the chants were sung in the Middle Ages. A dot after a note doubles its value. A horizontal line above a note indicates a slight lengthening. Vertical barlines delineate sections (double barline), periods (full barline), phrases (half barline), and smaller units (quarter barline through the top staff line) that may be marked by pauses of various lengths. In Solesmes performing style, notes are freely grouped in twos and threes (though other approaches are not so rigid); the editors added vertical strokes below some notes to suggest where such groups should begin.

Performances are also guided by symbols inserted among the words. Most chants are begun by the choir leader, the *cantor*, and an asterisk (✻) shows where the cantor is joined by the rest of the choir. Asterisks are also used to show other changes of performer—for example, between two halves of the choir. The signs *ij* and *iij* (the roman numerals 2 and 3), found in the Kyrie and Alleluia, indicate that the preceding material is to be sung twice or three times. Often these repetitions are performed by a different group of singers, as in the Kyrie.

(a) Introit: *Puer natus est nobis*

The Doxology is not written out in chant books, but is performed as follows:

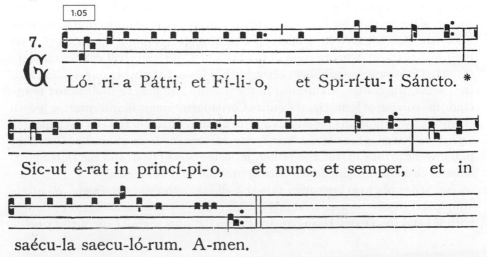

Puer natus est nobis, et filius datus est nobis: cujus imperium super humerum ejus: et vocabitur nomen ejus, magni consili Angelus.

Ps. Cantate Domino canticum novum: quia mirabilia fecit.

Gloria Patri, et Filio, et Spiritui Sancto. Sicut erat in principio, et nunc, et semper, et in saecula saeculorum. Amen.

A child is born to us, and a Son is given to us; whose government is upon His shoulder; and His Name shall be called the Angel of great counsel. (Isaiah 9:6)

Psalm verse: Sing ye to the Lord a new canticle, because He hath done wonderful things. (Psalm 97:1 [98:1])

Doxology: Glory be to the Father, and to the Son, and to the Holy Spirit. As it was in the beginning, is now, and ever shall be, world without end. Amen.

The sung portion of the Mass begins with the Introit (from Latin for "entrance"), introduced into the Mass sometime between the fourth and seventh centuries. In the early Middle Ages, the Introit consisted of a psalm preceded and followed by an antiphon (as in NAWM 4a) and was sung during the entrance procession of those conducting the Mass. Later the procession was shortened, and eventually it became the practice to sing the psalm after the priest and choir were in place. Without a long procession to accompany, the Introit text was abbreviated to the following standard form: the antiphon, one psalm verse, the Lesser Doxology (the formula praising God that is sung after every psalm), and a repetition of the antiphon, producing the form ABB'A.

The psalms derive from the Book of Psalms, part of the Hebrew Scriptures known to Christians as the Old Testament. Singing psalms has been part of Christian worship since the earliest days, and psalms are part of every Mass and Office service. Since each psalm is sung on many different occasions throughout the church year, the text of the antiphon places the psalm in the context of a particular service and feast day. Here the psalm text is the first verse of Psalm 97 in the Latin translation of the Bible, the Vulgate (Psalm 98 in the Hebrew Scriptures and most modern translations). Psalm 97 is a celebratory psalm, full of joy and praise, and so is appropriate for Christmas, but it has no specific connection to Jesus or his birth. That connection is made by attaching the antiphon text, a verse from the prophet Isaiah, whose vision of the birth of a son who shall rule was understood by Christians as a prophecy of the birth of Jesus. In light of this antiphon text, the "wonderful things" mentioned in the psalm verse may be understood to include the coming of Jesus and the entire Christian message. Reinterpreting Jewish Scripture by juxtaposing texts drawn from different parts of the Old Testament is a practice that goes back to the New Testament writers themselves. The Doxology, praising the Trinity of God the Father, Jesus the Son of God, and the Holy Spirit, situates both Old Testament texts firmly in a Christian context.

Two styles of chant appear in this and all other Introits. One style, relatively simple and *syllabic*, is used to sing the psalm verse (indicated by *Ps.* after a double barline) and the Lesser Doxology. In this recitational manner the melody holds mostly to one pitch, the reciting tone of the mode, with opening rises and cadential falls. Most syllables have one note, and others have two or three. The other style, used for the antiphon, is *neumatic*, with up to seven notes per syllable, and is much more varied in contour.

This Introit is in mode 7, as indicated by the number above the initial letter in this score. Both antiphon and psalm begin with a rising gesture from the mode's final, G, to its reciting tone, D, and end with a descent back to G, creating a melodic arch that is typical of chant. The antiphon often lingers on C, and some of the phrases cadence on A, two important secondary notes in this mode. Individual phrases tend to have an archlike pattern, rising near the beginning, rotating around one or two notes relatively high in the range, then sinking to a cadence.

The entrance psalm was originally performed antiphonally, alternating between two halves of the choir, but in modern practice it is often sung responsorially, alternating between a soloist and the choir. The cantor sings the opening (up to the asterisk), and the choir completes the antiphon. The psalm verse and Doxology are each begun by soloists (up to the asterisk) and finished by the choir. The Doxology is not written out in full in the chant books because the words were well known to the singers and because it was sung to the same melody as the psalm verse, only in three phrases rather than two. Instead, music is given for only the first two words (*Gloria Patri*) and the last six syllables, abbreviated to their vowels *E u o u a e* (for *saEcUlOrUm AmEn*). The Doxology is written out here to show how it fits the music. After the Doxology, the antiphon is repeated.

(b) Kyrie

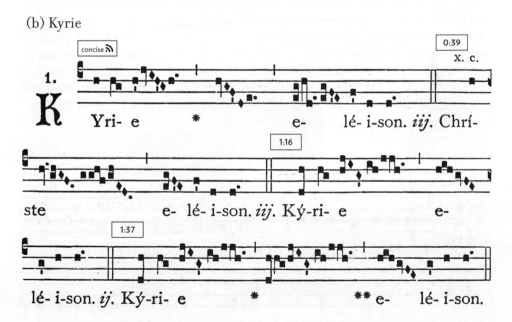

Kyrie eleison.	Lord have mercy.
Christe eleison.	Christ have mercy.
Kyrie eleison.	Lord have mercy

After the Introit, the choir sings the Kyrie. The Kyrie is the only chant from the Mass whose text is in Greek, showing its origin in the Byzantine Church. Among the musical settings of the Kyrie that may be sung on Christmas Day is this one from the tenth century, known as *Kyrie Cunctipotens Genitor*. (The name comes from an alternative text, known as a trope, that can replace the words "Kyrie" and "Christe.") The invocation "Kyrie eleison" is sung three times; then "Christe eleison" is sung three times; then "Kyrie eleison" is sung three times again. Here, a new melody is introduced for each section, and the final statement repeats a phrase, creating an overall form of AAA BBB CCC'.

The chant is classified as being in mode 1. This is very clear in the first "Kyrie eleison," which begins on the reciting tone A, circles around it, then gradually and repeatedly falls to the final D. The "Christe eleison" again starts on A and gradually falls to D. However, the remaining statements of "Kyrie eleison" reverse course, springing up to A, circling around it, and ending on A. The pattern of steps around A (whole step below, whole step and half step above) is the same as the pattern around D, so that medieval theorists recognized A as a *co-final* for mode 1.

Because of their very short text, most Kyries are *melismatic* (with melismas of many notes on several syllables), like this one. A few Kyrie melodies, used for Masses that are neither on Sundays nor on feast days, are syllabic to neumatic.

The Kyrie was originally sung in processions and took the form of a *litany*, in which the whole group repeats a short prayer in response to a leader. By the Middle Ages, Kyries were often performed antiphonally, in alternation between two halves of the choir, as illustrated on the accompanying recording. The cantor begins the first "Kyrie eleison," joined at the asterisk by one half (choir 1); the other half (choir 2) repeats the "Kyrie eleison"; then the two choirs alternate. In the final statement of "Kyrie eleison," choir 1 sings to the asterisk, choir 2 sings to the double asterisk, and both join together on "eleison."

(c) Gloria

ágimus tí-bi propter mágnam gló-ri-am tú-am. Dómi-

ne Dé-us, Rex caeléstis, Dé-us Pá-ter omní-pot-ens.

Dómine Fí-li uni-géni-te Jé-su Chrí-ste. Dómi-

ne Dé-us, Agnus Dé-i, Fí-li-us Pá-tris. Qui tól-

lis peccá-ta múndi, mi-se-ré-re nó-bis. Qui tóllis peccá-

ta múndi, súscipe depreca-ti-ónem nóstram. Qui sé-des

ad déxteram Pátris, mi-se-ré-re nó-bis. Quó-ni-am tu

só-lus sánctus. Tu só-lus Dóminus. Tu só-lus Altíssimus,

Jé-su Chrí-ste. Cum Sáncto Spí-ri-tu, in gló-

ri-a Dé-i Pá-tris. A-men.

Gloria in excelsis Deo	Glory be to God on high.
Et in terra pax hominibus bonae voluntatis.	And on earth peace to men of good will.
Laudamus te. Benedicimus te. Adoramus te. Glorificamus te.	We praise thee, we bless thee, we adore thee, we glorify thee.
Gratias agimus tibi propter magnam gloriam tuam.	We give thee thanks for thy great glory.

0:47 | Domine Deus, Rex caelestis, | O Lord God, King of heaven,
Deus Pater omnipotens.	God the Father Almighty.
Domine Fili unigenite Jesu Christe.	O Lord, the only begotten Son, Jesus Christ.
Domine Deus, Agnus Dei, Filius Patris.	O Lord God, Lamb of God, Son of the Father.

1:28 | Qui tollis peccata mundi, miserere nobis. | Thou who takest away the sins of the world, have mercy on us.
| Qui tollis peccata mundi, suscipe deprecationem nostram. | Thou who takest away the sins of the world, receive our prayer. |
| Qui sedes ad dexteram Patris, miserere nobis. | Thou who sittest at the right hand of the Father, have mercy on us. |

2:01 | Quoniam tu solus sanctus. | For thou only art holy,
Tu solus Dominus.	Thou only art Lord.
Tu solus Altissimus, Jesu Christe.	Thou only art most high, O Jesus Christ,
Cum Sancto Spiritu,	With the Holy Spirit,
In Gloria Dei Patris. Amen.	In the glory of God the Father. Amen.

The Kyrie is followed directly by the Gloria, with no intervening prayer or action. The Gloria, or Greater Doxology, is a text that praises God, states the doctrine of the Trinity, and asks for mercy. The first two phrases quote the words of the angels announcing Jesus' birth to the shepherds (Luke 2:14). The rest of the words are nonbiblical, arranged in several series of parallel phrases of glorification, naming the Father and Son, supplication, and praise. The Gloria is sung only on Sundays and feast days and is omitted in the seasons of Advent (before Christmas) and Lent (before Easter). Thus its presence adds to the festive quality of the Mass for Christmas Day, especially after having been absent during the preceding weeks.

Because the text is long, no Gloria melodies are melismatic; most, including this one, are neumatic, and a few are largely syllabic. This tenth-century melody is in mode 4, closing on E and moving in an octave from a third below to a sixth above. The mode is clear throughout because almost every phrase closes on the final.

There is no standard pattern of repetition for Gloria melodies, but in this Gloria the same melodic ideas recur repeatedly, often varied; for example, look and listen for the many variants of the motive first heard at "bonae voluntatis." Remarkably, references to the three aspects of the Trinity are all highlighted with the same motive, which occurs nowhere else: the Father at "Deus Pater omnipotens," the Son at "Jesu Christe," and the Holy Spirit at "Sancto Spiritu."

The Gloria and the Credo are unusual among the chants sung by the choir in that they are begun by the priest officiating at the Mass rather than by the cantor. This is a holdover from their original role as texts to be sung by the entire congregation.

After the Gloria, a prayer called the Collect is chanted, and then the Epistle (an extract from one of the letters in the New Testament) is recited. Both are vocalized with very simple formulas. At this Mass, the Epistle is the opening of the letter to the Hebrews (1:1–12), a passage that emphasizes the coming of Jesus Christ as the son of God, his superiority to the prophets and to the angels, and the permanence of his dominion. This reading links Jesus' birth to broader themes of Christian theology and thereby deepens the message of the Christmas Mass.

(d) Gradual: *Viderunt omnes*

Viderunt omnes fines terrae salutare Dei nostri: jubilate Deo omnis terra.

All the ends of the earth have seen the salvation of our God; sing joyfully to God, all the earth. (Psalm 97:3–4 [98:3–4])

℣. Notum fecit Dominus salutare suum: ante conspectum gentium revelavit justitiam suam.

℣. The Lord hath made known His salvation; He hath revealed His justice in the sight of the peoples. (Psalm 97:2 [98:2])

This Gradual exemplifies responsorial psalmody, in which a soloist singing the psalm verse alternates with a choir performing the respond. The texts are drawn from the same psalm featured in the Introit, continuing the mood of joy and celebration. But the specific passages chosen from this psalm (verse 2 for the psalm verse and parts of verses 3 and 4 for the respond) emphasize the idea of salvation made known to all peoples of the earth. Although the psalm was originally a Jewish hymn of praise to the God of Israel, in the liturgical context of the Christmas Mass, just after the Epistle, these verses were understood to speak of the coming of Jesus Christ and salvation through him, continuing the theological message of the Mass.

Unlike the Introit's psalm verse, which followed a recitational formula, this verse is extremely ornate, as was characteristic of chants featuring soloists from the choir, and the respond is also highly melismatic. Indeed, the Gradual and the Alleluia, which immediately follow it in most seasons of the church year, are the most elaborate chants of the Gregorian Mass, and together they form the Mass's musical high point. From the beginning, they were the only two chants of the Proper that were sung when no ritual action was taking place, and the words and the music were the single focus of attention.

The melody of this Gradual is clearly in mode 5, with cadences on the final F at the end of both respond and verse, a range that extends an octave above the final and one step below, many phrases that center on the reciting tone C, and phrase-endings on C and on A (both common in this mode). The note B is often flatted in this mode to avoid the tritone with F. Several flat signs appear in the music; they are valid only until the end of the word. More often, the B is not flatted, creating some variation in the location of the half step (A—B♭ or C—B), which is typical of mode 5. The frequent oscillations between A and C in the melody, which skip over B and thus withhold the location of the half step, seem to play on this ambiguity.

In performance, the soloist (usually the cantor, sometimes another singer or two singers) sings the opening phrase and is joined by the choir at the asterisk. Then the soloist sings most of the verse, and the choir joins in again at the asterisk. In the Middle Ages, the respond was then repeated by the entire choir (for an ABA form), but in modern practice that repetition is often omitted.

(e) Alleluia: *Dies sanctificatus*

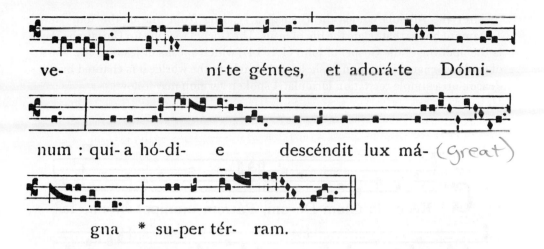

ve-   ní-te géntes,   et adorá-te   Dómi-

num : qui- a hó-di-   e   descéndit lux má- (great)

gna   * su-per tér-   ram.

Alleluia. Alleluia.

℣. Dies sanctificatus illuxit
    nobis: venite gentes, et adorate
    Dominum: quia hodie descendit lux
    magna super terram.

Alleluia. Alleluia.

℣. A sanctified day hath shone upon
    us; come ye peoples, and adore the
    Lord; for this day a great light hath
    descended upon the earth.

During most of the year, the Alleluia, another responsorial chant, comes after the Gradual. As in the Gradual, a soloist sings the verse, and the choir responds with "Alleluia" (from the Hebrew *Hallelujah*, meaning "praise Yahweh," or "Jehovah"). Here the verse is not from a psalm, but was created for the Christmas Mass. Its imagery of Jesus' birth as a day when "a great light descended upon the earth" anticipates the references to light in the following Gospel reading.

The soloist sings the first phrase of "Alleluia" to the asterisk. The choir repeats this (as shown by the repeat mark *ij.*) and continues with the following melisma, the *jubilus*, an ecstatic gesture of wordless joy. The soloist sings the verse, joined by the choir for the last words (marked by an asterisk). Finally, the respond is sung again without the repetition, creating an overall ABA' form. In the Middle Ages, the soloist often sang the "Alleluia," and the choir joined at the melisma, as on the accompanying recording.

The Alleluia for Christmas Day is one of the oldest. Many later Alleluias repeat the entire melody for "Alleluia" on the last word of the verse. Here instead there is a varied repetition of the first phrase of the verse ("Dies sanctificatus illuxit nobis") in the third phrase ("quia hodie descendit lux magna"). The melody is in mode 2, the plagal mode on D, and moves in the normal octave range from A to A. Most phrases end on the final, others on the note below, and several phrases linger on the reciting tone F. Compare this chant to the Kyrie, a mode 1 chant, to see how different are the plagal and authentic modes on the same final of D.

After the Alleluia comes the Gospel, a reading from one of the four New Testament books that relate the life of Jesus. The Gospel reading for Christmas Day is the opening of the Gospel of John (1:1–14), which speaks of Jesus as the Word of God incarnated in human flesh, bringing light to the world. It is chanted by the deacon on a simple recitation formula. A spoken sermon may follow.

(f) Credo

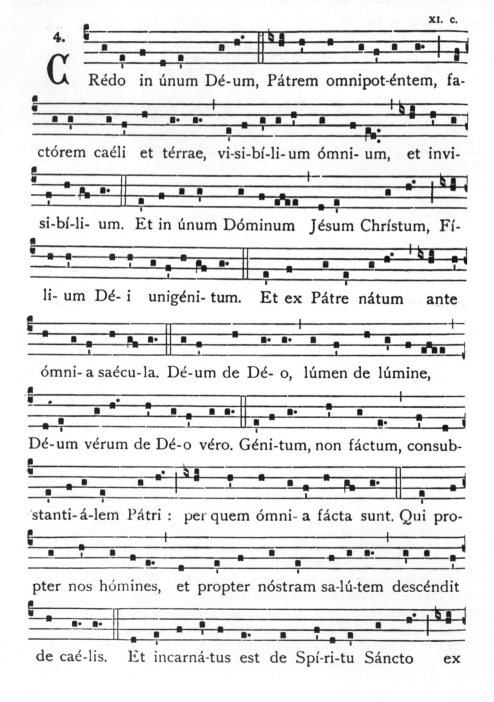

XI. c.

4.

Crédo in únum Dé-um, Pátrem omnipot-éntem, fa-

ctórem caéli et térrae, vi-si-bí-li-um ómni-um, et invi-

si-bí-li- um. Et in únum Dóminum Jésum Chrístum, Fí-

li- um Dé- i unigéni- tum.   Et ex Pátre nátum   ante

ómni- a saécu-la. Dé-um de Dé- o, lúmen de lúmine,

Dé-um vérum de Dé-o véro. Géni-tum, non fáctum, consub-

stanti-á-lem Pátri : per quem ómni- a fácta sunt. Qui pro-

pter nos hómines, et propter nóstram sa-lú-tem descéndit

de caé-lis. Et incarná-tus est de Spí-ri-tu Sáncto   ex

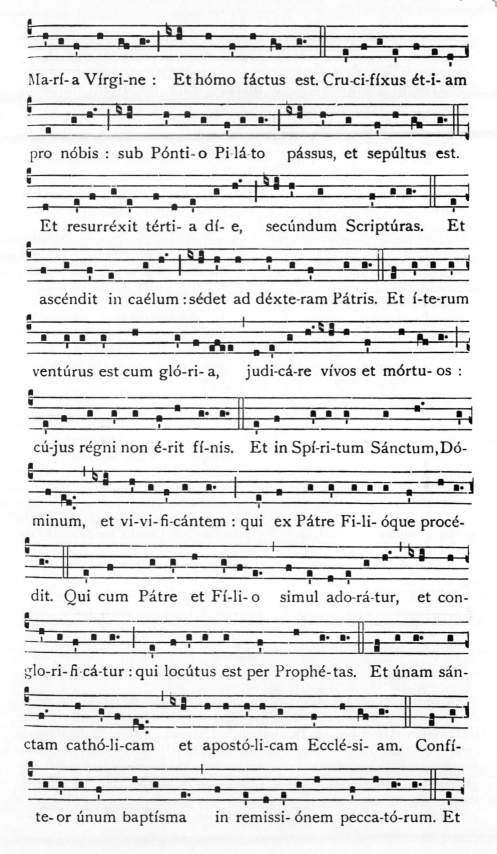

Ma-rí-a Vírgi-ne : Et hómo fáctus est. Cru-ci-fíxus ét-i- am

pro nóbis : sub Pónti-o Pi-lá-to pássus, et sepúltus est.

Et resurréxit térti- a dí- e, secúndum Scriptúras. Et

ascéndit in caélum : sédet ad déxte-ram Pátris. Et í-te-rum

ventúrus est cum gló-ri- a, judi-cá-re vívos et mórtu- os :

cú-jus régni non é-rit fí-nis. Et in Spí-ri-tum Sánctum, Dó-

minum, et vi-vi-fi-cántem : qui ex Pátre Fi-li- óque procé-

dit. Qui cum Pátre et Fí-li-o simul ado-rá-tur, et con-

glo-ri-fi-cá-tur : qui locútus est per Prophé-tas. Et únam sán-

ctam cathó-li-cam et apostó-li-cam Ecclé-si- am. Confí-

te- or únum baptísma in remissi- ónem pecca-tó-rum. Et

exspécto resurrecti-ónem mortu-ó-rum. Et ví-tam ventú-

ri saé-cu-li. A- men.

Credo in unum Deum, Patrem omnipotentem, factorem caeli et terrae, visibilium omnium et invisibilium.

Et in unum Dominum Jesum Christum Filium Dei unigenitum. Et ex Patre natum ante omnia saecula. Deum de Deo, lumen de lumine, Deum verum de Deo vero. Genitum, non factum, consubstantialem Patri: per quem omnia facta sunt. Qui propter nos homines et propter nostram salutem descendit de caelis. Et incarnatus est de Spiritu Sancto ex Maria Virgine: et homo factus est. Crucifixus etiam pro nobis: sub Pontio Pilato passus, et sepultus est. Et resurrexit tertia die, secundum Scripturas. Et ascendit in caelum: sedet ad dexteram Patris. Et iterum venturus est cum gloria judicare vivos et mortuos: cujus regni non erit finis.

Et in Spiritum Sanctum, Dominum, et vivificantem: qui ex Patre, Filioque procedit. Qui cum Patre, et Filio simul adorator, et conglorificatur: qui locutus est per Prophetas.

Et unam sanctam catholicam et apostolicam Ecclesiam.

Confiteor unum baptisma in remissionem peccatorum. Et exspecto resurrectionem mortuorum. Et vitam venturi saeculi. Amen.

I believe in one God, Father Almighty, maker of heaven and earth, and of all things visible and invisible.

And in one Lord Jesus Christ, the only-begotten Son of God. Born of the Father before all ages. God of God, light of light, true God of true God. Begotten, not made, being of one substance with the Father, by whom all things were made. Who for us humans and for our salvation descended from heaven. And was made incarnate by the Holy Spirit of the Virgin Mary, and was made man. And was crucified for us; under Pontius Pilate He died, and was buried. And rose again on the third day, according to the Scriptures. And ascended into heaven, and sits at the right hand of the Father. And He shall come again with glory to judge the living and the dead; of whose kingdom there shall be no end.

And in the Holy Spirit, Lord and giver of life, who proceeds from the Father and the Son. Who, together with the Father and the Son, is worshiped and glorified; who spoke by the prophets.

And one holy, Catholic, and Apostolic Church.

I acknowledge one baptism for the remission of sins. And I await the resurrection of the dead. And the life of the world to come. Amen.

The Credo, or Nicene Creed, is a statement of faith that summarizes the central doctrines of the Catholic Church. It was adopted at the church council at Nicaea in 325 C.E. and later revised. This was the last item to be added to the standard form of the Mass (in 1014), and it was the last of the Ordinary chants to be taken away from the congregation and given to the choir. The long association with congregational singing explains why all Credo melodies are syllabic and relatively simple, why there are relatively few Credo melodies, and why Credo melodies are not included in cycles of Ordinary chants. It also explains why the priest begins the chant, singing "Credo in unum Deum" (I believe in one God) before the choir sings the rest of the melody.

Like Gloria melodies, Credo melodies have no standard pattern of repetition, but they do feature a few motives that are repeated and varied to fit the changing accentuations of the text. Note for example the motive on "Patrem omnipotentem," used in various forms more than a dozen times and often preceded by a variant of the figure on "Credo in unum Deum." Although the melody ends on E and therefore is classed as mode 4, almost all the phrases close on G, and B♭ is an unexpectedly common tone (compare two other chants in mode 4, the Gloria in NAWM 3c and Offertory in NAWM 3g, in which B♭ never occurs). Here the B♭ is used as an upper neighbor decorating A, the reciting tone of mode 4.

The Credo marks the end of the first main division of the Mass, which centers on Bible readings and singing psalms more than on ritual actions. It is followed by the second main division, whose focus is the preparation for and giving of communion to the faithful.

(g) Offertory: *Tui sunt caeli*

Tui sunt caeli, et tua est terra: orbem terrarum, et plenitudinem ejus tu fundasti: justitia et judicium praeparatio sedis tuae.

Thine are the heavens, and Thine is the earth: the world and the fullness thereof Thou hast founded; justice and judgment are the preparation of Thy throne. (Psalm 88:11, 13 [89:11, 13])

As the priest begins to prepare the bread and wine for communion, the choir sings the Offertory. Originally, the Offertory was a long responsorial psalm, performed as members of the congregation made donations of bread and wine to the priests, with several florid verses sung by a soloist framed by a respond sung by the choir. All that survives today is the respond, whose melismatic character reflects its history as a chant associated with florid solo singing. This Offertory draws its text from a psalm (verse 11 and half of verse 13 from Psalm 88 in the Latin Vulgate, 89 in the Hebrew numbering and in the Protestant Bible). As is true of the other psalms sung in this Mass, the liturgical context reframes the text in Christian terms, linking the birth of Jesus to all of God's creation.

The melody is in mode 4, with a final on E and a range from C to C, but it tends to linger on F instead of emphasizing the reciting tone A. The cantor sings the first words to set the pitch, and the choir joins at the asterisk to complete the chant.

The priest then recites various prayers in a speaking voice for the blessing of the elements and vessels of the Eucharist, the reenactment of Christ's Last Supper. One prayer that is chanted is the Preface, to a formula that is more melodious than the other simple readings. The Preface serves to introduce the Sanctus.

(h) Sanctus

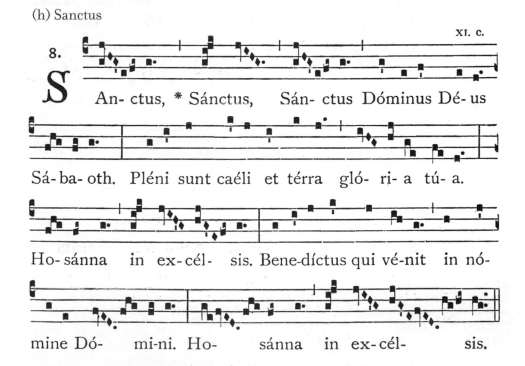

Sanctus, Sanctus, Sanctus Dominus Deus Sabaoth. Pleni sunt caeli et terra gloria tua. Hosanna in excelsis.

Benedictus qui venit in nomine Domini. Hosanna in excelsis.

Holy, holy, holy, Lord God of Hosts. The heavens and earth are full of thy glory. Hosanna in the highest.

Blessed is he who comes in the name of the Lord. Hosanna in the highest.

The Sanctus begins with the words sung by angels in a vision described in Isaiah 6:3. Sanctus melodies are typically neumatic, as in this eleventh-century setting. The threefold repetitions of "Sanctus" and the twofold "Hosanna" invite musical repetitions. Here, there are both exact repetitions (the third "Sanctus" repeats the first; the second "Hosanna" repeats the previous eleven notes) and varied repetitions (compare the sections from "Pleni" through "excelsis" and from "Benedictus" through the end to each other and to the melody from the second "Sanctus" through "Sabaoth"). The overall form of AA'A" is not uncommon, but the particular sequence of motives (abacd b'cdba' b"cdcdba") is individual and remarkable in its combination of simplicity with subtly complex variation.

The melody is in mode 8, with a final of G and an octave range from D to D. Frequent cadences on G and phrases that wind above and below it make the mode clear throughout. Compare this chant to the Introit in NAWM 3a, a mode 7 chant, to see the differences between the authentic and plagal modes on G.

Now the celebrant pronounces the Canon, the prayer consecrating the bread and wine, and the *Pater noster* (the Lord's Prayer, "Our Father").

(i) Agnus Dei

Agnus Dei, qui tollis peccata mundi: miserere nobis.	Lamb of God, who takest away the sins of the world: have mercy on us.
Agnus Dei, qui tollis peccata mundi: miserere nobis.	Lamb of God, who takest away the sins of the world: have mercy on us.
Agnus Dei, qui tollis peccata mundi: dona nobis pacem.	Lamb of God, who takest away the sins of the world: give us peace.

The Agnus Dei, like the Kyrie, was originally a litany, a repeated prayer in which participants respond to a leader. The text consists of a threefold acclamation, "Lamb of God, who takest away the sins of the world," followed by two identical responses, "have mercy on us," and a final response, "give us peace." Despite the two different responses, the three periods of this chant melody each end with the same music. The beginning of the middle period differs from the other two, creating an overall form of AB CB AB, one of the standard patterns for the Agnus Dei. The opening words "Agnus Dei" in each period are sung by the cantor, with the choir completing the period.

This chant is classed as mode 6, the plagal mode on F. The final is very clear, but the range from E to D could fit either mode 6 or mode 5, the authentic mode on F (compare the Gradual in NAWM 3d, which is in mode 5, and has a range from low E to high F). Here the reciting tone may be the deciding factor: there is a strong emphasis on A, the reciting tone of mode 6, whereas C, the mode 5 reciting tone, seldom occurs. Each melodic unit describes an undulating arch, and each period rises to a single peak (C in the outer periods, D in the middle one), arrives at a medial cadence on the reciting tone A, and winds back down to F.

(j) Communion: *Viderunt omnes*

Viderunt omnes fines terrae salutare Dei nostri.   All the ends of the earth have seen the salvation of
                                                        our God. (Psalm 97:3 [98:3])

After the faithful and celebrants have partaken of the bread and wine, the choir sings the Communion. This chant was originally a psalm with antiphon, sung antiphonally by the choir during the distribution of the bread and wine. In the later Middle Ages, it became customary at most services for the priest and other officiants to take communion on behalf of the congregation, so that the faithful seldom participated. This shortened the ritual, and, probably as a result, the Communion chant was abbreviated as well; around the twelfth century the psalm verses were dropped, leaving only the antiphon. Eventually, the chant was moved to follow rather than accompany the giving of communion.

The text of this Communion is the same as that beginning the Gradual in NAWM 3d. The Gradual, as a responsorial psalm associated with solo singing, was highly melismatic, but the Communion is neumatic, as is typical of antiphonal psalms in the Mass (the other being the Introit). There are no repeated motives in the music, but rather a variety of melodic patterns. The melody is in mode 1, evident in the cadences on the final D, the emphasis on the reciting tone A, and the range that extends almost an octave above D.

(k) Ite, missa est

| Ite, missa est. | Go, the Mass is over. |
| Deo gratias. | Thanks to God. |

At the end of the Mass, the priest or deacon dismisses the faithful, and the choir replies, "Thanks to God." In the Solesmes Mass cycles, this short text is always sung to the melody of the first "Kyrie eleison." In the accompanying recording, the dismissal is sung by the deacon.

Chants from Vespers for Christmas Day

Gregorian chant Office

4

(a) First Psalm with Antiphon: Antiphon *Tecum principium* and psalm *Dixit Dominus*

concise | 0:00/2:08

TECUM prin-cí- pi- um * in di- e virtú-tis tu- æ, in splendó-ri-bus sanctó-rum, ex ú-te-ro ante lu-cí-fe-rum gé-nu- i te. E u o u a e.

Tecum principium in die virtutis tuae, in splendoribus sanctorum, ex utero ante luciferum genui te.

Thine shall be the dominion in the day of Thy strength, in the brightness of the Saints, from the womb before the day star I begot Thee.

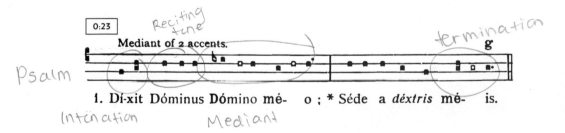

0:23

Mediant of 2 accents.

1. Dí-xit Dóminus Dómino mé- o ; * Séde a *déxtris* mé- is.

Antiphon and hymn from *Antiphonale monasticum* (Tournai: Desclée, 1934), 245 and 238 respectively. Psalm from *Liber usualis* (Tournai: Desclée, 1961), 128, Tone 1g. Reprinted by permission of St. Bonaventure Publications. English translations from *The Saint Andrew Daily Missal*, ed. Dom Gaspar Lefebvre, O.S.B. (New York: Benziger Publishing Co., 1956). Reprinted by permission.

1 Díxit Dóminus **Dómino méo**: * Séde a *déxtris* **mé**is.	The Lord said unto my Lord: Sit Thou at My right hand.
2 Donec pónam ini**mí**cos **tú**os, * scabéllum pé*dum tu*ó**rum.	Until I make Thine enemies Thy footstool.
3 Virgam virtútis túae emíttet Dómi**nus** ex **Sí**on: * domináre in medio inimicó*rum tu*órum.	The Lord shall send the rod of Thy strength out of Sion: rule Thou in the midst of Thine enemies
4 Técum princípium in díe virtútis túae in splendóri**bus** sanc**tó**rum· * ex útero ante lucíferum *génu*i te.	Thine shall be the dominion in the day of Thy power amid the brightness of the Saints: from the womb, before the day star have I begotten Thee.
5 Jurávit Dóminus, et non paeni**té**bit **é**um: * Tu es sacérdos in aetérnum secúndum órdi*nem Mel***chi**sedech.	The Lord hath sworn, and will not repent: Thou art a Priest for ever after the order of Melchisedech.
6 Dóminus a **déx**tris **tú**is, * confrégit in díe írae *súae* **ré**ges.	The Lord at Thy right hand shall strike through kings in the day of His wrath.
7 Judicábit in natiónibus, im**plé**bit ru**í**nas: * conquassábit cápita in tér*ra mul***tó**rum.	He shall judge among the heathen, He shall fill the places with dead bodies: He shall wound the heads over many countries.
8 De torrénte in **ví**a **bí**bet: * proptérea exal*tábit* **cá**put.	He shall drink of the brook in the way: therefore shall He lift up His head.
`1:49` 9 Glória **Pá**tri, et **Fí**lio, * et Spirí*tui* **Sán**cto.	Glory be to the Father, and to the Son, and to the Holy Spirit.
10 Sicut érat in princípio, et **núnc**, et **sém**per, * et in saécula saecu*lórum*. **Amen.**	As it was in the beginning, is now, and ever shall be, world without end. Amen.

(b) Hymn: *Christe Redemptor omnium*

Christe Redemptor omnium, Ex Patre Patris Unice, Solus ante principium Natus ineffabiliter.	Jesus! Redeemer of the world! Who, ere the earliest dawn of light, Was from eternal ages born, Immense in glory as in might.

Tu lumen, tu splendor Patris,
Tu spes perennis omnium:
Intende, quas fundunt preces.
Tui per orbem famuli.

Memento, salutis Auctor,
Quod nostri quondam corporis,
Ex illibata Virgine
Nascendo, formam sumpseris.

Sic praesens testatur dies,
Currens per anni circulum.
Quod solus a sede Patris
Mundi salus adveneris.

Hunc caelum, terra, hunc mare,
Hunc omne, quod in eis est,
Auctorem adventus tui
Laudans exultat cantico.

Nos quoque, qui sancto tuo,
Redempti sanguine sumus,
Ob diem natalis tui
Hymnum novum concinimus.

Gloria tibi, Domine,
Qui natus es de Virgine,
Cum Patre et Sancto Spiritu
In sempiterna saecula. Amen.

Immortal Hope of all mankind
In whom the Father's face we see,
Hear Thou the prayers Thy people pour
This day throughout the world to Thee.

Remember, O Creator Lord!
That in the Virgin's sacred womb
Thou was conceiv'd and of her flesh
Didst our mortality assume.

This ever-blest recurring day
Its witness bears, that all alone,
From Thy own Father's bosom forth,
To save the world Thou camest down.

O Day! to which the seas and sky,
And earth, and heav'n, glad welcome sing;
O Day! which heal'd our misery,
And brought on earth salvation's King.

We, too, O Lord, who have been cleans'd
In Thy own fount of Blood divine,
Offer the tribute of sweet song
On this blest natal day of Thine.

O Jesus! born of Virgin bright,
Immortal glory be to Thee;
Praise to the Father infinite
And Holy Ghost eternally. Amen.

Of the eight daily services that constitute the Office, Vespers is one of the most important. The principal feasts in the Catholic Church have two Vespers services: the first at sunset the evening before and the second at sunset on the feast day itself. Thus, the official name for Vespers on Christmas Day is Second Vespers of the feast of the Nativity of Our Lord (December 25). The excerpts from the Vespers included here exemplify two types of chant that occur in all Office services: the psalm with antiphon and the hymn.

The first full psalm sung in every Vespers service is Psalm 109, *Dixit Dominus* (Psalm 110 in the Protestant Bible). On this feast day, this psalm is preceded and followed by the antiphon *Tecum principium*, which borrows its text from the fourth verse of the psalm. The antiphon text places the psalm in a specific liturgical context. Here, although the words are drawn from a Jewish psalm written hundreds of years before Jesus was born, the antiphon is appropriate to a service celebrating his birth, due to its references to the womb and to one who was begotten by God and will have dominion. The reframing of the psalm in a Christian service is made explicit by the Lesser Doxology, the formula of praise to the Trinity that is sung at the end of every Office psalm, before the repetition of the antiphon. (It also appears in every Introit, as we saw in NAWM 3a.) The antiphon is a simple, mostly syllabic melody in mode 1. Its melodic contour elegantly delineates the phrasing and accentuation of the text while highlighting the most important notes in the mode (the final D, the reciting tone A, and F) through cadences or repetition. The psalm is sung to a *psalm tone*, a simple melodic formula designed to accommodate verses of any length. There is one psalm tone for each of the eight modes, and the mode of the antiphon determines the mode of the psalm, here mode 1. Each verse of the psalm is sung to the psalm tone, which is repeated twice more for the Lesser Doxology (here numbered as verses 9–10).

Psalm verses normally divide into two parts, punctuated by a colon or comma, and psalm tones use melodic motion to reflect this division. The formula for the first half of the verse has three components: an *intonation*, a rising figure used only in the first verse of the psalm (here the notes F–G–A); recitation on the reciting tone of the mode; and the *mediant*, a cadence to close the first half. As shown here, in mode 1 the mediant rises from the reciting tone A to B♭ on the next-to-last accented syllable, returns to A, falls to G on the last accented syllable, and returns again to A. (The open noteheads show what note to sing when there are two unaccented syllables after an accent, rather than one.) The last two accented syllables are shown in boldface here and in modern chant books as a guide for the singers. When the first half of the psalm verse is especially lengthy, a *flex* (inflection), a melodic fall of a step or third, serves as a resting point.

The second half of the verse begins with more recitation on the reciting tone and then concludes with a final cadence called a *termination*. Each psalm tone has a variety of terminations designed to provide a smooth flow back to the antiphon, and by convention the form of termination is indicated after the antiphon over the letters *E u o u a e*, which stand for the syllables "saEcUlOrUm AmEn," at the end of the Doxology. In this case, the termination closes on G with a G–A figure on the last accented syllable, shown in boldface, preceded by G and F for the previous two syllables, shown in italics. (Because the piece is not over until the antiphon repeats, the psalm tone itself does not have to close on the final of the mode.)

Office psalms were sung antiphonally, alternating verses or half-verses between two halves of the choir. On the accompanying recording, the cantor begins the antiphon to set the pitch, and the full choir joins in at the asterisk. Then the cantor sings the first half of the first psalm verse, half the choir completes it, and the two halves of the choir alternate verses until both join together in the reprise of the antiphon.

The hymn *Christe Redemptor* omnium hails the arrival of the Savior on this day of his birth. Hymn texts are not from the Bible, but are poems of praise and prayer. Hymns as a genre are strophic—that is, the number of lines, the syllable count, and the structure of all the stanzas are the same. This hymn has seven stanzas of four lines each, each line containing eight syllables. There is no regular pattern of accents, and rhymes occur only occasionally. The English translation included here is a rhyming, metrical version that can be sung to the chant, rather than a literal rendering. The setting of this hymn is simple, with no more than two notes per syllable. It may have been performed rhythmically rather than with the free durations of prose texts and psalms.

Ascribed to Wipo of Burgundy
(CA. 995–CA. 1050)

Victimae paschali laudes

Sequence (usually tuneful)

FIRST HALF OF THE ELEVENTH CENTURY

Sequence for Easter

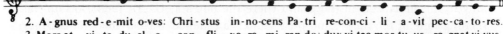

Seq.
1. Vic - ti - mae pa - scha+li lau - des *im - mo - lent Chri - sti - a - ni.

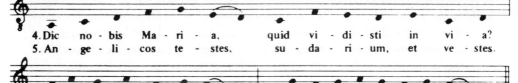

2. A - gnus red - e - mit o - ves: Chri - stus in - no - cens Pa - tri re - con - ci - li - a - vit pec - ca - to - res.
3. Mors et vi - ta du - el - o con - fli - xe - re mi - ran - do: dux vi - tae mor - tu - us, re - gnat vi - vus.

4. Dic no - bis Ma - ri - a, quid vi - di - sti in vi - a?
5. An - ge - li - cos te - stes, su - da - ri - um, et ve - stes.

Se - pul - crum Chri - sti vi - ven - tis, et glo - ri - am vi - di re - sur - gen - tis:
Sur - re - xit Chri - stus spes me - a: prae - ce - det su - os in Ga - li - lae - am.

[6. Cre - den - dum est ma - gis so - li Ma - ri - ae ve - ra - ci
7. Sci - mus Chri - stum sur - re - xis - se a mor - tu - is ve - re:

quam Ju - dae - o - rum tur - bae fal - la - ci.]
tu no - bis, vi - ctor Rex, mi - se - re - re. A - men. Al - le - lu - ia.

* Syllabic

1 Victimae paschali laudes immolent Christiani.

2 Agnus redemit oves: Christus innocens Patri reconciliavit peccatores.

3 Mors et vita duelo conflixere mirando: dux vitae mortuus, regnat vivus.

4 Dic nobis Maria, quid vidisti in via? Sepulcrum Christi viventis, et gloriam vidi resurgentis:

To the Paschal Victim let Christians offer songs of praise.

The Lamb has redeemed the sheep; sinless Christ has reconciled sinners to the Father.

Death and life have engaged in miraculous combat; the leader of life is slain, yet living he reigns.

Tell us, Mary, what you saw on the way? I saw the sepulchre of the living Christ and the glory of His rising;

Liber usualis, 780. "Chant: Sequence For The Solemn Mass of Easter Day," from Richard Hoppin, ed., *Anthology of Medieval Music* (New York: Norton, 1978), 15. © 1978. Used by permission of W. W. Norton & Company, Inc.

5 Angelicos testes, sudarium, et vestes. Surexit
   Christus spes mea: praecedet suos in Galilaeam.

6 [Credendum est magis soli Mariae veraci quam
   Judaeorum turbae fallaci.]

7 Scimus Christum surrexisse a mortuis vere: tu
   nobis, victor Rex, miserere. Amen. Alleluia.

The angelic witnesses, the shroud and vesture.
   Christ my hope is risen; He will go before His
   own into Galilee.

The truthful Mary alone is more to be believed than
   the deceitful crowd of Jews.

We know that Christ has truly risen from the dead.
   Thou conqueror and king, have mercy on us.
   Amen. Alleluia.

— (?) WIPO OF BURGUNDY

— TRANS. RICHARD HOPPIN

Among the many sequences that were sung in the Middle Ages, *Victimae paschali laudes* is one of only four that are retained in the liturgy and standard modern chant books (a fifth was added in the eighteenth century). When the Council of Trent (1545–63) eliminated most sequences, this one was kept because it was widely used and associated with Easter, the most important feast day of the Christian calendar. It was sung as part of the liturgy at Mass and was also incorporated into sacred dramas performed at Easter. The text describes Jesus' resurrection and the redemption that Christians believe he brings to humankind.

In one medieval manuscript, this sequence is ascribed to Wipo (ca. 995–ca. 1050), chaplain to Holy Roman emperor Henry III. He may have written the text, or both text and music, but it is also possible that the piece was written by someone else and attributed to Wipo simply because he was an eminent clergyman.

Sequences of the ninth through the eleventh centuries typically follow the form A BB CC . . . N, comprising an opening sentence with its own musical phrase, a series of paired sentences (each with the same number of syllables and set to the same music), and a final unpaired sentence. In its original form, *Victimae paschali laudes* lacked the final unpaired sentence, but verse 6 (marked here by brackets) was deleted after the Council of Trent, bringing this sequence into line with the usual pattern. There was a more urgent reason than mere conformity for making this change: that verse, with its reference to "the deceitful crowd of Jews," evokes the ancient calumny that Jews were responsible for the death of Jesus, part of an anti-Jewish tradition that modern church leaders have apologized for and have sought to uproot.

As is common in early sequences, the number of syllables increases through the first three verses and then recedes to the mean. Verses 4–7 each have internal rhymes, reflecting the predilection of Frankish writers for rhyming texts in newly composed chants. The melody likewise features musical rhymes that lend it coherence: verses 2–3 and 6–7 begin with the same phrase, and all verses and most internal phrases close with a stepwise descent to D, usually G—F—E—D.

6

Tropes on *Puer natus: Quem queritis in presepe* and melisma

Texted trope (liturgical drama) and untexted trope

LATE TENTH CENTURY

— more dramatic than the Mass

Trope to the Antiphon
[Midwives]

Quem que- ri- tis in pre- se- pe pas-

[Shepherds]

-to- res di- ci- te Sal- va- to- rem

xris- tum do- mi- num in- fan- tem pan- nis in-

-vo- lu- tum se- cun- dum ser- mo- nem an-

[Midwives]

-ge- li- cum Ad- est hic par- vu- lus cum

Ma- ri- a ma- tre su- a de qua du- dum va-

-ti- ci- nan- do i- sa- i- as di- xe- rat pro- phe- ta

Ec- ce vir- go con- ci- pi- et et pa-

Transcribed from Paris, Bibliothèque nationale, MS lat. 903, fol. 9v. From *Festive Troped Masses from the Eleventh Century: Christmas and Easter in Aquitaine*, ed. Charlotte Roederer, Collegium Musicum: Yale University, Second Series, vol. 10 (Madison: A-R Editions, 1989), 6–7 and 9. Reprinted by permission.

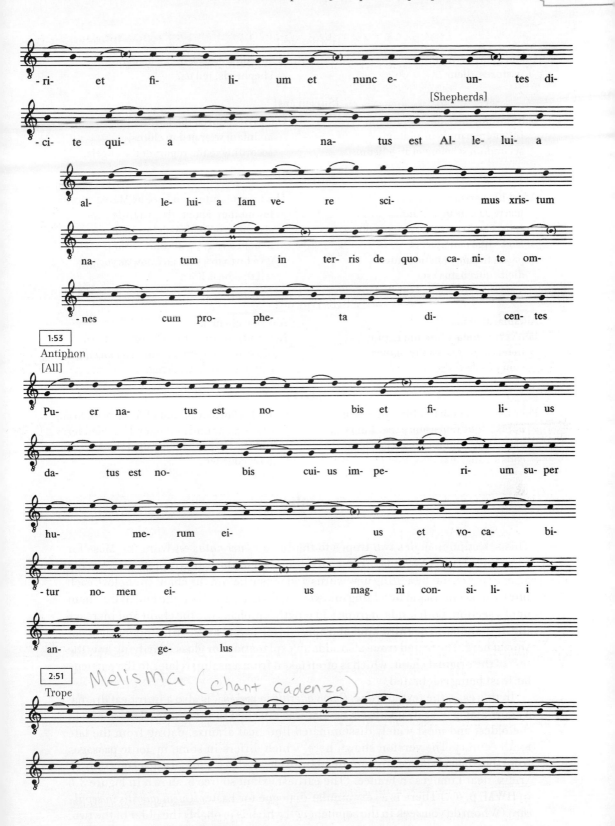

-ri- et fi- li- um et nunc e- un- tes di-

[Shepherds]

-ci- te qui- a na- tus est Al- le- lui- a

al- le- lui- a Iam ve- re sci- mus xris- tum

na- tum in ter- ris de quo ca- ni- te om-

-nes cum pro- phe- ta di- cen- tes

1:53
Antiphon
[All]

Pu- er na- tus est no- bis et fi- li- us

da- tus est no- bis cui- us im- pe- ri- um su- per

hu- me- rum ei- us et vo- ca- bi-

-tur no- men ei- us mag- ni con- si- li- i

an- ge- lus

2:51
Trope   Melisma (chant cadenza)

[MIDWIVES]

Quem queritis in presepe,
   pastores, dicite?

Whom do you seek in the manger,
   shepherds, tell us?

[SHEPHERDS]

Salvatorem, Christum Dominum,
   infantem pannis involutum,
   secundum sermonem angelicum.

Our savior, Christ the Lord,
   an infant wrapped in cloths,
   according to the report of the angels.

[MIDWIVES]

Adest hic parvulus cum Maria,
   matre sua, de qua dudum
   vaticinando Isaias dixerat propheta:
   Ecce virgo concipiet et
   pariet filium; et nunc euntes
   dicite quia natus est.

The infant is attended here by Mary,
   his mother, about whom a little while
   ago the prophet Isaiah foretold:
   behold a virgin will conceive and
   give birth to a son; and now as you go
   tell that he is born.

[SHEPHERDS]

Alleluia, alleluia!
Iam vere scimus Christum natum
   in terris, de quo canite omnes
   cum propheta dicentes:

Alleluia, alleluia!
Now truly we know that Christ was born
   on earth, concerning which let all sing
   with the prophet, saying:

[ALL]

Puer natus est nobis, et filius datus est
   nobis: cujus imperium super humerum
   ejus: et vocabitur nomen ejus, magni
   consilii angelus.

A child is born to us, and a Son is given to us;
   whose government is upon His shoulder;
   and His Name shall be called the Angel of
   great counsel.

This selection includes two tropes to the Introit *Puer natus est* from the Mass for Christmas Day (NAWM 3a). These illustrate two of the ways tropes could expand an existing chant: by adding new words and music before the chant (or before each phrase or section) and by adding untexted melismas, usually at the end of the chant or of a section. Both kinds of trope add length, emphasizing the chant and increasing its grandeur. The third kind of trope, adding text to an existing melisma, is not shown here. The texted trope also adds an explanation, or gloss, clarifying how the text of the original chant, which is often taken from a psalm, relates to the particular feast being celebrated.

In this case, the texted trope, *Quem queritis in presepe*, is also a liturgical drama, a short dialogue or dramatic scene that was attached to the liturgy. This is one of the oldest and most widely disseminated liturgical dramas, dating from the late tenth century. The version shown here, which differs in some melodic passages from the earliest sources, is contained in an eleventh-century manuscript from St. Yrieix, near Limoges in France. (The earliest extant source is shown in Figure 3.6 in HWM, p. 63.) There is a very similar dialogue for Easter, *Quem queritis in sepulchro* (Whom do you seek in the sepulcher?), which is probably the older of the two.

In the Christmas dialogue, the midwives caring for the Christ child ask the shepherds whom they seek in the manger. The shepherds answer that they are looking for an infant in swaddling clothes, Christ the Savior, as the angels foretold. The midwives explain that the child was born to Mary, a virgin. The shepherds rejoice in the knowledge that they have confirmed the birth of Christ, and they then introduce the singing of the Introit, whose text about the birth of a son is drawn from the prophet Isaiah (9:6, see NAWM 3a). The words of the trope set the stage for the Introit and indeed for the entire Mass.

The melody is in mode 7, the mode of the Introit, with a strong emphasis on the final G and reciting tone D. There are a number of notable melodic recurrences that help to create the sense of a dialogue. When the shepherds first respond, they begin by repeating the midwives' melody. The same opening motive begins the second half of the midwives' reply (at "Ecce virgo concipiet"). The shepherds' final acclamation echoes the first part of the midwives' reply, at least in its general outline of beginning on D, rising to high G, and falling back to D. In addition to these similarities at the beginnings of phrases, there are musical rhymes at cadences. The first three phrases all end with the same cadence, G—A—G—F—G. Then the last words of the shepherds' first statement, "sermonem angelicum," introduce a new ending formula that returns three more times: at the middle and end of the midwives' next response ("Isaias dixerat propheta" and "quia natus est") and at the end of the entire dialogue ("propheta dicentes"). These varied repetitions of one another's melodic material convey the sense of a conversation between the midwives and shepherds, and lend continuity and unity to the entire composition.

One late-tenth-century manuscript includes instructions for when and where the dialogue is to be performed: "On the day of the nativity of the Lord, at the station of St. Peter [a place along the side of the church], they begin the trope before the office is said [i.e., before the Mass begins with the Introit]." Exactly how and by whom it is to be performed is not specified, and even the identities of the characters in the dialogue have to be inferred from context. Perhaps the boys of the choir played the role of the midwives and the men the role of the shepherds, as in the recording accompanying this anthology. The recording continues with all voices singing the antiphon and added melisma, but the psalm verse and doxology are omitted. The performance differs in some small details from the transcription printed here.

Hildegard of Bingen (1098–1179)

Ordo virtutum: Closing chorus, *In principio omnes*

Sacred music drama

CA. 1151

In prin-ci-pi-o om—nes cre-a-tu-ræ vi—ru—e-runt, in me-di-o flo-res flo-ru—e-runt; po-ste-a vi-ri-di-tas de-scen—dit. Et is—tud vir proe-li-a-tor vi—dit et di—xit: Hoc sci-o, sed au—re-us nu-me-rus non-dum est ple—nus. Tu er—go, pa-ter-num spe—cu-lum a—spi-ce: in cor-po—re me—o fa—ti-ga-ti-o—nem sus-ti—ne—o, par-vu-li et-i-am me—i de—fi-ci—unt. Nunc me-mor e—sto, quod ple-ni-tu—do quae in pri—mo fac—ta est a—re-sce—re non de-bu—it, et tunc in te ha-bu—is-ti, quod o-cu—lus tu-us num—quam

ce - de - ret us - que dum cor - pus me - um

vi - de - res ple - num gem - ma - rum. Nam me

fa - ti - gat quod om - ni - a mem - bra me - a in ir - ri -

si - o - nem va - dunt. Pa - ter, vi - de, vul - ne - ra me - a

3:03

ti - bi o - sten - do. Er - go nunc, om - nes

ho - mi - nes, ge - nu - a ve - stra ad Pa - trem

ve - strum fle - cti - te, ut vo - bis

ma - num su - am por - - -

ri - gat.

VIRTUES AND SOULS

In principio omnes creature viruerunt,
in medio flores floruerunt;
postea viriditas descendit.
Et istud vir proeliator vidit et dixit:
Hoc scio, sed aureus numerus nondum est
    plenus.
Tu ergo, paternum speculum aspice: in corpore
    meo fatigationem sustineo, parvuli etiam mei
    deficiunt.
Nunc memor esto, quod plenitudo quae in primo
    facta est arescere non debuit, et tunc in te
    habuisti quod oculus tuus numquam cederet
    usque dum corpus meum videres plenum
    gemmarum.
Nam me fatigat quod omnia membra
    mea in irrisionem vadunt.
Pater, vide, vulnera mea tibi ostendo.
Ergo nunc, omnes homines, genua vestra ad
    Patrem vestrum flectite, ut vobis manum suam
    porrigat.

In the beginning all creatures flourished,
they bloomed in the middle of flowers;
after that greenness declined.
The warrior [Christ] saw this and said [to God]:
"This I know, but the golden number is not yet
    complete.
You, therefore, look upon the Father's reflection:
    in my body, I endure fatigue, even my children
    weaken.
Now be mindful, for the fullness that was made at
    the beginning did not need to wither, and at that
    time you deemed that you would not turn away
    your eye until you could see my body covered
    with gems.
It wearies me that all my followers [literally, my
    limbs] are subjected to mockery.
Father, behold, I show you my wounds."
Now, therefore, all humankind, bend your
    knees before your Father, that he may offer
    his hand to you.

Hildegard, founder and abbess of the convent in Rupertsberg, Germany, was famous for her prophetic powers and revelations. Her morality play with music, *Ordo virtutum* (The Virtues, ca. 1151), is unusual for its time because, unlike the liturgical dramas such as *Quem queritis in presepe* (NAWM 6), it is not a supplement to the Mass or Office of a certain feast. Rather, it is an independent Latin play, an edifying entertainment for Hildegard's select community of noblewomen, and was probably performed by them many times as a manifestation of the theology Hildegard delineated in her *Scivias*. The characters, singing in plainchant, include the Patriarchs and Prophets, sixteen female Virtues (including Humility, Love, Obedience, Faith, Hope, Chastity, Innocence, and Mercy), a Happy Soul, an Unhappy Soul, and a Penitent Soul. The Devil, bereft of divine harmony, can only shout and bellow; it is the only part that is spoken rather than sung.

The play begins with a chorus of Patriarchs and Prophets who express their wonder at the sight of the richly robed Virtues. Souls in a procession beg the Virtues for divine insight, alternating solos with choral responses. But the Devil tempts the Souls, and one Unhappy Soul succumbs and follows him, only to return later, bedraggled, hurt, and repentant. The Devil tries to reclaim her, but the Virtues, led by Humility, protect her and capture and bind the Devil. Though victorious, the Virtues and Souls lament the spoiling of the green, blossoming paradise and invoke Christ, who asks God to accept his suffering as the cure for the ills of a wounded world. Thus the play serves as a group enactment of the Christian story of sin, confession, repentance, and forgiveness. Only here it is the female Virtues who restore the fallen to the community of the faithful, not the male Prophets or Patriarchs—a message that would have had deep significance for the nuns in Hildegard's convent.

The final chorus, which serves as an epilogue, consists of four rhymed lines followed by a prose speech by Christ and ends with a short call to kneel in prayer. The melody is in mode 3, keeping mostly to the range of that mode, *d* to *e'*. It rises to *g'* at "oculus tuus" (your eye) and "ad Patrem" (to the Father), perhaps to emphasize those words, and elsewhere three times touches low *c*. This expanded range of a twelfth is typical of late Frankish chant. Periods and other strong endings in the text are marked by cadences on the final E. The reciting tone of this mode, C, plays no part in the structure; rather, the fifth degree, B, is the most frequent resting point.

The rhyme of the opening two lines is paralleled by an identical cadence formula in the music. The next two rhymed lines do not use the same closing pattern because the second serves as an introduction to Christ's speech. Frequently, phrases begin with the rising fifth *e–b'*, which opens the chorus and recurs seven times, sometimes leading to similar melodic contours. A few other melodic figures appear more than once, but for the most part, the melody unfolds in a constantly varied stream. The chorus ends with a melismatic flourish on the final word.

In the accompanying recording, the chorus of women and men sings over a drone on the modal final E, played in octaves on an organistrum (hurdy-gurdy). Singing to the accompaniment of a drone may have been common at the time, as it is in some traditions of folk music, but there is little evidence to tell us whether drones were used with notated music in Hildegard's time.

Bernart de Ventadorn (?CA. 1130–CA. 1200)

Can vei la lauzeta mover

Canso (troubadour song)
CA. 1170–80

(a) Milan manuscript

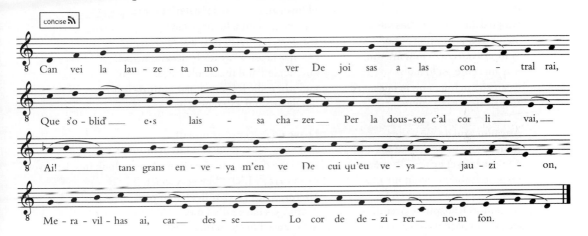

(b) Paris manuscript

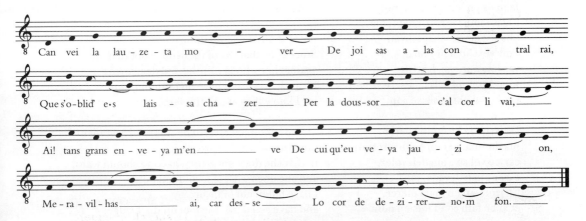

Music adapted from and text and translation taken from Hendrik van der Werf, *The Chansons of the Troubadours and Trouvères* (Utrecht, 1972), 91–95, where versions of the melody appearing in five different sources are given, showing surprising consistency among readings. The dot splitting two letters of a word, as in e · s, indicates a contraction. The text of the poem is from the edition by Moshé Lazar, *Bernard de Ventadour, troubadour du XIIe siècle: Chansons d'amour* (Paris, 1966), 180. We have made diligent efforts to contact the copyright holder to obtain permission to reprint this selection. If you have information that would help us, please write to Permissions Department, W. W. Norton & Company, Inc., 500 Fifth Avenue, New York, NY 10110.

Can vei la lauzeta mover
de joi sas alas contral rai,
que s'oblid' e · s laissa chazer
per la doussor c'al cor li vai,
ai! tan grans enveya m'en ve
de cui qu'eu veya jauzion,
meravilhas ai, car desse
lo cor de dezirer no · m fon.

When I see the lark beating
its wings joyfully against the sun's rays,
which then swoons and swoops down
because of the joy in its heart,
oh! I feel such jealousy
for all those who have the joy of love,
that I am astonished
that my heart does not immediately melt with desire!

`0:55`

Ai, las! tan cuidava saber
d'amor, e tan petit en sai,
car eu d'amar no · m posc tener
celeis don ja pro non aurai.
Tout m'a mo cor, e tout m'a me,
e se mezeis e tot lo mon;
e can se · m tolc, no · m laisset re
mas dezirer e cor volon.

Alas! I thought I knew so much
of love, and I know so little;
for I cannot help loving a lady
from whom I shall never obtain any favor.
She has taken away my heart and myself,
and herself and the whole world;
and when she left me, I had nothing left
but desire and a yearning heart.

Anc non agui de me poder
ni no fui meus de l'or' en sai
que · m laisset en sos olhs vezer
en un miralh que mout me plai.
Mirahls, pus me mirei en te,
m'an mort li sospir de preon,
c'aissi · m perdei com perdet se
lo bels Narcisus en la fon.

I have no power over myself,
and have not had possession of myself
since the time when she allowed me to look into her eyes,
in a mirror which I like very much.
Mirror, since I was reflected in you,
deep sighs have killed me,
for I caused my own ruin, just as
fair Narcissus caused his by looking in the fountain.

`1:59`

De las domnas me dezesper;
ja mais en lor no · m fiarai;
c'aissi com las solh chaptener,
enaissi las deschaptenrai.
Pois vei c'una pro no m'en te
vas leis que · m destrui e · m cofon,
totas las dopt' e las mescre,
car be sai c'atretals se son.

I despair of ladies;
I shall not trust them ever again;
just as I used to defend them,
now I shall condemn them.
Since I see that *one* of them does not help me
against her who is ruining and destroying me
I fear them all and have no faith in them,
for I know they are all the same.

D'aisso's fa be femna parer
ma domna, par qu'e · lh o retrai,
car no vol so c'om deu voler,
e so c'om li devada, fai.
Chazutz sui en mala merce,
et ai be faih co · l fols en pon;
e no sai per que m'esdeve,
mas car trop puyei contra mon.

My lady shows herself to be [merely] a woman
(and that is why I reproach her)
in that she does not want what one should want,
and she does what is forbidden her.
I have fallen out of favor,
and have acted like the fool on the bridge;
and I do not know why this has happened to me,
unless it was because I tried to climb too high.

Merces es perduda, per ver,
et eu non o saubi anc mai,
car cilh qui plus en degr'aver
no · n a ges, et on la querrai?
A! can mal sembla, qui la ve,

Mercy is gone, that is sure,
and I never received any of it,
for she who should have the most mercy
has none, and where else should I seek it?
Oh! how difficult it is for a person who sees her

qued aquest chaitiu deziron	to imagine that she would allow to die this poor yearning wretch,
que ja ses leis non aura be,	and would not help the man
laisse morir, que no l'aon!	who can have no help but her!

Pus ab midons no · m pot valer	Since pleas and mercy and my rights
precs ni merces ni · l dreihz qu'eu ai,	cannot help me to win my lady,
ni a leis no ven a plazer	and since it does not please her
qu'eu l'am, ja mais no · lh o dirai.	that I love her, I shall speak to her about it no more.
Aissi · m part de leis e · m recre;	So I am leaving her and her service;
mort m'a, e per mort li respon,	she has killed me, and I reply with death,
e vau m'en, pus ilh no · m rete,	and I am going sadly away, since she will not accept
chaitius, en issilh, no sai on.	my service, into exile, I do not know where.

2:49 Tristans, ges no · n auretz de me,	Tristan, you will hear no more of me,
qu'eu m'en vau, chaitius, no sai on.	for I am going sadly away, I do not know where,
De chantar me gic e · m recre,	I am going to stop singing,
e de joi d'amor m'escon.	and I flee from love and joy.

Bernart de Ventadorn was one of the most renowned and influential troubadours. Most of what we know about Bernart comes from his *vida* (life), a biographical tale about him, and from poems by Bernart and by other poets. His *vida* relates that he was born in the castle of Ventadorn in central France, and two poems by his contemporaries say that his parents were either bakers or servants at the castle. One of Bernart's own poems suggests that he learned how to sing and compose poetry from his patron, the Viscount of Ventadorn, and followed his example of promoting the ideals of *fin' amors* (refined love). By the early 1150s, Bernart entered the service of Eleanor of Aquitaine (1122–1204), who was duchess of Aquitaine (in southeastern France) and queen of two countries: she married Louis VII of France shortly before he became king in 1137, then after their divorce in 1152 she wedded Henry Plantagenet, Duke of Normandy, who in 1154 became Henry II of England. Bernart's time in her court brought him to northern France and possibly England, and he became one of the main conduits through which the troubadour tradition came north and stimulated the emergence of trouvères. Later in life, he served the count of Toulouse, and after the latter's death in 1194 Bernart entered a monastery.

Of Bernart's forty-five extant poems, eighteen have complete melodies, more than for any other poet of the twelfth century. One of the most widely known of his songs, and of all troubadour songs, is *Can vei la lauzeta mover*. It is a lover's complaint, the main subject of the entire troubadour repertory. The poem is in Occitan, a language then spoken in what is now southern France. This is a *canso*, a strophic song about love. More specifically, it is about *fin' amors*, refined or courtly love, an idealized love through which the lover is refined by his discreet and respectful adulation of an unattainable woman.

The song is strophic, each stanza but the last having eight lines rhymed abab-cdcd, and each line has eight syllables. The same rhymes appear in every stanza, a feat that demonstrates the poet's virtuosity. The music to which all the stanzas are sung has a new phrase for each line of poetry except the seventh, which repeats the music for the fourth line. The poem ends with a four-line stanza called the *envoi*, which uses the rhymes and music from the last four lines of the previous stanzas.

There are several versions of the melody, notated in different manuscript sources with slight variants among them. Three manuscripts present the melody with its original poem, and several others include the melody set to new words, a procedure called *contrafactum*. There are at least six contrafacta of *Can vei la lauzeta mover*, in four different languages, a sign of the great popularity of this melody. The variants among sources suggest that the melody was conveyed through oral tradition for some time before being written down. To illustrate this variation, the melodies from two of the sources are given here, one currently in Milan (Biblioteca Ambrosiana R 71 sup.) and the other in Paris (Bibliothèque nationale, fr. 22543). The performance on the accompanying recording follows the Milan manuscript. (The texts also vary between these manuscripts, but those variants are not shown here; rather, each melody is underlaid with the text of the poem in the authoritative modern edition.)

In both versions, the melody is in the first mode. The first two phrases establish the mode, beginning on the final D, rising to the reciting tone A, circling around it, and cadencing on A. The rest of the melody rises and falls through graceful arches in mostly stepwise motion, twice touching high D. The Paris version sustains momentum by avoiding a cadence on the final until the very end, as the internal phrases close on the more active tones of G, F, and E. The Milan version on the recording cadences on D after the fourth line, making the fourth and seventh phrases slightly different. The third phrase (at "Que s'oblid'") in the Paris version and the eighth phrase (at "Lo cor de dezirer") in both versions have figures that are written like noteheads with tails; these are sung as two pitches, the main note and the note a step down (if the tail goes down) or up (if the tail goes up). On the recording the singer treats all the notes B as B♭.

Whether the troubadour songs were sung in a particular rhythm is a much debated question, because the notation does not indicate rhythm but the poetry is metrical. The accompanying performance treats the rhythm freely, moving faster or more slowly to shape each phrase. Some performers move more quickly when there is more than one note on a syllable, keeping the syllables, rather than the notes themselves, roughly even in duration. Another approach is to give stressed syllables a value twice as long as unstressed syllables. The accompanying recording features the voice without accompaniment, which may be most likely how such songs were performed. Alternatively, the singer might have been joined by an instrument playing the melody, playing a drone, or improvising an accompaniment.

This canso has seven eight-line stanzas and the closing four-line envoi sung to the second half of the melody, emphasizing the melodic closure. Because of time constraints, only the first, second, and fourth stanzas and the envoi are included on the accompanying recording, but the entire poem should be read to fully understand its meaning. Each stanza introduces a new twist, and the poet's situation gradually becomes clearer with each one.

Comtessa de Dia

(FL. LATE TWELFTH TO EARLY THIRTEENTH CENTURY)

A chantar

Canso (troubadour song)

SECOND HALF OF TWELFTH CENTURY

A chantar m'er de so qu'ieu non volria,
tant me rancur de lui cui sui amia,
car ieu l'am mais que nuilla ren que sia;
vas lui no · m val merces ni cortesia,
ni ma beltatz ni mos pretz ni mos sens,
c'atressi · m sui enganad' e trahia
com degr' esser, s'ieu fos desavinens.

To sing I must of that which I would rather not,
so bitter I am towards him who is my love:
for I love him more than anyone;
my kindness and courtesy make no impression on him,
nor my beauty, my virtue, or my intelligence;
so I am deceived and betrayed,
as I should be if I were unattractive.

Melody transcribed by Hendrik van der Werf, *The Extant Troubadour Melodies* (Rochester: Author, 1984),
13. Gerald A. Bond, text editor. Text and translation used by permission of Hyperion Records Ltd., London,
England.

`0:58` D'aisso · m conort car anc non fi faillenssa,

amics, vas vox per nulla captenenssa,
anz vos am mais non fetz Seguis Valenssa;

e platz me mout quez eu d'amar vox venssa,
lo mieus amics, car etz lo plus valens;
mi faltz orguoill en ditz et en parvenssa,

e si etz francs vas totas autras gens.

Be · m meravill com vostre cors s'orguoilla,
amics, vas me, per qu'ai razon qu'ieu · m duoilla;

non es ges dreitz c'autr' amors vos mi touilla

per nuilla ren que · us diga ni acuoilla;
e membre vos cals fo · l comenssamens
de nostr' amor! ja Domnedieus non vuoilla
qu'en ma colpa sia · l departimens.

Proesa grans qu'el vostre cors s'aizina
e lo rics pretz qu'avetz m'en ataïna,
c'una non sai, loindana ne vezina,
si vol amar, vas vos non si'aclina;

mas vos, amics, etz ben tant conoissens
que ben devetz conoisser la plus fina:
e membre vos de nostres covinens.

Valer mi deu mos pretz e mos paratges,
e ma beltatz e plus mos fis coratges,
per qu'ieu vos mand lai on es vostr' estatges
esta chansson que me sia messatges;
ieu vuoill saber, lo mieus bels amics gens,
per que vos m'etz tant fers ni tant salvatges;
non sai si s'es orguoills o mal talens.

Mas aitan plus vuoill li digas, messatges,
qu'en trop d'orguoill ant grant dan maintas gens.

One thing consoles me: that I have never
  wronged you,
my love, by my behavior towards you;
indeed I love you more than Sequin loved
  Valensa;
and I am glad that my love is greater than yours,
my love, since you are the more worthy;
you are haughty towards me in your words and
  your demeanor,
yet you are friendly to everybody else.

I am amazed how disdainful you have grown,
my love, towards me, which gives me good
  reason to grieve;
it is not right that another love should take you
  away from me,
whatever she may say to attract you;
and remember how our love began!
God forbid
that I should be to blame for our parting.

The great prowess which you have
and your fine reputation worry me,
for I know no woman, near or far,
who would not turn to you, if she were inclined
  to love;
but you, my love, are discerning enough
to know who loves you most truly;
and remember the agreement we made.

My reputation and my noble birth should sway you,
and my beauty, and above all my faithful heart;
therefore I send to you where you dwell
this song to be my messenger;
I want to know, my noble love,
why you are so haughty and disdainful towards me;
I do not know whether it is pride or malice.

But most of all I want you to tell him, messenger,
that excess of pride has been the downfall of many.

According to a *vida* (life), or biographical tale, from about a century after she lived,
"Beatrix, comtessa de Dia [Countess of Dia], was a beautiful and good woman, the
wife of Guillaume de Poitiers. And she was in love with Rambaud d'Orange and
made about him many good and beautiful songs." It is not known which parts
of this account are legendary and which parts are true. She has tentatively been

identified with "Beatrix comitissa," named in a document of 1212 as the daughter
of Count Isoard II of Dia.

Like NAWM 8, *A chantar* is a canso in the Occitan language. However, in this
song the tables are turned, and it is the woman in love who writes of the pride and
disdain of her male lover. It has been suggested that the poetry of the female troubadours (called *trobairitz*) is more realistic and less artificial than that of their male
peers, as if the women were speaking from real life experience rather than of an
idealized love circumscribed by conventions. *A chantar* is the only song by a tro
bairitz for which the music is known to have survived.

The canso consists of five seven-line stanzas with the rhyme scheme aaaabab,
followed by a final couplet that is sung to the same music as the last two lines of the
preceding stanzas. While the a rhymes vary from stanza to stanza, the b rhymes are
the same throughout the poem ("-ens"), linking the stanzas together. The melody
used with each stanza repeats phrases in the pattern ab ab cdb, creating an overall
form of AAB:

Sections	A		A		B		
Musical phrases	a	b	a	b	c	d	b
Rhyme scheme	a	a	a	a	b	a	b

The A and B sections have a musical rhyme because both end with the same musical phrase. AAB form, with or without a musical rhyme, is found in several troubadour songs and many songs of the trouvères and Minnesinger. The melody is in
the first mode, and the pattern of cadences (E and D in the A sections; F, E, and
D in the B section) reinforces the form by closing on the final only at the ends of
sections. Each phrase is a shapely, mostly stepwise curve.

On the accompanying recording, the singer is unaccompanied and sings in relatively free rhythm, moving more quickly when there are two or three notes on a
syllable to maintain roughly equal durations among the syllables. As in NAWM 8,
the round noteheads with tails indicate two pitches, the main note and the note a
step down (if the tail goes down) or up (if the tail goes up). Only the first two verses
appear on the recording.

Adam de la Halle (CA. 1240–?1288)

Jeu de Robin et de Marion: Rondeau, *Robins m'aime*

Musical play

CA. 1284

Robins m'aime,	Robin loves me,
Robins m'a,	Robin has me,
Robins m'a demandée	Robin asked me
Si m'ara.	if he can have me.
Robins m'acata cotele	Robin bought me a skirt
D'escarlate bonne et belle	of scarlet, good and pretty,
Souskanie et chainturele.	a bodice and belt.
Aleuriva!	Hurray!
Robins m'aime,	Robin loves me,
Robins m'a,	Robin has me,
Robins m'a demandée	Robin asked me
Si m'ara.	if he can have me.

From Friedrich Gennrich, *Troubadours, Trouvères, Minne- und Meistergesang* (Cologne, 1951), 38.

Adam de la Halle, one of the last and most famous of the trouvères, was born in Arras and studied in Paris. In 1283 he traveled to Italy with his patron Robert II, count of Artois, and there he entered the service of Robert's uncle, Charles of Anjou. In Naples, Adam composed and staged for his two patrons the musical play *Le jeu de Robin et de Marion* (The Play of Robin and Marion, ca. 1284). Like many other secular dramas of its time, it is a spoken play that features music. However, it includes far more music than its contemporaries, and a few of the songs have polyphonic settings. Indeed, Adam is one of very few medieval composers who is known to have composed both monophonic and polyphonic works. It has been suggested that Adam may have borrowed some of the songs in the play, but the range of styles from popular to elevated is characteristic of his music.

The plot and poetry of the play draw on the genre of lyric poem known as a *pastourelle*, a dialogue between a shepherdess and a knight who courts her. In this play, Marion is a shepherdess who loves and is loved by a shepherd, Robin. When a knight tries to seduce her, she resists, and when he abducts her, Robin attempts to rescue her. Ultimately she escapes, and the lovers are reunited.

Typical of the tuneful songs in the play is *Robins m'aime*, sung by Marion at the opening in a celebration of Robin's love for her. It is a monophonic rondeau in the form ABaabAB, using separate letters for each musical phrase, capitals for the refrain, and lower case when the same music appears with new words in the stanza between the refrains. This form resembles the AAB form of *A chantar* (NAWM 9) with the addition of a refrain before and after the one stanza, using music drawn from the verse. As we shall see, many medieval song forms were based on AAB form, often with the addition of a refrain. The pattern in Adam's rondeau is slightly different from the standard form of the fourteenth-century rondeau (see NAWM 28). Here every phrase cadences on the modal final F. The A phrases circle around the final, and the B phrases skip up to the fifth degree of the scale and descend.

The songs of the trouvères, like those of the troubadours (NAWM 8–9), were written in a notation that did not indicate rhythm. The rhythm shown here is taken from this tune's appearance in a polyphonic motet whose notation shows the exact durations. Whether this rhythm represents that of the original song, or was added by the composer of the motet (possibly Adam himself), is an open question.

The music is written as a single melodic line, but its dancelike rhythm seems to invite instrumental accompaniment. In the recording that accompanies this anthology, the singer sings the refrain and verse, then is joined on the refrain by male voice and instruments (vielle, a bowed string instrument, and gittern, a plucked string instrument). She sings the verse again with the instruments, all join on the refrain, the instruments play the verse, and then singers and instruments join on the refrain two more times. Throughout, the instruments improvise embellishments and accompaniments. Medieval musicians freely adapted secular vocal music for instruments in any combination they desired, and this performance embodies that spirit.

Walther von der Vogelweide
(?CA. 1170–?CA. 1230)

Palästinalied (Nū alrēst lebe ich mir werde)

Minnelied
?CA. 1228

Nū alrēst lebe ich mir wer - de,
daz rei - ne lant und ouch die er - de,

sīt mīn sün - dic ou - ge siht
den man sō vil ē - ren giht.

mirst ge-schehen des ich ie bat, ich bin ko - men

an die stat, dā got men-nisch - lī - chen trat.

Nū alrēst lebe ich mir werde,	Now for the first time I live worthily,
sīt mīn sündic ouge siht	since my sinful eye sees
daz reine lant und ouch die erde,	the Holy Land and also the earth
den man sō vil ēren giht.	to which one so much honor assigns.
Mirst geschehen des ich ie bat,	To me has happened what I have always prayed for,
ich bin komen an die stat,	I have come to the city
dā got mennischlīchen trat.	where God walked as a human being.

1:07

Schoeniu lant rīch unde hēre,	Of the beautiful lands, rich and glorious,
swaz ich der noch hān gesehen,	that I so far have seen,
sō bist duz ir aller ēre:	you are the most deserving of honor:
waz ist wunders hie geschehen!	what a miracle happened here!
Daz ein magt ein kint gebar,	That a maiden bore a child,
hēre über aller engel schar,	Lord over all the multitude of angels,
was daz niht ein wunder gar?	was that not absolutely a miracle?

From Hugo Moser and Joseph Müller-Blattau, *Deutsche Lieder des Mittelalters: Von Walther von der Vogelweide bis zum Lochamer Liederbuch* (Stuttgart: Ernst Klett, 1968), 39–40.

2:52	Hie liez er sich reine toufen,	Here he in purity was baptized,
	daz der mensche reine sī;	so that each person could be pure;
	dō liez er sich hie verkoufen,	then he let himself be sold,
	daz wir eigen wurden frī.	so that we who are in bondage would be set free.
	Anders waeren wir verlorn;	Otherwise, we would be lost;
	wol dir, sper, kriuz unde dorn!	hail to you, spear, cross, and thorn!
	Wē dir, heiden, daz ist dir zorn!	Woe to you, heathens, this enrages you!

3:53	Kristen, juden unde heiden	Christians, Jews, and heathens
	jehent daz diz ir erbe sī.	all claim that this [land] is their inheritance.
	Got sol uns ze reht bescheiden	May God decide justly for us
	durch die sīne namen drī.	for the sake of His three names.
	Al diu welt diu strītet her:	All the world is fighting here;
	wir sin an der rehten ger:	we are desirous of the right;
	reht ist daz er uns gewer.	it is just for Him to defend us.

Walther von der Vogelweide was perhaps the most famous of the Minnesinger. Little is known of his life other than what he wrote in his songs, although a payment record confirms that he was a traveling singer. Most of his songs are love poems, but perhaps his best-known work is the *Palästinalied* (Palestine Song), a crusade song. Such songs described the experiences of those who undertook the Crusades and sought to inspire others to follow their example. Walther may have composed this song around 1228–29, when Holy Roman emperor Frederick II negotiated a treaty that gave Christians control of Jerusalem, which was formerly under Egyptian rule, or perhaps a few years earlier when Frederick was organizing a Crusade. Although the text describes seeing the Holy Land, it is not known whether Walther actually traveled there.

The poem is in Middle High German and has twelve stanzas, four of which are included here. Each stanza is sung to the same melody and has the same rhyme scheme: ab ab ccc. That pattern is reflected in the melody's form, AAB, with the two couplets each set to the same melody (A) and the final three lines set to a new melody (B) that shares the same last phrase. The musical form parallels that of *A chantar* (NAWM 9), though the rhyme scheme differs:

Sections	A		A		B		
Musical phrases	a	b	a	b	c	d	b
Rhyme scheme	a	b	a	b	c	c	c

Since the nineteenth century, scholars of German music have called this AAB structure *bar form*. The A section is known as the *Stollen*, the B section as the *Abgesang*.

As in the trouvère and troubadour songs we have seen (NAWM 8–10), each phrase of this Minnelied forms a shapely curve, moving mostly stepwise with occasional skips. The melody for the Stollen circles around the modal final D, rises to the fifth A, then gently descends to cadence on the final. The Abgesang, by contrast, starts on the A, rises several times to high C, and then descends through an octave before repeating the last phrase of the Stollen. The contrasts in range and shape differentiate the two sections and thus make the form more apparent.

In Walther's notation of this song, the pitches are clear, but the rhythm is not specified. The transcription printed here and the performance on the accompanying recording differ in some details, but both assume that each syllable receives the same duration except for the last syllable in each section, which is twice as long.

The song was originally notated as a monophonic line without accompaniment, but scenes depicted in contemporary artwork often include instrumentalists playing along with singers. On the recording, the vocal line is joined by a *rebec* (a bowed string instrument) and a lute, playing sometimes in unison with the voice, sometimes in heterophony, and sometimes in improvised polyphony. The instruments also play before and between stanzas.

Cantiga 159, *Non sofre Santa Maria,* from *Cantigas de Santa Maria*

Cantiga (song)

CA. 1270—90

Non so - fre San - ta Ma - ri - a de se - e - ren per - di - do - sos os que

as sas ro - ma - ri - as son de fa - zer de - se - jo - sos. E d'est'

o - yd' un mi - ra - gre de que vos que - ro fa - lar, que mos -

trou San - ta Ma - ri - a, per com' eu o - y con - tar, a ũ -

uns ro - meus que fo - ron a Ro - ca - ma - dor o - rar co - mo

mui bõ - os cris - chã - os, sin - ple - ment' e o - mil - do - sos.

Music from Alfonso X El Sabio, *Cantigas de Santa María: Nueva transcripción integral de su música según la métrica latina,* ed. Roberto Pla (Madrid: Música Didáctica, 2001), 290. Text from Afonso X, O Sábio, *Cantigas de Santa Maria,* ed. Walter Mettmann (Edicións Xerais de Galicia, 1981), 541–42. We have made diligent efforts to contact the copyright holder to obtain permission to reprint this selection. If you have information that would help us, please write to Permissions Department, W. W. Norton & Company, Inc., 500 Fifth Avenue, New York, NY 10110.

Non sofre Santa Maria
de seeren perdidosos
os que as sas romarias
son de fazer desejosos.

Holy Mary does not allow
losses to befall
those who desire
to undertake Her pilgrimages.

E dest' oyd' un miragre
de que vos quero falar,
que mostrou Santa Maria,
per com' eu oy contar,
aũuns romeus que foron
a Rocamador orar
como mui bõos crischãos,
simplement' e omildosos.

In this regard, listen to a miracle
that I want to tell to you,
that Holy Mary performed,
as I heard it recounted,
for some pilgrims who went
to Rocamador to pray,
like many good Christians,
simply and humbly.

Non sofre Santa Maria . . .

Holy Mary does not allow . . .

0:39   E pois entraron no burgo,
foron pousada fillar
e mandaron conprar carne
e pan pera seu jantar
e vynno; e entre tanto
foron aa Virgen rogar
que a seu Fillo rogasse
dos seus rogos piadosos

After they entered the town,
they went to an inn,
and ordered and paid for meat
and bread for their supper,
and wine; and in the meantime
they went to pray to the Virgin
that she pray to Her Son for them
with Her merciful prayers.

Non sofre Santa Maria . . .

Holy Mary does not allow . . .

1:07   E mandaran nove postas
meter, asse Deus m' anpar,
na ola, ca tantos eran;
mais poi-las foron tirar,
acharon end' hũa menos,
que a serventa furtar-
lles fora, e foron todos
poren ja quanto queixosos.

And they ordered nine chops of meat,
as God is my witness, to be put
into the pot, for that's how many they were;
but when they pulled them out,
they found one fewer,
for a servant girl had robbed
them, and they were all
complaining a lot about it.

Non sofre Santa Maria . . .

Holy Mary does not allow . . .

1:36   E buscaron pela casa
pola poderen achar,
chamando Santa Maria
que lla quiesse mostrar;
e oyron en un' arca
a posta feridas dar,
e d' ir alá mui correndo
non vos foron vagarosos.

And they searched throughout the house
trying to find it,
calling to Holy Mary
that she reveal it to them;
and they heard in a trunk
the chop hitting the side,
and they went running over to it quickly,
they were not loitering.

Non sofre Santa Maria . . .

Holy Mary does not allow . . .

E fezeron log' a arca	And they had the trunk
abrir e dentro catar	opened and looked inside,
foron, e viron sa posta	and they saw their chop
dacá e dalá saltar;	jumping back and forth;
e sayron aa rua	and they ran into the streets
muitas das gentes chamar,	and called to many people,
que viron aquel miragre,	who saw that miracle,
que foi dos maravillosos	which was one of the most marvelous

Non sofre Santa Maria . . .	Holy Mary does not allow . . .

2:20

Que a Virgen groriosa	That the glorious Virgin
fezess' en aqual logar.	had performed in that place.
Des i fillaron a posta	So they took the chop
e fórona pendorar	and hung it
per hũa corda de seda	on a silken cord
ant' o seu santo altar,	in front of Her holy altar,
loando Santa Maria,	praising Holy Mary,
que faz miragres fremosos.	who performs beautiful miracles.

Non sofre Santa Maria . . .	Holy Mary does not allow . . .

The *Cantigas de Santa Maria* is a collection of over 400 songs (*cantigas*) in honor of the Virgin Mary, preserved in four handsomely illustrated manuscripts. King Alfonso el Sabio (the Wise) of Castile and Léon, a kingdom in northwestern Spain, supervised its preparation around 1270–90 and may have written some of the poems and melodies. Although religious, such songs were sung not in church services but for entertainment, at a time when religious sentiments were a part of everyday life. Mary, the mother of Jesus, was the saint to whom believers most often prayed for assistance and protection. The veneration of Mary in art, poetry, and song increased during the thirteenth century, and these songs grew from that tradition.

A brief explanatory note, which is not sung, is at the beginning of each cantiga. The sung parts that follow include several stanzas, each preceded and followed by the refrain that states the moral of the song. Every tenth cantiga in the collection is a song of praise for Mary. The others describe miracles that Mary performed to protect the faithful from harm, to heal the sick or wounded, and to rescue those in peril. One of the most down-to-earth is this song, whose introductory note says that it relates "How Holy Mary caused to be discovered a chop of meat that was stolen from some pilgrims in the city of Rocamador."

The poem is in lines of eight or seven syllables with a rhyme at the end of each pair of lines. Only two rhymes are used throughout: "-osos" in the refrain and last line of each stanza, and "-ar" for the first three pairs in each stanza. The overall rhyme scheme aa bbba aa is typical of the Arabic *zajal* song form, showing the close relationship between Muslim and Christian cultures in Spain (it is unclear which used the form first).

The melody is simple and bouncy with a constantly repeating figure transcribed here as a quarter note and two eighth notes. The range is very narrow—only a sixth. The music for the refrain also appears in the second half of each verse, with different words. Indicating repetitions of music by letter and of text through capitalization, the overall form can be diagrammed A bba A bba A ... bba A. Note that the verse itself is in a form like that of *A chantar* (NAWM 9) and *Palästinalied* (NAWM 11), with a section repeated to new words followed by a longer contrasting section. Thus the cantiga's form is simply an expansion, with refrain, of the AAB form we have seen before; the relationship may not immediately be obvious because the refrain occurs first and it is customary to label sections alphabetically in the order they appear. Within both a and b sections, a short musical phrase repeats four times with varying endings, so that the entire song is spun out of only two brief ideas:

	Refrain				Verse								Refrain			
Sections	A				b		b		a				A			
Musical phrases	a	a'	a	a"	b	b'	b	b'	a	a'	a	a"	a	a'	a	a"
Rhyme scheme	a		a		b		b		b		a		a		a	

According to contemporary accounts, the refrain was typically sung by a chorus and the verses by a soloist, as on the accompanying recording. In that performance, the fourth and fifth verses are spoken rather than sung in order to emphasize the climax of the story, when the miracle occurs.

Although the troubadour, trouvère, and Minnesinger songs we have studied all fit neatly into modes familiar from chant (NAWM 8, 9, and 11 in mode 1 on D and NAWM 10 in mode 5 on F), the concept of modes as used in the church did not necessarily apply to the practice of vernacular melody in the Middle Ages. *Non sofre Santa Maria* illustrates how imperfect a mechanism the church modes can be for describing vernacular songs. The melody cadences on G, but the prominence of F as the lowest note in the refrain suggests that the recurring highest note B should be performed as B♭ to avoid the tritone. On the recording, the performers alter B to B♭ in the refrain and the second half of the verse (which uses the same music) but not in the first half of each verse; this produces an effect similar to that of shifting back and forth between Dorian and Mixolydian modes on G.

Like most medieval songs outside the liturgy, these cantigas could either be sung unaccompanied or with instruments. The recording offers one possibility for accompaniment: *nakers* (a small drum of the Middle Ages) beating a lively pattern and a *rebec* (a bowed string instrument) varying between phrases of the melody, a drone, and improvised counterpoint, joined on the refrains by a pipe and *oud* (lute).

La quarte estampie royal, from *Le manuscrit du roi*

Estampie

LATE THIRTEENTH CENTURY

From Timothy McGee, *Medieval Instrumental Dances* (Bloomington: Indiana University Press, 1989), 64.
Copyright 1989 Indiana University Press. Reprinted with permission of Indiana University Press.

Instrumentalists who played music for dancing during the Middle Ages usually played from memory or improvised, so very few dance melodies were written down. However, a thirteenth-century song manuscript known as *Le manuscrit du roi* (The Manuscript of the King), now in the French national library in Paris (Bibliothèque nationale fonds français 844), includes eight dance tunes identified as "royal estampies." The manuscript was probably commissioned around 1250–70 by Guillaume of Villehardouin, prince of Moria. The inclusion of these dance tunes suggests that they were highly esteemed, but what connection they may have had to the royal court is unclear.

The *estampie* is a dance in a fast triple meter that features a series of phrases, each played twice but with a different ending each time. The first time, the cadence is referred to as *open* (*ouvert*) because it ends on a note a step or two above the modal final and thus sounds incomplete; the second time, the phrase cadences on the final and is therefore referred to as *closed* (*clos*). In the transcription included here, the two cadences are shown as first and second endings with a repeat mark at the end of the first ending. The same open and closed endings were meant to be played with each successive phrase, so in the medieval manuscripts it was not necessary to write them out after the first few notes. The material shown here between vertical brackets was supplied by the editor, but any medieval performer would have known to play it.

The final of this estampie is F, and the mode initially seems to be mode 6, with a range extending a fourth below the final and a melodic emphasis on A, the reciting tone of that mode. Later, the melody ranges an octave above the final, reminding us that late medieval melodies often do not fit neatly into one of the standard church modes.

The editor has included the first phrase in the original thirteenth-century notation, which shows the relative durations of the notes exactly but does not include a time signature or barlines. The transcription into modern notation includes vertical strokes below the staff to indicate where the barlines would fall. On the accompanying recording, this estampie is played on a medieval *pipe and tabor*: a single performer plays the melody on a pipe, an end-blown flute similar to a recorder, while accompanying himself on a small drum called a tabor (for a thirteenth-century picture, see HWM, Figure 4.10, p. 81). As was typical at the time, the performer adds embellishments to the melody, including trills and ornamental notes. The drum part is entirely improvised. The first notated percussion parts did not appear until the late seventeenth century, but we know from pictures and descriptions that drums and other percussion were used frequently in music for dancing, processions, ceremonies, and the military.

Organa from *Musica enchiriadis*

Parallel organum and mixed parallel and oblique organum

CA. 850–890

(a) *Tu patris sempiternus es filius*, in parallel organum at the fifth below

Principal Voice
Organal Voice

Tu pa - tris sem - pi - ter - nus es fi - li - us.

Tu Patris sempiternus es filius.   You of the father are the everlasting son.

(b) *Sit gloria domini*, in parallel organum at the fifth below, with octave doublings

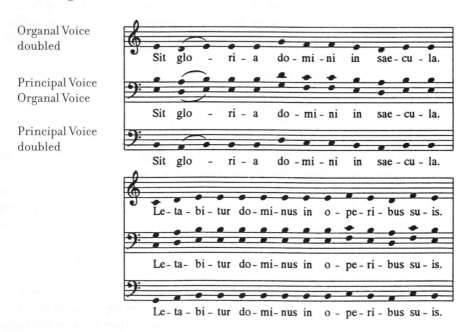

Organal Voice doubled

Sit glo - ri - a do - mi - ni in sae - cu - la.

Principal Voice
Organal Voice

Sit glo - ri - a do - mi - ni in sae - cu - la.

Principal Voice doubled

Sit glo - ri - a do - mi - ni in sae - cu - la.

Le - ta - bi - tur do - mi - nus in o - pe - ri - bus su - is.

Le - ta - bi - tur do - mi - nus in o - pe - ri - bus su - is.

Le - ta - bi - tur do - mi - nus in o - pe - ri - bus su - is.

Sit gloria domini in saecula.   May the glory of the Lord be forever;
Laetabitur dominus in operibus suis.   the Lord will rejoice in his works. (Psalm 103 [104]:31)

From *Musica enchiriadis and Scolica enchiriadis*, trans. with intro. and notes by Raymond Erickson, ed. Claude V. Palisca (New Haven: Yale University Press, 1995), 19, 24, and 27–28. Reprinted by permission.

(c) *Rex caeli domine*, in mixed parallel and oblique organum

Principal Voice
Organal Voice

Rex cae - li   do - mi - ne   ma - ris   un - di - so - ni.

Ty - tan - is   ni - ti - di   qual - li - di - que so - li.

Te hu - mi - les fa - mu - li   mo - du - lis ve - ne - ran - do pi - is.

Se iu - be - as fla - gi - tant va - ri - is   li - be - ra - re ma - lis.

Rex caeli domine maris undisoni,	King of Heaven, Lord of the roaring sea, of the
Tytanis nitidi squalidique soli.	shining Titan (Sun) and the squalid earth,
Te humiles famuli modulis venerando piis,	Your humble servants, worshipping you with pious melodies,
Se iubeas flagitant variis liberare malis.	Beseech you, as you command, to free them from diverse ills.

Musica enchiriadis (Music Handbook, ca. 850–890) was one of the most widely read music treatises in the Middle Ages. It survives in almost fifty manuscript sources, the earliest from ca. 890. Some early sources attribute it to Hoger (d. 906), abbot of the Benedictine abbey of Werden in northern Germany, but the surviving text appears to derive from earlier versions that may date back to the middle of the ninth century. It is a practical manual that includes instruction in the theory and practice of church music. One of the topics covered in the treatise is how to perform diaphony ("singing together"), or *organum*, which is music in two parts sung extemporaneously rather than from notation. The three selections shown here are examples from the treatise. They should be thought of not as compositions but as models for how such polyphony was expected to be sung. In every case, one of the voices—called the *principal voice*—was taken from a chant. The other voice—the *organal voice*—was derived from the principal voice according to a set of simple rules that were described in the treatise for singers to apply during performance. This made it unnecessary to write out the added part.

Tu patris sempiternus es filius (setting a line from the Latin hymn *Te Deum*) is an example of parallel organum at the fifth below, which was probably an ancient practice long before *Musica enchiriadis* described it. The principal voice, singing the chant, is joined by the organal voice a perfect fifth below, producing a more resonant sound than unison singing.

Sit gloria domini (to a verse from Psalm 103 [104]) illustrates the possibilities of doubling one or both voices at the octave to enrich the sonority further. Here the principal voice is doubled an octave lower and the organal voice an octave higher, but other combinations are also allowed by the treatise. Such doubling might have occured naturally in choirs that included both men and boys, whose voices lie in different ranges.

In both of these forms of parallel organum, everyone sings the same melody, separated by a perfect fifth or other perfect interval (octave or fourth). This manner of singing can be done without the use of notation, when everyone singing knows the same tune. (Try it with one or more friends, singing your favorite songs in parallel fifths.) The earliest appearance of parallel organum is in a ninth-century treatise, but it was not a new invention in the ninth century; rather, the new invention was notation, a way of writing down pitches, which allowed the writer to describe this phenomenon accurately for the first time. Since they are so simple, almost as obvious as singing in octaves, we assume that these styles of singing in parallel perfect intervals date back centuries and perhaps millennia.

Organum at the fourth below was more complex—at least in the notation system of the *Musica enchiriadis*—because of the way the writer described notes and scales. He laid out the system of notes as a series of disjunct tetrachords: G–A–$B\flat$–c, d–e–f–g, a–b–c'–d', e'–$f\sharp'$–g'–a', and so on. This scale system is ideal for parallel fifths because it lacks diminished fifths. (Try playing the tetrachords on the keyboard to confirm this.) However, this system does contain augmented fourths, such as $B\flat$–e and f–b, which must be avoided in organum at the fourth. In the examples included here, the presence of $B\flat$ in the lower octave and $B\natural$ in the upper octave is indicated in the transcriptions of the first and third selections; in *Sit gloria domini*, the low B is natural because it must duplicate the principal voice at a perfect octave.

The writer indicated that in order to prevent the organal voice from sounding a tritone below the principal voice, it must not move below c during a segment of chant that includes e or below g when the chant includes b. The organal voice must remain stationary until it can move in parallel perfect fourths without creating a tritone. The sequence *Rex caeli domine* is an example of how this system works in practice, producing organum that sometimes features parallel motion and at other times resembles a melody over a drone, called oblique motion. Seconds or thirds, still considered dissonances, are permitted while the organal voice is not moving. At the end of a phrase, if the organal voice would form a second or third with the principal voice, it moves instead to join the chant on a unison.

All three styles of organum illustrated here could be sung by a group with little or no rehearsal, since the rules for deriving the organal voice from the principal voice are clear and relatively simple. However, the system demonstrated by the *Rex caeli domini* example foreshadowed new possibilities. Although mixed parallel and oblique organum was still a method for singing polyphony extemporaneously rather than composing pieces, the system can be seen in retrospect as a step toward a polyphony of truly independent voices.

15

Alleluia Justus ut palma, from *Ad organum faciendum*

Alleluia in note-against-note organum

CA. 1100

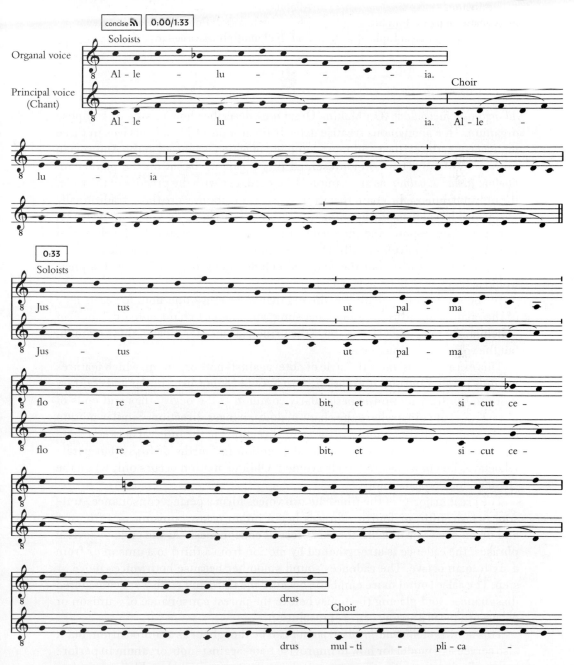

Organal voice

Principal voice (Chant)

concise | 0:00/1:33

Soloists

Al – le – lu – – ia.

Al – le – lu – – ia. Al – le –

lu – ia

0:33

Soloists

Jus – tus ut pal – ma

Jus – tus ut pal – ma

flo – re – – bit, et si – cut ce –

flo – re – – bit, et si – cut ce –

drus

Choir

drus mul – ti – pli – ca –

Milan, Biblioteca Ambrosiana, MS M. 17 sup. Adapted from Edmond de Coussemaker, *Histoire de l'harmonie au moyen-age* (Paris: V. Didron, 1852), 234, with emendations from other sources.

bi – tur.

Alleluia.   Alleluia.
Justus ut palma florebit,   The righteous shall flourish like a palm tree
et sicut cedrus multiplicabitur.   and shall multiply like a cedar.

Ad organum faciendum (On Making Organum) describes how to sing or compose organum. This anonymous treatise dates from around 1100 and survives in three manuscripts, the earliest and most complete of which is housed at the Ambrosian Library in Milan. The writer presented this organum, based on the plainchant *Alleluia Justus ut palma*, as an example. In accordance with the practice at the time, the only portions of the chant that were sung in polyphony were those traditionally performed by soloists: the opening intonation of "Alleluia," and most of the verse. The rest of the respond and the final word of the verse were sung by the choir and were not treated polyphonically. Only the upper voice of the polyphonic portions appears in the treatise, but the chant is included here to show how such a piece would actually have been performed.

In the sections in polyphony, the organal voice sings one note for each note of the chant, except for one melisma sung with the last chant note on "-lu-" of "Alleluia." The organal voice is above the principal voice for most of this organum, but the voices sometimes cross.

This example illustrates the style of note-against-note organum, which features not only parallel and oblique motion, as in NAWM 14, but also similar and contrary motion. Contrary motion is particularly common at the beginnings and ends of phrases and at points where the chant melody changes direction. Similar motion occurs when both voices move in the same direction but the interval between them changes. Most phrases use some parallel motion in fourths or fifths, but parallel octaves and unisons are largely avoided. Oblique motion occurs only when the chant melody repeats a note.

The great majority of the time, the two voices form a perfect consonance—unison, octave, fifth, or fourth. Phrases begin on an octave, unison, or fifth, and end on an octave or unison, the most restful consonances. At the ends of several phrases, the cadence is strengthened by motion from a third to a unison or from a sixth to an octave. The cadences sound smoother because both voices move by step. They also sound more emphatic because the third and sixth were considered dissonances, and placing them just before the purest consonance of a unison or octave produced a strong sense of resolution.

This setting of *Alleluia Justus ut palma* can be thought of as a composition, but it also served as a model for how to improvise note-against-note organum in performance. By demonstrating how a new, independent voice could be added to an existing melody, such music laid the foundation for the later development of polyphony.

Jubilemus, exultemus

Versus in Aquitanian polyphony

CA. 1100

16

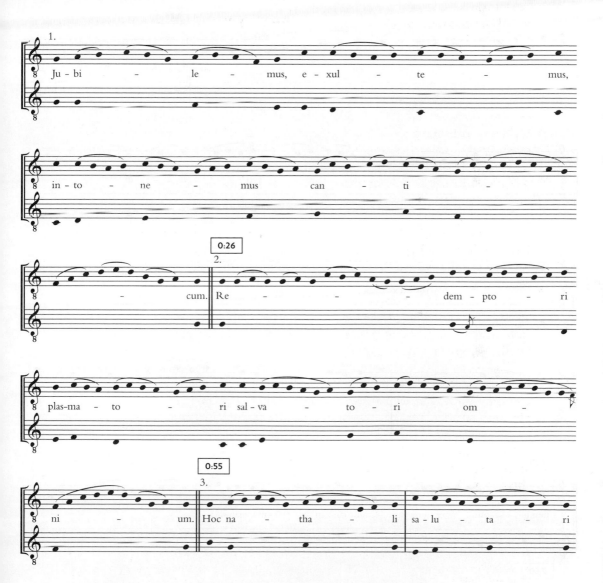

1. Ju-bi — le — mus, e-xul — te — mus, in-to — ne — mus can — ti — — cum.

0:26

2. Re — — — dem-pto — ri plas-ma-to — ri sal-va — to — ri om — ni — um.

0:55

3. Hoc na — tha — li sa-lu — ta — ri

Paris, Bibliothèque Nationale, fonds latin 1139, fol. 41. For two different metrical transcriptions, see *Saint-Martial Polyphony*, ed. Bryan Gillingham (Henryville, Ottawa, and Binningen: Institute of Mediaeval Music, 1994), 7–9, and *The Polyphony of Saint Martial and Santiago de Compostela*, ed. Theodore Karp (Berkeley: University of California Press, 1992), vol. 2, pp. 178–81. A facsimile of the page is in Carl Parrish, *The Notation of Medieval Music* (New York: Norton, 1957), Plate XXI, and a facsimile of the entire manuscript is published in *Paris, Bibliothèque nationale, fonds latin 1139 d'après les manuscrits conservés à la Bibliothèque nationale de Paris*, ed. Bryan Gillingham (Ottawa: Institute of Mediaeval Music, 1987).

Jubilemus exultemus, intonemus canticum	Let us rejoice, exult, and sing a song
Redemptori plasmatori, salvatori omnium.	to the redeemer, creator, savior of all.
Hoc nathali salutari omnis nostra turmula	For this blessed birth, let our whole congregation
Deum laudet sibi plaudet per eterna secula.	praise God and eternally applaud.
Qui hodie de Marie utero progrediens	He who today issued from Mary's womb
Homo verus rex atque herus in terris apparuit.	a true man, appeared on earth as a king and lord.
Tam beatum ergo natum cum ingenti gaudio	In such a blessed birth, then, with boundless delight,
Conlaudantes, exultantes benedicamus Domino.	praising and exulting together, let us bless the Lord.

This two-part setting of a rhymed metrical text is from a manuscript that was copied in the early twelfth century in or near Limoges, a city in the duchy of Aquitaine, now southwest France. The manuscript contains historical chronicles of Limoges along with tropes, versus, musical dramas, and Office services from the surrounding area. The music is written in the Aquitanian notation of that region. Now in the French national library in Paris, the manuscript was for centuries in the Abbey of St. Martial in Limoges. Because of these associations, the style represented by this piece is called Aquitanian polyphony or St. Martial polyphony. Most likely this style of polyphony originated in Limoges or nearby, in close proximity both geographically and chronologically to the troubadour tradition that emerged in Aquitaine in the early twelfth century. The polyphony in this and other Aquitanian manuscripts is the written record of what must have been primarily an oral tradition. Pieces such as this one were improvised within accepted conventions, and only some were written down.

The text is a versus, a rhythmic, rhymed poem in Latin. The internal rhymes (such as "Jubilemus," "exultemus," and "intonemus" in the first line) make the poetry especially lively and interesting. Since the poem ends with the phrase "Benedicamus Domino" (Let us bless the Lord), it may have been a polyphonic trope on the liturgical formula of the same name that was used both in the Office and as a substitute for the *Ite, missa est* at Mass during penitential seasons. This versus, however, makes no reference to an existing chant melody.

The anonymous composer set anywhere from one to seventeen notes in the upper part to each note in the lower part, called the tenor. Theorists at the time distinguished between two polyphonic styles or textures, both exemplified here. Extended passages with only one to three notes in the upper part for each tenor note, as at "Deum laudet, sibi plaudet" and "Tam beatum ergo natum," are in *discant style*. Passages in which the upper part is relatively melismatic compared to the tenor, as in the first two verses, are in *organum style*. This type of organum is today known as *florid organum* to distinguish it from other styles of organum.

When both voices move simultaneously, they move primarily in contrary motion, but oblique, parallel, and similar motion also occur. Because there are often two or more notes in the upper part for each tenor note, the sonorities between the voices are much more varied and include many more dissonances than the sonorities in note-against-note organum (compare NAWM 15). However, as in the earlier style, the ends of phrases are marked with unisons or octaves, usually approached in contrary motion, which creates a strong sense of closure. Treatises of the time suggest that the upper part, however florid, was conceived as an elaboration of an essential note-against-note counterpoint. Thus, for example, the upper part to the first two words of the second verse, "Redemptori plasmatori," can be reduced to the first note sung to each syllable, revealing the underlying contrapuntal framework (see HWM, p. 90, Example 5.4).

The notation in the manuscript is in heighted neumes, so that the pitches are fairly certain. The scribe notated the florid upper voice above the slower tenor part in score format, but the text underlay and alignment of the notes are not consistently clear. Although the poetry has consistent iambic meter, which might suggest a regular alternation of short and long notes in the tenor, the number of notes in the upper voice makes this unlikely. For this reason, most performers treat the rhythm freely, as in chant.

Leoninus (FL. CA. 1150S–CA. 1201) and colleagues

Viderunt omnes

Organum duplum

17

SECOND HALF OF THE TWELFTH CENTURY

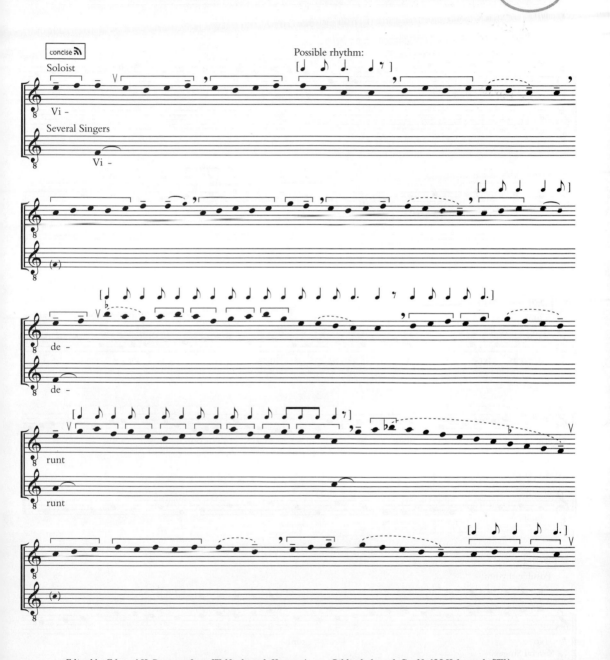

Edited by Edward H. Roesner from Wolfenbüttel, Herzog August Bibliothek, cod. Guelf. 628 Helmstad. (W1),
fol. 25r–25v. Chant from Paris, Bibliothèque nationale, fonds lat. 1112, 20r. © Copyright 2005
Edward H. Roesner. Used by permission.

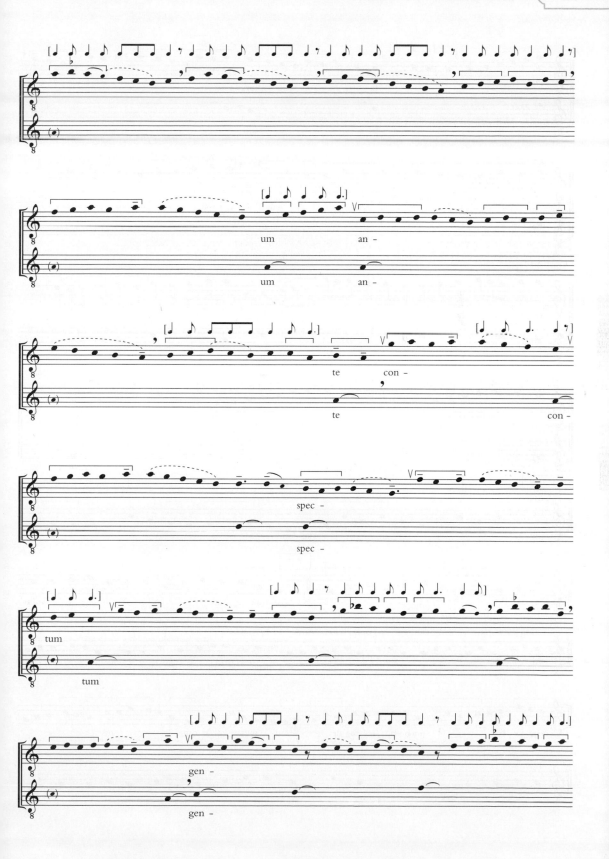

Viderunt omnes fines terrae salutare Dei nostri: jubilate Deo omnis terra.

All the ends of the earth have seen the salvation of our God; sing joyfully to God, all the earth. (Psalm 97[98]:3–4)

2:41 ℣. Notum fecit Dominus salutare suum: ante conspectum gentium revelavit justitiam suam.

℣. The Lord hath made known His salvation; He hath revealed His justice in the sight of the peoples. (Psalm 97[98]:2)

One of the most glorious accomplishments of the Middle Ages is the body of polyphony created during the twelfth and thirteenth centuries by musicians associated with the Cathedral of Notre Dame in Paris for the services there and in other churches. Leoninus, a canon at the cathedral, is credited with compiling a *Magnus liber organi* (Great Book of Polyphony) that contained two-voice settings of the solo portions of the responsorial chants for major feasts, although the repertory was almost certainly the work of many collaborators rather than a single individual. No such book survives from Leoninus' lifetime, but the repertory is preserved in several thirteenth-century manuscripts that include additions and substitutions by later composers.

This setting of the Gradual *Viderunt omnes* from the Mass for Christmas Day (see NAWM 3d) is found in one of the oldest of these manuscripts. Now housed in Wolfenbüttel, Germany, this source was prepared around 1240 for a priory (a religious house) connected to the cathedral in St. Andrews, Scotland; whether it was copied there or in Paris is not certain. Another early manuscript, probably copied in Paris in the 1240s and now in Florence, Italy, has a version of the same piece that differs in only a few details, variants that may have resulted either from oral transmission of the music or from choices of the scribes. The agreement between these two sources suggests that this may be the earliest surviving two-voice setting of *Viderunt* in the Notre Dame repertory; the other settings in the Florence and other manuscripts include passages from the version shown here but have different polyphony for several segments of the chant resulting from a process of substitution (see discussion for NAWM 18). The different settings are not attributed in the manuscripts, and we do not know how much of this version is by Leoninus, if any. But it is probably representative of the organum he and his contemporaries sang.

Performances of this piece must have seemed magnificent to listeners during the Middle Ages. As the first responsorial chant in the Mass for Christmas Day (also used at Notre Dame for the Feast of the Lord's Circumcision on January 1, a week after Christmas), it would probably have been the first polyphony to be heard during that service at Notre Dame, and it would have had a powerful effect. It is grand both in sound and in size, lasting about three times as long as the original chant.

As was typical during this period, only the solo portions are in polyphony, with the choral portions remaining in plainchant. The alternation between polyphony and monophony magnifies the contrast between solo and choral performance that was already present in the original chant. Here, the first two words of the respond and all but the last two words of the verse are set polyphonically. In these passages, the notes of the chant appear in relatively long values in the lower voice, sung by a small choir of about five voices, and above the chant is a much more florid upper line sung by a soloist. The lower voice came to be called the *tenor* (from Latin *tenere*, "to hold") because it holds the chant, and the upper voice is called the *duplum* (Latin for "double"). Only the polyphonic portions appear in the manuscripts; the choir would have performed the chant by memory or from a separate book of plainchant. The version of the chant included here is taken from a manuscript used in Paris during the Middle Ages and differs in a few details from the version in modern chant editions (compare NAWM 3d).

Besides the contrast between chant and polyphony, Leoninus and his colleagues employed two contrasting styles of polyphony: florid organum and discant. The opening passage is in organum style. The four notes of "Viderunt" are stretched out into unmeasured sustained notes of indefinite duration to form the tenor. Against this, the soloist sings melismatic phrases, always singing the same syllable as the tenor. The melismas are broken at irregular intervals by cadences and pauses that were marked by vertical strokes in the original notation and are rendered here as wedges or breath marks. The fluid melody—nonperiodic and loosely segmented— strongly suggests that this is a written version of a style developed through improvisatory practice.

At the word "omnes," there is a brief passage in discant style. In this section, the tenor moves more quickly, the duplum has one to three notes for each note of the tenor, and both parts sing in a strictly measured rhythm with repeating patterns known as rhythmic modes. The rhythm of the tenor is in mode 5, a series of equal long notes transcribed as dotted quarters, and the duplum is in mode 1, alternating long and short notes (called *longs* and *breves*, from Latin *longa* and *brevis*), transcribed as quarter and eighth notes respectively. In some cases the quarter note is split into smaller notes, demonstrating a practice known as *fractio modi* (division of the mode). The small noteheads that appear occasionally in both organum and discant sections represent a *plica* in the original notation, a stroke added to a note to represent a note a step higher or lower (compare the similar sign in NAWM 9).

The treatment of text in the original chant largely determined where to use organum or discant style. Organum style, with long sustained notes in the tenor, was appropriate for portions of the original chant that were syllabic or neumatic. Where the original chant was highly melismatic, it was necessary for the tenor to move along more quickly in discant style so that the whole piece would not be unduly lengthened. Thus, in this setting of *Viderunt omnes*, there are four passages in discant style: at the beginning of "omnes"; on "dominus" (the longest); at "suum" (the briefest); and on "revelavit." All of these end with a cadence in organum style, and in between them are sections in organum style. Such self-contained sections, setting one or more words or syllables from the chant and ending with a cadence, are known as *clausulae* (sing. *clausula*, Latin for a clause or phrase in a sentence). Clausulae may be in organum or discant style. Many discant clausulae close with a flourish in organum style to make a strong cadence.

In both organum and discant styles, the onset of a new tenor note is normally accompanied by a perfect consonance (unison, octave, fifth, or fourth) between the parts. At the close of extended phrases, the duplum sometimes sings a seventh moving to an octave (as at "-de-" of "Viderunt") or a second moving to a unison (as at "-nes" of "omnes") in what resembles a modern appoggiatura. The discant sections are articulated by rests that break up the melodies into easily understood phrases.

Horizontal brackets above the music show the original notegroups, or *ligatures*. These brackets are included in modern editions because the Notre Dame composers used ligatures to notate the rhythmic modes. At "dominus," the pattern of three notes in a ligature followed by several ligatures with two notes indicates that the rhythm is in mode 1. This edition uses dotted slurs to transcribe notegroups with diamond-shaped noteheads (used for descending figures) and adds a flat above the note B when singers would probably have sung B♭ to avoid the tritone with F or to provide a smoother contour.

It is not certain whether the upper part in the sections in organum style should be sung in modal rhythm or more freely. In most passages, the notation does not show the pattern of ligatures for any of the rhythmic modes, which suggests a free performance like the one on the accompanying recording. But in some passages, such as the first phrase on "-runt" of "Viderunt," there is a regular pattern of ligatures that suggests mode 1, as shown by the notes above the staff. Both rhythmic and free renditions can be heard on modern recordings of organum. Some scholars have suggested that the twelfth-century original was free, but that later generations preferred to hear the upper line in modal rhythm.

Clausulae on *Dominus*, from *Viderunt omnes*

18

Substitute clausulae

LATE TWELFTH OR EARLY THIRTEENTH CENTURY

(a) *Dominus*, clausula No. 26

From *Le Magnus Liber Organi de Notre-Dame de Paris*, vol. 5, *Les Clausules à deux voix du manuscrit de Florence, Biblioteca Medicea-Laurenziana, Pluteus 29.1, Fascicule V*, ed. Rebecca A. Baltzer (Monaco: Éditions de l'Oiseau-Lyre, 1995), 17 and 20. Reprinted by permission.

(b) *Dominus*, clausula No. 29

Singers at Notre Dame frequently devised new discant clausulae to replace passages on the same segment of chant that were used in existing organum. A manuscript of Notre Dame polyphony that was probably copied in Paris during the 1240s and is now in Florence, Italy, contains dozens of such *substitute clausulae*, including ten that set the phrase of chant from *Viderunt omnes* on the word "Dominus." Any of these could have been used at Mass in place of the parallel passage in the setting of *Viderunt omnes* in NAWM 17. Indeed, the first clausula shown here appears as part of a version of *Viderunt omnes* in another Notre Dame manuscript that also includes passages from NAWM 17. The collection of clausulae in the Florence manuscript is ordered according to the day in the church year when the clausula might be sung. The two included here are numbers 26 and 29 in the collection.

In both of these clausulae, the chant is in the tenor with a repeating rhythmic pattern, and the duplum adds a free counterpoint above it. The recurring rhythmic figures in the tenor give these clausulae greater shape and coherence than the clausula in NAWM 17 on this same segment of chant. Such rhythmic patterning is a common feature of clausula and motet tenors throughout the thirteenth century. In both of the clausulae included here, the pattern breaks near the end to signal the final cadence.

Clausula No. 26 uses rhythmic mode 5 in the tenor and alternates between modes 5 and 1 in the duplum. Mode 5 is a series of perfect longs (notes whose duration spans three *tempora*, the basic unit of time), notated here as dotted quarter notes, and mode 1 is the long-short pattern shown as a quarter and eighth note. The repeating rhythmic pattern in the tenor emphasizes the first and third dotted quarter note of every grouping, creating an effect similar to that of $\frac{6}{8}$ meter. However, the editor has not introduced barlines, and instead treats each perfect long as a unit, numbering them as if each perfect long were a measure of $\frac{3}{8}$. The duplum either rests with the tenor, producing short phrases, or keeps moving when the tenor rests, resulting in longer melodic phrases. Often the melodic and rhythmic contours in the duplum produce a sense of paired phrasing and varied repetition; for example, the first two phrases (longs 1–8) are varied in the second two phrases (longs 9–16), and the first four (longs 1–16) are varied again in the second four (longs 17–32). If the piece were barred in $\frac{6}{8}$ meter, almost every downbeat would have a perfect consonance, with either dissonance or consonance in between downbeats.

Both voices in clausula No. 29 use mode 2 (short-long, with the short note on the beat), which gives this clausula a very different rhythmic character. Although mode 2 is the prevalent rhythm, both voices include perfect longs (transcribed as dotted quarter notes), providing variety to the texture. Once again, the rhythmic repetitions in both voices create paired phrases (compare longs 1–8 with 9–16 and longs 17–24 with 25–32). All these repetitions, variations, and pairings create a very clear sense of structure, a characteristic that was of great importance for thirteenth-century music.

In the context of a complete performance of *Viderunt omnes* in the Mass for Christmas Day, any clausulae used for *Dominus* would have been performed by the same forces as in the setting in NAWM 17: about five voices on the tenor, and a soloist on the duplum. However, such clausulae found a new life as motets when words were added to the duplum. On the accompanying recordings these clausulae are sung by two soloists to facilitate comparison to the motets in NAWM 21.

Perotinus

(FL. LATE TWELFTH AND EARLY THIRTEENTH CENTURIES)

Viderunt omnes

Organum quadruplum

CA. 1198

From *Le Magnus Liber Organi de Notre-Dame de Paris*, vol. 1, *Les Quadrupla et Tripla de Paris*, ed. Edward H. Roesner (Monaco: Éditions de l'Oiseau-Lyre, 1993), 1–14. Reprinted by permission.

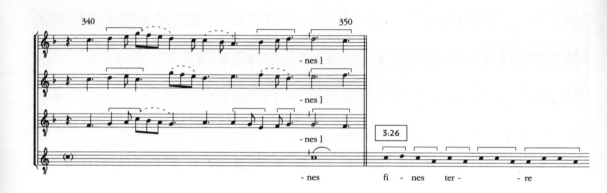

- nes]

- nes]

- nes]

3:26

- nes   fi - nes ter -   - re

sa - lu - ta -   - re   de -   - i   no - stri

iu - bi - la - te   de -   - o   om -

- nis   ter -   - ra.

Viderunt omnes fines terrae salutare Dei
  nostri: jubilate Deo omnis terra.

All the ends of the earth have seen the
  salvation of our God; sing joyfully to
  God, all the earth. (Psalm 97[98]:3–4)

4:14   ℣. Notum fecit Dominus salutare suum:
  ante conspectum gentium revelavit
  justitiam suam.

℣. The Lord hath made known His salvation; He hath revealed His justice in the
  sight of the peoples. (Psalm 97[98]:2)

Among several pieces ascribed to Perotinus is this setting of the Gradual *Viderunt omnes* (see NAWM 3d), the same chant elaborated in NAWM 17. The two settings had the same purpose, function, and intended audience. They also have the same general structure: only the solo portions of the original chant are set in polyphony; the choral portions remain in plainchant; and the polyphonic portions alternate between organum (with sustained notes in the tenor) and discant (in which the tenor moves more rapidly, in steady rhythm). However, Leoninus and his contemporaries sang in only two voice parts—tenor and duplum—and Perotinus composed for four voice parts, adding a *triplum* (the third voice from the bottom) and *quadruplum* (the fourth) to produce a much richer sound. Although *Viderunt omnes* appears in the Mass for Christmas Day (NAWM 3), at Notre Dame Cathedral in Paris it was also used for the Feast of the Lord's Circumcision on January 1. An 1198 letter from the bishop of Paris requests a four-voice organum for the latter feast, and Perotinus most likely composed this setting for that year's service.

In the organum sections of NAWM 17, the rhythm was probably unmeasured, but in Perotinus' setting, all the upper parts use the rhythmic modes throughout. This reflects his generation's preference for modal rhythm and also solves the practical problem of coordinating the parts.

As in NAWM 17, the longest discant clausula is on "dominus" (where the longest melisma is in the original chant), and shorter passages in discant appear at the beginning of "omnes," on "suum," and on "revelavit." Perotinus included two additional discant passages, on "-ta-" of "salutare" and on "gentium." In the discant sections, the upper voices often rest with the tenor, but sometimes one or more voices sing through the tenor rests to maintain forward motion.

In the very lengthy sections in organum style, Perotinus used various kinds of repetition to achieve a balance of unity and variety. Several phrases are repeated in one, two, or all three upper voices, exactly or with slight variations (see the quadruplum at the beginning of the piece and all three voices at longs 243–98 of the respond). Some figures are also repeated at a new pitch level (see the duplum at longs 20–27 of the respond and all three voices in the verse at longs 154–72). All this rhythmic and melodic repetition makes the music especially coherent and memorable.

As demonstrated several times near the beginning of this piece, Perotinus frequently employed a device called *voice exchange*, when two voices trade figures, as the duplum and triplum do at longs 8–19. Often the use of voice exchange or varied repetition results in pairs of phrases that exhibit antecedent-consequent relationships. Johannes de Garlandia, who wrote a treatise on rhythm in Notre Dame polyphony, remarked that complementary phrases of this kind occurred particularly in a style of organum called *copula*, which he said was intermediate between discant and organum.

Perotinus also used harmony to create interest and forward momentum. Phrases generally end with perfect consonances among all four voices, but many phrases (including the first several) begin with one or more dissonances (seconds, thirds, sixths, or sevenths) against the tenor, setting up an expectation of resolution. Especially emphatic arrivals, such as those at the end of the respond and the verse, are marked with what we today would call appoggiaturas.

At the beginning of the respond and again at the beginning of the verse, the editor of this edition has transcribed the clefs and first notes of the original notation and has indicated the range of each voice. The ranges overlap, and all three upper voices cross below the tenor at several points, although the triplum and quadruplum tend to lie a little higher than the duplum and tenor. Directions for performing such music at Notre Dame Cathedral indicate that the three upper parts were each performed by one singer, with about five singers on the tenor to ensure a seamless performance. The directions also indicate that this piece, like all chant and polyphony at Notre Dame, was performed from memory, a feat that seems astonishing today but is a testimony to the prodigious memories of medieval singers.

Ave virgo virginum

Conductus

LATE TWELFTH OR EARLY THIRTEENTH CENTURY

20

A - ve vir - go vir - gi - num Ver - bi car - nis cel - la,

In sa - lu - tem ho - mi - num Stil - lans lac et mel - la.

Pe - pe - ri - sti do - mi - num, Mo - y - si fi - cel - la,

O ra - di - o Sol ex - it, et lu - mi - num, fon - tem pa - rit stel - la.

Florence, Biblioteca Medicea-Laurenziana, MS Pluteus 29.1 (F), fol. 240r–240v.

Ave virgo virginum	Hail, virgin of virgins,
Verbi carnis cella,	shrine of the word made flesh,
In salutem hominum	who for man's salvation
Stillans lac et mella.	drips milk and honey.
Peperisti dominum,	You bore the Lord;
Moysi ficella,	you were a rush-basket for Moses;
O radio	O, from your rays
Sol exit, et luminum	the sun goes forth, and the star
Fontem parit stella.	brings forth a fountain of light.

0:38	Ave, plena gratia,	Hail, full of grace,
	Caput Zabulonis	chief of Zebulun,
	Contrivisti spolia	the spoils of robbers
	Reparans predonis.	you restore.
	Celi rorans pluvia	Like rain, falling from heaven
	Vellus Gedeonis,	on the fleece of Gideon,
	O filio	with your son
	Tu nos reconcilia,	reunite us,
	Mater Salomonis.	O mother of Solomon!

1:16	Virgo tu mosayce	You, Virgin,
	Rubus visionis,	bramble-bush of the Mosaic vision,
	De te fluxit sylice	from you flowed the fountain
	Fons redemptionis.	through the rock of redemption.
	Quos redemit calice	Those Christ has redeemed through the chalice
	Christus passionis,	of his passion,
	O gaudio	O, may he clothe them with the joy
	Induat glorifice	of his glorious
	Resurrectionis.	resurrection.

This thirteenth-century conductus is preserved in one of the three main manuscripts of Notre Dame polyphony, suggesting that it may have been composed for use at the Cathedral of Notre Dame in Paris. Conductus were rhymed, metrical, strophic Latin poems on sacred or serious topics, set either monophonically or in polyphony. Like much of the Latin poetry written during the later Middle Ages, this poem is addressed to the Virgin Mary, praising her and seeking her assistance. This polyphonic setting was probably used in special devotions and processions.

    The three strophes are each sung to the same music. In each strophe, the first two couplets have identical music in all parts. This creates an AAB form, which was more common in secular song than in sacred music during this era. Each line has seven or six syllables and occupies two measures of $\frac{6}{8}$ in the transcription, except for the seventh line of each stanza, which has only four syllables and fills just one measure. The text-setting is mostly syllabic, with a short melisma in the outer voices to mark the next-to-last syllable of the second, fourth, sixth, and last lines of each stanza. In the original manuscript, the short melodic phrases are clearly set off by strokes (transcribed here as rests or breath marks), and the poetry uses trochaic meter (alternating accented and unaccented syllables), suggesting transcription in rhythmic mode 1 as shown here. The regular alternation of quarter and eighth notes in that mode is enlivened by *fractio modi* (division of the mode), in which a note is divided into two or more smaller notes (shown here by eighth and/or sixteenth notes beamed together). A note with a slash through the stem (such as the second note of the middle voice) indicates a *plica*, a tail added to a note in the original notation to indicate a second note on the same syllable, a step up or down (compare NAWM 9, whose second note includes a tail; and NAWM 17 and 19, where plicas are transcribed as small noteheads). *Plica* means "folded," and the notation indicated that the latter note was "folded" into the former note, being performed in a manner akin to a liquescent neume (see the explanation of chant notation in NAWM 3).

In the original manuscripts, conductus are notated in score format, with notes to be sung simultaneously presented in vertical alignment. The text is written only under the lowest notated voice, the tenor, but all three voices sing the words at the same time. The three voices overlap in range, with the tenor extending from *e* to *f′*, the duplum (second voice from the bottom) from *e* to *d′*, and the triplum (third voice up) from *b♭* to *g′*.

As in discant, the sonority at the beginning of each rhythmic unit (here, each dotted quarter) is usually consonant, most often an open octave, fifth, or fifth plus octave, but dissonances occur freely in between. However, conductus differ from discant clausulae in that the tenor line is newly composed rather than borrowed from chant.

21

Motets on Tenor *Dominus*

Motets

THIRTEENTH CENTURY

(a) *Factum est salutare/Dominus*

Fa - ctum est sa - lu - ta - re con - spe - ctu no - tum gen - ti - um. A re - ge mun - dus Ce - sa - re de - scri - bi - tur. *Fa - ctor o - mni - um rex na - sci - tur sal - va - re quod pe - ri - it. Er - go La - za - re

Do–

[*actor in MS.]

Edited by Rebecca A. Baltzer from Florence, Biblioteca Medicea-Laurenziana, Plut. 29, fol. 408v. Translation adapted from Susan A. Kidwell, "The Integration of Music and Text in the Early Latin Liturgical Motet" (Ph.D. dissertation, University of Texas at Austin, 1993). Used by permission.

[* MS has A.]

DUPLUM

Factum est	Salvation
salutare	was made known
conspectu	in the sight
notum gentium.	of the people.
A rege	By King
mundus Cesare	Caesar, the world
describitur.	is defined.
Factor omnium	The maker of all,
rex nascitur	the King, is born
salvare	to save
quod periit.	that which has perished.
Ergo Lazare	Therefore, Lazarus,

post triduum	after three days,
iam compare.	now appear.
Tardare	To delay
nimis fatuum	the exceedingly foolish
sanare	or to heal
quartum mortuum	a man dead for four days
numquam voluit	was never desired
<u>Dominus</u>.	by the Lord.

TENOR

Dominus	Lord

—TRANS. SUSAN A. KIDWELL

(b) *Fole acostumance/Dominus*

Edited by Rebecca A. Baltzer from Munich, Bayerische Staatsbibliothek, Mus. ms. 4775, Complex A, fol. 1v–2r. Translation by Rebecca A. Baltzer. Used by permission.

li vail - lant;   quant en-vie et vi - la-ni - e vet de jor en jor mon-tant,

cor - toi - sic a - vec s'a-mi - e lar-ges-ce s'en vet fui - ant.   Pa-pe-lar-di-e, que

Dex la mau - di - e! Que que nus en di - e, vait mes a - vant;   n'est nus en vi - e, por

qu'il en mes-di - e, que l'en ne l'en   voist blas-mant.— Chas-cuns le vet re - do - tant,

n'il n'est mi - e grant fo-li - e, car li plus riche et   li   plus pois - sant

II.

vont mes tel vi - e me-nant;   va - lor ne sens ne cler-gi-e ne vont mes nu - le riens pri-sant;

DUPLUM

Fole acostumance	Foolish custom
me fait que je chant,	makes me sing,
car nus mes n'avance	for I can advance
par asotillance	neither by accomplishment
ne par chant.	nor by song.
Mes en remembrance	But for remembrance's sake
ai fet cest novel deschant,	I have composed this new motet [discant],
que duel et pesance	since the valiant
doivent avoir molt grant	ought to have much more
li vaillant;	grief and worry;
quant envie	because Envy
et vilanie	and Villainy
vet de jor en jor montant,	increase from day to day,
cortoisie	Courtesy
avec s'amie	with her friend
largesce s'en vet fuiant.	Largesse flees from them.
Papelardie,	Religious Hypocrisy [pope-flattering]—
que Dex la maudie!	may God curse it!
Que que nus en die,	Whatever anyone may say,
vait mes avant;	it continues to advance;
n'est nus en vie,	there is no one alive
por qu'il en mesdie,	who in return for slandering it
que l'en ne l'en voist blasmant.	is not blamed for doing so.
Chascuns le vet redotant,	Everyone lives in fear,
n'il n'est mie	and this is not
grant folie,	at all foolish,
car li plus riche et li plus poissant	for the richest and most powerful
vont mes tel vie menant;	lead this kind of life;
valor ne sens ne clergie	neither reputation nor wisdom nor knowledge—
ne vont mes nule riens prisant;	no one values anything anymore;
tot ont mes truant.	these wretches have everything.
Morte est France	Dead is France
par tel decevance	because of such deception
et par tel faus semblant.	and because of such false seeming.
Tant est mes plaine de tel viltance,	She is so full of such evil
que trestoz li monz s'en vait gabant;	that the whole world mocks her;
c'est grant duels et grant mescheance,	it is a great sorrow and great misfortune
quant tel guile dure mes tant,	that such guile endures so long,
qu'ipocrisie	that Hypocrisy
sor tote rien vivant	makes every living thing
va compaignie	abandon companionship
et grant despense eschivant.	and great generosity.
Trop sont chiche, anguoisseus et tenant,	They are very stingy, anguished, and greedy,
signorie	lordship
ne baillie	and power
ne vent refusant,	they do not refuse,
mes de lor bien ne se sent nus.	but no one gets any of their goods [favors].

1:01 *(marginal marker beside "n'il n'est mie")*

TENOR

Dominus	Lord

—TRANS. REBECCA A. BALTZER

(c) *Super te/Sed fulsit virginitas/Dominus*

From Hans Tischler, ed., *The Montpellier Codex, Part II: Fascicles 3, 4, and 5*, Recent Researches in the Music of the Middle Ages and Early Renaissance 4–5 (Madison: A-R Editions, 1978), 60–61. Reprinted by permission. Translation adapted from *English Music of the Thirteenth and Early Fourteenth Centuries*, ed. Ernest H. Sanders, Polyphonic Music of the Fourteenth Century 14 (Monaco: Éditions de l'Oiseau-Lyre, 1979), 239. Reprinted by permission.

TRIPLUM

Super te Ierusalem	Over thee, Jerusalem,
de matre virgine	from the virgin mother
ortus est in Bethlehem	has arisen in Bethlehem
deus in homine	God in man;
ut gygas substancie	like a giant of twin substance
processit gemine	he has come forth
virginis ex utero	from the virgin's womb
sine gravamine	without effort;
non fuit feconditas	this pregnancy did not occur
hec viri semine.	through human seed.

DUPLUM

Sed fulsit virginitas	Rather, her virginity received its splendor
de sancto flamine	from the Holy Spirit;
ergo pie virginis	therefore, pious virgin's
flos pie domine	flower, pious Lord,
da medelam criminis	bring us the remedy for our crime
matris pro nomine	for the name of Thy mother,
ne nos preda demonis	lest we fall prey to the devil
simus pro crimine	for our crime,
quos preciosi sanguinis	we who the flood of Thy precious blood
emisti flumine.	has ransomed.

TENOR

Dominus	Lord

These three pieces illustrate three stages in the development of the motet and demonstrate the medieval practice of reworking existing music into new guises. All three are based on the same chant melody, the melisma on *Dominus* from the Gradual *Viderunt omnes* (NAWM 3d), which we have seen set in discant style by Leoninus or his colleagues (in NAWM 17), by two anonymous composers (NAWM 18a and b), and by Perotinus (in NAWM 19). As is customary, each motet is identified by a title made up of the first words of each voice from highest to lowest.

Typical of the earliest motets, *Factum est salutare/Dominus* is a direct adaptation of a discant clausula. It was created by adding words to the upper voice of the clausula on *Dominus* in NAWM 18a, which appears earlier in the same manuscript of Notre Dame polyphony, probably copied in Paris in the 1240s and now in Florence. Since the music was already written, the poet had to accommodate his text to the number of notes in each phrase of the duplum, which resulted in varying line lengths and accentuations. When set with text, the duplum may also be termed the *motetus*.

As is true of many early motets, the text for the duplum is a trope on the words of the chant from which the tenor is taken, in this case the verse of *Viderunt omnes*:

Notum fecit Dominus salutare suum: ante conspectum gentium revelavit justitiam suam.	The Lord hath made known His salvation; He hath revealed His justice in the sight of the people.

It was customary for tropes and early motets to borrow words or sounds from the original chant text. This practice is demonstrated in this motet and indicated by the underlined words in the poetry: "Dominus" at the end of the motet, and "notum," "salutare," "conspectu(m)," and "gentium" near the beginning. The endings "-um" and "-are" are repeated as rhymes throughout the motet, and another word-ending from the original chant, "-it," is also used as a rhyme.

Besides borrowing words and sounds, the motetus reflects on the meaning of the chant text and of the holiday it celebrates, the nativity of Jesus. The first four lines summarize the chant's verse, from Psalm 97:2 (98:2), and the rest refer to incidents in the life of Jesus. The contrast between the power of Jesus as king of salvation and the power of earthly kings such as Caesar was drawn both by Jesus himself ("render unto Caesar the things that are Caesar's, and to God the things that are God's," in Mark 12:17) and in the story of his crucifixion (John 19:12–15). Raising Lazarus from the dead was a sign of Jesus' power as savior. The multiple allusions to the Bible create a sermon in miniature, drawing together ideas that the listener might not have thought to relate.

This first motet is like a gloss upon a gloss, a text (a gloss in words) added to what already was a musical elaboration (a gloss in music) of the original chant. Because of its sacred text, it could have been performed in place of the original clausula, as part of the Gradual at the Mass for Christmas Day, although we cannot be certain that it was. Since the motet is complete in itself, it could also have been sung in devotions or as entertainment for an audience of churchmen, university teachers and students, or courtiers who were well enough educated to follow the web of allusions.

A motet called *Error popularis/Dominus* appears just a few pages after *Factum est* in the same manuscript. It borrows the tenor from *Factum est*, states it twice, and adds a new, more quickly moving melody in the duplum with a secular Latin text. Such a piece, with words unrelated to the original chant or Christmas Mass, could have been performed as entertainment or in devotions, but not in the service. *Error popularis* was later reworked by another poet, who substituted a French text for the Latin one to produce the second motet included here, *Fole acostumance/Dominus*, which appears in three later manuscripts (the Munich source, used for this edition, was copied in Paris in the mid-thirteenth century and also includes *Factum est*). Such a chain of transformations illustrates the way that polyphony was viewed in the thirteenth century: as common property, material that could be used, altered, and adapted to new uses.

The tenor of *Fole acostumance* is identical to that of *Factum est* except that the section on "Do-" appears twice (the repetition begins at measure 41, marked with roman numeral II). Phrases in the duplum are longer than in *Factum est*, often overlapping the tenor rests, and the use of only three rhymes throughout the motet lends the poetry clarity and coherence. The poem is a blistering attack on envy, villainy, hypocrisy, deception, and greed, and was apparently inspired by conflict with or within the church. The only connection to the original chant text is through sound: the last line of the poem begins with "m" and ends with "nus," coordinated with the "-mi-" and "-nus" of "Dominus" in the tenor.

As we have seen, the first stage of motet composition consisted of adding text to an existing discant clausula, and subsequent developments included writing a new duplum to an existing tenor or writing a new text for an existing motet. In all of these cases, the composer reworked what was already a polyphonic piece. A different approach was to use a fragment of a chant to create a new tenor and add one or more voices above it, producing a motet that is not directly related to a discant clausula. This procedure quickly became the most common approach.

An example of such a motet is *Super te/Sed fulsit/Dominus*, which uses the first half of the *Dominus* melisma (minus its first two notes) stated twice (measures 1–18 and 19–36, paralleling measures 3–21 of *Factum est*). The rhythmic pattern differs from those in the previous motets, and occasionally notes are omitted, repeated, or inserted. This motet exists in two variants; a three-voice version (NAWM 21c) from a French manuscript copied in the 1270s, and a four-voice version (not included here) from a manuscript in Worcester, England copied in about 1270. The latter includes a "Primus Tenor" (first tenor) part, which thickens the texture and adds a third to the final sonority—traits of English music in the late Middle Ages. The two versions also differ in rhythm: the French variant uses the third rhythmic mode in the upper voices, transcribed here as dotted quarter-eighth-quarter, while the English prefers the quarter-eighth rhythms of the first rhythmic mode. The English version is probably the older.

The poetry in this motet was apparently written before the music, as shown by the regular line lengths and rhyme scheme. A single Latin poem was used for the upper two voices, the first half for the triplum, and the second for the duplum. The subject, the birth of Jesus to the Virgin Mary, is appropriate to the Christmas season, but the motet was likely sung in private devotions rather than as part of the Gradual at Mass. The composer may have chosen the *Dominus* melisma for the tenor because of its association with Christmas or as an echo of the word "Domine" in the text (duplum, measures 13–14).

With occasional exceptions, the upper voices do not rest at the same time as each other or at the same time as the tenor on *Dominus*. As a result, the music moves continuously. This is typical of motets with three or four voices and strongly differentiates these later motets from those of the early thirteenth century, such as *Factum est*. As became standard during the century, almost every measure in this transcription begins with a sonority of perfect consonances, usually fifth plus octave, but both consonance and dissonance occur freely in between.

In the English manuscript of *Super te*, the Primus Tenor has no words, and the second tenor has only the word *Dominus* at the beginning, without designations for where the syllables are to be sung. Some scholars and performers have interpreted the lack of text underlay in motet tenors to mean that these lines should be performed by instruments. Others have argued that all parts were sung by solo voices, and that is how all three motets are performed on the accompanying recordings.

Adam de la Halle (CA. 1240–?1288)

De ma dame vient/Dieus, comment porroie/Omnes

22

Motet

CA. 1260s–1280s

Adapted by Rebecca A. Baltzer from *The Montpellier Codex, Part III: Fascicles 6, 7, and 8*, ed. Hans Tischler, Recent Researches in the Music of the Middle Ages and Early Renaissance 6–7 (Madison: A-R Editions, 1978), 112–15. Translation adapted from the one by Susan Stakel and Joel C. Relihan in *The Montpellier Codes, Part IV: Texts and Translations*, Recent Researches in the Music of the Middle Ages and Early Renaissance 8 (Madison: A-R Editions, 1978), 92–93. Reprinted by permission.

Same tenor 4 measure unit repeated!
*new pattern begins; also repeated 4 times

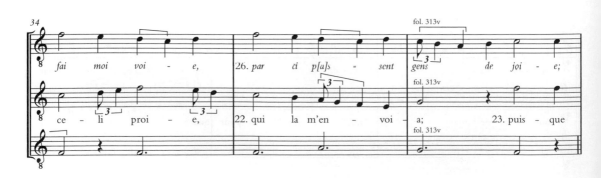

Triplum

De ma dame vient	From my lady comes
li gries maus, que je trai,	the grievous pain which I bear
don't je morrai,	and of which I will die,
s'esperance ne me retient,	if hope does not keep me alive,
et la grant joie que j'ai.	along with the great joy that I have.
Car j'aperçoi bien et sai,	For I see well and know
c'o[n] m'a grevé et mellé,	that others have hurt my chances and caused misunderstandings,
si qu'ele m'a tout ausi qu'entroublié,	and she has as good as forgotten me,
qui en soloie estre audeseure.	who used to be uppermost in her mind.
Dieus, quant verrai l'eure,	God, when will I see the hour
qu'aie a li parlé	when I shall have talked with her
et, de ce c'on m'a mis seure,	and, of that for which they have blamed me,

1:04

moi escusé?	be excused?
Tres douce amie,	Sweet friend,
aiés de moi pitié,	have pity on me,
por Dieu merci!	for God's sake, mercy!
Onques n'ama, qui por si peu haï,	Never has anyone loved, and then for so little been hated,
ne deservi ne l'ai mie;	nor have I deserved it;
ains est par envie,	rather it is out of envy
k'on en a mesdit,	that they have slandered me,
et en leur despit	and to spite them,
maintenant irai	now I will go
et pour aus crever ferai	and, to make them burst with anger,
melleur samblant, que je ne devroie.	will pretend to be happier than I should.

2:08

Fui toi, gaite, fai moi voie,	Get away, watchman, make way for me,
par ci p[a]ssent gens de joie;	for here pass joyful people;
tart m'est, que j'i soie,	it is past time that I be there—
encore m'i avés vous nuisi.	again have you done me harm.
Si serai je mieus de li,	I will get along better with her
c'onques ne fui, se seulete	than ever before, if alone
enqui en un destour	searching in a byway
truis m'amiete,	I find my beloved,
la doucete,	the sweet one,
la sadete brunete,	the charming, dark-haired one,
savourosete,	the luscious one,
cui Dieus doinst boin jour.	to whom God grant a fine day.

Motetus

Dieus, coument porroie	God, how can I
trouver voie	find a way
d'aler a celi,	to go to him
qui amiete je sui?	whose lover I am?
Çainturele, va i en lieu de mi,	Little belt, go there instead of me,
quar tu fus sieve ausi,	for you were his too;
si m'en conquera mieus.	in that way I'll accomplish more.
Mes comment serai sanz ti, Dieus?	But how will I get along without you? God!
Ceinturele, mar vous vi!	Little belt, a curse on you!
Au desceindre m'ociés;	In unbuckling, you kill me;

1:04

de mes grietés	from my sorrows
a vous me confor(t)toie,	I took comfort

quant je vous sentoie, aymi,	when I smelled on you, alas,
a la savour de mon ami.	the scent of my lover.
Ne pour quant d'autres en ai	Nevertheless, from others I have
a claus d'argent et de soie	articles of silver and of silk
pour mon user.	for my use.
Moi, lasse, comment porroie	Alas! how can I
sans celi durer,	endure without the one
qui me tient en joie?	who is the source of my joy?
Ceinturele, celi proie,	Little belt, beg him
qui la m'envoia;	who sent it to me;
puisque je ne puis aler la,	since I cannot go there,
qu'il en viengne ennuit ci,	let him come to me here at night,
droit au jour failli,	as soon as the day fades,
pour faire tout ses bo[i]ns.	to fulfill all his needs.
Et il m'orra, quant [il] iert, poinz,	He will hear me at the right time,
chanter a haute vois:	singing out loud:
Par ci va la mignotise,	There goes frolic,
par ci ou je vois.	there where I go.

`2:08`

TENOR

Omnes	All

— TRANS. SUSAN STAKEL AND JOEL C. RELIHAN

❦

Adam de la Halle's *De ma dame vient/Dieus, comment porroie/Omnes* is one of the few thirteenth-century motets whose composer we know. Since it combines the court tradition of trouvère song with the newer form of the motet, it is possible that Adam composed it for his patrons Robert II, count of Artois, or Charles of Anjou.

Adam borrowed from a variety of sources to create this piece. The tenor uses the melisma on "omnes" from the Gradual *Viderunt omnes* (see NAWM 3d), transposed down a fifth. Adam gives the melody a distinctive rhythmic profile and states it four times (measures 1–16, with the end of each statement marked by a double bar). He then repeats the same process twice, giving the melody two new rhythmic patterns that are each repeated four times (see measures 17–32 and 33–48). The motetus (or duplum) begins with the refrain from Adam's own monophonic rondeau *Diex, comment porroie*, transposed, and closes with another borrowed refrain (shown here in italics). The triplum also quotes several lines of poetry from other songs (shown in italics). This complex web of references to other music and poetry must have added to the intellectual appeal of this piece, and demonstrates motet composers' continued interest in alluding to more than one source (see NAWM 21a).

The piece uses the new notation known as Franconian, after Franco of Cologne, which indicates a precise rhythm for each note. The more exact notation allowed scribes to write down melodies that departed more from the rhythmic modes than was possible in earlier motets, such as those in NAWM 21. In Adam's motet, the tenor is still in modal rhythm, alternating modes 1 (as in measures 2–4) and 5 (as in measures 17–19), and mode 1 patterns often underlie the upper voices as well. (In this edition, perfect longs are transcribed as dotted half notes rather than dotted quarter notes, as in NAWM 17–21, so mode 1 alternates half and quarter notes.) But many smaller durations are used in the motetus and especially in the triplum, so that they move much faster than the tenor. Each voice has its own rhythmic character, with the triplum moving most rapidly, and they seldom move in rhythmic unison for an entire measure. Almost never does either upper voice have the same rhythm for two successive measures, giving the music a constant variety.

These rhythmic differences between the parts are characteristic of Franconian motets. In this case, they also add to the piece's meaning. The poem in the triplum is in the voice of a man who describes his pain at being separated from his lady; the motetus is in the voice of the lady, who is searching for a way to send word to tell him that he should come to her. It is hard for modern listeners to imagine how thirteenth-century audiences could hear motets with two texts, the most common type of motet in France, and understand both texts at once. But in this work, the use of two separate texts creates a special poignancy as the two lovers express their anguish at being apart, yearn to be together, and voice their feelings simultaneously, unable to hear each other.

Petrus de Cruce (Pierre de la Croix)
(MID-THIRTEENTH CENTURY TO EARLY FOURTEENTH CENTURY)

Aucun ont trouvé/Lonc tans/Annuntiantes

Motet

*Polytextual

CA. 1290

*Moving top voice represents later motet

23

Tr — 1. Au- cun ont trou-vé chant par u- sa- ge, 2. mes a moi en doune o- choi-

M — 1. Lonc tans me sui

T — ANNUN[TIANTES]

-son 3. A-mours, qui resbaudis mon courage, 4. si que m'e- stuet fai- re chan- çon; 5. car a-mer me

te- nu de chan- ter, 2. mes or ai rai- son

fait da- me bele et sage 6. et de bon re- non. 7. Et je, qui li ai fait hou-ma-ge 8. pour

de joi- e me- ner,

li ser-vir tout mon a- a- ge 9. de loi-al cuer sans pen-ser tra- hi- son, 10. chan-te- rai, car de li

3. car boune a- mour me fait de- sir- rer

From Hans Tischler, ed., *The Montpellier Codex, Part III: Fascicles 6, 7, and 8*, Recent Researches in the Music of the Middle Ages and Early Renaissance 6–7 (Madison: A-R Editions, 1978), 65–67; translation by Susan Stakel and Joel C. Relihan, from *The Montpellier Codex, Part III: Texts and Translations*, Recent Researches in the Music of the Middle Ages and Early Renaissance 8 (Madison: A-R Editions, 1978), 81-82.

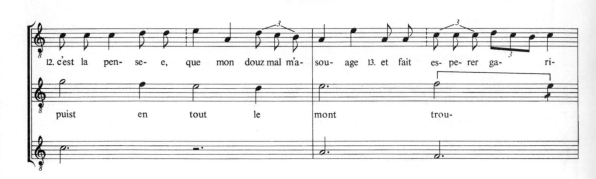

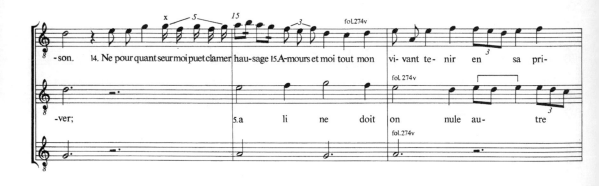

Triplum

Aucun ont trouvé chant par usage,	Some have composed songs out of habit,
mes a moi en doune choison	but I am given a reason to sing
Amours, qui resbaudist mon courage,	by Love, who so fills my heart with joy
si que m'estuet faire chançon;	that I have to make a song;
car amer me fait dame bele et sage	for he makes me love a woman who is beautiful and wise
et de bon renon.	and of fine reputation.
Et je, qui li ait fait houmage	And I, who have become her vassal
pour li servir tout mon aage	in order to serve her all my life
de loial cuer sans penser trahison,	with a loyal heart, without a thought of betrayal,
chanterai, car de li tieng un si douz heritage,	will sing, for from her I receive such a sweet gift
que joie n'ai se de ce non;	that I have joy from nothing else;
c'est la pensee, que mon douz mal m'asouage	[this gift] is the thought [of her], which assuages my sweet pain
et fait esperer garison.	and makes me hope to be cured.
Ne pour quant seur moi peut clamer hausage	Nevertheless, Love can claim authority over me
Amours et moi tout mon vivant tenir en sa prison.	and all my life long keep me in his prison.
Ne ja pour ce ne penserai vers li mesprison;	Never for this would I think ill of him;

`1:25`

tant set soutilment	he knows how deftly
assallir, k'encontre li defendre ne s'en puet on.	to attack that against him no one can defend himself.
Force de cors ne plenté de lignage	Neither bodily strength nor highest noble lineage
ne vaut un bouton;	is worth a button;
et si li plaist de raençon	and if it pleases him a ransom
rendre a son gré, sui pries et l'en fais gage	to grant on his own terms, I am ready and offer as a hostage
mon cuer, que je met du tout enabandon.	my heart, which I completely abandon.
Si proi merci, car autre avantage	I ask for mercy, for no other recompense
n'ai je ne pour moi nule autre raison.	do I have, nor for myself any other satisfaction.

Motetus

Lonc tans me sui tenu de chanter,	I have long refrained from singing
mes or ai raison de joie mener,	but now I have a reason to be joyous,
car boune amour me fair desirrer	for true love makes me desire
la mieus ensegnie, k'on puist en tout le mont trouver;	the finest woman one could find in the whole world;
a li ne doit on nule autre comparer.	to her no other can be compared.

`1:25`

Et quant j'aim dame si proisie,	And when I love a lady so estimable
que grant deduit ai du penser,	that great pleasure I get from the thought of her,
je puis bien prouver,	I can indeed prove
que mout a savoureuse vie,	that he has a rich life,
quoi que nus die,	whatever one may say,
en bien amer.	who truly loves.

Tenor

Annun[tiantes]	Announcing
— Petrus de Cruce	— Trans. Susan Stakel and Joel C. Relihan

Petrus de Cruce (the Latin form of his name, or Pierre de la Croix in French, meaning Peter of the Cross) was a student at the University of Paris sometime between 1260 and 1290. He apparently wrote his motet *Aucun ont trouvé/Lonc tans/ Annuntiantes* during those years, to judge by its presence in a manuscript copied around 1290. Later he resided in the castle of the king of France in Paris, then by 1301 returned to his native city of Amiens in northern France as a church official.

A younger contemporary of Franco of Cologne, Petrus modified Franco's notation system to allow up to seven semibreves within a breve. Because the notes in any group of four or more semibreves were shorter than the shortest note value in Franco's system, all the notes in the group were given the same duration in performance. This creates the effect of a quadruplet, quintuplet, sextuplet, or septuplet in modern notation. Later attempts to specify the exact durations of such small subdivisions led to the notational innovations of the Ars Nova (see NAWM 25).

The short notes were usually confined to the triplum (the highest voice), as is true in this motet. Their presence further differentiates the three voices of the motet, heightening the contrast we already observed in Franconcian motets (compare NAWM 22): the triplum moves relatively rapidly in breves and semibreves; the motetus more slowly in a clear modal rhythm, most often mode 1 with *fractio modi* (occasional divisions of the notes); and the tenor still more slowly, in perfect longs. In this edition, the perfect longs are transcribed as dotted half notes, imperfect longs as half notes, breves as quarter notes, and semibreves as notes of shorter durations. As theorists of the time noted, accommodating the increased number of short notes, each with its own syllable to pronounce, requires slowing down the tempo, and that is apparent in the accompanying recording (compare the pace of the perfect longs in NAWM 21a–c, NAWM 22, and this motet). The triplum also moves in a generally higher range than the other voices, crossing below the motetus several times but never below the tenor. The resulting effect is of a principal melody in the triplum accompanied by a relatively slow countermelody over a lowest voice that functions as harmonic support.

The texts of the triplum and motetus are love poems in French. Although they lack the regular line lengths and recurring stanza patterns of troubadour and trouvère songs, they share similar imagery, praising the lady the poet loves. Moreover, each poem uses only two rhymes (*-age* and *-on* in the triplum; *-er* and *-ie* in the motetus), recalling the use of a limited number of recurring rhymes in the troubadour and trouvère poems we have seen (NAWM 8–10). But in contrast to the complaints in the songs by Bernart de Ventadorn (NAWM 8) and the Comtessa de Dia (NAWM 9), Petrus's poems express the joy of loving a woman he can hardly praise enough and who gives him a reason to sing. The motetus text is suffused with such joy, and the triplum begins with very similar sentiments but goes on to swear fealty to his lady and to Love in the terms of a feudal vassal pledging allegiance to his lord, with images of service, prison, combat, hostage-taking, ransom, and pleas for mercy, all of which were common occurrences in the feudal society of knights, courtiers, and rulers and provided ready metaphors for the pangs of love.

The tenor melody, taken from a chant melisma, appears twice, first in the familiar recurring pattern long-long-long-rest (used in the tenor of NAWM 21c), and then in an unbroken stream of longs (measures 19–30). This repetition of the tenor and change in its rhythmic pattern at measure 19 coincides with the point of articulation between the two long sentences in the motetus text (lines 1–5 are the first sentence; lines 6–11 the second) and with the turn to images of combat and capture in the triplum. While the language of the two texts is quite similar up to this point in the motet, from here to the end the images are strikingly different, opening up a meaningful dialogue between the two voices.

Throughout the motet, the upper voices often cadence together, then one voice (usually the triplum) will begin before the other, bringing its text to the forefront. The motetus cadences at the end of each line of poetry, but the triplum comes to a cadence followed by a rest only at the ends of lines with the rhyme *-on*, thereby linking the poetic and musical structures. The beginning of almost every perfection (the length of a perfect long, a dotted half note in transcription) is marked by perfect consonances, but in between the two melodies may form dissonances with each other (as in measures 16 and 17).

On the accompanying recording, the tenor is performed instrumentally. This highlights the texted upper parts and seems appropriate to the untexted tenor in long notes. Yet many scholars and musicians argue that all three voices would have been sung (see commentary for NAWM 25). The recordings of the secular works in this anthology from the late thirteenth through the late fifteenth centuries include some with vocal and some with instrumental performance of the tenor, to illustrate the possibilities.

Sumer is icumen in

Rota

CA. 1250

English Music of the Thirteenth and Early Fourteenth Centuries, ed. Ernest H. Sanders, Polyphonic Music of the Fourteenth Century 14 (Monaco: Éditions de l'Oiseau-Lyre, 1979), 5–7. Translations from ibid., 210. Reprinted by permission.

Sumer is icumen in,	Summer is come,
Lhude sing cuccu!	sing loud, cuckoo!
GroweÞ sed and bloweÞ med	The seed grows and the meadow blooms,
and springÞ the wde nu.	and now the wood turns green.
Sing cuccu!	Sing, cuckoo!
Awe bleteÞ after lomb,	The ewe bleats after the lamb,
lhouÞ after calve cu.	the cow lows after the calf,
Bulluc sterteÞ,	the bullock leaps,
bucke verteÞ,	the buck [billy-goat?] farts,
murie sing cuccu!	sing merrily, cuckoo!
Cuccu, cuccu,	Cuckoo, cuckoo!
wel singes Þu cuccu,	You sing well, cuckoo.
ne swik Þu naver nu!	Don't ever stop now!
Sing cuccu nu; sing cuccu!	Sing, cuckoo, now; sing, cuckoo!

LATIN TEXT:

Perspice Christicola,	Observe, worshipper of Christ,
que dignacio;	what gracious condescension!
celicus agricola	The heavenly husband,
pro vitis vicio,	because of the vine's imperfection,
filio,	not sparing his son,
non parcens exposuit	exposed him
mortis exicio.	to death's destruction.
Qui captivos	The prisoners,
Semivivos	who are half-dead
a supplicio	on account of the death sentence,
Vite donat	he restores to life,
et secum coronat	and crowns them at his side
in celi solio.	on heaven's throne.

— TRANS. ERNEST H. SANDERS

One of the treasures of medieval polyphony is *Sumer is icumen in*, also known as the Summer Canon, the only known piece of six-part polyphony before the fifteenth century. It was composed around 1250, probably in Reading, England, where the manuscript in which it is preserved was copied and housed in an abbey. The main text, in medieval English, is a celebration of spring; the Latin text (not sung on the recording) was probably added to make this clearly recreational piece suitable for the manuscript of Latin polyphony in which it appears. Despite the English text, the counterpoint is too complex to imagine that this could be folk or popular music, or indeed anything other than entertainment music intended to be performed by those learned in church polyphony.

This piece combines two forms that were common in England at the time: the *rota* and the *rondellus*. The bottom two voices, marked "Pes" (foot), create a small rondellus, a form in which voices begin together and then exchange parts:

Pes 1	a	b
Pes 2	b	a

Together, they form a harmonic foundation, which they repeat throughout the piece. Above them, two, three, or four voices join in a rota, a round or perpetual canon at the unison. Each voice sings the same music, but enters at a different time: the first together with the Pes and the others at two-measure intervals.

Once all the voices have entered, the harmonies alternate between F—A—C—F sonorities on each downbeat and G—Bb—D or similar sonorities on the second half of each measure. The repeated movement between these two sonorities—from a sonority harmonizing the modal final F to a contrasting harmony and back—provides a basic framework of tension and resolution for the piece. The emphasis on imperfect consonances and on full triads is typical of English music of the thirteenth and fourteenth centuries. Other common traits of English music include melodies that modern listeners hear as in the major mode (it was not described as a mode until the sixteenth century, when it was called Ionian); alternation between chords on the first and second degrees of the scale; short, periodic phrases of two or four measures; and preference for rhythmic modes 1 and 5.

On the accompanying recording, the performers demonstrate three different possibilities for performance: over the repeating Pes, one voice sings the entire vocal line (beginning at 0:04), then two voices sing it in canon (0:33), then four voices (1:06). Since no ending for the piece is indicated, all singers could stop together or, as in the recording, each could stop in turn upon reaching the end of the melody, leaving the Pes singers to sing the final cadence.

Philippe de Vitry (1291–1361)

Cum statua/Hugo, Hugo/Magister invidie

Motet

CA. 1320

From Philippe de Vitry, *Complete Works*, ed. Leo Schrade, with new introduction and notes by Edward H. Roesner (Monaco: Éditions de l'Oiseau-Lyre, 1984), 26–28. Reprinted by permission.

TRIPLUM

	Cum statua Nabucodonasor	As with Nebuchadnezzar's statue
	metallina successive Syon	of metal, the Lord has suffered Zion successively
	ac gradatim deduci ac minus	and by stages to be reduced and
	fieri colis passus est Dominus,	made less:
	que cum primo fuerit aurea,	at first [the statue] was gold, and
	virtuosus; inde argentea,	[Zion] virtuous; then [it was] silver,
0:44	carne mundus; deinceps herea,	[and Zion] clean in its flesh; next bronze,
	sanctiloquus; fictilis ferea	[and Zion] holy in speech; [and last] a work of iron
	ac lutea. Pater novissime	and clay. Most recently, the father [pope]
	novissimis quibusdam maxime	to certain very young men,
	corde dantis una cum patribus	called "givers" and "fathers"
	ipocrisis antifrasis quibus	through hypocrisy and false words,
1:29	dat mendici nomen sophistice.	fallaciously gave the name "mendicants."
	Hec concino Philippus publice	This I, Philippe, sing publicly,
1:44	et quia impia	and because the impious
	lingua ledor unius territe	tongue of one in terror has wounded me
	pro vero refero:	I say as the truth:
	a prophetis falsis, attendite.	beware of false prophets!

DUPLUM

	Hugo, Hugo, princeps invidie,	Hugh, Hugh, prince of envy,
	tu cum prima pateas facie	since on first appearance you seem
	homo pacis, virtutum filius,	a man of peace, a son of the virtues,
0:44	te neminem decet in populo	it befits you to wound no one among the people
	lingue tue ledere iaculo	with the javelin of your tongue
	set ignarum docere pocius.	but rather to teach the ignorant.
	Qua me colpas igitur rabie	With what madness do you therefore charge me,
	assignata mihi nulla die?	never before imputed to me?
	Inconsultus causamque nescius	Unconsulted and knowing nothing of the cause,
1:44	stupeo, et eo,	I am astounded, and therefore,
	cum invidus sic sis palam pius,	since you are so envious even though you seem outwardly to be holy,
	perpere dicere	inconsiderate man, I can say
	ipocritam te possum verius.	quite truly that you are a hypocrite.

TENOR

Magister invidie	Master of envy

— TRANS. DAVID HOWLETT (MODIFIED)

Cum statua/Hugo, Hugo/Magister invidie is one of the motets most securely attributed to Philippe de Vitry: he names himself in the text of the triplum, he is identified as the author in a contemporary treatise, a fellow poet alludes to the work as his, and it is cited in the treatise *Ars nova*, which preserves his teachings. He probably wrote the motet in the late 1310s or 1320s, and it was likely performed in gatherings of clerics, of courtiers, or of faculty and students at the University of Paris, all part of Vitry's circle.

In most motets the tenor melody is drawn from a chant melisma and is labeled with the words originally sung to the melisma, as in NAWM 21–23, but this melody seems to have been Vitry's own. As the editor indicates under the first measure, in one manuscript the tenor is identified by the opening words of the triplum ("Cum statua") and in another by a phrase that invokes the duplum ("Magister invidie," echoing "princeps invidie" from the first line of the duplum).

The texts for the upper voices are polemical, addressing a personal dispute in the duplum and an issue in the church in the triplum. The duplum attacks someone named Hugh, who has not been identified but who apparently criticized Vitry unfairly. The triplum begins with a reference to a biblical story, Nebuchadnezzar's dream of a great statue as described by the Jewish prophet Daniel:

> You saw, O king, and behold, a great image. This image, mighty and of exceeding brightness, stood before you, and its appearance was frightening. The head of the image was of fine gold, its breast and arms of silver, its belly and thighs of bronze, its legs of iron, its feet partly of iron and partly of clay. As you looked, a stone was cut out by no human hand, and it smote the image on its feet of iron and clay, and broke them in pieces. (Daniel 2:31–34, Revised Standard Version)

Daniel interprets the image in the dream as representing a series of kingdoms, from Nebuchadnezzar's own reign (the head of gold) through a succession of inferior kingdoms (silver and bronze) to one that is divided (iron and clay) and will be brought down by God, after which God will establish a kingdom that will stand forever. Vitry uses this image to suggest the decay of the church in his own time. He particularly criticizes the rise of the mendicant orders, groups of friars such as Dominicans, Franciscans, and Augustinians, who took oaths of poverty ("mendicant" means "beggar"), owed allegiance directly to the pope, and were outside the control of the usual church hierarchy. How the arguments in the triplum and duplum relate to each other is unclear. Perhaps Hugh was a young friar who denounced some position propounded by Vitry or by his circle (the academic and clerical establishment in Paris) and this motet was Vitry's response.

Vitry's Latin poems may be hard to understand fully without more historical context, but they are beautifully crafted. Until the final four lines, both poems feature lines of ten syllables, the triplum proceeding mostly in rhymed couplets, and the duplum in groups of three lines with the rhyme scheme aab ccb aab. Then in both poems the final four lines alternate six-syllable lines featuring internal rhymes (such as "et qu*ia* imp*ia*") with rhymed ten-syllable lines. These structural similarities bind the two texts together. The interrelationships of the texts, in both meaning and poetic structure, were part of the appeal motets had for their primary audience of clerics, courtiers, nobles, teachers, and students.

The principal innovation that characterized the music of Vitry and his contemporaries and led to the label *Ars Nova* ("new art") was the invention of a notation that permitted note values to be divided into either three or two equal parts. This new notation allowed a greater variety of rhythmic patterns than were available in earlier systems of notation. In Franconian notation, which had been used in the late thirteenth century, the basic time unit (*tempus*, equivalent to a breve) always appeared in a group of three called a *perfection*, making triple time the universal meter. Moreover, the breve itself was divided into three equal semibreves; if there were only two semibreves, the second was twice as long as the first, maintaining the triple division. In contrast, Ars Nova notation allowed for duple or triple division at several different levels, known as mode (division of the long), *time* (division of the breve), and *prolation* (division of the semibreve). Triple divisions were called perfect, and duple divisions imperfect (or, for prolation, major and minor respectively).

In *Cum statua/Hugo, Hugo/Magister invidie*, the long is divided into three breves, making the mode perfect. This triple division is highlighted in the editor's transcription into modern notation, where in the upper voices each measure is a breve and in the tenor (the lowest voice) each measure is a perfect long, extending over three measures in the other parts. In turn, the breve (transcribed as a dotted half note) is divided into two semibreves (dotted quarter notes), making the time imperfect. The prolation, the division of semibreves into minims, is triple (major prolation, represented in the transcription by three eighth notes). The combination of imperfect time with major prolation produces a meter transcribed here as $\frac{6}{8}$, with groupings of three such measures resulting from the perfect mode.

The form of the piece is created by repetitions in the tenor. The tenor part consists of three statements of a 24-note melody called the *color* (in measures 1–45, 46–90, and 91–135). Each appearance of the color in the tenor is divided into three segments, or *taleae* (sing. *talea*, meaning "cutting"), that have identical rhythmic patterns (as in measures 1–15, 16–30, and 31–45), resulting in nine statements of the talea overall. This kind of organization, called *isorhythm* ("equal rhythm"), evolved from the shorter repeating patterns in the tenors of thirteenth-century motets, such as NAWM 21 and 22.

To point out these divisions, the editor has marked the beginning of each statement of the color with a capital letter (A, B, and C) and the beginning of the taleae within each color with a roman numeral (I, II, and III). The rhythmic pattern of the talea can be quite complex in some isorhythmic motets, but in this one it is rather easy to hear, marked out by alternating rests and relatively longer notes at the beginning of each talea followed by continuous shorter notes in the second half of the talea. The talea in the tenor can be seen in modern notation, but the repeating pattern is far easier to see in the original Ars Nova notation, where it is short and distinctive: a rest, a single note, a rest, two notes in a ligature, and five notes in a ligature. (As in NAWM 17–23, the brackets over each staff indicate ligatures in the original notation.)

Vitry coordinates the poetic form with the isorhythmic form. Each talea in the tenor accompanies two lines of poetry in the triplum, pointing out the rhymed couplets throughout most of the poem. In a similar manner, the duplum highlights the groupings of three lines and the final quatrain as described above, created through rhymes; the ends of lines 1, 3, 6, 9, 11, and 13 coincide with the end of a talea, and all but the first of these lines share a common rhyme (-*ius*).

It was noted earlier that the final four lines in each poem have the same shape, alternating six-syllable lines that have internal rhymes with ten-syllable lines. Vitry draws attention to these last four lines, which occupy the final two taleae in each part, through musical means. He sets the six-syllable lines using a technique called *hocket* (from the French *hoquet*, meaning "hiccup"), in which the upper voices alternate, one voice singing while the other rests and vice versa (measures 106–15 and 121–30). The alternation and thinning of texture demarcate the change of line length and make the internal rhymes in each voice easier to hear. Moreover, in the last two taleae, the rhythms of the upper parts and the tenor are isorhythmic: exactly the same in measures 121–35 as in 106–20 (except for slight variations in measures 131–32). This effect, known as *pan-isorhythm*, sets off this passage from the rest of the motet, providing a strong conclusion and highlighting the difference of the final quatrains from the rest of each poem.

At the beginning of each measure, with few exceptions, the parts form harmonic consonances, with the imperfect consonances of thirds and sixths more common than in thirteenth-century music, and perfect unisons, octaves, and fifths marking the points of greatest stability. At the end of the first and final statements of the color (mm. 43–45 and 133–35) and occasionally elsewhere, Vitry uses the strongest cadence available in Ars Nova style; known as a double leading-tone cadence, it consists of a harmonic major third and major sixth expanding out to a perfect fifth and octave, with both upper voices rising a half step like leading tones.

The use of accidentals other than B♭ was called *musica ficta* ("feigned music") because it involved notes outside the standard gamut. The manuscript sources include one such accidental, the F♯ in measure 39. Other notes would likely have been altered chromatically by the singers in order to avoid tritones, smooth the melody, or provide more satisfactory cadences, and the editor suggests these with accidentals above the staff.

Vitry's motets were most likely performed by one singer on each of the upper parts, but the tenor's performance has been a matter for debate. From the early twentieth century through the 1970s, most scholars and performers assumed that the long notes and lack of text underlay in the tenor suited that part best for instrumental performance. But more recently, scholars have argued that pay records, literary accounts, and pictures indicate purely vocal performance for all the parts in motets (see "In Performance: Voices or Instruments?" in HWM, p. 137).

If the tenor is to be sung, either it must have a text or it must be vocalized on a neutral vowel. On the accompanying recording, the singer on the tenor part sings *Cum statua* once for each color. This is the text given the tenor in one manuscript, and it results in an alternation of "ooh" and "ah" sounds that fit well under the upper parts.

Guillaume de Machaut (ca. 1300–1377)

La Messe de Nostre Dame: Kyrie and Gloria

Mass (Mass Ordinary cycle)

CA. 1364

(a) Kyrie

The Works of Guillaume de Machaut, ed. Leo Schrade, vol. 2, Polyphonic Music of the Fourteenth Century 3 (Monaco: Éditions de l'Oiseau-Lyre, 1956), 37–45. Reprinted by permission. The discussion of the form of the Gloria and its paraphrase of a chant melody is adapted from Daniel Leech-Wilkinson, *Machaut's Mass: An Introduction* (Oxford: Clarendon Press, 1990), 29–38.

Repeat Kyrie I.

Repeat chant Christe.

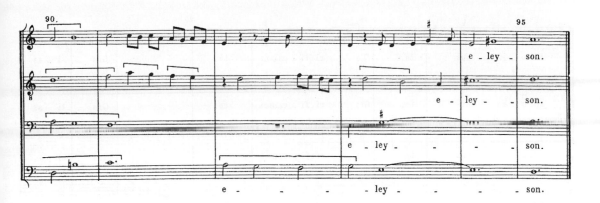

Kyrie eleison.   Lord have mercy.
Christe eleison.   Christ have mercy.
Kyrie eleison.   Lord have mercy.

(b) Gloria

Gloria in excelsis Deo	Glory be to God on high.
Et in terra pax	And on earth peace
hominibus bonae voluntatis.	to men of good will.
Laudamus te.	We praise thee.
Benedicimus te.	We bless thee.
Adoramus te.	We adore thee.
Glorificamus te.	We glorify thee.
Gratias agimus tibi	We give thee thanks
propter magnam gloriam tuam.	for thy great glory.

1:01

Domine Deus, Rex caelestis,	O Lord God, King of heaven,
Deus Pater omnipotens.	God the Father Almighty.
Domine Fili unigenite,	O Lord, the only begotten Son,
Jesu Christe.	Jesus Christ.
Domine Deus, Agnus Dei,	O Lord God, Lamb of God,
Filius Patris.	Son of the Father.

1:49

Qui tollis peccata mundi,	Thou who takest away the sins of the world,
miserere nobis.	have mercy on us.
Qui tollis peccata mundi,	Thou who takest away the sins of the world,
suscipe deprecationem nostram.	receive our prayer.
Qui sedes ad dexteram Patris,	Thou who sittest at the right hand of the Father,
miserere nobis.	have mercy on us.

2:30

Quoniam tu solus sanctus.	For thou only art holy,
Tu solus Dominus.	Thou only art Lord.
Tu solus Altissimus,	Thou only art most high,
Jesu Christe.	O Jesus Christ,
Cum Sancto Spiritu,	With the Holy Spirit,
In Gloria Dei Patris.	In the glory of God the Father.

3:14 Amen.   Amen.

Guillaume de Machaut probably wrote *La Messe de Nostre Dame* (Mass of Our Lady) in the 1360s for performance at a Mass for the Virgin Mary that was celebrated each Saturday in a chapel of the Cathedral at Reims, where he was a canon. When his brother Jean died in 1372, the observance became a memorial Mass for Jean, thanks to an endowment the brothers had given the church. An oration for Guillaume's soul was added after his death in 1377. Because of the endowment, this mass continued to be performed in their honor weekly for several decades.

The mass is in four voices throughout. The tenor and contratenor (the bottom voice in this transcription) togther provide a foundation for the more quickly moving upper voices, the motetus (duplum) and triplum. The contratenor (which means "against the tenor") is in the same range as the tenor, moving above or below it as needed to create the desired harmonic intervals, which sometimes results in large leaps (see the Kyrie, measures 9–10, 14–17, and 21–26).

Machaut used two styles in the mass. The Kyrie, Sanctus, Agnus Dei, and Ite, missa est are isorhythmic, based on chants for those texts, while the Gloria and Credo are generally syllabic and homophonic (except for melismatic Amens). The Gloria is partially paraphrased from a Gloria chant that moves freely between voices (see below), and the Credo is not based on chant.

The Kyrie is typical of the isorhythmic movements. The tenor melody is taken from the plainchant *Kyrie Cunctipotens Genitor*, which we saw in NAWM 3b (although Machaut used a slightly different version of the chant). The chant has four segments of melody—Kyrie eleison, Christe eleison, a new setting of Kyrie eleison, and a longer variant of the latter—and all four are set by Machaut. The last Kyrie (measure 67) begins like the second Kyrie (measure 50), emphasizing the similarity between the original chants.

In the first Kyrie (measures 1–27), the twenty-eight notes of the chant are divided into seven statements of a four-note talea in the tenor (see measures 1–4 for the first statement). In addition, the contratenor is mostly isorhythmic with a talea of twelve measures (compare measures 1–12 with 13–24), corresponding to three taleae in the tenor, and the upper voices are partially isorhythmic over the same span (see especially measures 9–12 and 21–24). The beginning of each talea in the tenor and contratenor is marked in this edition with a roman numeral in the score. In the Christe (measures 28–49) and second Kyrie (measures 50–66), both tenor and contratenor are exactly isorhythmic, with taleae of seven measures in the Christe and eight measures in Kyrie II, and the upper parts are again partly isorhythmic (for example, see measures 30–32, 37–39, and 44–47 of the Christe in all voices). The last, extended Kyrie (measures 67–95) has the longest talea in the tenor, fourteen measures, with the contratenor repeating a seven-measure pattern and the upper parts cycling with the tenor (compare measures 70–74 with 84–88 and 78–79 with 92–93). The rhythmic repetitions in other voices make the taleae in the tenor easier to hear, as do the recurring measures where all four voices sustain a long tone.

Characteristics of this Kyrie that are common in the rest of Machaut's music include the syncopations at the level of the quarter note (semibreve, in the original notation) and eighth note (minim) and the occasional use of hocket, as in measures 30–31 and 34 of the Christe. Both syncopation and hocket are used especially to highlight the isorhythmic repetitions in the upper voices. Also typical of Machaut is the alternation of sustained sonorities (as at measures 28, 32, 35, 39, 42, and 46) with passages of rapid motion in between them, which has been compared to the alternation of pillars with decorative stained-glass windows along the walls of a Gothic cathedral.

The harmony reflects the mode of the chant, mode 1 on D. Each section begins and ends on *d—a—d'—a'*, a very stable sonority of perfect consonances. Most final cadences and some internal cadences use the double leading-tone cadence with octave doubling in the upper part, producing parallel octaves and fifths. In between, a sense of forward motion is achieved through frequent sonorities with thirds or sixths, which lend the music a bright, sweet quality; they were recognized as imperfect consonances, but ultimately required resolution to perfect consonance at the end of a phrase. Machaut returns frequently enough to sonorities on D to keep the mode clear.

Chant Kyries were often performed in antiphony, with alternation between two halves of the choir (see NAWM 3b). A similar practice was often used for polyphonic settings, with alternation between soloists singing the polyphony and the choir singing the original chant, as on the accompanying recording. Such a performance proceeds as follows:

Kyrie:	Polyphony (Kyrie I)	0:00
	Chant	0:58
	Polyphony (Kyrie I)	1:16
Christe:	Chant	2:15
	Polyphony (Christe)	2:31
	Chant	3:22
Kyrie:	Polyphony (Kyrie II)	3:36
	Chant	4:16
	Polyphony (Kyrie III)	4:31

Alternatively, the polyphonic settings could be repeated to produce the threefold statements of "Kyrie eleison" and "Christe eleison." This was apparently Machaut's preference; all of the manuscript sources have repeat marks indicating that Kyrie I should be sung three times, the Christe three times, Kyrie II twice, and then Kyrie III.

The Gloria is mostly homophonic, allowing clear and relatively rapid declamation of its long prose text by all voices in a style that contrasts markedly with the isorhythmic and melismatic Kyrie. The triplum is slightly more active than the other voices, but each voice occasionally subdivides rhythms into smaller durations than do the other three. The rhythm throughout fits the words, with longer notes for the ends of phrases of text. At two spots (measures 43 and 93), the name

Jesu Christe is emphasized by being sung in double longs, transcribed here as double whole notes.

Daniel Leech-Wilkinson has demonstrated that the tenor and contratenor alternate in paraphrasing a chant Gloria, a regional variant of the Gloria in NAWM 3c, as illustrated here in a passage near the beginning of the movement. The pitches drawn from the chant are marked with an x.

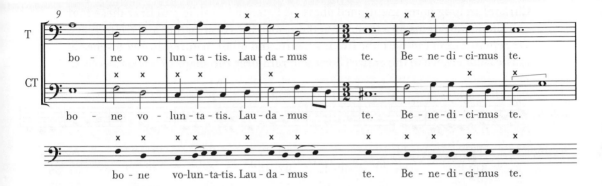

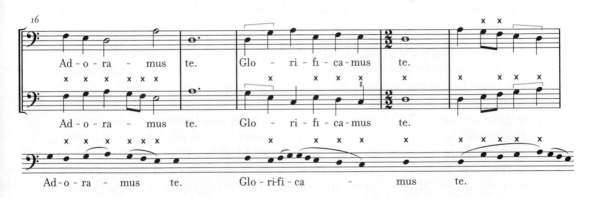

This Gloria chant is in mode 4, cadencing on E at the end of almost every phrase. Yet Machaut tailors his paraphrase so that the strongest cadences are on D, as in measures 17 and 19, reinforcing D as the modal center of this movement as it was for the Kyrie. Perhaps because the mode is so clearly on D, the singers on the accompanying recording chose a different Gloria chant, one in mode 2 on D, for the opening words, "Gloria in excelsis Deo," which were sung by the priest officiating at the Mass and thus were not set in polyphony by Machaut.

Between the priest's intonation and the closing melismatic Amen, the Gloria is in four main sections, indicated by double barlines in this edition (measures 1–30, 31–56, 57–83, and 84–105). These sections correspond to the four main units of the Gloria text, set off by spaces on page 142 above. Daniel Leech-Wilkinson has suggested that each of these sections follows a parallel melodic and harmonic outline. A similar structure can be seen in the chant Gloria, with its recurring motives (compare the settings of the same units of text in NAWM 3c to each other). But in Machaut's Gloria, Leech-Wilkinson finds the most evident repetition in the triplum, with a succession of six melodic contours elaborated in different ways in each section. The following chart shows these six contours and the measure numbers where they appear in each section. Each time they appear, segments *d* and *f* lead to closed cadences on the final D, segments *a* and *c* end with open cadences, and segment *e* is preceded by a linking figure (marked + in the chart) in which the triplum and motetus rest while the lower two voices cross melodically. In the first and third sections, the melodically similar segments *c* and *d* are conflated, and in the second and fourth sections segment *d* ends with the settings of "Jesu Christe" in long notes mentioned above. A listener is unlikely to hear these four sections as variations on a theme, but the similarities of structure and contour and the repetitions of motives, the linking figure, and other features do give a sense of musical coherence to the entire Gloria and reinforce the shape of its text.

Basic melodic outline	*a*	*b*	*c*	*d*	+	*e*	*f*
Section: 1	1–13	14–17		18–19	20	21–27	28–30
2	31–35	36–39	40–42	42–46	47	48–52	52–56
3	57–60	61–62	62–64		65	66–75	76–83
4	84–86	86–87	88–89	90–97	98	99–102	103–5

The crowning jewel of the Gloria is the Amen (measure 106), which glories in syncopation, hocket, isorhythmic repetition, and constantly changing figuration. The tenor line is freely adapted from the "Amen" of the same chant Gloria. The Amen begins with relatively long notes (the half notes correspond to breves in the original notation) and progressively moves to more rapid motion in semibreves and minims (quarter and eighth notes). At measure 108, the tenor begins to repeat a two-measure rhythmic figure, and by measure 111 all four voices are isorhythmic in two-measure units, with hocket between the upper voices and syncopation in the contratenor. After a cadence in measure 117, the figuration begins to change every one or two measures, and the hocket in the upper voices and syncopation in the contratenor grow more rapid and complex. Measures 127–30 are again briefly isorhythmic in all voices, with two levels of syncopation in the upper voices, providing a rhythmic climax before the final cadence. Despite the differences in texture and style between them, the Amen and the rest of the Gloria are linked by having similar beginning and ending passages; compare measures 1–5 with 106–10 and measures 102–5 with 128–31.

Machaut marks accidentals in his music much more frequently than Vitry (compare NAWM 25). Often these add emphasis to a cadence by creating leading tones, such as the C♯ and G♯ in the final cadence of the Gloria. But Machaut said he also added accidentals for the sake of beauty, as in the triplum at measure 31 of the Kyrie. Often an altered note in one voice will conflict with an unaltered note in another, as in the conflict of G against G♯ in the final cadence of the Kyrie or C against C♯ in measures 4 and 15 of the Gloria. In these cases, the editor suggests chromatically altering the unaltered note by placing an accidental above the note. Throughout, singers would no doubt also make chromatic alterations in order to avoid melodic or harmonic tritones (as at measures 16 and 26 of the Kyrie), create a smoother melody (as does the change from B to B♭ for the melodic high notes in the triplum and motetus of the Christe), or strengthen cadences with added leading tones (as at measures 19–20 of the Gloria). By placing these accidentals above the staff, the editor makes clear that they are not in the manuscripts, leaving performers free to choose whether to follow the editor's advice.

Guillaume de Machaut (CA. 1300–1377)

Douce dame jolie

Virelai

MID-FOURTEENTH CENTURY

A 1	Douce dame jolie,	Sweet lovely lady,
	Pour Dieu ne penses mie	for God's sake do not think of me
	Que nulle ait signourie	that any woman has sovereignty
	Seur moy fors vous seulement.	over me save you alone.
b 2	Qu'adès sans tricherie	For always, without treachery,
	Chierie	I have cherished
	Vous ay et humblement	you and humbly
b 3	Tous les jours de ma vie	all the days of my life
	Servie	have served you
	Sans vilein pensement.	without any base thought.
a 4	Helas! et je mendie	Alas! and I beg
	D'esperance et d'aïe;	for hope and for help;
	Dont ma joie est fenie,	for my joy is ended,
	Se pité ne vous en prent.	if you do not take pity on me.
A 1	Douce dame jolie . . .	Sweet lovely lady . . .
b 2	Mais vo douce maistrie	But your sweet sovereignty
	Maistrie	masters
	Mon cuer si durement	my heart so completely
b 3	Qu'elle le contralie	that it stays my heart
	Et lie	and binds it
	En amours tellement	in love so much

(labels in score margins: 0:15, 0:34, 1:05)

From *The Works of Guillaume de Machaut*, ed. Leo Schrade, vol. 2, Polyphonic Music of the Fourteenth Century 3 (Monaco: Éditions de l'Oiseau-Lyre, 1956), 168.

1:24	a 4	Qu'il n'a de riens envie	that my heart wants nothing

Fors d'estre en vo baillie;   save to be in your service;
Et se ne li ottrie   and yet your heart offers mine
Vos cuers nul aligement.   no relief.

A 1 Douce dame jolie . . .   Sweet lovely lady . . .

1:55 b 2 Et quant ma maladie   And since my malady
Garie   will be cured
Ne sera nullement   not at all
b 3 Sans vous, douce anemie,   without you, sweet enemy,
Qui lie   who are pleased
Estes de mon tourment,   with my torment,
2:14 a 4 A jointes mains deprie   with clasped hands I pray
Vo cuer, puis qu'il m'oublie,   to your heart, since it forgets me,
Que temprement m'ocie,   that it mercifully kill me,
Car trop langui longuement.   for I have languished too long.

A 1 Douce dame jolie . . .   Sweet lovely lady . . .

Machaut wrote many monophonic songs, including twenty-five virelais. *Douce dame jolie* carries on the tradition of the trouvères both in its subject matter, related to *fine amour*, and in its playful approach to language. The poem plays on images of feudal fealty: the lady is the sovereign and the singer is her vassal, who says he has humbly and loyally served her all his life and begs for her aid. This virelai appears in most of Machaut's manuscripts of his collected works, including the earliest, and thus must have been written by about 1350.

A virelai typically has three stanzas, each preceded and followed by a refrain. The stanzas have the AAB pattern of musical repetition familiar from many earlier secular songs (see NAWM 9 and 11), and the refrain uses the same music as the last section of the verse; because the refrain appears first, and musical elements are customarily labeled in alphabetical order, the overall form of the virelai is thus A bba A bba A bba A, with capital letters indicating repetitions of both text and music and lowercase letters indicating repetitions of music with new text. This is like the form of the cantiga in NAWM 12, but the number of stanzas in cantigas varies while virelais normally have three stanzas (or in some cases only one).

The number of poetic lines in each section can vary widely. In *Douce dame jolie*, there are four lines in the refrain and a sections and three lines in the b sections:

	Refrain				Stanza									
Lines of poetry	1	2	3	4	1	2	3	4	5	6	7	8	9	10
Rhyme	a	a	a	b	a	a	b	a	a	b	a	a	a	b
Sections of music	A				b			b			a			

Most of the lines have seven syllables, with three and six syllables respectively for the last two lines of each b section. Only two rhymes are used, -*ie* and -*ent*, and the brief poetic lines mean these sounds are constantly returning, with the second of the two rhymes marking the end of each section of the form.

The melody is in the transposed Dorian mode on G, with a B♭ in the signature. The refrain begins on the fifth scale degree, D, and repeatedly descends to the final, G, by leap or by step. The b section melody rises to high G, an octave above the final, then descends to hover around D. In a virelai, the two b sections often end with *ouvert* ("open") and *clos* ("closed") endings, like the parallel phrases of an estampie (see NAWM 13), and this is true here: the first b section has an open ending on the fifth degree, and the other sections all close on the final. Given the melodic emphasis on the final, fifth degree, and octave, the mode could hardly be more clear.

Musical rhymes or near-rhymes emphasize the rhymes in the poetry. In the refrain and a section, each appearance of the rhyme -*ie* is set with the same syncopated turning figure. In the b sections the same rhyme is set to a long D followed by a descent; the first occurrence (measures 20–21) echoes the syncopated figure from the refrain, and the immediate appearance of a varied repetition (measures 22–23) highlights the short three-syllable line in the middle of each b section. The phrases ending in -*ent* are less closely related but have similar contours and rhythms. The frequent repetitions of rhymes, rhythms, and melodic figures give this melody a catchy, stick-in-your-head character that has helped it become one of the most famous and widely performed melodies from the Middle Ages.

In addition to the clear mode and frequent repetitions, rhythmic factors that contribute to this song's popular character are duple meter and syncopations. Both of these reflect the innovations of Ars Nova notation, which allowed duple as well as triple division of breves and semibreves. The modern $\frac{2}{4}$ time signature is the equivalent of imperfect time with minor prolation. That is, the breve (transcribed as a measure) is divided into two semibreves (quarter notes) and the semibreve into two minims (eighth notes), so that the time (the division of the breve) is duple, or imperfect, and the prolation (the division of the semibreve) is duple, or minor. The exact values of notes in this notation permitted syncopated figures to be notated for the first time. Neither the duple meter nor the syncopations that pervade this song could have been notated in thirteenth-century notation systems.

Although *Douce dame jolie* consists of a single line of melody and is sung unaccompanied on the recording with this anthology, it could also have been performed with an extemporized instrumental accompaniment. Virelais, also called *chansons balladées* (songs for dancing), were originally associated with dancing, and the melody of *Douce dame jolie* seems particularly dancelike.

Guillaume de Machaut (CA. 1300–1377)

Rose, liz, printemps, verdure

Rondeau

MID-FOURTEENTH CENTURY

28

From Guillaume de Machaut, *Oeuvres complètes*, vol. 5, ed. Leo Schrade (Monaco: Éditions de l'Oiseau-Lyre, 1977), 11–12. Used by permission.

0:00	A	1	Rose, liz, printemps, verdure,	Rose, lily, spring, greenery,
		2	Fleur, baume et tres douce odour,	flower, balm, and the sweetest fragrance,
0:40	B	3	Belle, passes en doucour,	beautiful lady, you surpass in sweetness.
1:02	a	4	Et tous les biens de Nature,	And all the gifts of nature
		5	Avez dont je vous aour.	you possess, for which I adore you.
1:43	A	6	Rose, liz, printemps, verdure,	Rose, lily, spring, greenery,
		7	Fleur, baume et tres douce odour.	flower, balm, and the sweetest fragrance.
2:26	a	8	Et quant toute creature	And, since beyond any creature's
		9	Seurmonte vostre valour,	your virtue excels,
3:06	b	10	Bien puis dire et par honour:	I can honestly say:
3:29	A	11	Rose, liz, printemps, verdure,	Rose, lily, spring, greenery,
		12	Fleur, baume et tres douce odour,	flower, balm, and very sweet fragrance,
4:10	B	13	Belle, passes en doucour.	beautiful lady, you surpass in sweetness.

Rondeaux were love songs in the centuries-old tradition of the trouvères. They were probably performed most often as entertainment at court, where a cultivated audience would have appreciated the wordplay of their texts and the intricacies of their music. *Rose, liz* is preserved with Machaut's other polyphonic chansons in manuscripts prepared under his own supervision. The earliest manuscript (from ca. 1350) lacks the triplum, or top voice, suggesting that Machaut added it later. Indeed, Machaut composed most of his polyphonic chansons for three voices rather than four; here, the triplum is essentially decorative rather than integral to the structure of the work.

The rondeau is a poetic and musical form in which the full refrain, stated at the beginning and the end, contains all of the music in the piece. In *Rose, liz* the first part of the refrain (A in the diagram below) includes two lines of poetry and the second part (B) includes one. After the refrain, the next two lines of poetry are set to the music of the first part of the refrain. Then the first part of the refrain returns, both text and music. The following three lines are set to the music of the entire refrain, and the whole refrain returns at the end.

The musical form for the thirteen-line song is ABaAabAB, with capital letters indicating that both the music and the text of the refrain are sung and lower case letters indicating a repetition of music with a different text:

Lines of poetry	1	2	3	4	5	6(=1)	7(=2)	8	9	10	11(=1)	12(=2)	13(=3)
Rhyme	a	b	b	a	b	a	b	a	b	b	a	b	b
Sections of music	A		B	a		A			a	b	A		B

Each time the refrain returns, in part or in whole, it has new layers of meaning added by the intervening lines. In this rondeau, the first two lines of the refrain (A) enumerate beauties and pleasures of nature, from fragrant flowers to the greenery of spring, but we do not know the context for these images, nor their significance. Not until the third line (B) does the poet reveal that they all are surpassed in sweetness by his lady. The normal comparison of a woman to natural beauty is here reversed; nature is being compared to the lady and found wanting. In the following two lines (4–5), he says she possesses "all the gifts of nature," so that when the opening lines of the refrain return (A in lines 6–7), we hear them as naming those gifts; given the context of what we have learned so far, we understand these lines quite differently than we did at first. The next three lines (8–10) raise the stakes higher with the claim that her virtue is greater than any other creature's. After that, we hear the refrain that closes the poem as building on that claim, enumerating things, however desirable, that are still less virtuous, pleasing, or enticing than she.

The first section of the refrain ends without finality on the note D, and the second section closes on C. The two sections are linked by similar final rhymes (on -*our*) and by a kind of musical rhyme (compare measures 20–25 and 32–37). The harmonic relationship between the sections—in which the last tenor note of the final cadence is a step lower than that of main internal cadence—is common in medieval music, and the overall structure reflects the harmonic motion of the typical cadence, in which the tenor descends a step to the final.

The song centers on C, which is the first and last note and the most common note for internal cadences (measures 10 and 30). C was not recognized as a modal final by theorists of the time, but was already becoming common, and modes on C would be recognized in the sixteenth century and named Ionian and Hypoionian. But Machaut colors several passages with an emphasis on E♭, which would be rare in the later modes on C, giving this song a distinctive flavor very different from the familiar major mode of tonal music.

Like most of Machaut's polyphonic songs, *Rose liz* is constructed around a two-voice framework in which the cantus (Latin for "song") is the main melody and the tenor serves as a slower-moving support to the cantus. This structure is the opposite of earlier polyphony, in which the tenor was the main structural voice that provided the foundation for the others. Typically the cantus is the only voice provided with a text (although all of the voices may have been sung). The contratenor reinforces or complements the tenor in the same range, and the triplum shares the upper octave and exchanges figuration with the cantus. A diatonic figure of a stepwise descending fourth dominates the tenor part and at one point is taken up by the triplum (see tenor, measures 1–2, and triplum, measures 15–16). Thirds and sixths sweeten the harmony, but the ends of poetic lines are marked by cadences on open fifth and octave sonorities.

As in the *Messe de Nostre Dame*, Machaut alternated segments of music with different rhythmic profiles. Some measures sustain a chord without motion (for instance, measures 2 and 10); some move only in quarter notes (as do measure 8–9); but in most measures, at least one voice moves on most or all of the eighth notes. To create this activity, Machaut often reused the same rhythmic figures; those in measures 4, 5, 6, and 7 of the cantus recur several times throughout the song.

Characteristic of French fourteenth-century secular music are the long melismas at the beginning of lines and sometimes also in the middle. These melismas, occupying as much as four measures, do not fall on important words, nor even necessarily on accented syllables, but they serve a formal and decorative function.

Machaut's polyphonic chansons were probably performed by singers, one on each part (see "In Performance: Voices or Instruments?" in HWM, p. 137). The untexted lines might have been sung on neutral syllables, or all voices might have sung the text together, as on the accompanying recording. Some modern performances use instruments for the untexted lines, usually with a different timbre on each line to keep the parts clear.

Philippus de Caserta (FL. CA. 1370S)

En remirant vo douce pourtraiture

Ballade

CA. 1370

29

fol. 39

[E]n

0:53

1. En
2. m'a
4. He,
5. car
7. A
8. se

[T]enor. En remirant

re- -mi- -rant au cuer
point Bel A- -cueil,
se mon cuer
vous me plains,
Dieus e vous

vo dou- -ce pour- -trai-
d'u- -ne te- -le poin-
ou je prens nou- -re-
de- -voit en grant a- -ven-
car sui me pre- -nez en
ne me pre- -nez

From *French Secular Music: Manuscript Chantilly, Musée Condé 564*, ed. Gordon K. Greene, vol. 2, Polyphonic Music of the Fourteenth Century 19 (Monaco: Éditions de l'Oiseau-Lyre, 1982), 21–24. Used by permission. On the question of vocal or instrumental performance of the contratenor discussed in the commentary, see Peter Urquhart and Heather de Savage, "Evidence Contrary to the *a cappella* Hypothesis for the 15th-Century Chanson," *Early Music* 39 (August 2011): 359–78.

1:47

3. las !   si   ne   puet   doul -   - ce
6. si   ne lai - -ray   que   ne
9. telz   mauls ne   puis   lon -   - gue-

da - -
vous
- ment   - me   sans
doie a -
- en -   - du

per,   se   vo   doul - -çour   ne
- mer ;   mes vo   mer -   - cy   me
- rer ;   de   tri -   - ste   cuer   di-

35   2:21

me   va   se - -cour -rant :   pour   vostre   a -   - mor,
va   trop de - -tri -ant :   pour   vostre   a -   - mor,
- re puis en plou -rant :   pour   vostre   a -   - mor,

0:00	a	En remirant vo douce pourtraiture,		While I gazed at your sweet portrait,

0:00   a En remirant vo douce pourtraiture,   While I gazed at your sweet portrait,
          en laquele est tout doulz ymaginer,   in which the height of sweetness is depicted,
0:53   a m'a point au cuer d'une tele pointure   it stung my heart with a such a sting
          d'ardant desir si que mon cuer durer,   of burning desire that my heart cannot—
1:47   b las! si ne puet, doulce dame sans per,   alas!—survive, sweet peerless lady,
          se vo doulçour ne me va secourrant: if your sweetness does not come rescue me:
2:21   C pour vostre amor, dame, vois languissant. for your love, lady, I am languishing.

          a He, Bel Acueil, ou je prens noureture, Ah, Fair Welcome, in which I find sustenance,
            vo cuer vueilliez de m'amor alumer,   please kindle your heart with my love,
          a car se mon cuer devoit en grant ardure for even if my heart were, in great heat,
            ardre, bruir, a touz jorns sans finer, to blaze and burn forever, perpetually,
          b si ne lairay que ne vous doie amer;   yet I will not cease having to love you;
            mes vo mercy me va trop detriant: but your mercy is too delayed in coming to me:
          C pour vostre amor, dame, vois languissant. for your love, lady, I am languishing.

          a A vous me plains, car sui en aventure   To you I complain, for I am in danger
            de toust mourir pour loyalment amer,   of soon dying for faithfully loving,
          a se Dieus e vous ne me prenez en cure;   unless God and you take me into your care;
            en face Amour le dur en doulz muer,   may Love thereby turn harshness into sweetness;
          b telz mauls ne puis longuement endurer; such ills I cannot long endure;
            de triste cuer dire puis en plourant: with a sad heart I can say while weeping:
          C pour vostre amor, dame, vois languissant. for your love, lady, I am languishing.

Relatively little is known about the life of Philippus (or Philipoctus) de Caserta. His name implies that he was from Caserta in southern Italy near Naples. References in some of his song texts place him at the papal court in Avignon in southern France in the 1370s, and he was also associated with the court of the Visconti family at Pavia in northern Italy. He was the author of several treatises on music theory and composed at least six ballades and a Credo.

En remirant vo douce pourtraiture is a ballade, a form which has three stanzas set to the same music, each ending with the same line of poetry that serves as a refrain (indicated below as C). Each stanza features the same three rhymes and follows the aab pattern of musical repetition we have seen in other secular songs (see NAWM 9 and 11):

Lines of poetry	1	2	3	4	5	6	7
Rhyme	a	b	a	b	b	c	c
Sections of music	a		a		b		C

The first a section has an open ending on A and the second a closed ending on G. As is frequently true of ballades, the a section shares a musical rhyme with the end of the refrain: their last six measures are the same (compare measures 16–23 with the second ending to measures 46–51). As in Machaut's *Rose, liz* (NAWM 28), there are frequent melismas, which may occur at the beginning, middle, or end of a line of poetry. That Caserta sought to place himself in the Machaut tradition and invoke comparisons with him is plain from the text of this ballade, which quotes in its final stanza the refrain line ("Se Dieus et vous ne me prenez en cure") from Machaut's ballade *Plourez, dames* and the opening words of Machaut's ballade *De triste cuer*.

Both the Avignon and Pavia courts were centers for the Ars Subtilior, a style marked by a complexity of rhythm and notation unmatched before the twentieth century and exemplified in Caserta's *En remirant vo douce pourtraiture*. As is typical of fourteenth-century French polyphonic chansons, the top voice, or cantus, carries the main melody, the tenor supports it and forms cadences with the cantus, and the contratenor fills in between and around them. But the differences in rhythm between the parts evident in other polyphonic chansons, as in Machaut's *Rose, liz*, are taken to extremes in the Ars Subtilior.

The song is transcribed here in $\frac{9}{8}$ meter, corresponding to the Ars Nova mensuration of perfect time and major prolation—three-fold division of the breve, transcribed as three beats per measure, and of the semibreve, giving three eighth notes in each beat. The tenor moves mostly in dotted quarter notes, marking the principal meter and providing a steady background against which to hear the rhythmic adventures of the other voices, created by special signs in the original notation (see HWM, page 128, Figure 6.9). A dot in the cantus shifts the rhythm forward by an eighth note in measures 2–4 and 44–45, resulting in a series of ties across the beat. Red ink (as opposed to black), marked in the transcription by open brackets, shortens the length of notes by one-third, resulting in hemiola effects (see the contratenor at measure 2, cantus in measures 5–6, and both at measures 9–10 and 38–40, among others). A mensuration sign like a backward C denotes what is transcribed here as $\frac{2}{8}$ meter in the time of a dotted quarter (see the passages marked by dotted open brackets), as in the contratenor in measures 3–6 and in all three voices joining in succession in measures 12–15. A note shaped like a semibreve with a downward stem indicates four equal notes per measure in the cantus in measures 17 and 47. In these and many other measures, the voices subdivide the measure or the beat in different ways (here, 3 against 4 against 9), resulting in a rhythmic surface of astonishing variety.

Cadences mark the ends of poetic lines and provide guideposts for both performers and listeners. Each successive phrase has a distinctive rhythmic profile, which helps to give the piece shape. The rhythmic and metric complexity demands skilled performers, but it also generates momentum and sustains tension between points of rest, helping to create long-breathed phrases and a large-scale form. With all the conflicting meters and rhythms, it is remarkable how euphonious the music sounds.

Fourteenth-century chansons were most likely sung by solo voices on all three parts, but it is also possible that instruments were used for the untexted tenor and contratenor. As discussed in the sidebar "In Performance: Voices or Instruments?" on p. 137 of HWM, the preponderance of evidence supports vocal performance. Yet Peter Urquhart and Heather de Savage have recently argued that in at least some fifteenth-century chansons the contratenor may have been intended for a plucked string instrument. Could this apply to fourteenth-century songs as well? One point they raise is that in some chansons sustained notes in the contratenor create difficulties in the counterpoint, dissonances on prominent beats, that would disappear if played on a plucked string whose sound would decay before the note becomes dissonant. Such dissonances appear in the contratenor of *En remirant* in measures 10 (downbeat), 17 (beats 1 and 2), 34 (all three beats), 40 (downbeat), and 47 (beats 1 and 2). It can be argued in response that fourteenth-century music does not feature the strict treatment of dissonance typical of the Renaissance. On the other hand, such dissonances appear in no other voice in *En remirant*, suggesting that the contratenor may have been conceived differently and perhaps was intended for a plucked string instrument such as a harp or lute.

The debate continues, but in the meantime modern performers must make a choice. In the performance on the accompanying recordings, the cantus is sung and is doubled on recorder; the tenor is played on bass recorder; and the contratenor is played on a citole, a plucked medieval lute. Using instruments of contrasting timbres can highlight the independence of each line and the remarkable rhythmic complexity of this piece. Only the first of the three stanzas is included on the recording, for reasons of space.

Jacopo da Bologna (FL. 1340–?1386)

Non al suo amante

Madrigal

CA. 1350

30

From *Music of Fourteenth-Century Italy*, ed. Nino Pirotta, vol. 4, *Jacobus de Bononia, Vicentius de Arimino*, Corpus mensurabilis musicae 8 (Amsterdam: American Institute of Musicology, 1963), 114–15. © American Institute of Musicology. Used with permission.

Stanza 1 `0:00`

Non al suo amante più Diana piaque,
Quando per tal ventura tuta nuda
La vid' in meço de le gelid' aque,

No more did Diana please her lover,
when just by chance totally nude
he saw her amidst the chilly waters,

Stanza 2 `1:12`

Ch' a mi la pasturela alpestra e cruda,
Fixa a bagnar el suo candido velo
Ch' al sol e a l' aura el vago capel chiuda.

than did the rustic mountain shepherdess [please] me,
when I gazed at her washing her snow-white veil
that shields her graceful hair from the sun and the breeze.

Ritornello `2:25`

Tal che me fici, quando gli ard' el celo,

Tuto tremar d' un amoroso çelo.

— Francesco Petrarca

Such [was the experience] that it made me, [even] when the sun
    was scorching,
shiver all over with an amorous chill.

Not much is known of Jacopo da Bologna's life, but he was presumably born and educated in Bologna. He served the ruling family of Milan, the Visconti, in the 1340s and 1350s, interrupted by a period at the court of Verona in about 1349–52. *Non al suo amante* was probably composed during his time in Verona. It sets a poem by Francesco Petrarca (1304–1374), known to the English as Petrarch, who was the greatest Italian lyric poet of the fourteenth century. This is the only known musical setting of a Petrarch poem during the poet's lifetime, making it likely that Jacopo knew Petrarch, who studied law at the University of Bologna in the 1320s and traveled throughout northern Italy in his later years. Jacopo's version differs in some details of wording and spelling from Petrarch's, perhaps reflecting changes introduced in the transmission of poem or piece.

The poem alludes to an incident in Ovid's *Metamorphoses* (III, 138–252) in which Actaeon was hunting and accidentally came across the goddess Diana bathing in a spring. In her anger at being seen naked, she splashed his face with water; he was transformed into a stag and pursued by his hunting dogs. Petrarch compares this to his own experience seeing a young woman bathing not herself but her veil, thereby exposing her hair to view. The transformation in his case is not so violent, but the reference to Actaeon's fate nicely captures the mixture of surprise, admiration, love, and fear the poet feels.

Petrarch's poem has the form typical of the fourteenth-century madrigal: two stanzas of three lines followed by a two-line ritornello. (The number of stanzas can vary, as can the number of lines in the ritornello.) Similar to the *envoi* of troubadour songs (see NAWM 8–9), the ritornello (diminutive of Italian *ritorno*, "return") provides a summary reflection on the preceding stanzas, turning from description or narrative to offer a different perspective. The music for the stanza is heard twice, and the ritornello once. The two voices have the same text and were both meant to be sung, declaiming the syllables together most of the time with occasional points of contrast (as in measures 7–8 and 17–18). The voices are relatively equal, more so than in the treble-dominated style of Machaut (see NAWM 28), except during extended florid runs in the upper part on the first syllable and last accented syllable of each line. These melismas, which surround a mostly syllabic declamation of the remainder of each line of poetry, have been compared to floral garlands in a painting or decorations in the margins of a manuscript. At times the voices engage in a brief hocketlike alternation (as in measures 16, 19, and 21) or trade off resting while the other sings (as in measures 24–28). The ends of lines are marked by cadences. Between lines, while one voice rests, the other continues, creating a bridge to the next line (see measures 12, 24, and 47). The strongest cadences, like those at the end of each main section, converge on a unison, which differs from the usual French cadence formed by widening to an octave. The latter is used for some internal cadences, as at measures 34 and 47.

The rhythm is typical of the early Italian Trecento style. Both voices exhibit elaborate divisions of the beat that can easily be imagined as deriving from a tradition of improvised singing. The notation of the stanzas calls for imperfect division of the breve (transcribed as a half note) into two semibreves (quarter notes). In the Italian system, these can be further subdivided in various ways (producing eighth notes, sixteenth notes, and even sixteenth-note triplets in the transcription), allowing florid scales and runs. The star in the time signature in this edition indicates the presence of these small subdivisions. In the ritornello, the breve is perfect (now a dotted half note) and may be divided into three imperfect semibreves (three quarter notes) or two perfect ones (two dotted quarter notes), which can in turn be subdivided. The flexible Italian notation was perfectly suited for music in this style.

Francesco Landini (CA. 1325–1397)

Così pensoso

Caccia

MID–FOURTEENTH CENTURY

31

From Francesco Landini, *Complete Works*, ed. Leo Schrade, with introduction and notes by Kurt von Fischer, vol. 2, *Three-Part Ballate, Madrigals, Caccia* (Monaco: Éditions de l'Oiseau-Lyre, 1982), 219–21.

lor chon be' sem _ bian _

<table>
<tr><td>Così pensoso com'amor mi guida</td><td>Lost in thought as Love guided me</td></tr>
</table>

Così pensoso com'amor mi guida	Lost in thought as Love guided me
Per la verde rivera passo passo,	along the green bank step by step,
Senti', "Leva quel sasso!"	I heard, "Pick up that rock!"
"Ve'l granchio, ve', ve'l pesce, piglia, piglia!"	"See the crab, look, see the fish, catch it, catch it!"
"Quest'è gran maraviglia!"	"This is a great marvel!"
Cominciò Isabella con istrida:	Isabella began to screech,
"O mè, o mè!"	"O my, o my!"
"Che hai, che hai?"	"What's wrong? What's wrong?"
"I' son morsa nel dito!"	"I've been bitten on my finger!"
"O Lisa, il pesce fugge!"	"O Lisa, the fish is getting away!"
"I' l'ho, i' l'ho!"	"I've got it, I've got it!"
"L'Ermellina l'ha preso!"	"Ermellina caught it."
"Tie 'l ben, tie 'l ben!"	"Hold it tight, hold it tight!"
"Quest'è bella peschiera."	"This is a fine fish pond."
Intanto giuns' a l'amorosa schiera.	In the meantime, I had reached the affectionate group.

RITORNELLO

Dove vaghe trova' donne et amanti	There I found ladies and lovers
Che m'accolson a lor con be' sembianti.	who greeted me with pleasant looks.

Francesco Landini is best known as a ballata composer (see NAWM 32). *Così pensoso*, transmitted in the Squarcialupi Codex and two other manuscripts, is his only caccia, a fourteenth-century Italian genre that combines virtuosity—for both the composer and performer—with humor. The two upper parts form a canon at the unison, the second voice singing exactly the same melody and text as the first voice but entering several measures later. They are accompanied by a freely composed, untexted tenor in relatively long notes. The three voices cadence together in measure 88, followed by a short concluding ritornello with another canon in the top voices and freely composed tenor. *Così pensoso* is like a madrigal in featuring a ritornello in a different meter.

The word "caccia" means "hunt," referring to the second voice chasing after the first, and many such works are about hunting. Here the hunt is for fish—or perhaps metaphorically for love. The poem begins with the narrator deep in thought, then overhearing a dialogue from somewhere nearby but out of sight. We hear and observe the scene through the narrator. At first the situation is unclear, as the first words overheard are "pick up that rock!" The context gradually becomes clear as voices shout about a crab, fish, being bitten, and catching a fish in one's hands. In the ritornello, as the speakers come into view, we discover they are young ladies and their lovers on the bank of the fish pond, and we may wonder whether their games have deeper meanings.

The poetic lines are eleven, seven, or four syllables long, in an irregular arrangement that favors eleven-syllable lines for the narrative and shorter lines for the dialogue. (In counting syllables in Italian poetry, successive vowels are usually elided, even from one word to the next; for example, in the penultimate line the last vowel of "donne" is elided with the following "et," and the line is eleven rather than twelve syllables long.) Lines of these lengths, especially of eleven and seven syllables, were typical of Italian poetry for the next several centuries. The rhyme scheme is also irregular, though mostly in couplets.

Part of the craft and charm of a caccia is that through the canonic imitation the composer can create witty interplay between the voices. This can result from juxtapositions of sounds, like the echoing of "ve'" in the top voice by "*ver*-de ri-*ve*-ra" in the second voice at measures 25–28, quickly followed by the popping of "pesce, piglia, piglia" answered by "passo passo" in measures 28–30. Other juxtapositions create dialogue between voices, as when the second voice cries "Che hai, che hai?" ("What's wrong," but literally "What do you have") and the first responds "I' l'ho, i' l'ho!" ("I have it!") in measures 56–59. Almost always, the rests in one voice, marking the end of a phrase, are filled in by motion in the other. Throughout, the canonic combinations suggest the hubbub of a crowd at the water's edge.

Francesco Landini (CA. 1325–1397)

Non avrà ma' pietà

Ballata

32

LAST QUARTER OF THE FOURTEENTH CENTURY

concise · 0:00/3:17

2:23

Co

T

1.5. Non — a — vrà ma' pie — tà que — sta mie
4. For — se da lej sa — reb — bo — no in me

don — — na, Se
spen — — te Le

tu non faj, a — mo — — re,
fiam me che la pa — — rè

Ch'el — — la sia cer — ta del mio
Di gior — no in gior — no a — cres — co —

From *The Works of Francesco Landini*, ed. Leo Schrade, Polyphonic Music of the Fourteenth Century 4 (Monaco: Éditions de l'Oiseau-Lyre, 1958), 144–45. © Hänssler Verlag, D-71087 Holzgerlingen. Used by permission.

172

0:00		
A 1	Non avrà ma' pietà questa mia donna, Se tu non faj, amore, Ch'ella sie certa del mio grande ardore.	She will never have mercy, this lady of mine, if you do not see to it, Love, that she is certain of my great ardor.

0:52		
b 2	S'ella sapesse quanta pena i' porto Per onestà celata nella mente	If she knew how much pain I bear— for honesty's sake concealed in my mind—

1:37		
b 3	Sol per la sua bellecça, che conforto D'altro non prende l'anima dolente,	only for her beauty, other than which nothing gives comfort to a grieving soul,

2:23		
a 4	Forse da lej sarebbono in me spente Le fiamme che la pare Di giorno in giorno acrescono 'l dolore.	perhaps by her would be extinguished in me the flames which seem to arouse in me from day to day more pain.

3:17		
A 1	Non avrà ma' pietà questa mia donna, Se tu non faj, amore, Ch'ella sie certa del mio grande ardore.	She will never have mercy, this lady of mine, if you do not see to it, Love, that she is certain of my great ardor.

— B. D'ALESSIO DONATI

During the thirteenth and early fourteenth centuries, *ballate* (sing. *ballata*, from *ballare*, to dance) were associated with dancing, but the polyphonic ballate of the late fourteenth century were stylized works for elite audiences, meant to be sung and listened to for their own sakes. Landini was the leading ballata composer, with about 140 to his credit. His *Non avrà ma' pietà* was well known, with copies in the Squarcialupi Codex and several other northern Italian manuscripts, and is typical of the form and of Landini's style.

A three-line refrain called the *ripresa* (A, measures 1–29) is sung both before and after a seven-line stanza. The first two pairs of lines in the stanza, which were called *piedi*, have their own musical phrase (b, measures 30–57), and the last three lines, the *volta*, use the same music as the refrain (a). The first of the two piedi has an open (*verto*) ending on A, the second a closed (*chiuso*) ending on G, the same step-down relationship from internal to final cadence that we saw in NAWM 28 and 29. The form resembles that of a virelai (see NAWM 27), but with a single stanza instead of three.

Like Machaut's chansons, Landini's ballate are built around a two-voice framework comprising the cantus and the tenor. These two voices form cadences to mark the end of each line of poetry (as at measures 11, 17, and 29) and also occasionally within lines. At most of these cadences the upper voice decorates its rising stepwise motion by first descending a step and then skipping up a third, called a "Landini cadence" because Landini was the first composer to use it consistently, although it can be found in earlier fourteenth-century music (see for instance measures 58–59 in Vitry's *Cum statua/Hugo, Hugo/Magister invidie*, NAWM 25). It became common in both Italian and French music of the late fourteenth and early fifteenth centuries (see the final cadence of NAWM 29). The contratenor fills out the counterpoint and adds rhythmic interest. As in the music of Vitry, Machaut, and Caserta (see NAWM 25–29)—but not Landini's Italian predecessors—most of the cadences are double leading-tone cadences, either notated or created through the musica ficta expected from the performers.

Like Machaut, Landini used frequent syncopation, varied rhythms, and many sonorities containing thirds and sixths, which give this ballata its sweetness and charm. Elements that differentiate Landini's style from Machaut's include melismas on the first and penultimate syllables of each line, with clear, almost syllabic text-setting elsewhere; less angular contratenors; and smoother, more stepwise and rhythmically regular melodies in both cantus and tenor.

The tenor has a key signature with one flat, while the cantus and contratenor have none. This notational convention, sometimes called *partial signature*, was adopted apparently as a matter of convenience: the tenor line might consistently include B♭ (for example, to form a perfect fifth below F in one of the upper parts) while an upper part might include both B♮ and B♭ (whether notated or applied by the singers). We will see this notation in some fifteenth-century works as well.

As in French chansons, the tenor and contratenor are untexted. Modern performers often play those lines on instruments, but it is more likely that all three parts were sung. On the accompanying recording, all parts are sung, the cantus by two singers, and the tenor and contratenor are doubled by vielles.

33

Alleluia: A newë work

Carol

FIRST HALF OF THE FIFTEENTH CENTURY

From Oxford, Bodleian Library, MS Arch. Selden b. 26, ff. 21v–22. Edition from *Mediaeval Carols*, ed. John Stevens, Musica Britannica 4 (London: Stainer and Bell, 1952), 22–23. © 1952, 1958 by The Musica Britannica Trust. Reproduction by permission of Stainer & Bell, Ltd. English words modernized in spelling but not in form; modern equivalents given in brackets.

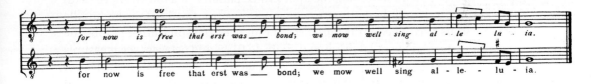

0:00/1:33/2:49

Alleluia, alleluia, alleluia.

0:38

1. A newë [new] work is come on hond [hand],
Through might and grace of Goddës sond
    [God's messenger],
To save the lost of every lond [land],
    Alleluia, alleluia,
For now is free that erst [once] was bond [in bondage];
We mow [may] well sing alleluia.

1:54

2. By Gabriel begun it was:
Right as the sun shone through the glass
Jesu Christ conceivëd was,
    Alleluia, alleluia,
Of Mary mother, full of grace;
Now sing we here alleluia.

3. Now is fulfilled the prophecy
Of David and of Jeremy [Jeremiah],
And also of Isaie [Isaiah],
    Alleluia, alleluia,
Sing we therefore both loud and high:
Alleluia, alleluia.

4. Simeon on his armës right
Clippëd Jesu full of might
And said unto that barne [child] so bright,
    Alleluia, alleluia;
I see my Savïour in sight;
And sung therewith alleluia.

5. Then he said, withoutë lece [without untruth]:
Lord, thou seeth thy servant in peace,
For now I have that I ever chece [choose],
    Alleluia, alleluia.
All ourë joyës [our joys] to increase
There saintës singeth alleluia.

6. Alleluia, this sweetë song,
Out of a greenë branch it sprong [sprang].
God send us the life that lasteth long!
    Alleluia, alleluia.
Now joy and bliss be them among
That thus can sing alleluia.

This anonymous carol survives only in a manuscript containing thirty-two carols that was copied about 1450 and is now at Oxford University. Like all fifteenth-century English carols, this one consists of a number of stanzas, each sung to the same music in alternation with a *burden*, or refrain. The text mixes the Latin "Alleluia" with an English poem about the incarnation of Jesus, a frequent theme of carols.

As in several other carols, there are two burdens, one for two voices and the other, a variation of the first, for three voices. Both are sung at the outset, and either both or just the second are repeated after each verse. In the first burden, the two parts move mostly in parallel thirds or sixths, sometimes crossing, and close on an octave or unison at the end of each phrase. In the second burden, the three voices move mostly in parallel $\frac{6}{3}$ sonorities: the middle voice presents a variant of the top melody from the first burden, the upper voice parallels it a fourth above (with some decoration), and the bottom voice moves mostly a third below the middle voice, and thus a sixth below the top voice. At cadences and some other points, the voices move out from parallel thirds and sixths to fifths and octaves (see measures 15–16 and 17–19 for examples). These streams of $\frac{6}{3}$ sonorities are typical of English polyphony, which featured longer successions of parallel thirds and sixths unmediated by perfect consonances than did Continental polyphony before the 1420s. The predominance of thirds and sixths, avoidance of parallel fifths, minimal presence of dissonance, regular phrasing, and primarily homorhythmic textures exemplified by this carol gave English music its distinctive "sweet" sound and exercised a profound influence on Continental composers.

Streams of imperfect consonances also appear in the music for the stanzas, marked *verse*. In most carols, the stanzas are set in free two-part counterpoint throughout. This carol is unusual in its alternation among monophonic, three-part, and two-part textures. The first two lines of each stanza are each sung first in unison, and then in three-part, mostly parallel polyphony. The three-part sections strongly resemble the English improvised tradition of *faburden*, in which a chant melody appears in the middle voice, paralleled a fourth above and a third below, moving to a fifth below to mark the beginnings and ends of phrases. (Compare the related practice of *fauxbourdon* in NAWM 37, which differs somewhat in procedure but sounds very similar and was probably derived from faburden.) The rest of the stanza alternates unison, two-part, and three-part writing, with a brief recollection of the burden at the word "alleluia."

In the manuscript, the text is printed beneath the lowest part, but all parts are to sing the text together. Although the editor has marked the three-part sections "chorus," such carols were probably sung by one singer on each part, as in most polyphony of the time. The recording accompanying this anthology includes only two of the six verses, each followed by the second burden.

John Dunstable (CA. 1390–1453)

Quam pulchra es

Motet or cantilena

FIRST HALF OF THE FIFTEENTH CENTURY

Quam pulchra es et quam decora,
carissima in deliciis.
Statura tua assimilata est palme,
et ubera tua botris.
Caput tuum ut Carmelus,
collum tuum sicut turris eburnea.

How beautiful you are, and how graceful,
dearest one, my delight.
Your stature is like a palm tree,
and your breasts like clusters of grapes.
Your head is like Carmel;
your neck is like an ivory tower.

1:04

Veni, dilecte mi,
egrediamur in agrum,
et videamus si flores fructus parturierunt
si floruerunt mala Punica.
Ibi dabo tibi ubera mea.
Alleluia.

Come, my beloved,
let us go out into the fields,
and let us see if the grape blossoms have borne fruit
and the pomegranates are in bloom.
There I will give you my breasts.
Alleluia.

— Adapted from The Song of Solomon 7:4–12

Dunstable wrote numerous three-part settings of liturgical or biblical texts. Most of them are based on chant melodies, but this antiphon on a biblical text is freely composed. It was written before 1430, either in England or in France where his patron John, duke of Bedford, was regent. It appears in a manuscript from about that time; the manuscript is now in Italy, although the portion in which this piece appears may have been copied in England. The large number of Dunstable's pieces present in manuscripts on the Continent testifies to his widespread popularity and influence.

Unlike earlier motets, there is no strong difference in character between the tenor (the lowest voice) and the other voices. All are similar in style and importance, and most often they move and declaim the text together. The musical texture of the piece—largely homophonic with short melismas at the ends of both main sections (measures 26–29 and 55–58)—resembles that of a conductus (see NAWM 20) or its English relative, the *cantilena*.

Unfettered by a cantus firmus or an isorhythmic scheme, Dunstable freely determined the form of the music, guided only by the text. He divided the piece into two sections, roughly equal in length. The first, measures 1–30, comprises abbreviated versions of verses 6, 7, 5, and 4 of Chapter 7 from The Song of Solomon; the second, beginning at "Veni," draws on verses 11–12, with an added "alleluia." This book from the Hebrew Bible is in a literal sense an erotic dialogue between lovers, but Christians traditionally interpreted it as expressing the love between Christ and the Church, or between the penitent soul and Mary, the Mother of God. Here the male lover speaks in the first half of the piece, and the woman responds in the second. The strongest cadences delineate the ends of Bible verses (measures 9, 18, 22, 29, 38, and 54), and others mark internal phrases.

In addition to the musical form being determined by the text, many musical phrases are molded to the rhythm of the words—for example, in the declamation of "statura tua assimilata est," "mala Punica," and "ibi dabo tibi." Although most of the text-setting is syllabic, many cadences feature brief melismas. The final word in both sections is set off by a cadence, particularly extensive melismas, and livelier rhythm. The care for rhythmic declamation draws our attention to certain words and thus to their meaning. For example, Dunstable emphasizes the woman's first words, "Come, my beloved," with fermatas and a melisma and thus highlights her invitation to her lover (interpreted as the Church's acceptance of Christ).

The frequent use of melodic thirds and the occasional outlining of a triad (as in the middle voice in measures 9–11 or the top voice in measures 43, 46, and 55–56) give Dunstable's melodies a character rather different from fourteenth-century melodies by Machaut or Landini. The counterpoint is also quite different. Parallel fifths and octaves, still common in fourteenth-century counterpoint (see NAWM 25 and 26), are now avoided, although parallel fifths may occasionally appear between upper voices as long as each voice forms good counterpoint with the lowest voice. (Can you find the parallel fifths in the opening phrase?) Almost every vertical sonority is consonant, and thirds and sixths are prominent, both typical traits of English music at the time. Some passages feature the parallel $\frac{6}{3}$ sonorities common in English polyphony, especially at cadences (as in measures 12–15 and 52–54), but most phrases offer much greater variety of sonority. Variety is also evident in the rhythm: despite the relative rhythmic simplicity, no two successive measures have the same rhythmic pattern.

The piece projects a strong tonal center of C, which is the opening note, the most frequent cadential note, and the root of the final open-fifth-octave sonority. It is not "in C major," but in a mode on C, later named Ionian by Glareanus. The cadences to C are not tonic-dominant cadences, but typical modal cadences of the time: D—F—B to C—G—C, as in measures 8–9, sometimes decorated with a Landini cadence, as at the end. Other cadences are on D, F, and G, all important notes in the Ionian mode.

All of these traits—relative equality of voices, free structure based on the text, sensitivity to text declamation, pervasive consonance, variety in sonority and rhythm, and strong tonal center—became characteristic of music in the fifteenth and sixteenth centuries.

Like other sacred polyphony of the time, this piece was probably performed by one singer per part, unaccompanied, as on the recording accompanying this anthology. Note the change of tempo at the words "et videamus," increasing the pace by the proportion of three new beats in the time of two former ones.

Binchois (Gilles de Bins) (CA. 1400–1460)

De plus en plus

Rondeau

CA. 1425

—more smooth than previous rondeaus

concise 0:00/0:52/1:25/1:58/2:51

0:31/2:30/3:23

Binchois, *De plus en plus*, from *Die Chansons von Gilles Binchois*, ed. Wolfgang Rehm, Musikalische Denkmäler 2 (Mainz: B. Schott's Söhne, 1957). © 1957 Schott Music GmbH & Co. KG. © Renewed. All rights reserved. Used by permission of European American Music Distributors Company, sole U.S. and Canadian agent for Schott Music GmbH & Co. KG.

0:00	A	1	De plus en plus se renouvelle	More and more renews again,
		2	Ma doulce dame gente et belle,	my sweet lady, noble and fair,
		3	Ma voulonté de vous veir.	my wish to see you.
0:31	B	4	Ce me fait le tres grant désir	It gives me the very great desire
		5	Que j'ai de vous oir nouvelle.	I have to hear news of you.
0:52	a	6	Ne cuidiés pas que je recelle,	Do not heed that I hold back,
		7	Comme a tous jours vous este celle	for always you are the one
		8	Que je veul de tout obeir.	whom I want to follow in every way.
1:25	A	9	De plus en plus se renouvelle	More and more renews again,
		10	Ma doulce dame gente et belle,	my sweet lady, noble and fair,
		11	Ma voulonté de vous veir.	my wish to see you.
1:58	a	12	Hélas, se vous m'estiés cruelle	Alas, if you were cruel to me,
		13	J'auvoie au cuer angoisse telle	I would have such anguish in my heart
		14	Que je voudroye bien mourir,	that I would want to die.
2:30	b	15	Mais ce seroit sans déservir,	But this would do you no wrong,
		16	En soustenant vostre querelle.	while supporting your cause.
2:51	A	17	De plus en plus se renouvelle	More and more renews again,
		18	Ma doulce dame gente et belle,	my sweet lady, noble and fair,
		19	Ma voulonté de vous veir.	my wish to see you.
3:23	B	20	Ce me fait le tres grant désir	It gives me the very great desire
		21	Que j'ai de vous oir nouvelle.	I have to hear news of you.

Binchois composed *De plus en plus* around 1425. At the time, he was probably in the service of William Pole, earl of Suffolk, one of the English noblemen assisting in the occupation of northern France. The upbeat opening, the relatively full harmony, the many harmonic thirds and sixths, and the great number of melodic thirds and triadic figures reflect the influence of English music. The appearance of this piece in a manuscript copied in Italy around 1430 demonstrates that Binchois's music was widely disseminated, even though he spent most of his career in and around the Burgundian court, where he was in service to the duke of Burgundy between 1427 and 1453.

The text is a love poem in the tradition of courtly love, or *fine amour*. The poetic form is a rondeau, like Machaut's *Rose, liz* (NAWM 28), but the first part of the refrain (A) consists of three lines and the second part (B) of two (rather than two lines and one line respectively, as in the Machaut). The rhyme scheme is different as well. The refrain contains all of the music, which is also set to the words of the couplets (a and b). The full refrain text with its music is heard only at the beginning and the end.

The quickly moving cantus (the topmost melody) indulges in runs, dotted figures, and syncopations. The slower-moving tenor (the middle voice) provides a foundation, harmonizing the cantus mostly in thirds and sixths, and resolving to octaves at cadences. The contratenor (the bottom voice in the score, though its melody crosses both above and below that of the tenor) enlivens the rhythm and fills in the harmony, often supplying the third note in a triad.

In this chanson, Binchois used imperfect time and major prolation, transcribed as two dotted quarters per measure (compare NAWM 25). Each measure is usually subdivided into two groups of three eighth notes, but often, particularly in the tenor, three quarter notes appear instead, producing a hemiola effect. This rhythm is indicated in several places by red ink in the original notation, denoting a change of mensuration (marked here by open brackets in the tenor, measures 3, 10–11, and 13–14, and in measures 3 and 8 of the contratenor).

The music fits the shape and structure of the poem. The cantus declaims the text in a mostly syllabic setting with melismas at cadences. Each line of poetry occupies four measures of music, producing a proportion of 3:2 between the two musical sections. A cadence marks the end of each poetic line, with the tenor-cantus pair moving from a sixth to an octave or from a third to a unison. The cadential motion to the octave from the sixth (changed to major when necessary by musica ficta) is usually decorated in the cantus with the third below the last note of the cadence, creating a Landini cadence. In most of the cadences, syncopation causes a dissonance in the upper voice before the penultimate note, a type of dissonance later called a *suspension*.

Binchois treated the end of the A section (measure 12) differently from the other cadences. After tenor and cantus cadence on G (measure 11), the tenor and contratenor close on D with F# in the cantus. The major third leaves us in suspense, intensified by a rest, as we anticipate the second section of the music. The end of the B section is more conventional, with a descending series of third-sixth sonorities that resolve to a fifth and an octave. Here, the only surprise is the cadential note D; earlier cadences had suggested C or G as the likely final.

Such polyphonic chansons may have been sung by three unaccompanied voices, as in the recording that accompanies this anthology. Alternatively, the two lower lines could be played by instruments, or the cantus and tenor could be sung and the contratenor played.

Guillaume Du Fay (ca. 1397–1474)

Resvellies vous

Ballade

1423

From Guillaume Dufay, *Opera omnia*, ed. Heinrich Besseler, vol. 6 (American Institute of Musicology, 1964), 25–26. © American Institute of Musicology. Used by permission.

0:00	a	Resvellies vous et faites chiere lye	Awake and be merry,
		Tout amoureux qui gentilesse ames	all lovers who love gentleness;
0:30	a	Esbates vous, fuyes merancolye,	frolic and flee melancholy.
		De bien servir point ne soyes hodés	Tire not of serving yourself well,
1:16	b	Car au jour d'ui sera li espousés,	for today will be the nuptials,
		Par grant honneur et noble seignourie;	with great honor and noble lordship,
		Ce vous convient ung chascum faire feste,	and it behooves you, everyone, to celebrate
		Pour bien grignier la belle compagnye;	and join the happy company.
2:10	C	Charle gentil, c'on dit de Maleteste.	Noble Charles, who is named Malatesta.

a   Il a dame belle et bonne choysie,   He has chosen a lady, fair and good,
    Dont il sera grandement honnourés;   by whom he will be greatly honored,
a   Car elle vient de tres noble lignie   for she comes from a very noble lineage
    Et de barons qui sont mult renommés.   of barons who are much renowned.
b   Son propre nom est Victoire clamés;   Her name is Victoria,
    De la colonne vient sa progenie.   and she descends from the Colonnas.
    C'est bien rayson qu'a vascule requeste   Thus it is right that his appeal be heard
    De cette dame mainne bonne vie.   to live honestly with this lady.
C   Charle gentil, c'on dit de Maleteste.   Noble Charles, who is named Malatesta.

"Awake and be merry," this ballade tells lovers. Guillaume Du Fay composed it
in 1423 for the marriage of Carlo Malatesta and Vittoria Colonna, niece of Pope
Martin V. At the time, Du Fay was serving the Malatestas, the ruling family of Rimini
and Pesaro. The acclamation "noble Charles," addressed to the bridegroom, is
set in long notes with fermatas, a traditional French technique for emphasizing
a person's name (compare Machaut's setting of "Jesu Christe" in the Gloria of his
mass, NAWM 26b). Following that statement, the family name Malatesta is set to a
spree of rapid triplets in the cantus. Perhaps the bouncy triplet rhythm at the line
"Pour bien grignier la belle compagnye" (and join the happy company) is also a
reflection of the text.

   The standard aabC musical form of the ballade repeats for each stanza. The
editor has labeled with capital letters the beginnings of the a section (measure 1),
the b section (measure 23), and the refrain C, the last line of each stanza (measure
50). The florid treatment at the end of each line of the poem follows the refined
ballade tradition. In the a section and refrain, Du Fay employed imperfect time
with major prolation, equivalent to $\frac{6}{8}$ (the breve, here transcribed as a dotted half
note, is divided into two parts, each containing three minims or eighth notes).
In the b section, he used perfect time with minor prolation, equivalent to $\frac{3}{4}$ (the
breve is divided in three semibreves, each containing two minims). Hemiolas and
syncopations abound throughout. Yet Du Fay is careful to make the text clear, and
in most passages he takes care to place accented syllables at the beginning of a
metrical unit. Both the a section and the refrain end with the same closing passage,
creating a musical rhyme. An unusual feature of this chanson is the imitation
between the cantus (top voice) and the tenor at measures 7–10, briefly involving
the contratenor as well at measures 15–19 and 60–64.

Resvellies vous combines elements of three main traditions of the fourteenth
century: from the French Ars Nova, the ballade form and syncopations; from the
Ars Subtilior, the rapid, complex rhythmic passages (such as the runs in the cantus
at measures 5–6, 34–35, 44–48, and 58–59 and the staggered long-short rhythms
in all three parts at measures 39–42); from the Italian Trecento, the smooth vocal
melodies, the syllabic declamation of some passages, and the change of meter; and
from all three traditions, the cantus-tenor framework and the elaborate melismas
at the ends of lines of poetry. These are signs of Du Fay's characteristic blending
of traits from diverse styles. English music is not yet a strong influence here, as

seems clear from the casual dissonances in some passages, such as measures 2 and 13–15; compare Du Fay's scrupulous control of dissonance in *Se la face ay pale* (NAWM 38a), composed about ten years later, after he became familiar with English music.

The melismatic passages in the cantus, with their rapid runs and triplet figures, may seem more suited to instrumental than vocal performance, yet they can be performed convincingly by a trained singer, as on the accompanying recording. The lower parts are mostly untexted and could have been sung or played on instruments. However, in the original sources, all three parts have text at the words "Charle gentil" (noble Charles) in the refrain, making it clear that Du Fay intended for all three performers to sing the name of the patron for whose wedding the piece was written. The accompanying recording presents only the first verse of the ballade, with voices singing the cantus and tenor and a vielle playing the contratenor. A sign at measure 15 indicates that the closing melismatic passage in the a section is to be performed only the second time through.

Guillaume Du Fay (ca. 1397–1474)

Christe, redemptor omnium

Hymn in fauxbourdon style

CA. 1430

37

From Guillaume Dufay, *Opera omnia*, ed. Heinrich Besseler, vol. 5 (American Institute of Musicology, 1966), 40–41. © American Institute of Musicology. Used with permission. English translation from *The Saint Andrew Daily Missal*, ed. Dom Gasper Lefebvre, O.S.B. (New York: Benziger Publishing Co., 1956). Reprinted by permission.

pre – ces Tu – i per – or – bem fa – mu – li.
pa – tris Mun – di sa – lus ad – ve – ne – ris.
tu – i Hym – num no – vum con – ci – ni – mus.

pre – ces Tu – i per – or – bem fa – mu – li.
pa – tris Mun – di sa – lus ad – ve – ne – ris.
tu – i Hym – num no – vum con – ci – ni – mus.

(Mod)

A – men.

0:00	Christe Redemptor omnium,	Jesus! Redeemer of the world!
	Ex Patre Patris Unice,	Who, ere the earliest dawn of light,
	Solus ante principium	Was from eternal ages born,
	Natus ineffabiliter.	Immense in glory as in might.

0:25	Tu lumen, tu splendor Patris,	Immortal Hope of all mankind
	Tu spes perennis omnium:	In whom the Father's face we see,
	Intende, quas fundunt preces.	Hear Thou the prayers Thy people pour
	Tui per orbem famuli.	This day throughout the world to Thee.

1:21	Memento, salutis Auctor,	Remember, O Creater Lord!
	Quod nostri quondam corporis,	That in the Virgin's sacred womb
	Ex illibata Virgine	Thou was conceiv'd and of her flesh
	Nascendo, formam sumpseris.	Didst our mortality assume.

1:47	Sic praesens testatur dies,	This ever-blest recurring day
	Currens per anni circulum.	Its witness bears, that all alone,
	Quod solus a sede Patris	From Thy own Father's bosom forth,
	Mundi salus adveneris.	To save the world Thou camest down.

Hunc caelum, terra, hunc mare,   O Day! to which the seas and sky,
Hunc omne, quod in eis est,   And earth, and heav'n, glad welcome sing;
Auctorem adventus tui   O Day! which heal'd our misery,
Laudans exultat cantico.   And brought on earth salvation's King.

Nos quoque, qui sancto tuo,   We, too, O Lord, who have been cleans'd
Redempti sanguine sumus,   In Thy own fount of Blood divine,
Ob diem natalis tui   Offer the tribute of sweet song
Hymnum novum concinimus.   On this blest natal day of Thine.

Gloria tibi, Domine,   O Jesu! born of Virgin bright,
Qui natus es de Virgine,   Immortal glory be to Thee;
Cum Patre et Sancto Spiritu   Praise to the Father infinite
In sempiterna saecula. Amen.   And Holy Ghost eternally. Amen.

During the late Middle Ages and Renaissance, it was a frequent custom for a chorus and soloists to sing alternate stanzas when performing a plainchant hymn. The chorus always sang the monophonic chant, but the soloists might have sung polyphony, either improvised or composed. Du Fay and other composers wrote numerous polyphonic settings for the even-numbered stanzas of hymns, which were meant to be performed by soloists or by a small choir with three or more singers on each part, but the odd-numbered stanzas continued to be sung by the choir to monophonic chants.

This piece, composed about 1430 when Du Fay was in service at the pope's chapel in Rome, is a setting of the hymn for Vespers on Christmas Day (NAWM 4b). It is in the style of fauxbourdon, a notational practice that apparently derived from the improvised English tradition of faburden (see discussion for NAWM 33). Du Fay placed the chant, lightly decorated, in the cantus (the x's mark the notes of the chant). Through his paraphrase, Du Fay converted the centuries-old chant into a melody in the style of a modern chanson, complete with constantly varying rhythms and an embellished Landini cadence at the end of every phrase. He added to this a tenor part that begins an octave lower and then moves mostly in sixths against the chant, expanding to an octave at cadences. A third voice, not written down (but often indicated in the music by the word "faulxbourdon"), can be sung at the interval of a perfect fourth below the cantus, producing a succession of $\frac{6}{3}$ sonorities, except where the bottom voice moves out to an octave. In this edition, the unwritten middle voice is transcribed in small notes. As long as the outer voices form a harmonic sixth or octave, the middle voice is consonant with both, but there are some passing dissonances where the outer voices contract to a fifth (as on the last eighth note of measure 5). Fauxbourdon's emphasis on consonant sonorities, especially thirds and sixths, became characteristic of Renaissance music, even though its strict parallelism eventually came to sound archaic.

In a full performance of this hymn, the chant would be sung for each odd-numbered verse and the polyphony for each even-numbered verse. The accompanying recording includes just the first four verses, to give examples of each type of setting, followed by the closing Amen. The polyphony is performed by a small choir of men and boys, rather than by soloists.

Guillaume Du Fay (ca. 1397–1474)

Se la face ay pale

Ballade

1430s

Missa Se la face ay pale: Gloria

Cantus-firmus mass

CA. 1453

38

First mass based on a secular cantus firmus

(a) *Se la face ay pale*

From Guillaume Dufay, *Opera omnia*, ed. Heinrich Besseler, vol. 6 (American Institute of Musicology, 1964), 36. © American Institute of Musicology. Used with permission. The connection this ballade and the mass that is based on it may have with the Holy Shroud, discussed in the commentary, was proposed by Anne Walters Robertson, "The Man with the Pale Face, the Shroud, and Du Fay's *Missa Se la face ay pale*," *The Journal of Musicology* 27 (Fall 2010): 377–434.

Se la face ay pale,	If my face is pale,
La cause est amer,	the cause is love,
C'est la principale,	that is the principal reason,
Et tant m'est amer	and for me it is so bitter
Amer, qu'en la mer	to love, that in the sea
Me voudroye voir;	I would like to throw myself;
Or, scet bien de voir	then, seeing this, she would know well,
La belle a qui suis	the fair lady to whom I belong,
Que nul bien avoir	that to have any happiness
Sans elle ne puis.	without her I am not able.

Se ay pesante malle	If I have a heavy load
De dueil a porter,	of grief to bear,
Ceste amour est male	[it is because] this love is difficult
Pour moy de porter;	for me to endure;
Car soy deporter	because to enjoy oneself
Ne veult devouloir,	she does not want to allow,
Fors qu'a son vouloir	so that her own will
Obeisse, et puis	one must obey, and since
Qu'elle a tel pooir,	she has such power,
Sans elle ne puis.	without her I am not able.

C'est la plus reale	She is the most regal woman
Qu'on puist regarder,	that one could ever see.
De s'amour leiale	From loyal love for her
Ne me puis guarder,	I cannot keep myself.
Fol sui de agarder	Foolish am I for looking at her
Ne faire devoir	and for not wanting
D'amours recevoir	to receive love
Fors d'elle, je cuij;	from anyone but her, I think;
Se ne veil douloir,	if I want not to be sad,
Sans elle ne puis.	without her I am not able.

(b) *Missa Se la face ay pale*: Gloria

From Guillaume Dufay, *Opera omnia*, ed. Heinrich Besseler, vol. 3 (American Institute of Musicology, 1964), 4–13. © American Institute of Musicology. Used with permission.

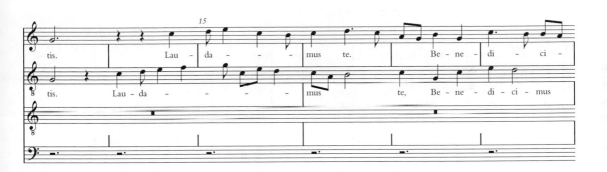

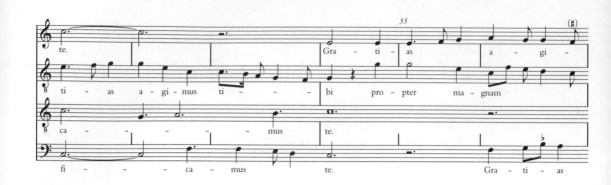

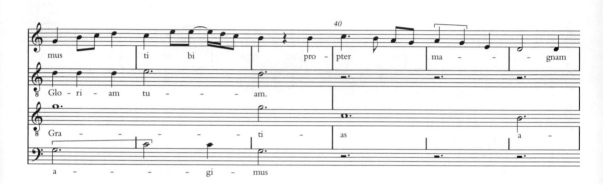

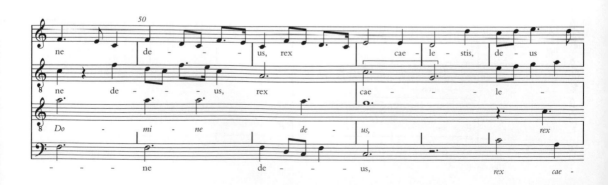

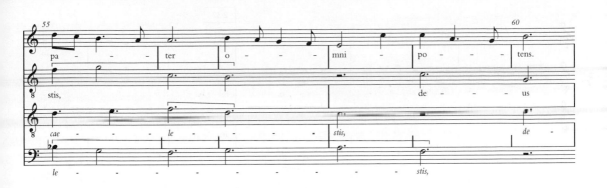

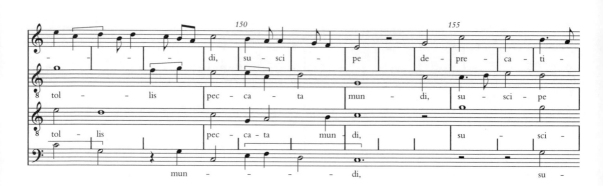

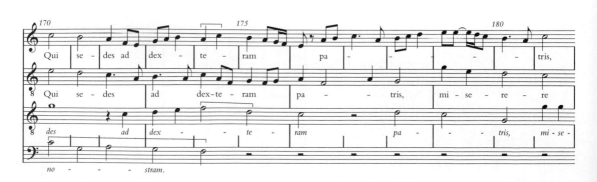

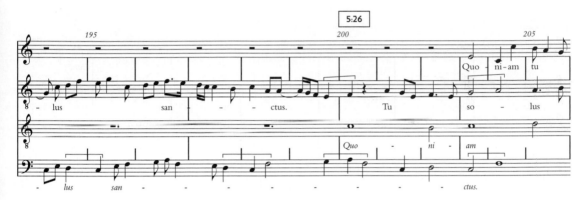

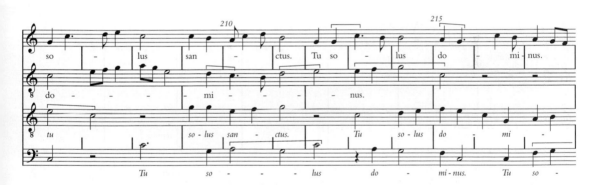

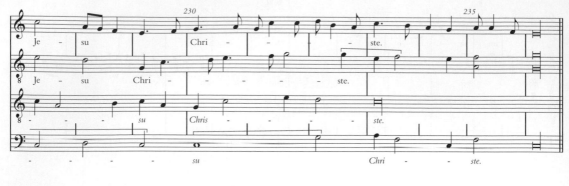

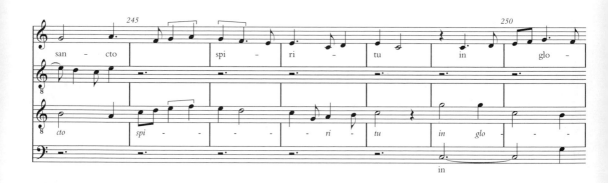

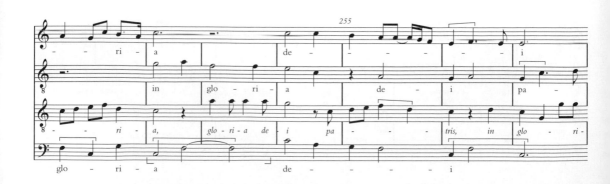

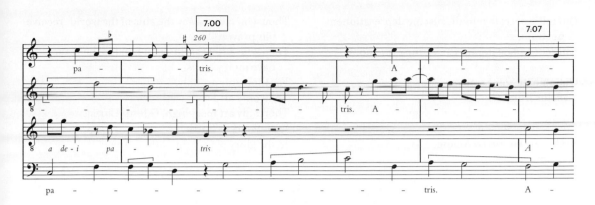

Gloria in excelsis Deo	Glory be to God on high.
Et in terra pax hominibus bonae voluntatis.	And on earth peace to men of good will.
Laudamus te. Benedicimus te. Adoramus te. Glorificamus te.	We praise thee, we bless thee, we adore thee, we glorify thee.
Gratias agimus tibi propter magnam gloriam tuam.	We give thee thanks for thy great glory.
Domine Deus, Rex caelestis,	O Lord God, King of heaven,
Deus Pater omnipotens.	God the Father Almighty.
Domine Fili unigenite Jesu Christe.	O Lord, the only begotten Son, Jesus Christ.
Domine Deus, Agnus Dei, Filius Patris.	O Lord God, Lamb of God, Son of the Father.
Qui tollis peccata mundi, miserere nobis.	Thou who takest away the sins of the world, have mercy on us.

Qui tollis peccata mundi, suscipe deprecationem nostram.	Thou who takest away the sins of the world, receive our prayer.
Qui sedes ad dexteram Patris, miserere nobis.	Thou who sittest at the right hand of the Father, have mercy on us.
Quoniam tu solus sanctus.	For thou only art holy,
Tu solus Dominus.	Thou only art Lord.
Tu solus Altissimus, Jesu Christe.	Thou only art most high, O Jesus Christ,
Cum Sancto Spiritu,	With the Holy Spirit,
In Gloria Dei Patris. Amen.	In the glory of God the Father. Amen.

Du Fay composed *Se la face ay pale* during the 1430s while he was serving as master of the chapel at the court of the duke of Savoy. He may have written it for Anne of Lusignan, princess of Cyprus, who married Louis, the son of duke Amadeus VIII of Savoy, in 1434. Anne Walters Robertson has suggested that the text, probably by Du Fay himself, can be read with either secular or sacred meanings. In a secular register, it is a lover's complaint, similar to older poems in the troubadour and trouvère traditions (see NAWM 8 and 27). The repeated use of the same rhymes in each stanza derives from those traditions, and the three-fold pun that links love ("amer") with something bitter ("amer") that causes the desire to throw oneself in the sea ("la mer") is found in other medieval love poems. But the image of a man with a pale face who experiences grief and bitterness for love of another was also used in writings about Christ's sacrifice on the cross, during which he suffered and died (symbolized by his deathly pallor) for love of the souls of humankind, and this poem may be understood allegorically as Christ's plea to accept the love he offers. Reading love poems as religious allegories was a long-standing practice, reaching back to the Bible itself (see the discussion of NAWM 34 and The Song of Solomon).

In comparison with his earlier ballade *Resvellies vous* (NAWM 36), this one shows many changes in Du Fay's style, including his blending of national characteristics. Instead of following the fixed form of the fourteenth-century ballade (aabC), he composed the music freely to suit each line of text. Only the use of three stanzas, the closing refrain line, and the final melisma are retained from the ballade tradition. Other French characteristics include frequent syncopation and an angular contratenor line with many large leaps. English influence is demonstrated in pervasive consonance with only a few ornamental dissonances, the prevalence of thirds and sixths, relatively short and well-articulated phrases, relative equality between cantus and tenor melodies, and triadic figures that suffuse the final melisma. Both English and Italian traits are evident in the smooth, mostly stepwise melodies in cantus and tenor and in the primarily syllabic treatment of the text.

In the manuscript sources and in this edition, both cantus and tenor are underlaid with text, suggesting that both are to be sung, as on the accompanying recording. The contratenor seems better suited for an instrument than for a singer due to its wide range and large leaps, and one manuscript ends with a three-note "chord" that is impossible for a soloist to sing but easy for a string instrument such as the vielle on the accompanying recording.

In 1452–58, Du Fay was back at the court of Savoy after several years in Cambrai. He apparently wrote *Missa Se la face ay pale* during this time at Savoy, using the tenor of his earlier ballade as a cantus firmus. This mass was the first complete mass to be based on a secular melody, and a recent study by Anne Robertson offers an explanation for why Du Fay used it. She suggests that the mass was composed to honor the Holy Shroud, which was acquired by Louis, duke of Savoy, in 1453 and is known today as the Shroud of Turin, after the city where it was moved in 1578 when Turin became the new capital of Savoy. This relic is the reputed shroud used to wrap the body of Jesus after his crucifixion, and it has on it an image of a bearded man who has been crucified and laid out for burial (see Figure 8.9 in HWM, p. 184). The Shroud's acquisition was by far the most important event in Savoy during the 1450s, instantly elevating the status of the duchy. Although Du Fay's ballade *Se la face ay pale* was ostensibly secular, its words match perfectly the image on the Shroud, showing the deathly pale face and painful wounds that embody the suffering of Christ. There was no more appropriate melody to use as the basis for a mass in honor of the Shroud.

The structure of the mass is carefully designed. Du Fay maintained the durations of the ballade tenor in the tenor of the mass but added verbal indications to multiply those durations in performance by varying amounts. As a result, the cantus firmus is heard at different speeds in various movements and sections. In the Kyrie, Sanctus, and Agnus Dei, each note of the ballade tenor is doubled in duration through the marking "Crescit in duplo" ("increase to twice the length"). In the Gloria and in the Credo, the cantus firmus is heard in the tenor three times, first at triple the normal durations ("triplo"), then at double the durations ("duplo"), and finally at its original pace (indicated by "ut jacet," "as it lies"). Thus in the first section of the Gloria (measures 1–118), each beat of the original ballade tenor is now three beats long, corresponding to a full measure of triple time in the other voices. In the second section, at "Qui tollis" (measures 119–236), each beat of the original chanson tenor is now two beats long, corresponding to a measure of duple time in the other voices. Finally, in the third section, at "Cum sancto spiritu" (measures 237–76), the tenor moves at its original pace, and the beats and measures in all four voices correspond.

The form of this Gloria, delineated by the calculated restatement of the tune, is further marked by the inclusion of a duet preceding each entrance of the cantus firmus. Additionally, a briefer duet divides the cantus firmus into two halves in each section. Each of the Gloria's three sections has the same internal proportions, which are also of interest. They are easiest to see in the last section: six measures of duet without the tenor, eighteen measures with the tenor, three measures of rest in the tenor, and twelve final measures of tenor (stopping the count where the tenor reaches its last note). This arrangement of 6, 18, 3, and 12 units can be simplified by dividing each number by three, producing the proportions 2:6:1:4. This set of proportions features numbers whose ratios form those of the perfect fifth (6:4 or 3:2), octave (4:2 or 2:1), and twelfth (6:2 or 3:1), the same ratios represented in the proportional scheme of the whole movement (3:2:1). Moreover, the ratio of the first segment of duet and tenor melody (measures 237–60) to the second (measures 261–75)—2+6 to 1+4, or 8 to 5—approximates the Golden Section, a ratio beloved of mathematicians, architects, and composers, especially Du Fay. This intricate numerical structure shows the enduring influence of the links between music and number that were promulgated by theorists from Pythagoras through Boethius and beyond.

More evident to the listener than these proportions is the way that the source ballade gradually emerges from obscurity to recognizability. Although the tenor melody is present from the outset and is apparent to the singers because Du Fay notated it in its original note values, it becomes easy to recognize by ear only during the final statement, when it is included with its original durations. Then, at the end, the tenor is joined by other borrowings from the original ballade. At measures 270–74 of the Gloria, Du Fay borrowed material from all three voices of the final melisma of the ballade (measures 25–29), sometimes exactly and otherwise in paraphrase. A briefer and less obvious borrowing from all three voices of the ballade occurs at measures 146–54 (compare the top three voices there to measures 4–6 of the ballade). Borrowings from multiple voices of the model occur frequently in masses whose cantus firmus is drawn from a polyphonic work. Such masses are sometimes called *cantus-firmus/imitation masses* to distinguish them from cantus-firmus masses on monophonic tunes and from *imitation masses* that borrow from all voices of a polyphonic work but lack a cantus firmus (see NAWM 52b).

Each voice of the mass is a distinct layer with its own melodic and rhythmic logic and function. The tenor provides the scaffolding, around which everything else is coordinated. The bassus, the lowest voice, joins with the tenor to establish the harmonic foundation, often providing the lowest note at cadences. The top two voices, the superius and the contratenor altus, are the most active, moving in smooth, mostly stepwise lines varied with skips and leaps, and occasionally echoing each other (see measures 1–4 and 14–15 for brief examples). The rhythmic diversity the top voices provide, each measure different from the last, is typical of Du Fay and was part of the variety that was prized by commentators at the time. Despite the diverse roles the voices play, they are more equal than in earlier music, with sixth-to-octave cadences forming between superius and altus (as at measures 12–13), altus and bassus (measures 27–28), tenor and bassus (measures 33–34), and superius and bassus (measures 36–37), as well as the usual cadences between superius and tenor.

Besides the use of the ballade tenor throughout the mass, another feature that links each movement is the use of a *head-motive*, a musical idea that appears at the beginning of every movement, thereby establishing a relationship between the sections. Each movement of the mass begins in the superius with a variant of the motive that in the Gloria is set to the words "Et in terra pax." The motive is also alluded to within movements, as in the Gloria at measures 40, 88, 119, 243, and 262. The movements of the mass are also linked because all are in the same mode. Although the ballade is clearly centered on C and many of the internal cadences in the mass movement also close on C, Du Fay centered the mass on F. With the tune in the tenor, he was able to close the first and final sections of the Gloria on F in bassus and superius (measures 118 and 276), and closes the middle section on C (measure 236). (There was no concept of fixed pitch in the fifteenth century, and singers placed music in any range that was comfortable for them; reflecting this practice, the performance on the accompanying recording is pitched a minor third lower than notated.)

Consonance and dissonance are carefully controlled. The strongest dissonances are suspensions, all properly resolved (for example, at measures 33, 36, 72, and 81), while other dissonances, mainly between beats, pass quickly. Du Fay obviously worked to include as many thirds and sixths as possible, which produced many triads (to use modern terminology) on the strong beats.

According to long-standing liturgical tradition, the opening words of the Gloria, "Gloria in excelsis Deo" (Glory be to God on high), are always sung by the priest. For this reason, composers before the eighteenth century never included these words in their settings of the Gloria. Du Fay's mass could have been sung by four soloists but was more likely sung by a small choir. The Burgundian court chapel in 1469, one of the largest in Europe, included at least fourteen male singers: six on the cantus, two on the altus, and three each on the tenor and bassus. Savoy's chapel in the 1450s was somewhat smaller, with about nine to eleven singers. Other studies of chapel and cathedral musicians also suggest that polyphonic sacred music was sung with a few singers on each part. The long tones of the tenor in isorhythmic movements such as this one have prompted many modern performers to use instruments on the tenor and sometimes on the bassus as well, either instead of or doubling the singers. However, the historical evidence suggests that instruments were rarely used to accompany sacred polyphony. All four parts are texted in the manuscript sources except for some passages in the lower two voices, where the editor has added the text in italics. In the performance on the accompanying recording, all parts are sung by soloists.

Antoine Busnoys (CA. 1430–1492)

Je ne puis vivre

Virelai

CA. 1460

From Leeman L. Perkins and Howard Garey, eds., *The Mellon Chansonnier*, vol. 1 (New Haven: Yale University Press, 1979), 65–67.

0:00 A Je ne puis vivre ainsy tousjours
    Au mains que j'aye en mes dolours
    Quelque confort
    Une seulle heure ou mains ou fort;
    Et tous les jours
    Léaument serviray Amours
    Jusqu'a la mort.

I cannot live this way forever
    unless I have, in my pain,
    some comfort,
    a single hour, or less, or more;
    and every day
    loyally I will serve Love
    until death.

1:08	b	Noble femme de nom et d'armes,	Lady, noble in name and in arms,
		Escript vous ay de dittier cy,	for you I have written this song,

1:38	b	Des ieux plourant a chauldes larmes	while from my eyes I am crying hot tears
		Affin qu'ayés de moy merchy.	so that you will have mercy on me.

2:13	a	Quant a moi, je me meurs bon cours,	As for me, I am dying in good course,
		Vellant les nuytz, faisant cent tours,	awake every night, pacing around a hundred times,
		En criant fort:	crying loudly:
		"Vengeance!" a Dieu, car a grant tort	"Vengeance!" to God, for most unjustly
		Je noye en plours	I am drowning in tears;
		Lorsqu'au besoing me fault secours—	when I need it, I get no help—
		Et Pitié dort.	and Pity sleeps.

3:17	A	Je ne puis vivre ainsy tousjours . . .	I cannot live this way forever . . .

Antoine Busnoys was the most prolific and widely praised composer of chansons in his generation. After holding positions at churches in Tours (where he knew Ockeghem) and Poitiers, in 1466 he entered the service of the heir to the duke of Burgundy, who succeeded to the title as Charles the Bold the next year. On the latter's death in 1477, Busnoys served Charles's daughter Mary of Burgundy and her husband Maximilian of Hapsburg.

Je ne puis vivre is one of four Busnoys chansons linked to Jacqueline de Hacqueville, whose name is spelled out by the first letters of each line of the poem: JAQUELJNE D'AQVEVJLE (treating as interchangeable the letters I and J and likewise U and V, as in Roman times). She has been identified as a lady-in-waiting to the wife of French king Charles VII. One of the songs that alludes to her name, *Ja que lui ne s'i actende*, speaks from a woman's perspective, making it likely that she wrote that poem and that these chansons are part of a dialogue in poetry, a tradition that dates back to the troubadours and beyond.

The song is in the form of a virelai with a single stanza (AbbaA, called *bergerette* by some modern writers; compare NAWM 27). The poem features lines of eight and four syllables in irregular alternation and uses different rhymes in the a and b sections. As in many of Busnoys's virelais, the b section is in a contrasting mensuration, transcribed here as duple meter after the triple meter of the refrain. The ends of most lines are signaled with a cadence, although several internal cadences are elided by movement in one voice (as at measure 19). The mode is the authentic mode on C, used by composers for many generations before it was named the Ionian mode (mode 11) by Glareanus in his *Dodekachordon* (1547). Most cadences are on C, the remainder on G (including at the end of the b section), and both cantus and tenor range more than an octave above the final.

Unlike in earlier chansons, the tenor is in the same vocal range as the cantus, often crossing above it. All three voices are equally flowing and interesting, a significant change from the differentiation of roles in Du Fay's chansons, whose contratenors tend to be angular with many skips and leaps. The relative equality of the three voices is emphasized by the performance on the accompanying recording, in which all three are sung and the contratenor sings the same text as the other voices.

Much of the song is shaped by imitation, a technique Busnoys was among the first to use consistently. In each case, one voice exactly imitates another for two or more measures, then diverges to lead toward the cadence. At the opening, the contratenor imitates the cantus. The tenor enters in measure 6 with the same phrase, now displaced metrically (beginning on the third rather than the first beat of a measure) and texted with the second line of the poem, under a new melody in the cantus. At measure 13, the tenor states a figure three times in a stepwise rising sequence, with the contratenor moving in parallel thirds below it and the cantus imitating it a measure behind. Here again Busnoys plays with the meter: he shortens the figure on its repetitions, deleting its first note, so that its ending note moves forward one beat with each statement until it finally arrives at the beginning of a measure (compare measures 14–15, 16–17, and 17–19 in the cantus). The next phrase (at measure 19) has an even closer imitation between tenor and cantus, only two beats apart, as if the meter had changed to duple. Indeed, the rest of the A section can be heard in duple rather than triple meter. The b section begins in homophony, but its second line is treated in imitation between cantus and tenor (measures 33–37). Except for the very opening and for a brief moment near the end (compare measure 33 in the contratenor to measure 34 in the cantus), the points of imitation involve only the cantus and tenor, and the contratenor weaves free counterpoint beneath them.

Jean de Ockeghem (CA. 1420–1497)

Missa prolationum: Kyrie

Mass

SECOND HALF OF THE FIFTEENTH CENTURY

Canon

— Perfect ; imperfect mensuration

how do things work together in texture?

From Johannes Ockeghem, *Missa prolationem*, ed. David Condon (Espoo, Finland: Fazer Music, 1992), 9–13.
© Copyright 1992 by Fazer Music, Inc., Helsinki. Reprinted by permission.

1:06

texture of 2 voices

Kyrie eleison.	Lord have mercy.
Christe eleison.	Christ have mercy.
Kyrie eleison.	Lord have mercy.

Ockeghem's *Missa prolationum* is one of the most famous pieces of the fifteenth century, but it is more often discussed than heard. Since we lack any evidence for why or on what occasion Ockeghem may have written the mass, it has long been assumed that he did so as a demonstration of his abilities as a composer. The mass is such a contrapuntal tour de force that it can be surprising how simply beautiful it sounds.

Missa prolationum (Mass of Prolations) presents a series of double mensuration canons, notated in two voices but sung in four parts using the four prolations (comparable to meters) that had been basic to notation since the Ars Nova. This figure shows the four combinations of time and prolation, with modern equivalents:

	Breve	Semibreves	Minims
Perfect time, major prolation	⊙ $\frac{9}{8}$		
Perfect time, minor prolation	◯ $\frac{3}{4}$		
Imperfect time, major prolation	₵· $\frac{6}{8}$		
Imperfect time, minor prolation	₵ $\frac{2}{4}$		

In a mensuration canon, two voices read from the same line of music but interpret the notes according to different mensuration signs. The beginning of each notated part is shown here before the transcription of each section of the Kyrie. The way the canon works is complicated, and therefore cumbersome to explain, only because the notation is unfamiliar to us.

In the first Kyrie, the top voice, or *superius*, reads the upper notated line in imperfect time and minor prolation (indicated by the mensuration sign C), so that both the breve (transcribed as a half note ♩) and semibreve (quarter note ♪) divide into two equal units. Meanwhile the second voice down, the *altus*, interprets the same part in perfect time and minor prolation (indicated by the open circle ○); here the semibreve remains duple (a quarter note) but the breve contains three units rather than two and therefore is transcribed as a dotted half note (♩. = ♪ ♪ ♪). At the outset, this means the altus moves more slowly than the superius, by a ratio of three to two. But after the first six notes, all relatively long, the rhythm shifts to shorter note values that are read the same in both mensurations, while the canon continues.

The bottom two parts are laid out in a similar way. The tenor reads the lower notated part using imperfect time and major prolation (⊙), so that the semibreve divides into three and therefore is transcribed as a dotted quarter (♩. = ♫♪), while there are two semibreves in a breve (♩. = ♩. ♩.). The bassus interprets the same line in perfect time and major prolation (⊙); the semibreve is triple (♩.), but there are three units in a breve, transcribed as a dotted half tied to a dotted quarter (♩ ♩. = ♩. ♩. ♩.). When there are only two semibreves between breves, the second one is doubled in duration; thus the second and third notes in the bassus are transcribed as dotted quarter and dotted half respectively (♩. ♩.). Once again, things change after the first six notes. Ockeghem introduces coloration (here, filled-in black notes where open white notes are expected), which changes both time and prolation to duple for most of the remainder of the canon, in both voices.

The net effect is that Kyrie I begins as a double mensuration canon, with all voices beginning together but the superius and tenor moving faster than their following voices, and then changes into a "normal" double canon at the fourth measure of the transcription, as the altus and bassus follow one measure behind the superius and tenor, using the same note values.

The canons in the first Kyrie are at the unison. Subsequent canons appear at each interval from the second (in the Christe) through the octave (in the "Osanna" of the Sanctus), then return to the fourth (for the "Benedictus" and Agnus Dei I) and fifth (Agnus Dei II and III). This procedure organizes the whole mass as a cycle of canons at different intervals. The second Kyrie is shaped like Kyrie I, only with canons at the third; this requires each voice to use a different clef, as well as a different mensuration sign (see the discussion in HWM, pp. 193–94). Both Kyries end on F, the main modal center for the entire mass. The Christe is very different, offering a contrast to the Kyries. Only one mensuration is used throughout, and only two voices appear at once. The altus and bassus sing a passage together; the superius and tenor repeat it a step higher; then this process repeats with a new passage, leading to a final cadence on D. Here the "canon" at the second is only a repetition while the leading voices rest. The result is a Christe that is much longer than the Kyries. Normally, there are three statements of the phrase "Christe eleison" (as in NAWM 3b), but here because of Ockeghem's canonic design, there are at least four (twelve, if the singers perform all the repetitions added by the editor in italics).

Although *Missa prolationum* is a unique work, it shares several characteristic features with Ockeghem's other music. One such trait is a tendency for phrases to start with longer durations and move toward shorter ones in all voices, building up a density of rhythm toward the end of a phrase that has been called Ockeghem's "drive to the cadence." Like his predecessor Du Fay, Ockeghem varies the rhythm constantly so that two successive measures almost never have the same rhythm.

Throughout, he achieves a full harmonic sound by including three different consonant pitches in almost every simultaneous sonority (forming what we call triads), except in the last chord of an important cadence, when only perfect consonances were allowed in order to convey a sense of finality. Ockeghem's emphasis on triadic sonorities helps to make all his intricate canonic counterpoint work, as is evident from the triadic skips and leaps at the opening of both Kyrie I and Kyrie II. Where the tenor or the lowest voice descends at a cadence, one or more upper voices may syncopate to cause a suspension, as at the conclusion of the Christe and Kyrie II. With few exceptions, the only other dissonances are brief passing tones. This strict control of dissonance gives the music an overwhelmingly euphonious sound.

As is typical of Ockeghem's music, the phrases are long and winding, and many of the cadences are blurred by motion in other voices, producing a sense of sustained, ongoing movement. In Kyrie I, cadences between cantus and tenor in measure 5 and measures 6–7 are obscured by the other two voices, which keeps the momentum going. Even in the two-voice counterpoint of the Christe, what sound like cadences at the beginning of measures 3 and 4 are barely touched before the voices move on, delaying the sense of arrival until the end of measure 4. In the same way that the frequent pauses and clear phrasing in Du Fay's music seem to reflect Italian and English influences, Ockeghem's more continuous flow and fondness for syncopation may represent a concentrated French style, reflecting his almost half-century at the French royal court.

Henricus Isaac (CA. 1450–1517)

Innsbruck, ich muss dich lassen

Lied

CA. 1500

D-iskantlied

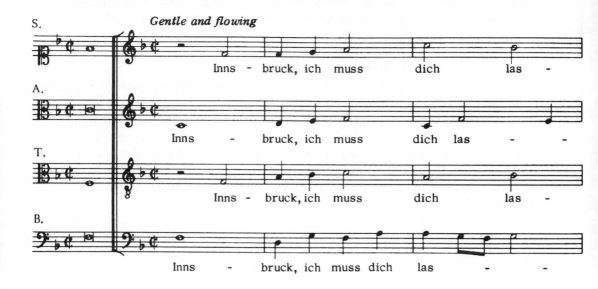

0:00	Innsbruck, ich muss dich lassen,	Innsbruck, I must leave you;
	ich fahr dahin mein Strassen,	I am going on my way
	in fremde Land dahin.	into a foreign land.
	Mein Freud ist mir genommen,	My joy is taken from me,
	die ich nit weiss bekommen,	I know not how to regain it,
	wo ich im Elend bin.	while in such misery.

0:49	Gross Leid muss ich jetzt tragen,	I must now endure great pain
	das ich allein tu klagen	which I confide only
	dem liebsten Buhlen mein.	to my dearest love.
	Ach Lieb, nun lass mich Armen	O beloved, find pity
	im Herzen dein erbarmen,	in your heart for me,
	dass ich muss dannen sein.	that I must part from you.

1:38	Mein Trost ob allen Weiben,	My comfort above all other women,
	dein tu ich ewig bleiben,	I shall always be yours,
	stet treu, der Ehren fromm.	forever faithful in honor true.
	Nun muss dich Gott bewahren,	May the good Lord protect you
	in aller Tugend sparen,	and keep you in your virtue
	bis dass ich wiederkomm.	for me, till I return.

—TRANS. NOAH GREENBERG
AND PAUL MAYNARD

Henricus Isaac wrote two settings of this melody and text, probably while he was in the service of the Holy Roman emperor Maximilian I between about 1497 and 1512. Innsbruck was the emperor's favorite city and one of his official residences. This setting may have been composed for the departure of the emperor and his court from Innsbruck in either February 1500 or December 1501.

During the very late fifteenth and early sixteenth centuries, the polyphonic *Lied* was usually either an arrangement of a folk or popular song or a setting of a newly composed melody. In either case, Lieder were intended for use at court or in elite circles. By this period, the preferred texture for secular music was four parts rather than three, as had been standard during most of the fifteenth century (see NAWM 35, 36, 38a, and 39). In four-voice Lieder, the tune may be in the tenor or the cantus, and the setting may use cantus-firmus style, imitation, or homophony. It is not known whether Isaac used an existing song for this Lied or if he devised the tune and poetry himself, although the latter perhaps is more likely. The melody is in the cantus, and the other voices mostly harmonize with it in simple homophony, modeled on the style of Italian songs that Isaac had encountered while living in Florence. Such homophonic, strophic settings in four parts became typical for many kinds of vernacular songs in the sixteenth century. Isaac's other setting of the same melody is in a very different style, more typical of the German Lied at this time, with the tune in canon in the tenor and altus.

Each line of the poem is set to its own musical phrase and separated from the next line by a rest. Phrases usually end with suspensions leading to cadences on the mode's final, F, or reciting tone, C, and a cadence on G marks the midpoint of each stanza. Although the piece may sound tonal to modern ears, music of this time period was still conceived according to the modal system. This is apparent from the cadences, which move out from a sixth to an octave, and also from the occasional triads on E♭, a whole step below the final, which would rarely occur in a piece in F major.

There are three stanzas of poetry, all sung to the same music. On the accompanying recording, this Lied is sung with one voice on each vocal line, and the repetition of the final phrase in measures 20–23 is omitted in the first two verses. Later in the sixteenth century, this melody was adapted to sacred words and became widely known as the chorale *O Welt, ich muss dich lassen* (O world, I now must leave thee; see NAWM 104b).

Josquin Desprez (CA. 1450–1521)

Faulte d'argent

Chanson

CA. 1500

42

From Josquin Desprez, *Werken, Wereldlijke Werken I*, ed. Albert Smijers (Amsterdam: G. Alsbach, 1925), 38–40.
Score reengraved by Laura Dallman using modern clefs.

Faulte d'argent, c'est douleur non pareille;	Lack of money, that's sorrow without equal.
Se je le dis, las, je sçay bien pourquoy.	If I say this, alas! I know well why.
Sans de quibus il se fault tenir quoy.	Without money one must keep quiet.
Femme qui dort, pour argent se resveille.	A sleeping woman will wake up for money.

Faulte d'argent is one of Josquin's most securely attributed chansons, ascribed to him in a number of independent sources including two reliable manuscripts copied during his lifetime: one in Augsburg, Germany in 1505–14; the other in Florence, Italy around 1508–27. Given the dates of the manuscripts, he probably composed this song in the 1490s or early 1500s.

Chansons by Binchois (NAWM 35), Du Fay (NAWM 38a), and other composers active before the mid-fifteenth century are treble-dominated—the cantus is the most important voice, the tenor accompanies the cantus in two-part counterpoint, and the other voices are added around the cantus-tenor framework. We saw in Busnoys's *Je ne puis vivre* (NAWM 39), a chanson from the third quarter of the fifteenth century, that the three voices were more equal, all participating in imitation at the beginning, although for most of the song the cantus and tenor played the central role, exchanging ideas in imitation while the contratenor accompanied with free counterpoint. In *Faulte d'argent* and other chansons by composers from Josquin's generation, all the voices are similar in style, all are equally important, and all are essential to the counterpoint. The cadences are not all formed between the cantus and tenor but may be formed between any two voices.

Faulte d'argent is a setting for five voices of a song that was apparently well known at the time, as it was set by several composers. The text for the song is a brief quatrain extracted from a longer poem; the last line was originally from another stanza, but in this abbreviated version it offers a surprising change of tone from a complaint about lack of cash to an ironic comment about what money can do.

Arrangements of popular songs were fashionable beginning in the 1490s, perhaps to satisfy the taste of patrons, or perhaps because composers were seeking a more directly appealing style. Here Josquin combines popular appeal with learned techniques he inherited from Ockeghem and other predecessors by using the existing tune like a cantus firmus in canon.

The tenor (notated here on the second staff down) states the melody. A canon (an instruction written in the part) directs that it is to be sung "par Nature"—in the natural hexachord from C to A—but also "par B mollis"—down a fifth in the soft hexachord (with B♭). This creates a canon at the fifth between the tenor and its following voice, here called *quinta pars* ("fifth part," on the next-to-bottom staff). It would be surprising if a popular song made good counterpoint with itself, and indeed this song would not work as a canon if left unaltered. So Josquin adds rests between phrases to allow the two parts to fit together and repeats phrases to create a variety of contrapuntal combinations. (To hear the original tune without these alterations, sing measures 10–15, 29–30, 33–41 first beat, and 53–58 of the quinta pars without breaks between them.)

The other parts spin a web of counterpoint around this two-voice canonic cantus firmus. At times they create points of imitation with the canonic voices, as at the beginning, either stating a phrase of the borrowed tune exactly or paraphrasing it more or less closely. At other times the other parts add new contrapuntal lines, some of which themselves become motives treated in imitation, like the figure tossed between the outer voices in measures 13–24, joined by the contratenor at measure 20.

The fourth line of the original song has the same music as the first, and Josquin follows suit at measure 44 by presenting an almost exact repetition of the opening section with the new words. At measure 64 a coda begins; the tenor and quinta pars are still in canon, but now both diverge from the original song melody to vary a figure heard earlier in other voices (compare the tenor in measures 65–66 with the discantus in measures 12–13 and 55–56 and the bassus in measures 36–37).

Josquin sets the text mostly syllabically and with careful attention to accentuation, often highlighting accented syllables by lengthening the duration or syncopating the rhythm. He repeats phrases of text throughout, constucting a longer piece in syllabic style than would otherwise be possible. Earlier chanson composers avoided such repetition of individual words or phrases of the text, but it became a frequent feature of sixteenth-century vocal works.

The tonal plan of the chanson is unusual. Because of the canon at the fifth, the tenor presents the song in the Hypodorian mode on D, and the quinta pars states it in the same mode transposed to G. (The tune is Hypodorian rather than Dorian because it falls in the range from a fourth below the final to a fifth above.) This creates ambiguity: what is the mode of this piece? The other parts are notated with a flat in the signature, suggesting a transposed Hypodorian mode on G, and the first cadence is indeed on G (measure 5). But the next is on D (measure 12), supporting the end of the first line of poetry in the tenor, and then G and D alternate until the first section is over (measure 24). The second line of poetry is concluded by cadences on A (measures 33 and 36), which would point to a modal final on D, but the third poetic line ends with a cadence on B♭ (measure 43), which points to G. When the opening section returns, the stage seems to be set for a final cadence on G, but at measure 67 the music swerves and leads to a closing cadence on D. The harmonic surprise matches the surprise in the last line of the poem, showing Josquin's interest in reflecting the meaning of the text.

Despite the complexities of the canon, the double cantus firmus, and the ambivalent mode, the chanson sounds like an upbeat, witty song of its time, with excellent declamation of the text, attractive melodies, constantly changing rhythms and textures, and an immediately comprehensible form based on a succession of phrases and sections organized primarily by points of imitation. The suave combination of popular appeal with learned compositional techniques exemplifies the virtuoso command of his craft that won Josquin a reputation as the best composer of his era.

Josquin Desprez (CA. 1450–1521)

Mille regretz

Chanson

CA. 1520

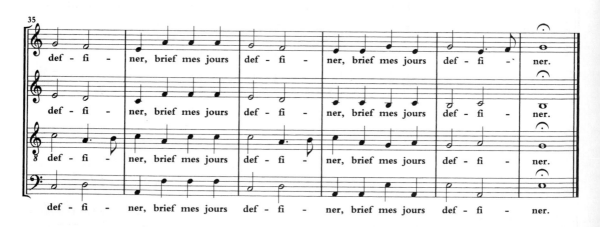

Mille regretz de vous habandonner
Et d'eslonger vostre fache amoureuse,
Jay si grand dueil et paine douloureuse,
Qu'on me verra brief mes jours definer.

A thousand regrets at deserting you
and leaving behind your loving face.
I feel so much sadness and such painful distress,
that it seems to me my days will soon dwindle away.

Mille regretz is simpler and more homophonic than most of Josquin's chansons and is credited to him in only two sources. For these reasons, and because a large number of works that were once attributed to Josquin are now known or suspected to be by other composers, several scholars have questioned its attribution to Josquin. If it is by Josquin, it is one of his last chansons, and it demonstrates his interest in keeping up with the most modern styles.

There is evidence to suggest that Josquin composed it for Holy Roman emperor Charles V and presented it to him in person in 1520, when the emperor was in Brussels, near where Josquin was living in Condé-sur-l'Escaut. A document from Charles V's 1520 account book records a generous payment to "Joskin" from Condé "for some new songs" that the composer delivered in person. This group of songs very likely included *Mille regretz*, given the chanson's subsequent history; perhaps the poem's theme of taking leave, and the closing image of one's days dwindling away, resonated with the aged composer, then around seventy, and the young emperor whose family the composer had served. After Josquin's death, it became one of his most popular chansons, especially in Spain, where Charles spent most of his time. It was known in Spain as "La cancion del Emperador" (The Song of the Emperor), confirming the link to Charles and thus to Josquin. It was later reworked in a mass by Cristóbal de Morales and arranged for vihuela (a guitar-shaped lute) by Luis de Narváez (see NAWM 68a).

As is typical of music by Josquin and his contemporaries, each phrase of text is given a distinctive musical phrase that fits the rhythm and meaning of the words. The texture also changes from phrase to phrase, alternating between homophony and imitation, and between various combinations of two, three, or all four voices. The sadness of the song is conveyed especially by the many descending lines, as at "regretz," "paine douILourouse" (painful distress), and "brief mes jours definer" (my days will soon dwindle away). The last line of the poem is reiterated for expressive emphasis, a gesture that became the norm in sixteenth-century text settings. Here the repetitions of the final words also suggest the image in the text of dwindling away.

The piece is in mode 3 (Phrygian), as demonstrated by the frequent cadences on E (including the final cadence) and the ranges of cantus and tenor from low C or D to high E. The only cadence note other than E is A, an important note in the mode (and the reciting tone of its plagal relative, mode 4). Several of the cadences, including the final sonority, include thirds, as was becoming more common during this period. In the fifteenth century, pieces and sections typically closed on perfect consonances, such as an octave or a fifth and octave.

All the parts were meant to be sung, as evident in the appropriate text-setting and in the various textures—such as alternating pairs of voices and imitation between the parts—that suggest complete equality among the parts. Most likely, the song was intended for one singer on each part, as was standard in the sixteenth century, and that is how it is sung on the accompanying recording.

Josquin Desprez (CA. 1450–1521)

Ave Maria . . . virgo serena

Motet

CA. 1480–85

Edited by Alejandro Enrique Planchart. Used by permission. Reprinted from Allan W. Atlas, *Anthology of Renaissance Music* (New York: W. W. Norton, 1998), 159–65.

0:00	Ave Maria, gratia plena,	Hail Mary, full of grace,
	Dominus tecum, Virgo serena.	the Lord is with you, serene Virgin.

0:45	Ave, cujus conceptio	Hail to her whose conception,
	Solemni plena gaudio,	full of solemn jubilation,
	Caelestia, terrestria	fills heaven and earth
	Nova replet laetitia.	with new joy.

1:21	Ave, cuius nativitas	Hail to her whose birth
	Nostra fuit solemnitas:	was our solemn feast,
	Ut lucifer, lux oriens,	like the morning star, the light of day,
	Verum solem praeveniens.	anticipating the true sun [Christ].

1:59	Ave, pia humilitas,	Hail, pious humility,
	Sine viro fecunditas,	fruitful without a man,
	Cuius annuntiatio	whose annunciation
	Nostra fuit salvatio.	was our salvation.

2:27	Ave, vera virginitas,	Hail, true virginity,
	Immaculata castitas,	immaculate chastity,
	Cuius purificatio	whose purification
	Nostra fuit purgatio.	purged our sins.

3:04	Ave, praeclara omnibus	Hail, most excellent in all
	Angelicis virtutibus,	angelic virtues,
	Cuius fuit assumptio	whose assumption was
	Nostra glorificatio.	our glorification.

3:59	O Mater Dei,	O Mother of God,
	Memento mei.	remember me.
	Amen.	Amen.

Ave Maria . . . virgo serena was perhaps Josquin's most popular motet, as demonstrated by its inclusion in numerous manuscripts and its placement as the first work in Ottaviano Petrucci's first published collection of motets in 1502. Its cumbersome title is necessary to distinguish it from another motet Josquin wrote that also begins "Ave Maria." *Ave Maria . . . virgo serena* was copied into a manuscript in about 1485, making it the earliest datable piece by Josquin.

The text, in praise of the Virgin Mary, begins with two lines from the sequence sung on the Feast of the Annunciation. It continues with a metric and rhymed hymn, frequently used in the fifteenth century for private devotions, whose five stanzas celebrate the five major feasts commemorating the events of Mary's life: the Immaculate Conception, her Nativity, the Annunciation, Purification, and her Assumption. The motet text ends with a two-line prayer in common use at the time. The form of the poem determined the form of the music, reflecting Josquin's interest in clear delineation of the text. For each couplet or strophe, Josquin composed a unique musical treatment. Each section ends with a cadence on C, the tonal center, demonstrating Josquin's concern for pitch organization. Glareanus, in his *Dodekachordon*, classified the mode of this motet as Hypoionian (mode 12) because of its final on C and ranges of at least a fifth above and fourth below the final in the tenor and the superius, which were the two voices that Glareanus and other Renaissance theorists considered to define the mode in a polyphonic work.

Josquin's setting of the words shows both variety and expressivity. The opening couplet (measures 1–15) is composed as a series of points of imitation based on the original melody of the sequence:

A - ve   Ma - ri - a,   gra - ti - a ple - na,   Do - mi-nus te - cum,   Vir-go se - re - na.

Josquin gives each phrase of text a musical subject, paraphrased from the corresponding phrase in the chant, that is taken up by each voice in turn, working from highest to lowest. Before the last voice finishes its phrase, a different voice begins the next phrase with a new subject, preserving the musical continuity. At "virgo serena" (serene Virgin), the final phrase of the first couplet (measures 12–15), all the voices sing together for the first time, and the rhythmic activity accelerates to the eighth-note level, emphasizing the conclusion of the first section. This increase in activity, often called a "drive to the cadence," is a technique Josquin probably learned from Ockeghem (see NAWM 40).

When the first stanza of the hymn begins, the texture changes from imitation to homophony. The first line, hailing Mary's conception, is presented twice, in parallel sixths and then in parallel §️ sonorities that are reminiscent of fauxbourdon (measures 16–20). By the time that Josquin composed this piece, fauxbourdon was considered old-fashioned; perhaps the use of an older style was meant to evoke a sacred and dignified mood. The second line, "full of solemn jubilation," suggests both fullness and solemnity because all four voices are in homophony for the first time in the motet (measures 20–22). The end of the strophe is marked with the most emphatic cadence so far in the piece.

Josquin varied the texture constantly through the rest of the piece, alternating duets with three- and four-part writing, and points of imitation with homophony. The meter shifts to triple time at measures 47, providing contrast. A particularly expressive moment comes at the closing prayer, when the music slows and the singers declaim in rhythmic unison and simple harmonies, "O mother of God, remember me. Amen" (measures 73–79). It is as if the composer—on his own behalf, and also for his singers, his patron, and the congregation—set aside his artistry to speak directly and modestly to the Virgin Mary, pleading for his soul.

This motet is often sung by choirs today, but in Josquin's time it was probably performed by only a few singers, perhaps as few as one per part. It is a rewarding piece to sing; each part is equally interesting and important, the texture changes continually, and the melodies unfold smoothly and logically, yet with constant rhythmic and melodic interest.

Josquin Desprez (CA. 1450–1521)

Missa Pange lingua: Kyrie and part of Credo

Paraphrase mass

CA. 1515

45

(a) Kyrie

Kyrie eleison.   Lord have mercy.
Christe eleison.   Christ have mercy.
Kyrie eleison.   Lord have mercy.

(b) Credo, excerpt: *Et incarnatus est* and *Crucifixus*

Et incarnatus est de Spiritu Sancto ex Maria Virgine: et homo factus est.	And was made incarnate by the Holy Spirit of the Virgin Mary, and was made man.
Crucifixus etiam pro nobis: sub Pontio Pilato passus, et sepultus est.	And was crucified for us; under Pontius Pilate He died, and was buried.
Et resurrexit tertia die, secundum Scripturas.	And rose again on the third day, according to the Scriptures.
Et ascendit in caelum: sedet ad dexteram Patris.	And ascended into heaven, and sits at the right hand of the Father.
Et iterum venturus est cum gloria judicare vivos et mortuos: cujus regni non erit finis.	And He shall come again with glory to judge the quick and the dead; of whose kingdom there shall be no end.

Since Ottaviano Petrucci did not print *Missa Pange lingua* in any of his collections of Josquin des Prez's masses (published in 1502, 1505, and 1514), it is likely that it was one of the last that Josquin composed. It appears in manuscripts dating from late in Josquin's lifetime and was published in the anthology *Missae tredecim* (Thirteen Masses) in 1539, eighteen years after Josquin's death.

The mass is based on the melody of the hymn *Pange lingua gloriosi* (text by St. Thomas Aquinas), assigned to second Vespers on the feast of Corpus Christi (*Liber usualis*, p. 957). The six strophes of the hymn are sung to the melody given below with the first strophe.

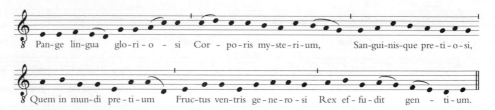

Pan-ge lin-gua   glo-ri-o-si   Cor-po-ris my-ste-ri-um,   San-gui-nis-que pre-ti-o-si,

Quem in mun-di pre-ti-um   Fruc-tus ven-tris ge-ne-ro-si   Rex ef-fu-dit   gen-ti-um.

Pange lingua gloriosi	Sing, tongue, of the glorious
Corporis mysterium,	body's mystery
Sanguinisque pretiosi,	and of the precious blood,
Quem in mundi pretium	ransom of the world, that
Fructus ventris generosi	the fruit of the generous womb,
Rex effudit gentium.	the king of all peoples, poured forth.

Josquin based all the movements of the mass—though not all its subdivisions—on the hymn melody. Throughout most of the mass, he adapted the six phrases of the hymn melody as subjects for polyphonic imitation, making imitation the primary structural device rather than the layering of voices around a cantus firmus. At times the source melody is also adapted in other ways, for instance as the superius melody on a homophonic passage. A mass based on this procedure—paraphrasing a melody in all voices and treating motives derived from it in points of imitation as well as in other textures—is called a *paraphrase mass*.

The Kyrie follows the hymn closely. The movement has three sections (Kyrie I, Christe, and Kyrie II), and in each section Josquin paraphrased two of the hymn's six phrases. The last notes of the second, fourth, and sixth phrases of the hymn determine the modal degrees on which each section of the Kyrie closes—respectively G, D, and E.

The tenor takes the lead at the outset, following the contour of the hymn's first phrase exactly, then adding effusive decoration before cadencing on the last note of the hymn's first phrase, C (see measures 1–5). The bassus imitates the same figure a fifth lower but diverges more from the original hymn. The superius and altus repeat the tenor and bassus phrases an octave higher (measures 5–9); such alternation of paired voices is typical of Josquin's music. The second phrase of the hymn is then paraphrased in a three-voice point of imitation. The first several notes of the hymn phrase (C–D–C–C–B–A) are reworked to create a motive in the bassus (C–C–D–C–A–B–A in measures 9–11) that is imitated exactly by tenor and superius at one-measure intervals. But the rest of the hymn phrase (C–B–A–G) is more loosely paraphrased, as all three voices indulge in repeated descending figures, each decorated in a different way, with energy sustained by faster rising scale figures (measures 12–16). This heightened activity is typical of Josquin's "drive to the cadence."

The third and fourth phrases of the hymn are paraphrased in the Christe, again with imitation in paired voices. To achieve maximum variety, Josquin varied the combinations of voices, the order of entrances, and the intervals of imitation. Also typical of Josquin's music is the way that each motive begins as a clear statement of the original hymn phrase in long notes and then becomes progressively more active and more distant from the source.

In the final Kyrie, the fifth and sixth phrases of the hymn are treated a bit more freely. For example, the fifth phrase is missing its opening note, and the sixth phrase is paraphrased differently in each voice. Searching for the hymn's contour in all four voices in measures 60–70 provides a striking lesson in Josquin's inventiveness in reworking given material. Several motives are repeated either in sequence or at pitch in a most striking manner.

Excerpts from the *Credo* demonstrate Josquin's attention to text expression. The solemn proclamation at "Et incarnatus est" (And he was made incarnate by the Holy Spirit out of the Virgin Mary, and was made man) is declaimed in block chords, with the top voice paraphrasing the first line of the hymn. Such homophonic passages often appear in sixteenth-century works, alone or in alternation with points of imitation. For the word "Crucifixus" (crucified), Josquin took advantage of the plaintive semitone motion in the hymn's opening. The following passage, mostly on new material, features alternating imitative and homophonic phrases. Some motives suggest word-painting, including the burst of activity at "Et resurrexit" (and was resurrected) and the rising line at "Et ascendit in caelum" (and ascended into Heaven).

As we have seen in several other scores, the editor has included the original notation at the beginning of each section. The composer specified the text underlay in the excerpt from the *Credo*, and the music perfectly suits the rhythm and accentuation of the words. In the *Kyrie*, the original music contained only the word "Kyrie" or "Christe" at the beginning of each part and "eleison" at the end; the editor has added text repetition (the text shown in brackets) to fit the musical rhythm. With these additions, one can consider each section to be a three-fold statement of the text (for instance, the three statements of "Kyrie eleison" begin at measures 1, 5, and 9 of Kyrie I). In a performance at a Mass, the *Kyrie* as written here could be performed once and be sufficient for the liturgy, which requires each sentence to be said three times. Otherwise, each section would be sung three times or alternated with chant, as in NAWM 26a.

Martin Luther (1483–1546)

Nun komm, der Heiden Heiland and *Ein feste Burg*

46

Chorales
1524 AND 1529

(a) Attributed to St. Ambrose: Hymn, *Veni redemptor gentium*

Ve – ni, re – dem – ptor gen – ti – um. o – sten – de par – tum vir – gi – nis;

mi – re – tur om – ne sae – cu – lum, ta – lis de – cet par – tus de – um.

Veni, redemptor gentium,	Come, Savior of nations,
ostende partum Virginis;	display the offspring of the Virgin.
miretur omne saeculum:	Let all ages marvel
talis decet partus deum.	that God granted such a birth.
Non ex virili semine,	Not from man's seed,
sed mystico spiramine	but by the Holy Spirit's power
Verbum Dei factum est caro	the Word of God is made flesh
fructusque ventris floruit.	and blooms as the fruit of the womb.
Alvus tumescit Virginis,	The womb of the Virgin swells,
claustrum pudoris permanet,	yet the fortress of her purity is not breached,
vexilla virtutum micant,	the sparkling banners of virtue
versatur in templo Deus.	turn it into a temple of God.
Procedat e thalamo suo,	He comes forth from his chamber,
pudoris aula regia,	the royal hall of purity,
geminae gigas substantiae	a giant of twofold substance in one,
alacris ut currat viam.	eager to run his course.
Egressus eius a Patre,	He comes to us from the Father,
regressus eius ad Patrem;	and he returns to the Father;
excursus usque ad infernos	he goes down to Hell
recursus ad sedem Dei.	and returns to the seat of God.

From Einsiedeln, Benediktinerkloster, Musikbibliothek, MS 366 (twelfth century), after *Hymnen: Die mittelalterlichen Hymnenmelodien des Abendlandes*, ed. Bruno Stäblein, Monumenta mododica medii aevi 1 (Kassel: Bärenreiter, 1956), 273–74.

Aequalis aeterno Patri,	Equal to the eternal Father,
carnis tropaeo cingere,	victory clothed in our flesh,
infirma nostri corporis	the weaknesses of our bodies
virtute firmans perpeti.	your virtues shall forever strengthen.
Praesepe iam fulget tuum	Now your crib gleams,
lumenque nox spirat novum,	the night gives forth a new light,
quod nulla nox interpolet	because darkness cannot enter in,
fideque iugi luceat.	faith perpetually shines.
Gloria tibi, Domine,	Praise be to you, Lord,
Qui natus es de virgine,	who is born of a virgin,
Cum Patre et sancto Spiritu,	with the Father and the Holy Spirit,
in sempiterna saecula. Amen.	in eternity. Amen.

—ATTRIBUTED TO ST. AMBROSE

(b) Martin Luther, *Nun komm, der Heiden Heiland*

1. Nun komm, der Heiden Heiland,   Now come, Savior of the gentiles,
   Der Jungfrauen Kind erkannt,   known as Child of the Virgin,
   Dass sich wunder alle Welt,   at which all the world marvels
   Gott solch' Geburt ihm bestellt. that God such a birth for him ordains.

2. Nicht von Manns Blut noch von Fleisch, Not from man's blood nor from flesh,
   Allein von dem Heil'gen Geist   but alone from the Holy Spirit
   Ist Gott's Wort worden ein Mensch   has God's Word become a human being,
   Und blühet ein Frucht Weib'sfleisch.   and blooms fruit of a woman's flesh.

3. Der Jungfrau Leib schwanger ward,   The Virgin became pregnant,
   Doch blieb Keuschheit rein bewahrt,   But her virginity was kept pure,
   Leucht herfür manch' Tugend schon,   There shines forth many a virtue indeed,
   Gott da war in seinem Thron.   There God was on his throne.

From *Eyn Enchiridiom oder Handbuchlein . . . geystlicher gesenge und Psalmen* (Erfurt, 1524). Spellings modernized.

4. Er ging aus der Kammer sein,
   Dem kön'glichen Saal so rein,
   Gott von Art und Mensch ein Held
   Sein Weg er zu laufen eilt.

He went out of his chamber,
the royal hall so pure,
God by nature and as man a hero,
he hurries to run his course.

5. Sein Lauf kam vom Vater her
   Und kehrt' wieder zum Vater,
   Fuhr hinunter zu der Höll',
   Und wieder zu Gottes Stuhl.

His path came to us from the Father,
and returned to the Father;
went down to Hell,
and back to God's throne.

6. Der du bist dem Vater gleich,
   Führ hinaus den Sieg im Fleisch,
   Dass dein ewig Gott's Gewalt
   In uns das krank' Fleisch enthalt.

You, who are equal to the Father,
bring forth the victory in the flesh,
that your eternal God's power
our sickly flesh preserves.

7. Dein Krippen glänzt hell und klar,
   Die Nacht gibt ein neu Licht dar.
   Dunkel muss nicht kommen drein,
   Der Glaub' bleibt immer im Schein.

Your crib shines bright and clear,
the night gives forth a new light.
Darkness must not come into it,
Faith stays always in the light.

8. Lob sei Gott dem Vater ton;
   Lob sei Gott seim ein'gen Sohn,
   Lob sei Gott dem Heiligen Geist
   Immer und in Ewigkeit.

Praise be made to God the Father,
Praise be to God his only Son,
Praise be to God the Holy Spirit
Forever and in eternity.

— Martin Luther

(c) Martin Luther, *Ein feste Burg*

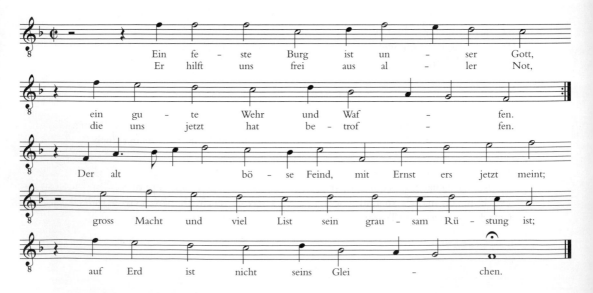

Ein fe - ste Burg ist un – ser Gott,
Er hilft uns frei aus al – ler Not,

ein gu - te Wehr und Waf – fen.
die uns jetzt hat be - trof – fen.

Der alt bö - se Feind, mit Ernst ers jetzt meint;

gross Macht und viel List sein grau - sam Rü - stung ist;

auf Erd ist nicht seins Glei – chen.

Transcribed from Joseph Klug, *Geistliche Lieder auffs new gebessert* (Wittenberg, 1533).

0:00	1. Ein feste Burg is unser Gott,	A sturdy fortress is our God,
	ein gute Wehr und Waffen.	a good defense and weapon.
	Er hilft uns frei aus aller Not,	He helps us free from all afflictions
	die uns jetzt hat betroffen.	that have now befallen us.
	Der alt böse Feind,	The old, evil enemy
	mit Ernst ers jetzt meint;	now means to deal with us seriously;
	groß Macht und viel List	great power and much cunning
	sein grausam Rüstung ist,	are his cruel armaments;
	auf Erd ist nicht seins Gleichen.	on Earth is not his equal.

0:48	2. Mit unsrer Macht ist nichts getan,	With our own strength is nothing done,
	wir sind gar bald verloren;	very soon we are entirely lost;
	es streit' für uns der rechte Mann,	but fighting for us is the righteous man,
	den Gott hat selbst erkoren.	whom God himself has chosen.
	Fragst du, wer der ist?	Do you ask, who he is?
	Er heißt Jesus Christ,	His name is Jesus Christ,
	der Herr Zebaoth,	the Lord Sabaoth,
	und ist kein andrer Gott,	and there is no other God;
	das Feld muß er behalten.	he must hold the battlefield.

3. Und wenn die Welt voll Teufel wär   And if the world were full of devils
   und wollt uns gar verschlingen,   who wanted to devour us entirely,
   so fürchten wir uns nicht so sehr,   we would not fear so much,
   es soll uns doch gelingen.   we will succeed nevertheless.
   Der Fürst dieser Welt,   The prince of this world,
   wie saur er sich stellt,   no matter how angry he appears,
   tut er uns doch nichts;   he will nevertheless do nothing to us;
   das macht, er ist gericht'.   that means, he is already judged.
   Ein Wörtlein kann ihn fällen.   A little word can bring him down.

4. Das Wort sie sollen lassen stahn   The Word they shall leave standing
   und kein' Dank dazu haben;   and receive no thanks for this;
   er ist bei uns wohl auf dem Plan   he is certainly with us on the battlefield
   mit seinem Geist und Gaben.   with his spirit and talents.
   Nehmen sie den Leib,   They may take your life,
   Gut, Ehr, Kind und Weib,   goods, honor, child, and wife,
   laß fahren dahin,   let all this occur,
   sie haben's kein' Gewinn,   yet from it they have no profit;
   das Reich muß uns doch bleiben.   The Kingdom still remains for us.

— MARTIN LUTHER

(d) Johann Walter (1496–1570), *Ein feste Burg*, setting for four voices

Ein feste Burg, from Johann Walter, *Sämtliche Werke*, ed. Otto Schröder, vol. 1, *Geistliches Gesangbüchlein*
(Wittenberg 1551), part 1, *Deutscher Gesänge* (Kassel: Bärenreiter, 1953), 26–27. Used by permission.

1 WB   2 BZ (Darin mit dem Text der 1. und 3. Strophe; diese beiden auch in LC und Ba.)   3 GC

In the early years of the Lutheran Church, Martin Luther regarded music as a crucial tool for propagating the new faith. Especially important were the congregational hymns in the vernacular that became known as *chorales* (from the German word for "chant"), which gave the people in the pews a role in the music of church services and also could be sung at home as part of private devotions. Luther and his colleagues often used or adapted existing German devotional songs as chorales or created chorales by writing new religious words for well-known secular songs, as in the retexting of *Innsbruck, ich muss dich lassen* (see NAWM 41) for the chorale *O Welt, ich muss dich lassen* (O world, I now must leave thee). The examples presented here demonstrate two other main sources for chorales: adaptations of Gregorian chants and new melodies in contemporary style.

The text of the hymn *Veni redemptor gentium* was attributed to St. Ambrose of Milan (ca. 340–397), but it was most likely not actually written by him. The earliest known form of the melody, shown here, is found in a twelfth-century hymnal from Einsiedeln, Germany. It was used as an Office hymn during the Advent season before Christmas. Luther adapted the text as a chorale for Advent by translating the eight verses into rhyming metric poetry in German, changing the number of syllables per line from eight (common in Latin hymns) to seven. In addition to transposing the melody up a fourth, he indicated specific rhythms and changed several of the notes so that each phrase has a single highest note and so that the last phrase is the same as the first. These changes converted a chant in free rhythm into a melody in the style of Luther's time, which the congregation would probably have found more appealing and easier to sing. Luther made his adaptation in 1523 or 1524, and in the latter year the chorale was published in one of the first collections of chorales to be printed. J. S. Bach later used this chorale as the basis for two cantatas (see NAWM 103).

The most famous of all chorales is *Ein feste Burg*, whose text and music are credited to Luther. It was first printed in a 1529 chorale collection, but no copies of that volume survive. The edition shown here is transcribed from the oldest extant publication, from 1533. The words, based on Psalm 46, are a stirring statement of faith in God's power to protect believers, and they must have been a great comfort during the bitter and often bloody battles over religious doctrine in Europe during the sixteenth and seventeenth centuries. (See Meyerbeer's opera *Les Huguenots*, NAWM 147, which is about one such conflict and which quotes *Ein feste Burg*.) The melody reinforces this image of strength with the repeated opening notes, frequent returns to the opening high note, and several descending scale figures that lead to the mode's final (F) or reciting tone (C). The mode is Ionian, mode 11 in Glareanus's set of twelve modes, transposed a fourth higher to F; Luther associated the Ionian mode with hymns of faith. The rhythm demonstrates Luther's careful attention to the proper setting of text, with long notes for the stressed syllables and shorter notes for most unstressed ones. Since the eighteenth century, Luther's forceful, almost jaunty rhythm has usually been smoothed out into mostly even note values.

The tune of *Ein feste Burg* may draw some elements from a melody by Luther's younger contemporary, the Meistersinger Hans Sachs (1494–1576). Like most chorales that were newly composed rather than adapted from existing songs or chants, it follows bar form—AAB—as was customary in the songs of the Minnesinger (see NAWM 11) and Meistersinger. As in many of the Meistersinger's songs, the A and B sections end with the same musical phrase.

Beginning soon after the first chorales were composed, Lutheran composers created four-part settings of chorales for performance by the choir during services—separately or alternating verses with the congregation singing in unison—or for singing in schools, in private devotions, or as recreation. The leader in this practice was Johann Walter, whose first collection of four- and five-voice chorale settings, the *Geystliches Gesangk Buchleyn* (Little Book of Spiritual Songs), was published in 1524. In later editions, Walter added several settings of *Ein feste Burg*, including the one printed here. He followed the tradition of the German Lied in placing the tune in the tenor, essentially unchanged, and surrounding it with free counterpoint in the other voices. Phrase endings in the tenor are often overlapped by one or more voices, maintaining the forward momentum until the end of each section. The cadence at the end of the first section (measures 8–9) includes a triad on the lowered seventh degree (E♭) just before the final three chords. This was a very common cadential formula throughout the sixteenth century.

On the accompanying recordings, *Veni redemptor gentium* is sung by a chant choir, as it would have been in Catholic services, and *Nun komm, der Heiden Heiland* is sung in unaccompanied unison by a mixed congregation of men and women, as was the practice in Lutheran services during Luther's lifetime. Only the first verse of the chant hymn and verses 1 and 8 of the chorale are included on the recordings, but both texts are printed here in their entirety in order to show how Luther adapted the Latin original. The recordings also include two verses of *Ein feste Burg* in congregational unison and one verse in Walter's polyphonic setting. The edition of Walter's setting includes alternate text underlay for some passages, printed in smaller letters.

Loys Bourgeois (CA. 1510–CA. 1561)

Psalm 134 (*Or sus, serviteurs du Seigneur*)

Metrical psalm

CA. 1551

47

(a) Psalm 134, *Or sus, serviteurs du Seigneur*

1. Or sus, serviteurs du Seigneur,
   Vous qui de nuict en son honneur
   Dedans sa maison le servez,
   Louez-le, et son nom eslevez.

   Arise, you servants of the Lord,
   you who by night in his honor
   serve him in his house,
   praise him, and lift up his name.

2. Levez les mains au plus sainct lieu
   De ce tressainct temple de Dieu,
   Et le los qu'il a merité
   Soit par vos bouches recité.

   Lift up your hands to the holiest place
   of this most holy temple of God,
   and may the praise that He deserves
   be recited by your mouths.

3. Dieu qui a fait et entretient
   Et terre et ciel par son pouvoir,
   Du mont Sion, où il se tient,
   Ses biens te face appercevoir.

   May God who made and maintains
   the earth and heavens by his power,
   from Mount Zion, where he resides,
   let you experience his blessings.

— CLÉMENT MAROT AND
THÉODORE DE BÈZE

From Clément Marot and Théodore de Bèze, *Les psaumes en vers français avec leurs mélodies* (Geneva, 1562), 447.

(b) William Kethe (D. CA. 1608): Psalm 100, *All people that on earth do dwell* (CA. 1559)

Music and text from Robin A. Leaver, *"Goostly psalmes and spirituall songs": English and Dutch Metrical Psalms from Coverdale to Utenhove 1535–1566* (Oxford: Clarendon Press, 1991), 237. William Kethe: Psalm 100, *All people who on earth do dwell.* Reprinted by permission of Oxford University Press.

1. All people that on earth do dwell,
   Sing to the Lord with cherefull voyce:
   Him serve with feare, his praise forthe tell:
   Come ye before him, and reioyce.

2. The Lord, ye knowe, is god in dede:
   Without our aide, he did vs make:
   We are his folke: he doeth vs fede,
   And for his shepe he doeth vs take.

3. Oh, entre then his gates with praise:
   Approche with ioye his courtes vnto:
   Praise, laude, and blesse his Name always:
   For it is semely so to do.

4. For why? the Lord our God is good:
   His mercie is for euer sure:
   His trueth at all times firmely stoode,
   And shal from age to age indure.

1. All people that on earth do dwell,
   Sing to the Lord with cheerful voice:
   Him serve with fear, his praise forth tell:
   Come ye before him, and rejoice.

2. The Lord, ye know, is God indeed:
   Without our aide, he did us make:
   We are his folk: he doth us feed,
   And for his sheep he doth us take.

3. Oh, enter then his gates with praise:
   Approach with joy his courts unto:
   Praise, laud, and bless his Name always:
   For it is seemly so to do.

4. For why? the Lord our God is good:
   His mercy is forever sure:
   His truth at all times firmly stood,
   And shall from age to age endure.

—WILLIAM KETHE

In Calvinist churches such as the Reformed Church and Presbyterian Church, congregational singing in the vernacular was as important as in the Lutheran Church. The spiritual leader of the Reformed movement, Jean Calvin (1509–1564), believed that humans could not give God anything better than God had given humans, and so he insisted that only texts from the Bible, especially psalms, should be sung in church. Since psalms had verses of varying lengths and thus were difficult for congregations to sing together, Calvinist poets prepared rhymed, metric, strophic translations of psalms in the vernacular, which were called *metrical psalms*. These were set to simple, syllabic tunes—most newly composed, some adapted from chants, chansons, dances, or other melodies—and published in collections called *psalters*.

The most famous metrical psalm tune is the one included here, composed (or perhaps adapted) by Loys Bourgeois for the version of Psalm 134 by Clément Marot and Théodore de Bèze. The melody first appeared in the Genevan Psalter, *Trente Quatre Pseaumes de David* (Thirty-Four Psalms of David), published in 1551. The popularity of this melody may owe something to its almost perfect shape. It matches the four-line poetic stanzas with four brief phrases of eight notes each. The first three phrases share the same rhythm and move almost entirely by step, with one skip or leap before the last three notes. The last phrase slightly alters the rhythm and introduces more skips, creating a sense of finality by breaking the pattern set in the preceding phrases. The four phrases end with near-rhymes: three stepwise half notes that rise in the first and third phrases and descend in the second and fourth. Each phrase has a single high note, the highest of which is C in the last phrase. In perfect symmetry, the high point of the phrase gradually shifts from the last note of the first phrase (A) to the third note from the end of the second phrase (B♭), the third note from the beginning of the third phrase (A), and the first note of the final phrase. The successive phrase endings on A, G, F, and F create a gradual descent that balances the ascent from F to A in the first phrase. Additionally, each individual phrase includes a unique balance of ascending and descending elements. It takes longer to describe this melody than is required to sing it, but that a simple melody can feature such richness of detail may explain why it is so memorable and enduring.

Metrical psalm singing was adopted by English Protestants living in exile on the Continent during the reign of Mary I (r. 1553–58), who had restored Catholicism in England. When Elizabeth I succeeded Mary and revived the Church of England, she allowed psalm singing, and it soon became a regular part of church services as well as devotions at home. In English-language psalters, including the English Psalter of 1561, William Kethe's metrical translation of Psalm 100 was associated with Bourgeois's tune, which eventually became known as "Old Hundredth." It has been the most frequently printed tune in English-language psalters and hymnals for over four hundred years. Over the years, several rhythmic variants have been introduced, including a version in which all the notes are the same length.

On the recordings, both the French and the English psalms are sung by a mixed congregation of men and women without accompaniment, as was the sixteenth-century practice. Only the first verse of each is included.

Thomas Tallis (CA. 1505–1585)

If ye love me

Anthem

CA. 1546–49

48

begins homophonic & homorhythmic

ALTO 1: If ye love me, keep my com-mand-ments,

ALTO 2: If ye love me, keep my com-mand-ments,

TENOR: If ye love me, keep my com-mand-ments,

BASS: If ye love me, keep my com-mand-ments,

A¹: and I will pray the Fa-ther, and

A²: and I will pray the Fa-ther, and he shall

T: and I will pray the Fa-ther, and

B: and I will pray the Fa-ther,

From Thomas Tallis, *English Sacred Music I: Anthems*, transcribed and edited by Leonard Ellinwood, rev. Paul Doe, Early English Church Music 12 (London: Stainer and Bell, 1973), 16–18. © 1971 The British Academy. Reproduced by permission of Stainer & Bell Ltd.

The Church of England was founded by King Henry VIII in 1534, but only after his son Edward VI succeeded to the throne in 1547 did the Church replace Latin with English as the language for the liturgy. Edward and his advisors undertook the reform as part of an effort to make services as accessible and comprehensible to worshipers as was possible. The music also was to be in English, clearly declaiming the text and focusing on worship of God and Jesus, without the songs for Mary or other saints that were common in the Catholic Church (see NAWM 44 and 50). As Edward decreed in 1548:

> They shall from henceforth sing or say no anthems of our Lady [Mary] or other saints but only of our Lord, and them not in Latin but, choosing out the best and most sound-ing [inspiring] to Christian religion, they shall turn the same into English, setting thereunto a plain and distinct note, for every syllable one, [and] they shall sing them and none other [i.e., shall not embellish the written notes with improvisations].

"Anthem" was the English form of the Latin word "antiphon," and it became the standard term for works that played the same role in Anglican worship as motets in Catholic services.

Thomas Tallis had recently joined the Chapel Royal, which served the king and his court, and was one of the first to compose music for the new liturgy. *If ye love me*, copied into a manuscript in 1547 or 1548, was among his first. He may have composed it before Edward's decree, but it follows those strictures closely: the text is "of our Lord," inspiring, in English, and set to music with one note per syllable with only a few exceptions.

The text is a brief excerpt from the words Jesus said to his disciples at the Last Supper the evening before he was crucified, as related in the Gospel of John 14:15–17. In the Anglican liturgy, this passage is the beginning of the Gospel reading for Whitsunday (the Sunday seven weeks after Easter that commemorates Pentecost, when the Holy Spirit descended on the disciples and they spoke in tongues), but the message is suitable for almost any worship service or for private devotions.

Tallis's music combines clear declamation of the text with remarkable musical interest and variety. The melodies fit the words like a glove, with both rhythms and contours that follow the natural patterns of speech. The melodic lines are simple yet beautifully shaped, often beginning with skips or leaps that lead to a gentle stepwise descent. In a brief compass, Tallis offers a compendium of musical textures, with each phrase of text receiving a different treatment. The first is presented in homophony in all four voices, for maximum clarity. The other phrases are all set as points of imitation, but each is unique: a pair of imitative duets, as at the beginning of *Missa Pange lingua* (NAWM 45); three entries, the middle one in two voices simultaneously, with each voice given a different intervallic contour (measures 9–13); four entries, culminating in chordal homophony (measures 13–19); and again four entries, with each voice stating the idea twice, at two different pitch levels (measures 19–26). As in many of Tallis's anthems, the second half is repeated, producing an ABB form that emphasizes the words through repetition and creates a satisfying conclusion. Through works such as this, Tallis helped to establish a new tradition for Anglican church music, combining comprehensibility and immediacy with attractive music that appeals to listeners and is rewarding to sing.

Before the first measure, next to the original clefs, the editor has added black noteheads to show the range of each part. The organ part, which doubles the voices, is found in one manuscript, but this anthem was probably most often performed by voices alone, as on the accompanying recording. There it is sung a perfect fourth higher than notated.

William Byrd (CA. 1540–1623)

Sing joyfully unto God

Full anthem

1580s–1590s

– More voices = More texture

49

From *The Byrd Edition*, gen. ed. Philip Brett, vol. 11, *The English Anthems*, ed. Craig Monson (London: Stainer & Bell, 1983), 82–90. © 1983 Stainer & Bell Ltd. Reproduced by permission. The pitch has been transposed up a minor third from C to Eb to conform with how, according to the editor, the original scheme of clefs was read.

William Byrd composed *Sing joyfully unto God*, a setting of the first four verses of Psalm 81, sometime during the 1580s or early 1590s. It was one of his most popular anthems, appearing in many manuscripts from the time, and had a long career, being printed in anthologies of English church music in 1641 and again in the eighteenth century. It is a full anthem, the English equivalent of the choral motet, as opposed to a verse anthem, which is scored for soloists with instrumental accompaniment, often alternating with the choir. Anthems were performed in Church of England services and used for home devotions. The composition of such sacred music with text in the vernacular rather than in Latin was a defining contribution of the Reformation.

Several distinctive traits distinguish Byrd's style in sacred choral music from those of other composers such as Josquin (NAWM 44–45), Palestrina (NAWM 51), Victoria (NAWM 52), or Lassus (NAWM 53). In the music of Byrd, cadences are more frequent, imitation is freer and almost constant, homophony is rare, and the voice lines are often more angular and energetic.

This anthem is in the Ionian mode, number 11 in Glareanus's scheme of twelve modes, with a final of C (transposed here to Eb, as explained below) and a range in soprano 1 and tenor of about an octave above the final. Byrd made both the mode and the structure of phrases clear through the many cadences, most on the final or reciting tone of the mode (as transposed here, Eb and Bb respectively). The typical cadence includes bass motion of a fifth down or fourth up (as in measures 4–5 and 9–10). This type of cadence became increasingly common over the course of the sixteenth century and is the ancestor of the modern dominant-to-tonic cadence. However, during the sixteenth century, most such cadences still included a suspension, which was a remnant of the older sixth-to-octave cadence.

In the first point of imitation (measures 1–10), involving only four of the six parts, the subject is treated freely; the rising fifth of the first entrance is answered with a second, fourth, and octave. Vigorous leaps bring to life texts such as "Sing loud" (measure 10) or "Take the song" (measure 26). Melodies consisting mostly of skips and leaps, such as soprano 2, tenor, and bass in measures 10–12, are not unusual. This style contrasts strongly with the largely stepwise motion in music by Josquin or Palestrina. Leaps are especially common in the bass, even two successive leaps in the same direction (see measures 14–15), as the bass sounds the root of each successive triad (to use modern terminology).

Homophonic texture is infrequent in this piece. More often, two or more voices move together in rhythmic unison, as at "Blow the trumpet in the new moon" (measures 30–38), where the fanfare-like figures evoke the text. Byrd paid close attention to the rhythm of the words as well as their meaning. Unstressed syllables most often fall on weak beats, while stressed syllables appear on the main beats (whole notes in the transcription) or are accented by syncopation.

This anthem was originally notated a minor third lower, with no key signature; the first note of each part, in its original clef, is shown at the beginning. The particular combination of clefs has been interpreted by some modern scholars as a notational convention that implies a transposition up a minor third, as shown here and as sung on the accompanying recording. Such a convention would have been useful at a time when singers rarely encountered key signatures other than a single flat. Yet not all modern authorities agree on this interpretation. Some sources for the piece include an organ accompaniment, as shown here, but it is probably not by Byrd. The piece was probably composed for unaccompanied voices, as it is performed on the recording.

Nicholas Gombert (CA. 1495–CA. 1560)

Ave regina caelorum

Motet

PUBLISHED 1541

50

From Nicholas Gombert, *Opera Omnia*, vol. 8, ed. Joseph Schmidt-Görg, Corpus mensurabilis musicae 6 (N.p.: American Institute of Musicology, 1970), 36–41. The chant *Ave regina caelorum* is transcribed from the Poissy Antiphonal, Melbourne, State Library of Victoria, Ms. *096.1/R66A, f.396r, described by John Stinson, "The Poissy Antiphonal: A Major Source of Late Medieval Chant," *La Trobe Library Journal* 51 and 52 (October 1993): 50–59, with a facsimile of this chant on page 57.

Ave, regina caelorum.	Hail, Queen of Heaven.
Ave, domina angelorum.	Hail, mistress over the angels.
Salve radix sancta,	Hail, holy root,
Ex qua mundo lux est orta.	out of whom the Light arose over the world.
Gaude gloriosa,	Rejoice, glorious lady,
Super omnes speciosa.	beautiful above all others.
Vale valde decora,	Go well, most gracious lady,
Et pro nobis semper Christum exora.	and for us always pray to Christ.

Nicholas Gombert, a native of Flanders, was a singer, master of the choirboys, and unofficial court composer in the chapel of Charles V, Holy Roman emperor and king of Spain. As part of the royal chapel, Gombert traveled with Charles throughout his broad domain, which included Austria and parts of Italy and Germany as well as Spain and Flanders. He composed ten masses, eight Magnificats, and more than 70 chansons but is best known for his over 160 motets. He published four books of motets, two for four voices (1539 and 1541) and two for five voices (1539 and 1541), likely all composed for Charles's chapel.

Ave regina caelorum is from the second book of motets for five voices. It is a setting of the text of one of the four Marian antiphons, chants addressed to the Virgin Mary, mother of Jesus, and sung at Compline, the last Office service of the day. The motet was presumably intended for performance at Compline but may also have been used at mass or in other services for Mary, in the same way that lines from this text found their way into hymns and other songs addressed to the Virgin. About a quarter of Gombert's motets were settings of Marian texts, showing the important role of devotions to Mary in the Catholic Church of his time.

Writing in 1556, Hermann Finck described Gombert as a "pupil of Josquin," a connection that is strengthened by the *déploration* (memorial piece) Gombert wrote on Josquin's death. Finck continued that Gombert "shows all musicians the path, nay more, the exact way to refinement and the requisite imitative style. He composes music altogether different from what went before. For he avoids pauses, and his work is rich with full harmonies and imitative counterpoint."

Ave regina caelorum exemplifies this new style. The melodies are smooth, mostly stepwise, and largely syllabic, interleaved with decorative melismas. Every phrase of text is set in a point of imitation. Imitation can be relatively exact, as at the beginning on "Ave," or show considerable variety among voices in rhythm and contour, as in the next point of imitation, on "regina." The order of entries is constantly varied, and one or more voices may repeat the phrase as another entry after all five voices have entered, as the altus does at measure 7 and cantus, tenor, and bassus do at measures 13–14. Gombert indeed "avoids pauses"; the points of imitation overlap in unbroken succession, without the breaks between phrases that typify Josquin's motets (compare NAWM 44). Gombert frequently thins the texture to four or even three voices (see for instance measures 45–50), but does not employ the strong contrasts of texture that Josquin uses to set off each phrase or section from its surroundings, such as alternating pairs of voices or juxtaposing imitation with homophony. Instead, the music unfolds in one continuous strand.

Yet, as in Josquin, there are strong cadences at the end of each phrase of text, such as those at measures 9, 17, 22, and 31, that articulate the music and establish the modal center on F. Sixteenth-century composers and theorists saw the modes as a link between the Christian tradition and the emotional effects of ancient music, so making the mode clear was of vital concern. Theorists considered the cantus and tenor to be the two voices that defined the mode. Here, both range from a fourth below to a fifth above the final, indicating that this piece is in the plagal mode on F, called Hypolydian (mode 6), rather than in the authentic Lydian mode (mode 5).

Many of Gombert's motets are based on plainchants, paraphrasing each phrase of the chant in succession and treating it in a point of imitation. We have seen this procedure in the opening section of Josquin's *Ave Maria . . . gratia plena* (NAWM 44). In this motet, Gombert not only sets the text of the chant *Ave regina caelorum* but also paraphrases its melody phrase by phrase.

There were several variants of the text and melody of *Ave regina caelorum*. Gombert based his motet on a version of the chant specific to the Dominican order, transcribed here from a fourteenth-century manuscript used by nuns in a Dominican convent:

A - ve, re - gi - na cae - lo - rum.

A - ve, do - mi - na an - ge - lo - rum.

Sal - ve ra - dix san - cta ex qua mun - do lux est or - ta.

Gau - de glo - ri - o - sa, su - per om - nes spe - ci - o - sa.

Va - le val - de de - co - ra, Et pro no - bis sem - per Chris - tum ex - o - ra.

There are two pairs of verses, each pair with its own melody, followed by a longer final verse that varies the melody of the second pair. Most versions of this chant use B♭ in the opening melodic figure on "Ave," so that the first interval is a descending whole step. But the Dominicans reformed their liturgy and chant in the mid-thirteenth century, and one of the changes they made was to avoid using B♭ whenever possible. In this chant, that alteration results in an opening figure that begins with a descending half step rather than a whole step. As is apparent in the first point of imitation in the motet, where every voice begins with a descending half step, Gombert follows the Dominican version shown above.

The Dominican form of the melody is also distinctive in other ways that match Gombert's motet, featuring more melodic repetition than other variants and using the same cadential figure for every sentence in the text and twice in the final verse (at "pro nobis" as well as "exora"). Since it appears so often in the source melody, this motive also occurs frequently in Gombert's motet, paraphrased in different ways, and it saturates the closing passage (beginning with the tenor at measure 88).

For each point of imitation throughout the motet, Gombert paraphrases the segment of chant melody for that same phrase of text, occasionally borrowing from elsewhere in the chant as well. The relationship between the motet and its source varies considerably, from the almost exact borrowing at the opening "Ave" to more modified reworking at "Gaude gloriosa" and little or no resemblance at "Et pro nobis," where Gombert may have avoided echoing the chant in order to save that motive for his closing section. After they enter, voices freely diverge from the chant melody. For listeners familiar with the chant, the motet weaves a luxurious fantasy on its melodic ideas. For us today, armed with a score, looking at how Gombert reworks each idea in turn is a lesson in the variety and flexibility of the Renaissance art of paraphrase.

Giovanni Pierluigi da Palestrina
(1525/6–1594)

Pope Marcellus Mass: Credo and Agnus Dei I

Mass

CA. 1560

51

(a) Credo

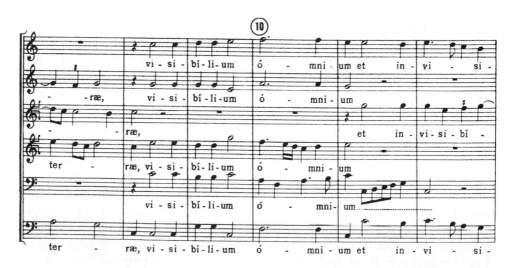

First published in Palestrina, *Missarum Liber secundus* (Second Book of Masses, Rome, 1567). From *Opere complete di Giovanni Pierluigi da Palestrina*, ed. Raffaele Casimiri, vol. 4 (Rome: Edizione Fratelli-Scalera, 1939): 177–87 and 194–96. Reprinted by permission of the Fondazione Istituto Italiano per la Storia della Musica, Rome.

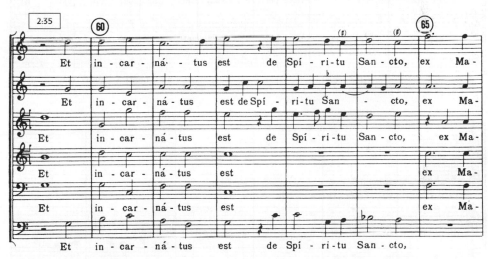

Credo in unum Deum, Patrem omnipotentem, factorem caeli et terrae, visibilium omnium et invisibilium.

Et in unum Dominum Jesum Christum Filium Dei unigenitum.

Et ex Patre natum ante omnia saecula.

Deum de Deo, lumen de lumine, Deum verum de Deo vero.

Genitum, non factum, consubstantialem Patri: per quem omnia facta sunt.

Qui propter nos homines et propter nostram salutem descendit de caelis.

Et incarnatus est de Spiritu Sancto ex Maria Virgine: et homo factus est.

Crucifixus etiam pro nobis: sub Pontio Pilato passus, et sepultus est.

Et resurrexit tertia die, secundum Scripturas.

Et ascendit in caelum: sedet ad dexteram Patris.

Et iterum venturus est cum gloria judicare vivos et mortuos: cujus regni non erit finis.

Et in Spiritum Sanctum, Dominum, et vivificantem: qui ex Patre, Filioque procedit.

Qui cum Patre, et Filio simul adorator, et conglorificatur: qui locutus est per Prophetas.

Et unam sanctam catholicam et apostolicam Ecclesiam.

Confiteor unum baptisma in remissionem peccatorum.

Et exspecto resurrectionem mortuorum.

Et vitam venturi saeculi. Amen.

I believe in one God, Father Almighty, maker of heaven and earth, and of all things visible and invisible.

And in one Lord Jesus Christ, the only-begotten Son of God.

Born of the Father before all ages.

God of God, light of light, true God of true God.

Begotten, not made, being of one substance with the Father, by whom all things were made.

Who for us humans and for our salvation descended from heaven.

And was made incarnate by the Holy Spirit of the Virgin Mary, and was made man.

And was crucified for us; under Pontius Pilate He died, and was buried.

And rose again on the third day, according to the Scriptures.

And ascended into heaven, and sits at the right hand of the Father.

And He shall come again with glory to judge the living and the dead; of whose kingdom there shall be no end.

And in the Holy Spirit, Lord and giver of life, who proceeds from the Father and the Son.

Who, together with the Father and the Son, is worshiped and glorified; who spoke by the prophets.

And one holy, Catholic, and Apostolic Church.

I acknowledge one baptism for the remission of sins.

And I await the resurrection of the dead.

And the life of the world to come. Amen.

(b) Agnus Dei I

Agnus Dei, qui tollis peccata mundi: Lamb of God, who takest away the sins
  miserere nobis.   of the world: have mercy on us.

The relation of this mass to Pope Marcellus II, who reigned for only twenty days in 1555, is uncertain. It became Palestrina's most famous mass thanks to a legend that he composed it in order to demonstrate to the Council of Trent (1545–63) that it was possible to write a polyphonic mass that was reverent in spirit and did not obscure the words, thus saving polyphonic music from condemnation by the church. The legend is probably untrue, but it was widely believed in part because the text of the mass is set so clearly. Unlike most other masses we have seen (NAWM 26, 38b, and 45), and unlike most of Palestrina's masses, this one is not based on an existing piece of music.

The Credo is a particularly challenging section of the mass to compose because of the importance and length of the text. In this setting, Palestrina abandoned imitation for the sake of clear diction and brevity. The voices pronounce a given phrase, not in the staggered manner of imitative polyphony typified by Gombert's motet *Ave regina caelorum* (NAWM 50), but simultaneously in the same rhythm, etching the text in the hearer's consciousness. Palestrina avoided monotony by dividing the six-voice choir into smaller groups and combining the different voices in constantly varying ways. He reserved the full six-voice ensemble for climactic or particularly significant phrases, such as "per quem omnia facta sunt" (by whom all things were made); this is the first instance in the Credo when all six voices sing together, and it creates a musical image for the word "all." The six voices also sing together on the phrase "Et incarnatus est" (And was made incarnate), a point Palestrina emphasized because it is one of the central mysteries of the Christian faith. Other portions of the text are sung by three, four, or five voices at a time. Because there is little of the usual imitation or repetition, some voices do not sing some phrases of the text. Where clarity of the text is not an issue, as in the closing passage on "Amen" (measures 186–97), Palestrina returns to his more customary imitative style.

The section beginning at measure 13 illustrates Palestrina's flexible approach to musical textures. One group of four voices sings "Et in unum Dominum" (And in one Lord), and another group of four voices answers by repeating those words and completing the thought ("Jesum Christum"). Then "Filium Dei unigenitum" (only-begotten Son of God) is sung by three voices, symbolizing the three-in-one essence of the Trinity. The texture here is like that of fauxbourdon (see NAWM 37), which by Palestrina's time was considered old-fashioned or even crude. Yet Palestrina applied the sound of fauxbourdon to great effect here and elsewhere in the Credo; harmonies of sixths and thirds provide relief from the almost constant fifth-third combinations, and the texture also suggests the sacred by evoking the aura of a distant but still remembered past.

Throughout this section of the Credo, each phrase closes on a sixth-to-octave cadence. Palestrina preserved forward motion by postponing a full cadence until measure 27 and by beginning the next phrase immediately after each cadence with a syncopated sonority that enters on the next half beat (the next quarter note, in this transcription). He also used syncopation to stress accented syllables, such as the first syllables of "Dominum" and "Jesum." These syncopations contribute to a constantly varying rhythmic surface in which no two successive measures have the same rhythm.

As was common in setting the Credo, Palestrina divided the text into smaller sections. He set the portion beginning at "Crucifixus" for only four voices (measure 74), then returned to six voices at "Et in Spiritum Sanctum" (measure 116). He occasionally illustrates the text through musical imagery, though less often than Josquin or Lassus in their motets (see NAWM 44 and 53). Some of the imagery is obvious, such as when the voices descend together at "descendit de caelis" (descended from Heaven) in measures 53–58, and when the upper voices ascend at "Et ascendit in caelum" (And ascended into Heaven) in measures 92–94. Other imagery is more subtle, such as when four voices sing "consubstantialem" (of one substance) in measures 40–42; this is a variant of the previous phrase and thus "of one substance" with it.

Palestrina used a similar approach for the Gloria of this mass, which also has a long and theologically crucial text. But the movements with shorter texts would be too brief if set in the same way, so there Palestrina turned to imitation and development of motives to create movements of sufficient weight and splendor, aware that the familiar text would be heard and understood as it was reinforced by repetition in all voices.

In Agnus Dei I, the opening subject is sung nine times, each statement differing somewhat from the others, in a point of imitation that lasts fifteen measures. This same subject is treated in imitation at the opening of the Kyrie and appears in the bassus at the beginning of the Credo (see measures 1–7, Bassus I and II), so that it serves to some extent as a head motive for the mass. "Qui tollis peccata mundi" (who takes away the sins of the world) is also treated imitatively, but the subject is even more varied from one voice to another, and whole phrases repeat in different voices with alterations in the counterpoint (compare measures 15–19 to measures 19–23), producing an intense development of the musical material. Each voice sings accented syllables on different beats, spinning out its line at its own pace, though at times two voices move together in parallel tenths (see measures 15–18, cantus and bassus I). The final phrase, "miserere nobis" (have mercy on us), receives similar treatment.

Palestrina's melodies typically move by step, and any skips or leaps are usually followed by stepwise motion in the opposite direction to fill in the gap. The counterpoint is mainly consonant. According to strict rules, only certain dissonances are allowed, all preceded and followed by consonances. These include passing tones, neighbor tones, suspensions, and cambiatas (figures in which a voice skips a third down from a dissonance to a consonance and then moves up a step to the expected tone of resolution, as in the cantus at measures 6–7 of the Agnus Dei). Final sonorities of each section and of major subsections most often include thirds, creating full triads instead of the open fifths and octaves typical in earlier music.

In the original publications of the *Pope Marcellus Mass*, repetitions of text were not indicated even when they were clearly intended by the composer. In the edition included here, the repetitions have been supplied in italics by the editor, as in the cantus and tenor II in measures 16–18 of the Credo. As printed, the music is almost wholly diatonic, but singers likely added alterations through musica ficta, as indicated above the staff by the editor. Of the three required statements of "Agnus Dei" (see NAWM 3i), only the first is included here. For the second, singers either would have repeated the first or would have sung plainchant. Palestrina scored the last statement for seven voices (Agnus Dei II, omitted in this anthology).

Tomás Luis de Victoria (1548–1611)

O magnum mysterium   *Missa O magnum mysterium*: Kyrie

Motet   Imitation mass

CA. 1570   CA. 1580s

52

Imitative entrances

(a) *O magnum mysterium*

First published in Victoria, *Motectae* (Venice, 1572). From Tomás Luis de Victoria, *Opera omnia*, vol. 2, *Motetes I–XXI*, ed. Felipe Pedrell, rev. ed. Higinio Anglès, Monumentos de la música española 26 (Barcelona: Instituto español de musicología, 1965–68), 7–9. We have made diligent efforts to contact the copyright holder to obtain permission to reprint this selection. If you have information that would help us, please write to Permissions Department, W. W. Norton & Company, Inc., 500 Fifth Avenue, New York, NY 10110.

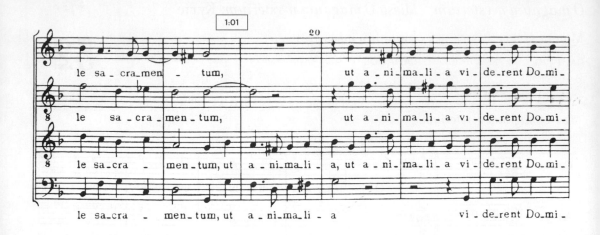

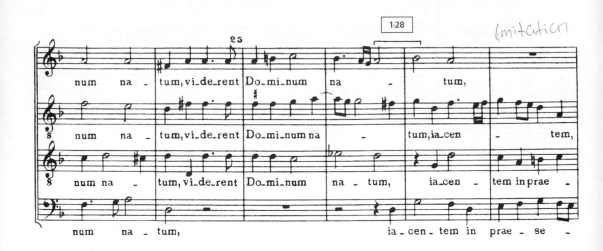

O magnum mysterium, et admirabile
sacramentum, ut animalia
viderent Dominum natum,
iacentem in praesepio.
O beata Virgo,
cuius viscera meruerunt portare
Dominum Iesum Christum. Alleluia.

O great mystery and awesome
sacrament, that the animals
should see the Lord, newly born,
lying in the manger.
O blessed Virgin,
whose womb was worthy of bearing
the Lord Jesus Christ. Alleluia.

(b) *Missa O magnum mysterium*: Kyrie

First published in Victoria, *Missae . . . liber secundus* (Rome, 1592). From *Thomae Ludovici Victoria Abulensis Opera omnia*, ed. Felipe Pedrell, vol. 2 (Leipzig: Breitkopf & Härtel, 1902–13), 6–9. We have made diligent efforts to contact the copyright holder to obtain permission to reprint this selection. If you have information that would help us, please write to Permissions Department, W. W. Norton & Company, Inc., 500 Fifth Avenue, New York, NY 10110.

Kyrie eleison.   Lord have mercy.
Christe eleison.   Christ have mercy.
Kyrie eleison.   Lord have mercy.

O magnum mysterium is Victoria's most widely known piece and is a favorite of modern choirs. He likely composed it during his early years in Rome, where he went to study at age seventeen, and it was published in his first book of motets in 1572. Written for the Feast of the Circumcision on January 1, the motet conveys the mystery, awe, reverence, and joy of the Christmas season through the use of expressive motives, affecting harmonies, and contrasting textures. About twenty years after composing the motet, Victoria used it as the basis for an *imitation mass*, a mass in which each movement is based on the same polyphonic work and all voices of that work are adapted in the mass, but none is used as a cantus firmus. The motet (NAWM 52a) exemplifies Victoria's style, and the first movement of the mass (NAWM 52b) illustrates how an imitation mass differs from a cantus-firmus mass (see NAWM 38b) or paraphrase mass (see NAWM 45).

Like Josquin (see NAWM 43–45), Victoria was fond of paired imitation. That is evident at the beginning of the motet, where the cantus and altus are paired and are echoed several measures later by the tenor and bassus. Victoria used some expressive license in composing the subject. Palestrina almost always would follow a leap with stepwise motion in the opposite direction, but Victoria sometimes continued with another leap or with stepwise motion in the same direction. In this motet, the large leaps of a fifth, both down and up, capture the sense of "magnum" (big, large, or great), and the combination of these fifths with the rising and falling semitone on "mysterium" suggests a sense of mystery.

Victoria turned to homophony in measures 16–26 and changed the number of voices every two or three measures to create maximum variety of texture. (In this score, measure numbers are at the upper right of the measure, rather than at the beginning of the measure.) The poignant false relation (F♮ in one voice followed immediately by F♯ in another) in measures 20–21 is an element of Victoria's expressive vocabulary that would not appear in the music of Palestrina. Elsewhere similar fluctuations occur between E and Eb, C and C♯, and Bb and B♮, lending the music color and fluidity. Imitation, again with paired voices, resumes for the final clause of the first sentence, "iacentem in praesepio" (lying in the manger, in measures 27–39). After a brief silence, all four voices exclaim in awe, "O beata Virgo" (O blessed Virgin), and the outer voices weave a florid garland around the sustained inner voices. The final "Alleluia" is first set homophonically in a dancelike triple meter, then imitatively in duple.

The mode is transposed mode 2 (Hypodorian), with a final on G, one flat in the key signature, and a range in both cantus and tenor of about a fifth above and a fourth below the final. As would be expected in this mode, most strong cadences are on G, with others on D (measures 9, 25) and Bb (measure 48), the fifth and third of the mode. At both of the main cadences—at the end of the first sentence (measure 39) and at the end of the piece—B♮ is included in the final sonority, creating a full major triad (as we would describe it); such a substitution of a major third (later sometimes called a "Picardy third") for the modally prescribed minor third became common for final cadences in music composed during the seventeenth and eighteenth centuries.

The first section of the motet has two main points of imitation—at the opening and at "iacentum in praesepio"—and these are both adapted by Victoria in the Kyrie movement of his *Missa O magnum mysterium*. The first Kyrie parallels measures 1–16 of the motet, featuring paired imitation between cantus and altus followed by an almost exact repetition in tenor and bassus. Yet the motives are considerably reworked so that the mass actually features two related subjects (one in cantus and tenor, the other in altus and bassus) fashioned from the motet's single subject. The entire polyphonic texture of the motet is reproduced in all voices, yet each voice is altered in subtle and interesting ways, showing what more can be done with the existing material. The second Kyrie is based on the point of imitation at "iacentum in praesepio" in the motet, especially on measures 30–39, again reworking the entrances and the counterpoint.

The Christe may appear at first to be based on a freely invented subject, as is the case in some imitation masses. But it is actually a clever reworking of a homophonic passage in the motet, on "ut animalia" (measures 19–21), into a new point of imitation. The opening four notes of the bassus, d–e–f♯–g, are from measures 19–20 of the motet bassus, and the answer in the tenor paraphrases the g–a–bb–g–d' motion at the same location in the motet tenor. The altus in the Christe imitates the bassus figure an octave higher, as in the motet at measures 20–21, and the superius completes the point of imitation. Such radical transformations were one way for a composer to display his virtuosity in reworking given material.

In discussing imitation masses, there is potential for confusion in terminology. In the term "imitation mass," the word "imitation" refers to the relationship between the mass and the polyphonic work it imitates, which is known as its *model*. But "imitation" is also used to describe the relation between voices, as one voice imitates a melody that another has just presented, and this sort of imitation is a characteristic that imitation masses typically share with paraphrase masses. Indeed, just by looking at or hearing this Kyrie and the Kyrie from Josquin's *Missa Pange lingua* (NAWM 45), one may not be able to tell which is the imitation mass and which the paraphrase mass. This is because they differ in how they relate to the source of musical material (respectively, a polyphonic work and a monophonic melody), but not in style or texture (both use imitative counterpoint, with some passages in homophony or other textures). To avoid this potential confusion, some music historians use the terms *model mass* or *parody mass* instead of *imitation mass*.

As was becoming common in the later sixteenth century, most of the chromatic alterations, even at cadences, were marked by the composer rather than determined by the singers, as had previously been the frequent practice. In comparing the motet and mass, note that the two editors have chosen different ratios of reduction for the original notation; as a result, the primary beat is transcribed as a quarter note in the motet but as a half note in the mass. (The opening of the original notation is shown at the beginning of the motet.) Both pieces are sung on the accompanying recordings by male choirs with boys on the upper parts, as was customary because of the proscription against women singing in church.

Orlande de Lassus (1532–1594)

Cum essem parvulus

Motet

1579

53

Six voices

From Orlande de Lassus, *Mottetta, sex vocum, typis nondum uspiam excusa* (Munich, 1582).

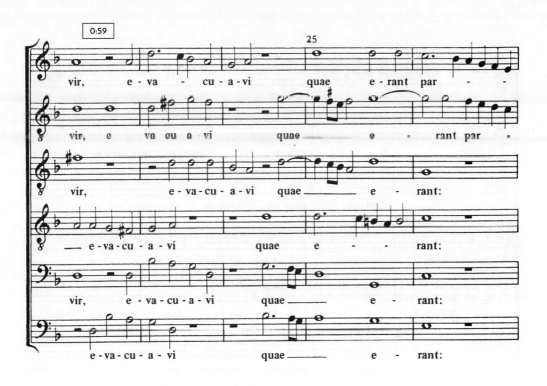

gno-scam sic - ut, sic - ut et co - gni-tus____

gno-scam sic - ut et co - gni-tus____ sum.

gno-scam sic - ut, sic - ut et____ co - gni-

gno - scam sic - ut et co-gni-tus sum, et co - gni-

gno-scam sic - ut____ et co - gni-tus sum.

gno - scam____ sic - ut et____ co - gni-

____ sum. Fi - - - -

Nunc au - tem____ ma - nent_____ Fi -

tus sum. Nunc au - tem ma - nent Fi - des,

tus sum. Nunc____ au-tem ma - nent Fi - - - -

Nunc au - tem ma-nent Fi - - -

tus sum. Fi - des,

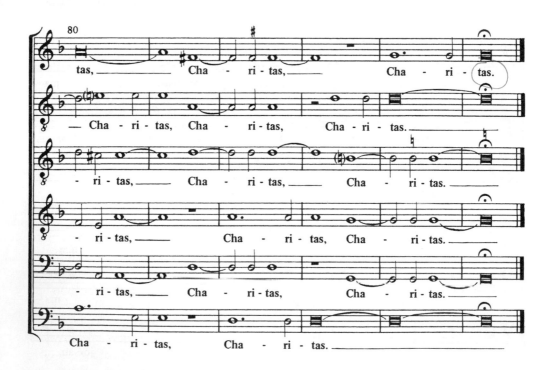

Cum essem parvulus,	When I was a child,
loquebar ut parvulus,	I spoke as a child,
sapiebam ut parvulus,	I understood as a child,
cogitabam ut parvulus;	I reasoned as a child;
quando autem factus sum vir,	but when I became a man,
evacuavi quae erant parvuli.	I put away things that are childish.
Videmus nunc per speculum	Now we see as if through a mirror
in aenigmate; tunc autem	in riddles; but then [we will see]
facie ad faciem.	face to face.
Nunc cognosco ex parte,	Now I know in part;
tunc autem cognoscam	but then I shall understand [fully]
sicut et cogitus sum.	just as I have been understood.
Fides, Spes, Charitas, tria haec:	Faith, hope, love [abide], these three:
major autem horum est Charitas.	but the greatest of these is love.
— 1 CORINTHIANS 13:11–13	

Cum essem parvulus was composed in 1579, according to the date on a manuscript now in the Bayerische Staatsbibliothek in Munich, and was published in a volume of Lassus's motets for six voices in 1582. The words are drawn from the first epistle of St. Paul to the Corinthians.

Like many sixteenth-century motets, *Cum essem parvulus* is divided into two parts, corresponding to the major division of the text. The motet is in G Hypodorian (the Hypodorian mode transposed up a fourth by adding a B♭ in the key signature). As was the frequent custom, the first part ends on the fifth degree D and the second part on the final G. (Note that the lowest voice in the texture is usually bassus I rather than bassus II.)

Lassus was famous in his own time for his forceful and imaginative projection of the words, and this motet features examples in almost every phrase. Texture, contrapuntal technique, form, melody, and figuration are all used to convey particular images in the text.

The opening words, "Cum essem parvulus" (When I was a child), are given to the two highest voices, cantus and altus I. The high range and thin two-voice texture evoke the voice of a child; indeed, these parts may well have been sung by boys in Lassus's time, since women were excluded from singing in Catholic church choirs, and boys often sang the highest parts. (The performance on the accompanying recording uses a mixed chorus of men's and women's voices.) From the child, our attention is drawn to the speaker, Paul, as the lower four voices of the choir sing "Loquebar" (I spoke), answered by the upper two parts on "ut parvulus" (as a child). The alternation of textures sounds like a dialogue, but it evokes the idea of memory, of a man remembering how he was as a boy. The parallel construction of the text—"I spoke as a child, I understood as a child, I reasoned as a child"— led the composer to create parallel constructions in the music. Each statement of "ut parvulus" is exactly the same, and the relatively short, quickly moving notes symbolize the diminutive movements of a child. Meanwhile, the lower voices vary their idea each time, always moving from a surprising G major sonority to B♭ major, yet growing more active with each repetition, as if to illustrate the growth in complexity of adult reasoning. Lassus's ways of depicting images and ideas in the text here vary from the obvious to the clever to the remarkably subtle.

The word-painting continues throughout. After the four lower parts begin the phrase "quando autem factus sum vir" (but when I became a man), the upper parts join in on the last three words, perhaps representing the boys becoming men. At "evacuavi" (I put away), all six voices enter in turn, but then drop out until only two are singing, a nice image for setting things aside. The word "parvuli" (childish) is illustrated by repeating the figure we have already heard four times on "parvulus." At "nunc per speculum" (now through a mirror), bassus I rises by step while the other voices fall (measures 30–31), like a reflection in a mirror. This is part of a longer phrase, translated as "Now we see as if through a mirror in riddles," whose sense of seeing only indirectly and with limited understanding is nicely captured by free, nonimitative counterpoint full of suspensions (measures 28–34). What a contrast at the next phrase, where the image of seeing clearly and face to face ("facie ad faciem") is conveyed by a sudden turn to homophonic declamation in root-position triads, first in duple, then in triple meter (measures 39–43). Coming together in rhythmic unison symbolizes the coming together of the soul with the divine, resolving the earlier enigmas.

The second part has equally strong musical images: consider how Lassus illustrates the words "ex parte" (in part) and "tria haec" (these three) through the number of voices he uses, how he emphasizes "Charitas" (Love) as greater than "Fides" (Faith) and "Spes" (Hope) through repetition and harmonic motion, and how he conveys the meaning of "major" (greatest) through the most elaborate point of imitation in the whole motet, in which each voice states the subject twice.

Thus all the aspects of the musical setting were stimulated by the words: the division of phrases and sections; the rhythm, accentuation, and melodic contour of each motive; the harmonic effects and cadences; the changes of texture; the various devices such as suspensions and imitation; and, of course, his clever illustration of the meanings and images in the text. Throughout, Lassus's music matches every rhetorical gesture and image of Paul's epistle.

Juan del Encina (1468–1529)

Oy comamos y bebamos

Villancico

CA. 1495

54

1. Oy co - ma - mos y be - ba - mos y can - te - mos y hol - gue - mos, que ma - ña - na a - yu - na - re - mos.
4. que cos - tum - br'es de con - çe - jo que to - dos oy nos har - te - mos,

Tenor — Oy co - ma - mos

1. Contra — Oy co - ma - mos

2. Contra — Oy co - ma - mos

[Fine]

2. Por on - rra de sant An - true - jo pa - ré - mo - nos oy bien an - chos,
3. en - bu - ta - mos es - tos pan - chos, rre - cal - que - mos el pe - lle - jo,

Por hon - ra

Por hon - ra

Por hon - ra

[D.C. al Fine]

From *La obra musical de Juan del Encina*, ed. Manuel Morais (Salamanca: Centro de Cultura Tradicional, 1997), 199–200. Departamento de Cultura, Diputacion de Salamanca. Used by permission.

0:00	Oy comamos y bebamos	Today let's eat and drink
	y cantemos y holguemos,	and sing and have a good time,
	que mañana ayunaremos.	*for tomorrow we will fast.*
0:09	Por onrra de sant Antruejo	To honor Saint Carnival
	parémonos oy bien anchos,	today let's end up very fat,
0:16	enbutamos estos panchos,	let's stuff our bellies,
	rrecalquemos el pellejo,	let's stretch our skin,
0:22	que costumbr'es de conçejo	for it's a custom of the council
	que todos oy nos hartemos,	that today we all gorge ourselves,
	que mañana ayunaremos.	*for tomorrow we will fast.*

0:31	Honrremos a tan buen santo	Let's honor this good saint
	porque en hambre nos acorra;	so that in hunger he may assuage us;
	comamos a calca porra,	let's eat at top speed,
	que mañana ay gran quebranto.	for tomorrow there will be great affliction.
	Comamos, bebamos tanto,	Let's eat, let's drink so much,
	hasta que nos rrebentemos,	until we burst,
	que mañana ayunaremos.	*for tomorrow we will fast.*

0:53	Beve, Bras; más tú, Beneyto;	Drink Bras; and you more, Beneyto;
	beva Pidruelo y Llorente.	drink Pidruelo and Llorente.
	Beve tú primeramente,	You drink first;
	quitarnos has deste preito.	let's give up arguing about it.
	En bever bien me deleyto.	Drinking delights me.
	Daca, daca, beveremos,	Give here, let's all drink,
	que mañana ayunaremos.	*for tomorrow we will fast.*

1:15	Tomemos oy gasajado,	Let's take pleasure today,
	que mañana biene la muerte;	for tomorrow comes death;
	bevamos, comamos huerte;	let's drink, let's eat heartily;
	vámonos para el ganado,	[then] let's return to our herd,
	no perderemos bocado,	let's not lose a mouthful,
	que comiendo nos iremos,	for eating we will go,
	que mañana ayunaremos.	*for tomorrow we will fast.*

Encina was the first major Spanish playwright and a leading exponent of the villancico during the late fifteenth century, when he was in the service of the duke of Alba. Like many of his compositions, this villancico was included in the Cancionero Musical de Palacio, a manuscript anthology compiled ca. 1500–1520, perhaps for the duke's court.

Drawing on ancient Greek and Latin models, Renaissance poets cultivated *pastoral* poetry and drama, which centered on the idealized lives of shepherds and their loves in beautiful natural settings. In this tradition, for entertainment at court, Encina created *eclogues*, pastoral plays in one act, and had his characters sing *villancicos*, songs whose poetry and musical style were modeled on those of Spanish rustic and popular songs. *Oy comamos y bebamos* is the concluding villancico from an eclogue performed at the duke of Alba's court on Fat Tuesday in 1495, in which shepherds prepare and consume their annual feast. Fat Tuesday (also known as Shrove Tuesday and Mardi Gras) is a traditional time of feasting on the last day of the Carnival season before the fasting and renunciation of Lent begin on Ash Wednesday. Here the shepherds in the eclogue extol the pleasures of eating and drinking, while providing entertainment for the nobles and courtiers who were doing the same as they watched the play. The music is designed to sound rustic, with a primarily homophonic texture, simple harmonies (mostly what we would call root-position triads), and dancelike rhythms that use hemiola effects to shift between $\frac{6}{8}$ and $\frac{3}{4}$ meters.

Villancicos vary in form, but all include a refrain, called an *estribillo*, and one or more stanzas, called *coplas*. Here the refrain has three lines, and the stanzas have seven. Musically, the stanzas begin with a section called *mudanza* ("change") that includes two statements of a musical unit, each set to two lines of poetry. In many villancicos, the mudanza presents new material, but here it uses the last two-thirds of the refrain. The last three lines of each stanza, called the *vuelta* ("return" or "repetition"), repeat the music of the refrain. As in most villancicos, only the last line of the refrain text is repeated at the end of each stanza. When the mudanza includes only new material, the resulting form is aB ccaB ccaB, and so forth (using letters for musical repetitions and capitalization to show textual repetition), which resembles the AAB stanza form we have seen since troubadour songs and cantigas (see NAWM 9 and 12). However, in this villancico, the three brief phrases of the refrain repeat throughout, in the pattern abC bcbcabC bcbcabC, and so forth, as shown in the table below. The essential aspect of the villancico form is the two-fold repetition of a segment of music at the beginning of each stanza, followed by the repetition of the music of the refrain, culminating in a textual refrain. The resulting musical and poetic form resembles and apparently derives from that of the medieval cantigas (see NAWM 12) and is a relative of the virelai (see NAWM 27) and ballata (see NAWM 32).

Musical form	Phrases of music	Poetic lines	Rhyme	Poetic form
		Estribillo		
A	a	Oy comamos y bebamos	a	Estribillo
	b	y cantemos y holguemos,	b	
	C	*que mañana ayunaremos.*	b	Refrain line
		Copla 1		
B	b	Por onrra de sant Antruejo	c	Mudanza
	c	parémonos oy bien anchos,	d	
B	b	enbutamos estos panchos,	d	
	c	rrecalquemos el pellejo,	c	
A	a	que costumbr'es de conçejo	c	Vuelta
	b	que todos oy nos hartemos,	b	
	C	*que mañana ayunaremos.*	b	Refrain line

As in most fifteenth-century villancicos, the text appears only in the upper voice, which carries the main melody. The other parts may have been sung or may be performed on instruments, as they are in the recording accompanying this anthology. On that recording, the singer and players both add decorative embellishments to later stanzas, following the typical performance practice of the time.

Marchetto Cara (CA. 1465–1525)

Mal un muta per effecto

Frottola

CA. 1500

55

From William F. Prizer, *Courtly Pastimes: The Frottole of Marchetto Cara* (Ann Arbor: UMI Research Press, 1980), 399–402. Text underlay for lower three voices added for this anthology by David Botwinik; the original source and Prizer's edition have only a text incipit for these three voices of the first line of the poem. Translation by Peggy Forsyth, from liner notes for *Circa 1900*, *Renaissance Music from the Courts of Mantua and Ferrara* (London: Chandos Records CHAN 833, 1984). We have made diligent efforts to contact the copyright holder to obtain permission to reprint this selection. If you have information that would help us, please write to Permissions Department, W. W. Norton & Company, Inc., 500 Fifth Avenue, New York, NY 10110.

El suo pro-prio na-tu-ra-le, El suo pro-prio na-tu-ra-le.

El suo pro-prio na-tu-ra-le, El suo pro-prio na-tura-le.]

El suo pro-prio na-tu-ra-le, El suo pro-prio na-tu-ra-le.]

El suo pro-prio na-tu-ra-le, El suo pro-prio na-tu-ra-le.]

0:00	Mal un muta per effecto El suo proprio naturale; Ben far no, ben si pò male Ad ogn'un al suo dispecto.	One cannot truly change one's nature; unable to do good, well able to do harm, each to his own vice.
	Mal un muta per effecto El suo proprio naturale.	One cannot truly change one's nature.
0:35	Ogni cosa sua natura Seguitar e di mestiero; Non è arte nè misura Che mai faci el falso vero; Non è biancho quel ch'è nero, Come chiar vede la vista; Non si pente un alma trista Cangie el tempo pur suo aspecto.	Everything naturally follows its own course. Neither Art nor Science ever fashioned truth from lies. What is black is not white, as is plain for all to see. A sinning soul does not repent despite Time's changing face.
1:01	Mal un muta . . .	One cannot truly . . .
1:11	L'armelin per non manchiarse Pria al nemico vien in mano; Mal la rana vil aparse Lieta fori del paltano; Chi è gentil, chi è vilano Ala fin si manisfesta; Non arar la regal vesta Cangie el tempo pur suo aspecto.	The ermine, to avoid being stained when confronted by its enemy, comes into one's hands. The fearful frog is never happy outside its pond. The good and the bad all come to light in the end. Do not pawn the royal robe despite Time's changing face.
1:38	Mal un muta . . .	One cannot truly . . .

1:48	Orna ben di sella e freno	A richly jewelled saddle and bridle
	Lassi nel misero e vile,	are only mean and cruel shackles
	Chè per questo non è apieno	to curb the freedom
	Un caval acto e gentile;	of a noble horse.
	Sta el porcho nel porcile,	A pig lives in a pigsty
	Glie convien che gli è el suo loco;	and that is its proper place.
	Sempre da calore el focho	Fire always gives its heat
	Cangie el tempo pur suo aspecto.	despite Time's changing face
2:14	Mal un muta . . .	One cannot truly . . .
2:24	Mille prove ò già fatto io	A thousand tokens have I showered
	In costei d'amor ver priva,	upon her who shows no love,
	In cui posi el pensier mio	keeping her in my thoughts
	Per voleria tener viva;	where she has ever lived,
	E nel mondo faria diva	desiring her to be in this world
	D'alta eterna e d'amor fama;	a goddess of great and eternal renown;
	Ma el sul mal e'l tristo brama,	but cruelty and harshness is all her love
	Cangie el tempo pur suo aspecto.	despite Time's changing face.
2:51	Mal un muta . . .	One cannot truly . . .

— TRANS. PEGGY FORSYTH

Marchetto Cara spent most of his career at the court in Mantua in northern Italy, working for the ruling Gonzaga family from 1494 to 1525. Music at court was strongly supported by the marquis, Francesco II Gonzaga, and his wife Isabella d'Este, from the ruling family of Ferrara. After their marriage in 1490, Isabella worked to increase the number of musicians at Mantua and encouraged them to set Italian poetry to music, making Mantua a leading center for Italian song around the turn of the sixteenth century. The principal genre was the frottola, and Cara was the most prolific composer of frottole.

Mal un muta per effecto, one of about 125 frottole that Cara composed for performance at the Mantuan court, was published in Ottaviano Petrucci's seventh book of frottole (Venice, 1507). Through most of its stanzas, the poem offers a series of illustrations for the maxim that things, animals, and people are true to their natures and cannot change; you cannot create truth from lies, change black to white, or conceal the nature of a bridle by decorating it with jewels or of a pig by giving it a beautiful home. Once we have sagely nodded our heads, the poet springs the point of the poem in the last stanza: despite all his efforts to woo her, his beloved is still as cruel and harsh as ever. The effect is simultaneously bitter and witty, deflating the woman he sought to please by implicitly comparing her to lies, sin, shackles, and pigs.

Although the term "frottola" is applied to musical settings of various types of poetry in popular style, this song manifests the poetic and musical form of the frottola proper, also called *barzelletta*. The poem consists of lines of eight syllables, grouped in a four-line *ripresa*, whose first two lines are immediately repeated and then return as a refrain, and eight-line stanzas, consisting of two two-line *piedi* ("feet") and a four-line *volta* ("return" or "repetition"). The terms for the parts of a frottola derive from those asociated with the earlier ballata (see NAWM 32). The music is coordinated with this poetic structure through the scheme shown here:

Phrases of music	Music mm.	Poetic lines	Rhyme	Poetic form
		Ripresa		
‖: a	‖: 1–3	Mal un muta per effecto	a	
b :‖	4–6 :‖	El suo proprio naturale;	b	
b	7–9	Ben far no, ben si pò male	b	Ripresa
c c	‖: 10–12 :‖	Ad ogn'un al suo dispecto.	a	
a a	‖: 13–15 :‖	Mal un muta per effecto	a	
b d	16–21	El suo proprio naturale.	b	Refrain
		Stanza 1		
a	1–3	Ogni cosa sua natura	c	
b	4–6	Seguitar e di mestiero;	d	Piede
a	1–3	Non è arte nè misura	c	
b	4–6	Che mai faci el falso vero;	d	Piede
b	7–9	Non è biancho quel ch'è nero,	d	
c	10–12	Come chiar vede la vista;	e	
c	10–12	Non si pente un alma trista	e	Volta
a	13–15	Cangie el tempo pur suo aspecto.	a	
a	13–15	Mal un muta per effecto	a	
b d	16–21	El suo proprio naturale.	b	Refrain

The repeated phrases in the ripresa (measures 1–6, 10–12, and 13–15) create the musical form abab bcca abd. This same sequence of musical phrases is then used for the eight lines of each stanza and the following refrain. An unusual feature of this frottola is that the last line of each stanza is the same, which helps to drive home the poetic point that time may pass but the basic nature of a person, animal, or thing does not change. Both the rhyme and the musical phrase for this final line of each stanza link it to the following refrain by echoing the first line of the refrain. Moreover, the rhyme scheme for each stanza matches the musical form, in that each rhyme gets its own musical phrase.

The meter as notated is different from the meter as felt in performance. In Renaissance notation, the meter signature ¢ indicated duple meter in what theorists called *proportia dupla* (doubled proportion) or *alla breve* (by the breve), meaning that the basic beat was felt on the breve (transcribed here as a half note) rather than the semibreve (transcribed as a quarter note). Today this sign, the last surviving symbol from the Renaissance system of proportions, means the same thing in practice—the beat is on the half note rather than the quarter note—but we call it *cut time*. Given that signature, we would expect to feel the music in $\frac{2}{2}$, as transcribed here. But instead the meter sounds like $\frac{3}{2}$ with an upbeat, as if it were written this way:

The measures seem to alternate between $\frac{6}{4}$ (as in the first full measure here) and $\frac{3}{2}$ (as in the second measure), producing a hemiola effect that was characteristic of frottole, canzonettas, and other popular song types during the sixteenth and early seventeenth centuries. A similar rhythmic effect is found in Encina's villancico in NAWM 54. Like villancicos, frottole were written for aristocratic entertainment but in a mock-popular style, evident in their simple melodies and harmonization primarily with what are now called root-position triads.

In the original source, only the cantus (topmost voice) is underlaid with the text of the *ripresa*. The other three voices are provided with a text incipit, the first line of the poem. They may have been played on instruments, as in the performance on the accompanying recording, but could also have been sung. To facilitate vocal performances, the score indicated here provides a possible text underlay for the three lower voices.

Jacques Arcadelt (CA. 1507–1568)

Il bianco e dolce cigno

Madrigal

CA. 1538

Note values halved. Published in *Il primo libro di Madrigali d'Archadelt a quatro con nuova gionta impressi* (Venice, 1539); first edition lost but probably from 1538. This edition from Arcadelt, *Opera omnia*, ed. Albert Seay, vol. 2, *Madrigali: Libro primo*, Corpus mensurabilis musicae 31 (American Institute of Musicology, F76 1970), 38–40. © American Institute of Musicology. Used with permission. For more on the metaphorical meanings of death in Florentine madrigals, see Stefano La Via, "*Eros* and *Thanatos*: A Ficinian and Laurentian Reading of Verdelot's 'Si lieta e grata morte,'" *Early Music History* 21 (2002): 75–116.

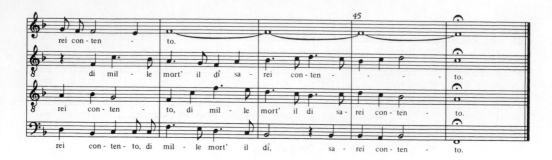

Il bianco e dolce cigno	The white and sweet swan
Cantando more. Et io	dies singing. And I,
Piangendo giung' al fin del viver mio.	weeping, come to the end of my life.
Stran' e diversa sorte,	Strange and different fate,
Ch'ei more sconsolato,	that it dies disconsolate,
Et io moro beato.	and I die happy—
Morte che nel morire,	a death that in dying
M'empie di gioia tutt'e di desire.	fills me fully with joy and desire.
Se nel morir' altro dolor non sento,	If when I die no other pain I feel,
Di mille mort' il dì sarei contento.	with a thousand deaths a day I would be content.

— ALFONSO D'AVALOS

Jacques Arcadelt's first book of madrigals was enormously popular. First printed in 1538, it went through 58 editions, the last of which was printed in 1654, over a century after its first appearance. Among its contents was perhaps the most famous of the early madrigals, *Il bianco e dolce cigno*, composed in the mid-1530s, while Arcadelt was in Florence, and reprinted in many anthologies.

Unlike a frottola, the poem used in a madrigal is not strophic and has no refrain or other repetition. This poem freely alternates lines of seven and eleven syllables with a free rhyme scheme (abb cdd ee ff). (Note that in Italian, vowels often elide; for example, the "-co" at the end of "bianco" and the "e" that follows are elided and treated as one syllable.)

The poetic imagery is based on the traditional belief that swans sing only when they die. The poet contrasts the swan's death with his own "happy" death, which fills him with "joy and desire." In the realm of desire, death had at least two possible metaphorical meanings at the time. In the Neoplatonic philosophy of the Florentine humanist Marsilio Ficino (1433–1499), whose *Sopra lo Amore* (On Love) introduced the concept of "platonic love" to western Europe, death was a metaphor for falling in love, as one's thoughts turn entirely to the beloved. If love is mutual, both lovers die a happy death as their souls leave their own bodies and live in each other. If we read the poem this way, the poet expresses his satisfaction that his love is returned. An earthier interpretation would read these lines as alluding to the belief that sexual climax resembles a "little death," a euphemism often used by Renaissance poets. In either reading, ironies abound: at the moment of death, the swan sings and yet is disconsolate, while the poet—experiencing a different kind of death—weeps but is filled with ecstasy, wishing for as many such deaths as possible. The sentiment is at once surprising and erotic.

Arcadelt's setting is primarily homophonic and has clearly marked rhythms, as in a frottola (see NAWM 55). But the first three lines do not follow the structure of the poem, as was customary in a frottola. The first cadence (measure 5) occurs in the middle of the second line of poetry, completing the thought and the sentence. The end of that line runs into the third, following the second sentence as it continues through the line ending (an effect called *enjambment*). Thus, Arcadelt preserved the syntax and meaning of the text and also underscored the word "more" (dies) with a dissonant suspension. At "Et io piangendo" (And I weeping), he illustrated the sharp contrast between the swan's song and the lover's tears with an excursion to an E♭ triad. The juxtaposition of major triads a whole step apart, causing a tritone relation between A and E♭ (measure 6), becomes a musical metaphor for death; this same relation exists between the triads on B♭ and C at "morire" (to die) in measure 26 and at "morir" in measure 31. Although the work is through-composed, without the repetitive form of a frottola or villancico, Arcadelt did occasionally introduce repetitions of both words and music, often with subtle variations (measures 10–15 repeat measures 5–10 with voices exchanging material, and later measures 38–42 repeat measures 34–38).

Arcadelt departed from the prevailing homophony at "stran' e diversa sorte" (strange and different fate) to suggest a musical image of difference. Then, at "mille mort' il di" (a thousand deaths a day), twelve single or paired entries sing a lilting motive. The multiple imitative entries evoke the idea of a high number, and the contentment conveyed by the motive and its rising and falling contour remind us of the metaphorical meaning of "death."

Madrigals were customarily performed with one voice on each part at upper-class gatherings that could include mixed groups of men and women. Sometimes instruments replaced one or more of the voice parts. In general, madrigals were intended for the pleasure of the performers themselves, rather than for an audience. Since each singer read only his or her line out of a partbook, one enjoyable aspect of sight-singing was the surprise of hearing how the parts fit together. Here, for example, the images created by changing between homophony and polyphony would be recognized only in performance.

Cipriano de Rore (1516–1565)

De la belle contrade d'oriente

Madrigal

CA. 1560–65

57

From Cipriano de Rore, *Opera omnia*, ed. Bernhard Meier, Corpus mensurabilis musicae 14 (American Institute of Musicology, 1969), 96–99. © American Institute of Musicology. Used with permission.

Da le belle contrade d'oriente
Chiar' e lieta s'crgca Ciprigna, ed io
Fruiva in braccio al divin idol mio
Quel piacer che non cape' humana mente,
Quando senti dopp'un sospir ardente:
"Speranza del mio cor, dolce desio,
T'en vai, haimè! Sola mi lasci! Adio!
Che sarà qui di me scur' e dolente?

From the fair regions of the East,
clear and bright rose Venus, and I
enjoyed in the arms of my divine idol
the pleasure that no human mind can understand,
when I heard after a burning sigh:
"Hope of my heart, sweet desire,
you go, alas! Alone you leave me! Farewell!
What will become of me, gloomy and sad?

Ahi crud' amor! Ben son dubbios' e corte	O cruel love! Much too tentative and brief are
Le tue dolcezze, poi ch'anchor ti godi,	your sweet caresses. Besides, you even take delight
Che l'estremo piacer finisc' in pianto."	in seeing this extreme pleasure end in tears."
Ne potendo dir più cinseme forte	Unable to say more, she held me tight,
Iterando gl'ampless' in tanti nodi,	repeating her embraces in many coils,
Che giamai ne fer più l'edro o l'acanto.	more than ever heather or acanthus made.

—ANONYMOUS

Cipriano de Rore probably composed *Da le belle contrade d'oriente* near the end of his life, since it was published posthumously, in his last collection of madrigals. The text is both erotic and moving: pleasant lovemaking is followed by the woman's complaint that her lover is about to leave her, leading to embraces that suggest both her passion and her desire to keep her lover close to her.

The poem is a sonnet, a form with fourteen eleven-syllable lines divided between an octave (the first eight lines) and sestet (the last six lines). Following the model set by the poet Francesco Petrarca (or Petrarch, 1304–1374), the anonymous poet further divided the octave into two quatrains and the sestet into two tercets, with an overall rhyme scheme of abba abba cde cde. (This differs from the Shakespearean sonnet, which has ten-syllable lines in the rhyme scheme abab cdcd efef gg.) Typically, the octave sets up a situation, and the sestet provides a twist or culmination.

In his setting, Rore marked the division between octave and sestet with the longest rest in the piece for all voices (measure 41), and he clearly delineated the divisions between quatrains and tercets with cadences at measures 21 and 56. He also observed the rhythm of the words very closely, placing longer notes on accented syllables, as in the first phrase. At times this produces syncopation, as it does in measures 13–15 and 49–51. As is typical of madrigals, Rore's setting is through-composed but occasionally repeats a phrase with some variation, especially at the end (compare measures 69–73 to measures 76–80).

This work represents the second generation of the madrigal, when five and six parts were common. The fifth voice is labeled *quintus* (Latin for "fifth"). Rore varied the texture from one voice to five, with diverse combinations of two, three, and four voices in between. Such changes of texture help to indicate the shift between the poet's narration and the woman's speech. The opening narration closes with a passage for the four lowest voices (measures 21–25). Then as the woman begins to speak, the top voice reenters and carries the leading melody throughout her entire speech (measures 25–56) while the others accompany. When she ceases to speak, the top voice briefly drops out and the lower voices resume the narration (measures 56–57).

Words and feelings are conveyed through striking musical devices. The ascent of the planet Venus is depicted with ascending scales that rise as much as a twelfth in the bassus. The woman's first phrase, "Speranza del mio cor" (Hope of my heart), brightly rises in the top line supported by major triads, suggesting hopefulness. At "Te'n vai, haimè" (You go, alas!), melodic half steps and minor thirds convey sadness, heightened by frequent rests that evoke sighs or sobs. At "sola mi lasci" (alone you leave me), the uppermost voice sings alone, with a rising chromatic line; such chromaticism, which lay outside the normal rules of music (and which we have not seen since the chromatic intervals of ancient Greek music in NAWM 2), was understood as a sign for grief. Later in the piece, Rore indulged in graphic musical images sometimes called *madrigalisms*. Closely consecutive entrances of the motive on "cinseme forte" (hold me tight) depict the meaning of the words, and in the last two lines multiple repetitions and fast runs represent the coils of embraces that resemble the climbing vines of heather or acanthus.

The harmony also reflects the poetry. The modal center is clearly F, and the piece is in mode 6 (Hypolydian), with both tenor and cantus moving primarily in the range from low C to high D. But during the woman's emotional speech, the harmony goes far afield, touching triads as distant as E major on the sharp side (measures 36–37) and Db major in the flat direction (measure 48) and including stark juxtapositions such as A major with C minor (measures 40–41, with both the cantus and the tenor moving by chromatic semitone). Half a century later, Claudio Monteverdi credited Rore with starting a "second practice" in which the melody and harmony were dramatic equal partners with the text and were freed from the restrictions of strict modal counterpoint; he must have had compositions such as this in mind.

In the edition included here, the barlines are indicated between staves but not within each staff in order to preserve the feel of the original notation, which had no barlines. The value of some notes extends beyond the next barline, such as the dotted quarter note at the end of the first measure.

Luca Marenzio (1553–1599)

Solo e pensoso

58

Madrigal

1590s

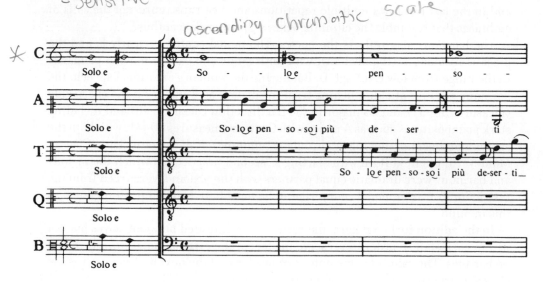

First published in Luca Marenzio, *Il nono libro de madrigali a 5 voci* (Venice: Gardano, 1599). This edition from *Music and Patronage in Sixteenth-Century Mantua*, ed. Iain Fenlon, vol. 2 (Cambridge: Cambridge University Press, 1982), 99–105. Reprinted with the permission of Cambridge University Press.

Word painting

Solo e pensoso i più deserti campi
Vo misurando a passi tardi e lenti;
E gl'occhi porto, per fuggire, intenti,
Dove vestigio uman l'arena stampi.
Altro scherno non trovo che mi scampi
Dal manifesto accorger de le genti;
Perchè negli atti d'allegrezza spenti
Di fuor si legge com'io dentro avampi:

Si ch'io mi credo homai che monti e piagge
E fiumi e selve sappian di che tempre
Sia la mia vita, ch'è celata altrui.
Ma pur sì aspre vie nè sì selvagge
Cercar non sò, ch'Amor non venga sempre
Ragionando con meco, et io con lui.

— FRANCESCO PETRARCA (PETRARCH)

Alone and pensive, the deserted fields
I measure with steps deliberate and slow;
and my eyes I hold in readiness to flee
from a place marked by human footsteps.
No other defense I find that can save me
from the peering eyes of people;
because when laughter and cheer are spent,
from outside can be read my inner flame.

So I have come to believe that mountains and beaches
and rivers and woods know of what fibers
is made my life, hidden from others.
Yet paths neither so rough nor wild
can I find where Cupid does not seek me always
to debate with me, and I with him.

This madrigal, published in Marenzio's ninth book of madrigals in the year of his death, is one of his most celebrated. A setting of a sonnet by Petrarch, it is a masterpiece of sensitive musical imagery, harmonic refinement, and deft counterpoint. The chromatic scale in the topmost voice, rising deliberately one half step per measure from g' to a'' and then descending to d'', represents the poet's measured steps as he wanders pensively in the deserted fields. Not only is this chromatic scale effective as tone painting, it also represents a new musical resource, because composers prior to Marenzio's generation had never extended chromatic motion for more than a few semitones in one direction. The descending arpeggios in the lower voices paint a forbidding, desolate landscape.

The jagged melodic subject imitated by all the voices in measures 25–33 depicts the poet's darting eyes as he looks for a hiding place—he fears that his eyes will reveal his inner fire. He feels safe among the mountains, beaches, rivers, and woods that already know him. These surroundings are depicted musically: the mountains by a series of leaps (measures 88–92) and the flowing rivers by eighth-note runs spanning a seventh passed from voice to voice (measures 93–100). When the poet complains that he cannot find terrain rough enough to discourage Cupid from following him, the voices stumble over each other in syncopations, suspensions, and cross-relations (measures 111–21). A subject that gallops headlong down an octave in dotted notes represents Cupid in hot pursuit, while two of the voices repeat the phrase "cercar non sò" (I cannot find).

Despite the chromaticism, *Solo e pensoso* is clearly in the mode of G, specifically mode 7 (Mixolydian), as indicated by the range of the cantus and tenor. G is the most common cadential note, followed by D, the mode's fifth degree (and reciting tone). The end of the sonnet's octave (the first eight lines) is marked by a strong cadence on D and a pause that delineate the two sections of the poetic form, octave and sestet, through harmonic means. The divisions between quatrains in the octave and between the tercets in the sestet are also strongly marked (measures 44 and 111).

In comparing *Solo e pensoso* with the madrigals of Arcadelt and Rore (see NAWM 56 and 57), we see the vocal lines becoming more complex and harder to sing with each generation. Although earlier madrigals were intended almost solely for convivial singing, for the entertainment of the singers themselves, late-sixteenth-century madrigals such as Marenzio's were often conceived for professional groups of singers, who played an increasingly important role at courts in northern Italy.

Carlo Gesualdo (CA. 1561–1613)

"Io parto" e non più dissi

Madrigal

CA. 1600

loves dissonance

59

16ths for "life"

First published in Carlo Gesualdo, *Madrigali a cinque voci libro sesto* (Gesualdo, 1611). This edition of Gesualdo, *"Io parto" e non più dissi*, from Gesualdo, *Sämtliche Madrigale für fünf Stimmen*, ed. Wilhelm Weismann, vol. 6, *Sechstes Buch* (Hamburg: Ugrino Verlag, 1957), 29–32. © 1957 Bärenreiter-Verlag. © Renewed. All rights reserved. Used by permission of European American Music Distributors Company, U.S. and Canadian agent for Bärenreiter-Verlag.

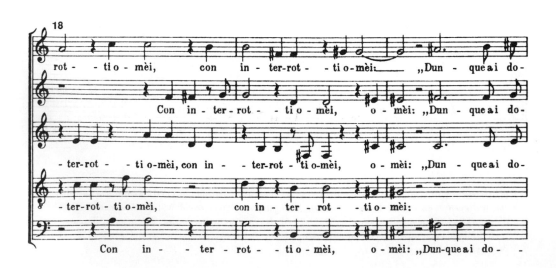

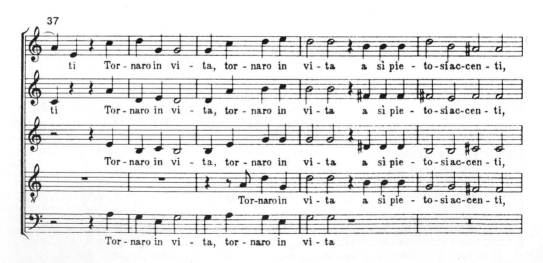

"Io parto" e non più dissi che il dolore	"I depart." I said no more, for grief
Privò di vita il core.	robbed my heart of life.
Allor proruppe in pianto e disse Clori	Then Clori broke out in tears and said,
Con interrotti omèi:	with interrupted cries of "Alas":
"Dunque ai dolori io resto. Ah, non fia mai	"Hence in pain I remain. Ah, may I never
Ch'io non languisca in dolorosi lai."	cease to pine away in sad laments."
Morto fui, vivo son che i spirti spenti	Dead I was, now I am alive, for my spent spirits
tornaro in vita a sì pietosi accenti.	return to life at the sound of such pitiable accents.

Although this madrigal was first published in 1611, it may have been composed in the late 1590s. It exemplifies Carlo Gesualdo's use of contrasts between chromatic and diatonic, dissonant and consonant, homophonic and imitative, and slowly and quickly moving passages to heighten the emotions and dramatic impact of the poem.

The text is full of strong images and changes in tone that made it well suited for Gesualdo's musical style. The poem hinges on surprise: it begins with a grief-stricken scene of two lovers parting and then turns erotic as the speaker implies that the couple has just made love (when he refers to his "spent spirits") and that the woman's distress arouses him again ("Dead I was, now I am alive"). The sudden change to present tense in the last sentence suggests that something more may ensue before he departs.

Gesualdo typically breaks up the lines of poetry into smaller units to isolate each strong and memorable image, and then gives each segment of text individual treatment. The first line is set to three distinct musical ideas: simple, matter-of-fact recitation for "Io parto" (I depart), set off with a rest to suggest the quotation marks; a chromatic rise to a half cadence for the speaker's comment that he said no more, implying unspoken pain; and an expression of grief through a descending line and a suspension on "dolore" (grief). The last figure is immediately intensified by a repetition a semitone higher with the descending whole steps altered to half steps (measure 6) and an ending on a very distant harmony (F# rather than C, as in measure 5). Similarly, the second line is split into two musical ideas: simple recitation on "Privò" and then descending imitative entries that represent a heart breaking. Chromaticism marks words associated with sadness, such as "pianto" (tears, measures 13–15) and "ai dolori io resto" (I remain in pain, measures 20–23), and the interrupted cries of "alas" are depicted with short rests that break into each part like breaths between sobs (measures 17–19). When Clori begins to speak (measure 20), the three upper parts declaim against the bass in the same way that the three middle parts did for the opening words of her male lover.

The music of the penultimate line (measures 28–37) contains three separate images: of death, through a chromatic succession of sustained chords; of renewed life, through a diatonic motive in rapid motion, close imitation, and syncopation; and of exhaustion—or the expending of spirits—through a rapid descending scale figure. In the last line, Gesualdo indulged in a pun by setting the word "accenti" (accents) with ornamental runs of the kind that when improvised were called *accenti*.

Despite his fragmentation of the poetic text through this great variety of musical figures and textures, Gesualdo achieved continuity by avoiding conventional cadences and thus linking each phrase to the next. Although often chromatic, the madrigal is clearly in mode 3 (Phrygian), as demonstrated by the first and final sonorities and by the ranges of the cantus and tenor (second part from the bottom). Gesualdo emphasized the main steps of the mode at beginnings and endings of lines and at pauses—E, the final (measures 1, 4, 7, 15, 23, 29, and 43–44); C, the mode's reciting tone (measures 5 and 12); A, the reciting tone of the related plagal mode (measures 17, 21, 26, and 37); and G (measures 11, 40, and 42) and B (measures 3, 25, and 40), the other strong notes in the mode.

The performance on the accompanying recording features one singer per part, accompanied by a lutenist who plays the bass line and fills in some of the harmony from the other parts. Lutes often accompanied madrigal singing and were useful in helping the singers find their pitches.

Claudin de Sermisy (CA. 1490–1562)

Tant que vivray

Chanson

CA. 1527

60

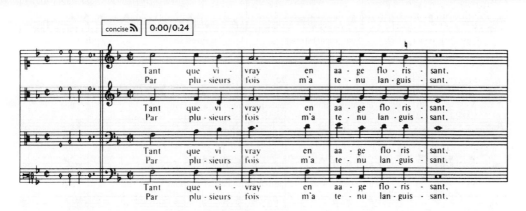

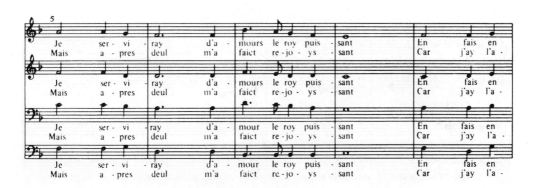

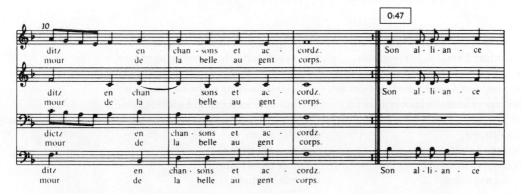

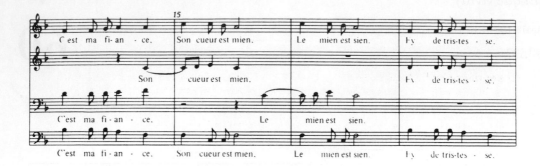

Tant que vivray en aage florissant,
Je serviray d'amours le roy puissant
En fais en ditz en chansons et accordz.
Par plusieurs fois m'a tenu languissant,
Mais apres deul m'a faict rejoyssant
Car j'ay l'amour de la belle au gent corps.
Son alliance
C'est ma fiance,
Son cueur est mien,
Le mien est sien.
Fy de tristesse,
Vive lyesse,
Puisqu'en amour a tant de bien.

As long as I am able-bodied,
I shall serve the potent king of love
through deeds, words, songs, and harmonies.
Many times he made me languish,
but after mourning, he let me rejoice,
because I have the love of the fair lady with the lovely body.
Her alliance
is my betrothal.
Her heart is mine,
mine is hers.
Shun sorrow.
Live in merriment,
because there is so much good in love.

1:05

Quand je la veulx servir et honorer,	When I want to serve and honor her,
Quand par escriptz veulx son nom decorer,	when I want to adorn her name with words,
Quand je la veoy et visite souvent,	when I see and visit her often,
Ses envieux n'en font que murmurer;	those jealous of her do nothing but whisper;
Mais nostre amour n'en scauroit moins durer;	but our love would not last any less,
Autant ou plus en emporte le vent.	however far the wind carries the rumors.
Maulgré envie,	Despite jealousy,
Toute ma vie,	all my life,
Je l'aymeray	I will love her
Et chanteray;	and sing of her;
C'est la premiere,	She is the first,
C'est la derniere	she is the last
Que j'ay servie et serviray.	that I have served and will serve.

— CLÉMENT MAROT

Claudin de Sermisy probably wrote *Tant que vivray* for the French royal court, where he spent most of his career. The Parisian publisher Pierre Attaingnant included it in a collection of chansons that was printed in early 1528. It became one of the most popular chansons of its era and was reprinted many times during the following century.

Tant que vivray represents a new type of chanson cultivated in France beginning in the 1520s and characterized by repetitive form, lighthearted words, lively rhythms, and syllabic and homophonic textures. The text of this chanson has two strophes, each sung to the same music, and Sermisy highlights the parallel structure and rhyme schemes of lines 1–3 and 4–6 of each stanza by repeating the same music, creating an AAB form for each strophe. Sectional repetitions like these are found in other light forms of the period, such as the frottola and canzonetta, but not in the madrigal. The poem expresses the happy feelings of a contented lover; the many short lines and quick rhymes in the second half of each stanza seem especially to suggest the bubbling up of joy.

The setting is syllabic and mostly homophonic. Even the apparent imitation between altus and tenor in measures 13–18 is simply the result of repeating short phrases in three-part homophony with the two inner voices alternating who takes the middle part. The principal tune is in the cantus, but the other parts are also tuneful and rewarding to sing, as is appropriate in a piece intended for amateurs to sing for their own enjoyment. The harmony consists mostly of what we would call root-position triads and strongly defines the pitch center of F. At some cadences, as the voices declaim the text together, a traditional suspension becomes an accented dissonance (for example, the *c″* in measure 3).

Because the same music is used for more than one set of words, it is evident that the composer did not set out to illustrate specific words or phrases in the text, but the general spirit of the setting captures the good cheer and optimism of the poem. The rhythms are lively and well suited to the words. The ends of the long lines of text are set to relatively long notes, and short lines end with repeated notes, thereby emphasizing the form of the poetry. The long-short-short rhythm that opens the piece became a characteristic feature of chansons; the same rhythm in diminution begins the B section, which moves along more rapidly than the first section, as suits its more active text.

Chansons such as this were usually sung by one voice per part. Alternatively, some or all parts could be played by instruments, or a performer could sing the top part while playing the bass line and notes from the other parts on the lute. The adaptability of such chansons is attested by a large number of arrangements for various forces. In the performance on the accompanying recording, a lute accompanies the singers, and some of the singers add embellishments during the second verse.

Orlande de Lassus (1532–1594)

La nuict froide et sombre

Chanson

CA. 1570S

61

From Jane Bernstein, *The Sixteenth-Century Chanson*, vol. 12, *Orlande de Lassus* (New York: Garland, 1987), 119–21. Reprinted by permission of Jane A. Bernstein.

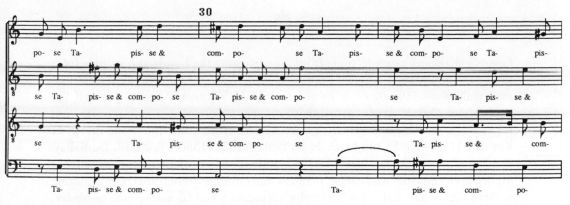

La nuict froide et sombre,	The night cold and dark,
Couvrant d'obscure ombre	covering with obscure shadows
La terre et les cieux,	the earth and the skies,
Aussi doux que miel,	as sweet as honey
Fait couler du ciel	pours down from the sky
Le sommeil aux yeux:	sleep to the eyes.
Puis le jour luïsant	Then the shining day,
Au labeur duisant	to encourage labor,
Sa lueur expose:	exposes its first light,
Et d'un tein divers	and with varied colors
Ce grand univers	it carpets and gives form to
Tapisse et compose.	this large universe.

— JOACHIM DU BELLAY

Lassus's chansons range in topic from the serious to the bawdy and in style from the light homophonic type we have seen in NAWM 60 to a style akin to Italian madrigals, especially those of Rore (see NAWM 57) and of Lassus himself (he wrote about 200). Most of Lassus's chansons are settings of anonymous poetry, but for some he used poems by well-known writers of his time, including Pierre de Ronsard (1524–1585) and Joachim Du Bellay (1522–1560). Ronsard, Du Bellay, and Jean-Antoine de Baïf (see NAWM 62) were members of the literary movement known as the Pléiade, who sought to renew and ennoble French poetry by imitating ancient Greek and Latin poetry in the vernacular. For *La nuict froide et sombre*, published in a collection of Lassus's chansons issued in 1576 by the Parisian printers Le Roy & Ballard, the composer used a Du Bellay poem whose focus on nature and humanity's place in the universe, reminiscent of imagery in ancient literature, is far from the love poetry found in most songs of the time.

The influence of the madrigal is readily seen in Lassus's approach to the text. He captures both the mood and the imagery of the poem through musical means. At the beginning, the cold and dark night, and the feeling of reverence it inspires, are suggested by relatively long notes and harmonies that move in the flat direction to B♭-major and G-minor triads (as we would call these sonorities). The sense of "covering" is slyly conveyed when the cantus dips below the altus (measures 4–5), and the "obscure shadows" are set to a harmonic move in a sharp direction, from A- to E- to B-major triads, appropriately mysterious in context. Rising lines lead from "la terre" (the earth) to "les cieux" (the skies), ending on the highest sonority in the piece (at measure 10). "Fait couler du ciel" (pours down from the sky, measures 13–15) is set with a running descent that ends with a leap up to "ciel" (sky), and the overlapping imitations in each voice lend a sense of flowing down. After moving more slowly again for "sommeil" (sleep), the music becomes more active as the light of day illuminates the world and summons labor (beginning in measure 18). A syncopated duet in cantus and altus, imitated a measure later by tenor and bassus (measures 23–24), creates varied rhythms and a contrast of textures from two to four voices, a subtle illustration of the idea of "varied colors." The word "tapisse"—a verb which means "decorate," "cover," or "carpet" and is related to the nouns "tapis" (carpet) and "tapisserie" (tapestry)—is given the longest point of imitation in the chanson, with twelve entries (some doubled in thirds or tenths), as if to depict the many threads in a tapestry or multiple beams of light suffusing the world at dawn.

Lassus uses the harmony to provide both structure and meaningful contrast. The chanson is in mode 1 (Dorian), as defined by the final cadence and the ranges of the superius and tenor. In the first half of the poem, focused on the night, cadences alternate between the modal final D (measures 4, 10, and 18) and the second scale degree E (measures 7 and 13), a less common cadence point in mode 1 and thus appropriate to the shadowy imagery of the poem. The second half, about the light of day, focuses on F (measures 22 and 26), whose relatively bright major sonority is a common point of contrast in mode 1 polyphony, before turning to close on D.

Claude Le Jeune (CA. 1528–1600)

Revecy venir du printans

Chanson

LATE SIXTEENTH CENTURY

62

Published in *Le Printemps* (Paris: Ballard, 1603). This edition adapted from that of Henry Expert in *Les maîtres musiciens de la Renaissance française*, 12 (Paris: Alphonse Leduc, 1900), 11–27.

D: Et la grû' qui four - che son vol Re - tra - ver - se l'air et s'en va.

HC: Et la grû' qui four - che son vol Re - tra - ver - se l'air et s'en va.

0:38
Rechant à 5

D: Re - ve - cy ve - nir du Prin - tans L'a-mou-reuz' et bel - le sai - zon.

C: Re - ve - cy ve - nir du Prin - tans L'a- mou-reuz' et bel - le sai - zon.

HC: Re - ve - cy ve - nir du Prin - tans L'a-mou-reuz' et bel - le sai - zon.

T: Re - ve - cy ve - nir du Prin - tans L'a-mou-reuz' et bel - le sai - zon.

B: Re - ve - cy ve - nir du Prin - tans L'a-mou-reuz' et bel - le sai - zon.

0:45
[2] Chant à 3

D: Le So-leil é - clai - re lui - zant D'u-ne plus sé - rei - ne clair - té:

C: Le So-leil é - clai - re lui - zant D'u-ne plus sé - rei - ne clair - té:

T: Le So-leil é - clai - re lui - zant D'u-ne plus sé - rei - ne clair - té:

D: Du nu - a - ge l'om - bre s'en - fuit, Qui se ioû' et court et noir - cît Et fo - retz et champs et cou - taus.

C: Du nu - a - ge l'om - bre s'en - fuit, Qui se ioû' et court et noir - cît Et fo - retz et champs et cou - taus.

T: Du nu - a - ge l'om - bre s'en - fuit, Qui se ioû' et court et noir - cît Et fo - retz et champs et cour - taus.

Le la - beur hu-main re - ver - dît, Et la prê' dé - cou - vre ses fleurs.

Le la - beur hu-main re - ver - dît, Et la prê' dé - cou - vre ses fleurs.

Le la - beur hu-main re - ver - dît, Et la prê' dé - cou - vre ses fleurs.

1:08

Rechant à 5

Re - ve - cy ve - nir du Prin - tans L'a - mou - reuz' et bel - le sai - zon.

Re - ve - cy ve - nir du Prin - tans L'a - mou - reuz' et bel - le sai - zon.

Re - ve - cy ve - nir du Prin - tans L'a - mou - reuz' et bel - le sai - zon.

Re - ve - cy ve - nir du Prin - tans L'a - mou - reuz' et bel - le sai - zon.

Re - ve - cy ve - nir du Prin - tans L'a - mou - reuz' et bel - le sai - zon.

1:14

[3] Chant à 4

De Ve - nus le filz Cu - pi - don L'u - ni - vers se - mant de ses trais,

De Ve - nus le filz Cu - pi - don L'u - ni - vers se - mant de ses trais,

De Ve - nus le filz Cu - pi - don L'u - ni - vers se - mant de ses trais,

De Ve - nus le filz Cu - pi - don L'u - ni - vers se - mant de ses trais,

De sa flam - me va ré-chau - fér, A-ni-maus, qui vo - let en l'air,

De sa flam - me va ré-chau - fér, A-ni-maus, qui vo - let en l'air,

De sa flam - me va ré-chau - fér, A-ni-maus, qui vo - let en l'air,

De sa flam - me va ré-chau - fér, A - ni-maus, qui vo - let en l'air,

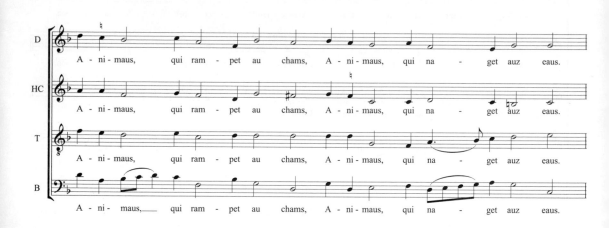

A - ni - maus, qui ram - pet au chams, A - ni - maus, qui na - get auz eaus.

A - ni - maus, qui ram - pet au chams, A - ni - maus, qui na - get auz eaus.

A - ni - maus, qui ram - pet au chams, A - ni - maus, qui na - get auz eaus.

A - ni - maus, qui ram - pet au chams, A - ni - maus, qui na - get auz eaus.

Ce qui mes - me-ment ne sent pas, A - mou-reux se fond de plai - zir.

Ce qui mes - me-ment ne sent pas, A - mou-reux se fond de plai - zir.

Ce qui mes - me-ment ne sent pas, A - mou-reux se fond de plai - zir.

Ce qui mes - me-ment ne sent pas, A - mou-reux se fond de plai - zir.

Revecy venir du Printans
L'amoureuz' et belle saizon.

Le courant des eaus recherchant
Le canal d'été s'éclaircît:
Et la mer calme de ces flots
Amolit le triste courrous:
Le Canard s'egaye plonjant,
Et se lave coint dedans l'eau;
Et la grû' qui fourche son vol
Retraverse l'air et s'en va.

Revecy venir du Printans
L'amoureuz' et belle saizon.

Le Soleil éclaire luizant
D'une plus séreine clairté:
Du nuage l'ombre s'enfuit,
Qui se ioû' et court et noircît.
Et foretz et champs et coutaus
Le labeur humain reverdît,
Et la prê' découvre ses fleurs.

Revecy venir du Printans
L'amoureuz' et belle saizon.

De Venus le filz Cupidon
L'univers semant de ses trais,
De sa flamme va réchaufér,
Animaus, qui volet en l'air,
Animaus, qui rampet au chams,
Animaus, qui naget auz eaus.
Ce qui mesmement ne sent pas,
Amoureux se fond de plaizir.

Here again comes the Spring,
the amorous and fair season.

The currents of water that seek
the canal in summer become clearer;
and the calm sea the waves'
sad anger soothes.
The duck, elated, dives
and washes itself quietly in the water.
And the crane that branches off in flight
recrosses the air and flies away.

Here again comes the Spring,
the amorous and fair season.

The sun shines brightly
with a calmer light.
The shadow of the cloud vanishes
from him who sports and runs and darkens.
Forests and fields and slopes
human labor makes green again,
and the prairie unveils its flowers.

Here again comes the Spring,
the amorous and fair season.

Cupid, the son of Venus,
seeding the universe with his arrows,
with his flame he will rekindle
animals that fly in the air,
animals that crawl in the fields,
animals that swim in the seas.
Even those that feel not,
in love they melt in pleasure.

Revecy venir du Printans L'amoureuz' et belle saizon.	Here again comes the Spring, the amorous and fair season.
Rion aussi nous: et cherchon Les ébas et ieus du Printans: Toute chose rit de plaizir; Sélebron la gaye saizon,	Let us, too, laugh, and let us seek the sports and games of Spring: everything smiles with pleasure; let us celebrate the merry season.
Revecy venir du Printans L'amoureuz' et belle saizon.	Here again comes the Spring, the amorous and fair season.

— JEAN-ANTOINE DE BAÏF

Claude Le Jeune composed *Revecy venir du printans* sometime during the late 1500s, and it was published after his death. It exemplifies *musique mesurée* (measured music), which reflected a new approach to poetry and music that was practiced in elite circles in late-sixteenth-century France.

The poets and composers of the Académie de Poésie et de Musique (Academy of Poetry and Music), founded in 1570 under the patronage of King Charles IX, sought to unite poetry and music as in ancient times. Led by Jean-Antoine de Baïf, the poets of the Académie wrote strophic French verses in ancient classical meters, which they called *vers mesurés à l'antique* (measured verses in ancient style), substituting the ancient Greek and Latin quantities of long and short syllables for the modern stress accents. Since the French language lacked any consistent distinction between long and short vowels, the theorists of *vers mesuré* created a system in which syllables were assigned long and short values. Composers such as Le Jeune set these verses accordingly, with long notes for the long vowels and notes half as long for the short vowels, producing *musique mesurée*. Through this fusion of poetry and music, the poets and composers associated with the Académie sought to revive the ethical effects of ancient Greek music and thereby improve society. Such goals reflect the ideals of Renaissance humanism, although neither a revival of Greek *ethos* nor social improvement seems to have been the result. Instead, the varying patterns of long and short notes in *musique mesurée* were adopted in later French styles of setting texts, including the *air de cour* (court air) and French opera in the seventeenth century (see NAWM 85b and c).

In this chanson, the following pattern of long (L) and short (S) syllables is used almost throughout: SS LS LS L L. This results in rhythmic groupings of quarter notes in the pattern 2 3 3 2 2. Although identical to a popular hemiola rhythm used by Cara in his frottole (see NAWM 55) and later by Monteverdi in his canzonettas (see NAWM 74a), the rhythm here derives from a different source, namely an attempt to emulate ancient Greek poetic meter. Melismas, most of no more than four notes, relieve the uniformity of rhythm and add lightness and charm to the individual parts.

The refrain, or *rechant*, is for five voices, and the strophes, or *chants*, are successively for two, three, four, and five voices. The five voice parts are labeled with French rather than Latin terms: *Dessus* for superius, *Taille* for tenor, *Haute-Contre* for contratenor altus, *Basse-Contre* for contratenor bassus, and *Cinquiesme* for quintus (both mean "fifth"). These terms continued in use for French vocal and instrumental music from the Renaissance through the eighteenth century. In the performance on the accompanying recording, some of the vocal lines are doubled by instruments, as was a frequent practice of the time.

Thomas Morley (1557/8–1602)

My bonny lass she smileth

Ballett

CA. 1595

From Thomas Morley, *First Book of Ballets to Five Voices* (London, 1595; reprinted 1600), ed. Edmund Horace Fellowes, The English Madrigal School 4 (London: Stainer and Bell, 1913), 23–25. Dynamic markings added by the editor.

The *ballett* was the English form of the Italian *balletto*, a light, homophonic, strophic song for three or more singers, distinguished by dancelike rhythms and "fa-la-la" refrains. Thomas Morley composed *My bonny lass she smileth* in the early 1590s and published it in his *First Book of Balletts to Five Voices* in 1595. He based it on *Questa dolce sirena* by Giacomo Gastoldi (ca. 1544–1609), the leading Italian composer of balletti.

The poem is light and witty. There are two strophes, marked 1 and 2 in the score. In the first half of each strophe, the poet speaks about the beloved in the third person. In the second half, he addresses her directly to make a surprising request: smile less and look at me less directly, or I will quite burn up with passion. The lighthearted mood and sly wit are nicely matched by the musical setting.

The ballett is in two repeated sections, creating the form AABB. The entire ballett, including repeats, is sung to the words of the first strophe and then repeated for the second strophe, so that every line of text is sung twice. Each section has two parts: two lines of verse set homophonically with the main melody in the top voice accompanied by root-position triads in the other voices, followed by a more contrapuntal setting for the "fa-la-la" refrain, which includes some imitation and rhythmic disjunction between the voices. Although the second "fa-la" passage changes to triple meter, the two sections have the same proportions, heavily weighted toward the nonsense syllables; in both sections, the verse fills four measures and the refrain fills nine.

The lack of a key signature and the presence of several F naturals remind us that the ballett is in mode 7 (Mixolydian) rather than in G major.

Music like this was principally designed for the performers themselves. Several elements make this piece especially satisfying to sing, including the spritely rhythms, changing textures, and attractive melodies in every voice part. Such pieces were probably sung with one voice on each part but could also have been performed with one or more parts played by a viol. Today balletts are often treated as choral music, usually for small choirs of two to five on a part, and editors often supply dynamic markings (as here) and piano reductions to facilitate rehearsal.

Thomas Weelkes (CA. 1573–1623)

As Vesta was

Madrigal

CA. 1601

From *Madrigals: The Triumphs of Oriana*, ed. Edmund Horace Fellowes, The English Madrigal School 32 (London: Stainer and Bell, 1923), 175–88. Dynamic markings added by the editor. In the commentary below, the discussion of this madrigal's political context and allegorical allusions draws on Jeremy L. Smith, "Music and Late Elizabethan Politics: The Identities of Oriana and Diana," *Journal of the American Musicological Society* 58 (Fall 2005): 507–58.

This madrigal was Weelkes's contribution to *The Triumphs of Oriana*, a collection of twenty-five madrigals by twenty-three different composers published by Thomas Morley in 1601. It has long been assumed that Morley planned the collection to honor Queen Elizabeth, but recent research has shown that the situation is more complex.

All the madrigals in the collection end with the words "Long live fair Oriana," using the name of the heroine of *Amadis de Gaule*, an epic romance popular in the sixteenth century. The phrase has been taken to honor Elizabeth, but Jeremy L. Smith has argued that it was originally meant to refer to Anna of Denmark, wife of James VI, king of Scotland, who succeeded to the English throne as James I after Elizabeth's death in 1603. Elizabeth was unmarried (unlike the character Oriana) and had no direct heir. James, a descendent of her grandfather Henry VII, was Elizabeth's closest relative and presumed successor, and Catholics (Morley included) hoped that although he was also Protestant he would improve the lot of Catholics in England. However, in 1601, the Earl of Essex led a revolt that sought to replace Elizabeth with James, and when it failed, Essex was executed. To escape the whiff of treason, Morley recast his collection of madrigals, which was about to be published, so that it could be read as a tribute to Elizabeth.

Knowing this history gives double meanings to Weelkes's madrigal, whose text, a poem in five rhymed couplets, he wrote himself. In the original political context prior to Essex's revolt, Elizabeth can be identified with Vesta, Jupiter's unmarried sister, who was the Roman goddess of fire, hearth, and home. She descends as Oriana ascends, a potent metaphor for one queen being succeeded by another. But the poem works almost as well in honoring Elizabeth, who can be equated with the "maiden Queen" surrounded by adoring attendant shepherds (the gentlemen of her court). The Roman goddess Vesta defers to her, as does Diana, goddess of virginity and the hunt, whose nymphs abandon her and run down Mount Latmos to join the shepherds in singing praises to the queen.

Weelkes wrote this poem using words and images that could be readily depicted in music, making this madrigal a textbook example of word-painting. "Vesta" and the "maiden queen," as females, are described only by the upper four voices of the ensemble (measures 1–22). "Latmos hill" is suggested by a four-note climbing figure, followed by falling scalar figures for "descending" (measures 4–9) and a rising scale for "ascending" (measures 12–22). The lower voices join in at "Attended on by all the shepherds swain" (measures 23–32), representing the male shepherds with deeper voices and "all" with the first appearance of all six voices at once. The crowd of Diana's nymphs running down the hill is depicted with descending scales in imitative polyphony and alternating groups of paired voices (measures 36–46). The phrases "two by two," "three by three," and "together" are set respectively for two pairs of voices, two groups of three, and all six voices together (measures 47–51). Likewise, when Diana is left "all alone," the words are sung by a single mournful soprano (measures 56–57). The nymphs and shepherds mingle in groups of high and low voices (measures 59–63), and their "mirthful tunes" are suggested by short melodic motives that pass back and forth between voices. These depictions range from the clever and subtle to the kind of obvious translation of words to music that has earned the term *madrigalism*.

Weelkes treated the final phrase, "Long live fair Oriana," in a most extraordinary manner, surpassing all his other images. The words are set to a motive (first heard in measures 79–80) that enters forty-nine times in a variety of circumstances—in all voices, in seven different transpositions, outlining both major and minor triads, and with varied intervals of time between one entrance and the next. The effect is as if a great crowd is hailing their queen again and again, from every direction. The long life wished for the queen is illustrated both by the length of this section, occupying almost the last third of the madrigal, and by augmentation of the motive in the bass by a factor of eight (at measure 83) and later by four (measure 102). If most of the word-painting is clever or conventional, the impact in this final section is also deeply meaningful.

Although it may have been performed for the queen, this piece, like most madrigals, was intended primarily for amateurs to sing at home for their own pleasure. This madrigal must have been particularly entertaining to sing because it combines wordplay and wit with attractive melodies, noble sentiments, and interesting textures that change from homophony to imitative polyphony and from one grouping of voices to another.

John Dowland (1563–1626)

Flow, my tears

Air or lute song

CA. 1600

65

John Dowland published his lute song *Flow, my tears* in his *Second Book of Songs* (1600). He adapted it from his most popular piece for lute, a pavane titled *Lachrimae* (Tears), which he later arranged for viol consort and published in a collection called *Lachrimae or Seaven Teares* (1604). Many other composers wrote arrangements or variations on this same piece. Such reworking of existing music into new forms was typical during the Renaissance and has parallels in the many arrangements of popular tunes published during recent decades.

A pavane (or pavan) is a slow processional dance with three repeated strains in the form AABBCC (see NAWM 66b). Most sixteenth-century pavanes were functional dance music, but Dowland's pavanes are more contrapuntal than those of earlier composers, and he apparently intended them primarily as abstract instrumental music for the enjoyment of the player or of listeners. In the lute song arrangement of *Flow, my tears*, Dowland set the topmost melody in the vocal line with a poem in five strophes—two for the statement and repetition of the first strain, two for the second strain, and the last sung twice to the third strain.

The opening motive of *Lachrimae* is the basis for the entire piece: a stepwise descent through a fourth that suggests a falling tear and thus earned the pavane its name. The motive appears many times in various forms and in all four contrapuntal parts (here, including the top, middle, and bass lines of the lute accompaniment as well as the voice). In arranging the piece as a song, Dowland (or perhaps an anonymous poet) capitalized on this motive by setting appropriate words to it at the opening: "Flow, my tears, fall from your springs!" The association of this motive with tears then brings new meaning to later phrases of text that are not obviously about tears but come to life when linked with that image through this motive; this occurs at the phrases "[sad] infamy sings," "There let me live forlorn," "Down, vain lights," and so on, through "they that in hell" in the last stanza (measures 19–20). The rising motive in measures 11–12 clearly conveys the text of both verses, demonstrating that although concrete painting or expression of individual words and phrases is usually not possible in songs where more than one stanza is sung to the same music, it is possible to arrange the poetry to evoke feelings that suit the gestures in the music.

Although there is a tendency for modern listeners to hear this piece in the key of A minor, it exhibits traits of the modal system of the Renaissance. Old-fashioned sixth-to-octave cadences (in measures 8–9 and 19) occasionally appear alongside the more modern form with a falling fifth in the bass (as in measures 6–7), and even the latter form follows modal voice-leading with a sixth-to-octave cadence between melody and tenor (the middle part in the lute). The long series of harmonies that rise by third or fifth in measures 11–14 (d–F–a–C–G–d–a) would be unlikely to occur in a tonal piece, where root motion is directional, normally moving *down* by third or fifth (rather than up) or up by second or fourth. The melody ranges from a fifth below to a fifth above the final A, placing it in the plagal mode on A (mode 10 or Hypoaeolian).

The lute tablature, shown here below the transcription, indicates which strings are to be played, which frets the fingers should be placed at to stop the strings, and what rhythm to play. Those who are accustomed to tablature find it easier to use than standard notation, but anyone who is not a lute player will likely find it a curious and confusing code. What looks like a musical staff is actually a sign for the six main pairs (or *courses*) of strings, tuned from bottom up $G–c–f–a–d'–g'$. (A seventh, tuned to D, is needed for notes below G; see measures 11 and 13–15 for examples.) The letter *a* means to play the string below the letter as an open string, *b* to stop it at the first fret (producing a note a half-step above the open string), and so on. Thus, in the first chord, the low string tuned to G is stopped at its second fret (shown by the letter *c*), producing the note A; the strings tuned to *c* and *f* are both stopped at the fourth fret (the letter *e*), producing the notes *e* and *a* respectively; and the string tuned to *a* is stopped at the third fret, producing the note c'. The rhythmic signs above the six strings indicate what durations to use (one flag is a half note, two flags a quarter note, and so on); to keep the notation simple, a duration stays in force until another one is indicated (compare the tablature in measure 1 to the transcription above it). Lute players throughout Europe used various systems, but all were based on these same principles.

Tielman Susato (CA. 1515–1570)

Dances from *Danserye*: Basse danse *La morisque* and Pavane and Galliard *La dona*

Basse danse, pavane, and galliard

PUBLISHED 1551

66

(a) No. 5: Basse danse *La morisque*

(b) No. 38: Pavane *La dona*

From *Het derde musyck boexken begrepen int ghet al van onser neder duytscher spraken, daer inne begrepen syn alderhande danserye . . .* (Antwerp, 1551). Note values reduced by half.

(c) No. 50: Galliard *La dona*

Susato was born near Cologne in Germany, but moved as a young man to the Flemish city of Antwerp, where he was a member of the town band, a composer, and a prolific music printer. He was the first successful music publisher in the Low Countries, printing music by Josquin, Lassus, Clemens, and other composers, and also several of his own works. Among the latter was the book of dances from which these pieces are drawn, published in 1551. The long title translates as "The third little music book published in our Nether-Dutch language, wherein are included all types of dances, that is, basse danses, rounds, allemandes, pavanes and others, with also fifteen new galliards, very enjoyable and easy to play on all musical instruments." The last phrase, and the title that reads like an advertisement, both make clear that Susato was marketing this collection to amateur performers to play for their own enjoyment.

The pieces included here illustrate three dances that were widespread in the fifteenth and sixteenth centuries. Although many of Susato's dances are arranged from chansons, a common practice of the time, these do not have any source that has been identified.

The first is a *basse danse* (low dance), a stately court dance for couples that earned its name from its graceful movements performed low to the ground, in contrast to the leaps and fast motions of other dances. Music for basse danses in the fifteenth century, when the dance was at the height of its popularity, consisted of tenors over which treble instruments improvised. But in the sixteenth century, the music tended to take the shape of a series of four-measure phrases, in either triple or duple meter, which combine to make larger sections, each repeated. The basse danse *La morisque* (The Moor) consists of two repeated sections. This structure—later called binary form—would become the standard form for dances in the seventeenth and eighteenth centuries, and it was expanded upon in various ways in the mid- to late-eighteenth century to create sonata form, rondo form, and other standard formal patterns. (On the accompanying recording, the players repeat the first section after the second, to create an ABA form, reminding us that such dances could be rearranged by the performers to suit their tastes.) In *La morisque*, each section contains two varied statements of the same phrase, the first closing on a full triad on G, and the second on a C triad. Modern ears will hear it in C major, but musicians of the time would have called it mode 12, the Hypoionian.

As suggested in his title, Susato grouped dances of the same type together. But it was a frequent practice to pair together a dance in duple meter with a faster one in triple meter, and one of the most common pairings was of a *pavane* with a *galliard*. The pavane (from Italian *pavana*, "from Padua") was a dignified court dance similar in character to the basse danse. It is always in duple meter and usually consists of three repeated sections, for a form AABBCC. The galliard (from Italian *gagliardo*, "vigorous") was a more vigorous dance marked by kicks and jumps. It was usually in the same form as a pavane, but in triple meter. In many pavane-galliard pairs, both dances use the same melodic outline, so that they sound like two variations on the same tune. Such is the case with this pavane and galliard, both called *La dona* (The Lady). Comparing the superius parts (the top lines) of each makes clear how the galliard's melody parallels the pavane's, but the harmony is rather different in places.

These instrumental dances were published in partbooks, with one bound booklet for each of the four players. Each partbook had only the music for that part, and there was no score. The instrumentation was not specified, leaving the choice up to the players. These dances could be played by four instruments of the same type in different sizes to suit the ranges of the parts, such as a consort of soprano, alto, tenor, and bass recorders, or a similar consort of viols. They could also be played with a different type of instrument on each part. The players, especially the performer on the top line, were free to embellish the music, and did so especially at cadences and when sections repeated, as on the accompanying recording. Percussion was never notated, but pictures from the period show that drums or other percussion instruments were used at least some of the time. The freedom players had to decide how to perform the piece has more in common with modern practice for popular music than with current standards for performing classical music, where scrupulous adherence to the score is expected.

Anthony Holborne (CA. 1545–1602)

The Night Watch and *The Fairie-round*

Consort dances (almain and galliard)

PUBLISHED 1599

(a) *The Night Watch*, almain

(b) *The Fairie-round*, galliard

These two dances for instrumental consort by Anthony Holborne were published in his 1599 collection titled *Pavans, Galliards, Almains and Other Short Aeirs both Grave, and Light, in Five Parts, for Viols, Violins, or Other Musicall Winde Instruments*. It is the largest surviving English collection of consort music from its time, containing sixty-five pieces, almost all of them dances. In the dedication, Holborne describes himself as a gentleman and servant to the queen of England and implies that the pieces in the collection were written over several years. Two-thirds of them, including the two printed here, appear elsewhere as solos for lute, cittern, or bandora—plucked string instruments that Holborne played—and the consort pieces may have been arranged from those solo versions. In issuing this compilation of music for an ensemble of five players, with parts in ranges playable by viols, recorders, or a variety of other instruments, Holborne was clearly seeking to appeal to a wide range of amateurs who would enjoy playing these dances as chamber music, in the same way that madrigal collections were marketed to amateur singers.

The Night Watch is an *almain* or *allemande* (French for "German dance"), a couple dance in $\frac{4}{4}$ meter that was popular throughout the sixteenth century. Partners stand side by side in a line of couples that moves across the floor and back, using a basic pattern that consists of walking three steps and lifting the free foot, then repeating, starting with the other foot. By Holborne's time, the allemande was being danced less often but had become one of the dances most often used in stylized dance compositions. It was commonly followed by a livelier dance in triple meter, such as the galliard *The Fairie-round*, although in Holborne's collection he groups the dances with others of their type, leaving any such pairing to the performers. These two dances have the same form AABBCC that we saw in Susato's pavane and galliard *La dona* (NAWM 66b and c), but they are musically independent, without the melodic similarities of the Susato pair. Compared to Susato's dances, they offer more rhythmic variety and much more interesting counterpoint, making them remarkably satisfying to play and to hear.

Like many allemandes, *The Night Watch* begins most phrases with an upbeat and moves in units of two or four measures. Here all three sections are eight measures long in a 2 + 2 + 4 pattern, creating a satisfying regularity of rhythm and phrasing. Two figures introduced at the outset—the rising pattern of eighth, eighth, and quarter note in the top line, and the descending dotted rhythm in the second line down—suffuse and energize the music, recurring throughout the dance in varying forms and combinations. Occasional syncopations further enliven the texture, and a sudden pile-up of syncopations in measures 20–22 brings the dance to a close.

The Fairie-round creates more metrical complexity by layering duple and triple divisions of its $\frac{6}{4}$ meter. For the first three measures, the lowest and middle parts divide the measure into three as if in $\frac{3}{2}$, while the top part divides it into two and the other two parts syncopate against both. Throughout the piece, this pattern of two against three trades off among instruments, submitting to a unified pulse only at the end of each section. As in *The Night Watch*, short melodic figures are tossed among instruments, keeping the counterpoint constantly lively. Near the end, a rising sequence in all instruments (measures 21–22) unifies the texture to create a satisfying close.

The harmony in both pieces is clear, closing on the modal final in the first section, on the fifth degree in the middle section, and back on the final at the end, and each phrase cadences on a full triad. Although modern ears may hear these pieces as tonal, they are still modal; for example, the F—A—C triad that opens the middle section of *The Night Watch* would be startling in G major but is normal in G Mixolydian.

We do not know why Holborne gave these dances the titles *The Night Watch* and *The Fairie-round*. In the seventeenth century, it became common practice to give dances fanciful titles like these rather than simply calling them by the name of the dance (see NAWM 87). If the idea was to catch the imagination and thus make the pieces more appealing and popular, it worked for these two. Both are favorites among consort musicians, and *The Fairie-round* was included on the set of recordings sent into space in 1977 on Voyager 1 and Voyager 2, the first man-made objects designed to leave the solar system. These recordings contained greetings in fifty-five languages and twenty-seven pieces of music from around the world meant to represent the cultures of Earth to anyone who found the space probes.

On the accompanying recording, *The Night Watch* is played by viols joined by a lute and *The Fairie-round* by viols alone. In both performances, the repeated sections are embellished with passing tones and turns, especially at cadences.

Luis de Narváez (FL. 1526–49)

From *Los seys libros del Delphín*

Intabulation and variation set

CA. 1538

68

(a) *Cancion Mille regres*, intabulation of Josquin's *Mille regretz*

concise 🔊

Edited by Geneviève Thibault in "Instrumental Transcriptions of Josquin's French Chansons," in *Josquin des Prez*, ed. Edward E. Lowinsky (London: Oxford University Press, 1976), 464–66. Used by permission. All rights reserved.

(b) *Cuatro diferencias sobre "Guárdame las vacas"* [Four Variations on "Guárdame las vacas"], variation set

Adapted from Luys de Narváez, *Los seys libros del Delphín*, ed. Emilio Pujol, Monumentos de la Música Española 3 (Barcelona: Consejo Superior de Investigaciones Científicas, 1945), 85–87.

Luis de Narváez was apparently a native of Granada in southern Spain, although nothing is known of his early years. He was employed from about 1526 by Francisco de los Cobos, secretary to Emperor Charles V, and after his patron's death in 1547 he entered the service of the royal family. Narváez is best known for *Los seis libros del Delphín* (The Six Books of the Dauphin), published in Vallidolid, Spain, in 1538. It is a collection of pieces for *vihuela* (a Spanish plucked string instrument that was closely related to the viol and to the lute) that testify to Narváez's skill as a vihuelist and as a composer. The contents include fantasias, sets of variations, arrangements of vocal pieces, songs, and a contrapuntal setting of a basse danse melody. Two of those genres are illustrated here: arrangements and variations.

Cancion Mille regres is an arrangement—called an *intabulation* because it was written in tablature—of *Mille regretz* (NAWM 43), the chanson attributed to Josquin. Comparing the original to Narváez's version shows that the latter is not a simple transcription but an imaginative reworking of the piece for a new medium. Narváez preserved the four-voice texture of the original but changed some notes and added many figures. The vihuela cannot sustain tones the way that voices can, since a plucked string rapidly loses volume; to compensate and to make the rhythm livelier, Narváez added scales, turns, and other figuration. Such figures were called *divisions* or *diminutions* because they divided the long notes into smaller durations.

Some figures fill in large intervals with stepwise motion—for example, the sixteenth notes in the first half of measure 2 bridge the gap between *c'* and *f'*, and those in measure 6 fill in the rising fifth from *d* to *a*. Other figures ornament what were sustained tones in the original, like those in the second half of measure 2 and in measure 7. Through such embellishments Narváez drew attention to the movement of different voices at different times, often emphasizing important beats and cadences. The constant variations in texture and figuration sustain the interest of player and listener alike.

Los seys libros del Delphín was the first publication to contain sets of variations, called *diferencias* in Spanish. It includes two sets of variations on *Guárdame las vacas*, a standard air for singing poetry that consists of a simple melodic outline over a bass progression:

This variation set does not begin with the melody in unadorned form, as would become common in later theme-and-variation movements. Rather, it comprises a succession of four variations in which the original bass is readily apparent, but the melody is richly elaborated, although the melodic outline remains perceptible underneath the decoration. Each variation introduces a new figuration while preserving the phrase structure, harmonic plan, and cadences of the theme. These characteristics became standard for variation sets. Narváez added a four-measure phrase at the end of the fourth variation to confirm the cadence and reinforce the conclusion.

One interesting difference between vihuela or lute music and vocal music is the notation of accidentals. Singers were expected to alter pitches by half steps up or down as called for by the rules of musica ficta, so manuscripts and printed vocal music often omitted those accidentals. It is up to modern editors to suggest where such alterations would likely have been made. Unlike composers of vocal music, intabulators had to specify each note exactly, by indicating on which fret the finger would be placed, so that there would be no ambiguity. A comparison of Narváez's intabulation of *Mille regretz* to the original chanson demonstrates that Narváez regularly expanded the minor sixth to a major sixth at cadences by sharping the upper note, as at measures 4, 5, and 9; these alterations would have been made by singers according to the rules of musica ficta (although they are not always indicated by the editor of the chanson in NAWM 43). The exact notation of intabulations often suggests what typical practice may have been, but it is not certain whether singers would have consistently used the same alterations as instrumentalists.

William Byrd (CA. 1540–1623)

John come kiss me now

Variations

CA. 1600

William Byrd's *John come kiss me now* is preserved in the Fitzwilliam Virginal Book, a manuscript collection copied in the 1610s and now in the Fitzwilliam Museum at Cambridge University. This collection is the primary source for English music for the *virginal* (the English term for harpsichord), containing almost 300 compositions from the late sixteenth and early seventeenth centuries by over thirty composers, and is also the largest single source of Byrd's music, with more than seventy works attributed to him. Since this piece does not appear in the earlier manuscript collection of Byrd's keyboard music known as *My Ladye Nevells Booke*, copied in 1591, it can be presumed that Byrd composed it in the 1590s or early 1600s.

John come kiss me now is a set of sixteen variations on a popular song melody. The variation set was a favorite genre for keyboard composers, especially in England, because it allows the composer and player to explore a wide variety of textures and figurations against the background of the recurring elements of the theme. Composers of variations often used short themes that were simple, memorable, and regular in phrasing, and *John come kiss me now* is no exception. Indeed, for a popular song, this theme is remarkably economical in its motivic material and already imbued with variation. The opening four-note motive, a stepwise rising dotted figure followed by a skip down of a third (G—A—B—G), appears three times, each with a different continuation: first a leap up to C, then a leap up to D, and then a rising sequence answered by a descending sequence on the falling third. The initial melodic units of two measures each are answered by a longer four-measure phrase to form a balanced period. The bass line (G—C—G—D—G—F—G—D—G) moves away from and back to the modal final of G; to ears accustomed to tonal music, the move to F (measure 6) and back may sound surprising, but it was standard in the Mixolydian mode.

In contrast to Narváez's variations on *Guárdame las vacas* (NAWM 68b), which preserved only the barest outline of the melody, here Byrd keeps the melody always readily audible. Most often it is at the top of the texture, sometimes embellished, as in variation 3 (measures 17–24); later it travels to a middle voice in variations 10–12 and 16, and to the bass in variation 14. The most distant from the melody is variation 6 (measures 41–48), where the opening four-note motive in sixteenth-note diminution suffuses the texture before the tune gradually comes into focus.

Each variation features a distinctive rhythmic pattern, motive, or technique. A few variations are consistent in their figuration throughout, but most change textures or rhythmic patterns midway. Some variations build on elements of the theme itself, and others introduce a new or derived motive and pass it between voices. As in many variation sets, there is a gradual intensification of rhythm, leading to the triplets and sextuplets of variations 12–14. The rhythm relaxes somewhat in the last two variations, where the slowing of the pace and surprising turns of harmony bring the series of variations to a satisfying close.

Variation	Measure	Description
1	1	Rhythm of main motive echoed in lower parts
2	9	Main motive varied in imitation and inversion
3	17	Motives in eighths, then sixteenths
4	25	Motive derived from theme, with stepwise fall and rise through a fourth
5	33	New motives in eighths, then sixteenths
6	41	Main motive in inversion and in diminution
7	49	Main motive varied in top voice, treated in inversion and imitation in other voices
8	57	Rhythmic figuration in lower voices
9	65	Three distinct layers of rhythm and figuration in all voices subtly derived from opening motive
10	73	Rapid scalar figures passed between the hands
11	81	Theme in tenor, with new motives in top voice
12	89	Triplets appear, theme moves from tenor to bass
13	97	Sextuplets as top voice trades theme with tenor
14	105	Sextuplets with theme in bass
15	113	Rhythm relaxes to showcase new harmonies and bass line alongside new motives in lower voices
16	121	New harmonies continue, rhythm of main motive passed among voices in diminution, and alto voice finally takes the theme

Although today the term *virginal* is usually reserved for a small harpsichord with only one keyboard and strings running perpendicular to rather than parallel to the keys, the English used the word for all types of harpsichord in the sixteenth and seventeenth centuries, and this piece can be played on any of them. As in the pieces that Narváez composed for vihuela (NAWM 68), the embellishing figures in this piece help to compensate for the inability of a plucked string instrument to sustain pitches. The double diagonal line drawn through the stem of a note (see the first note of the melody) indicates an ornament, but writings from Byrd's era do not tell us exactly how to perform it; most likely this sign indicates a *shake*, a brief trill oscillating between the designated note and the note above or below it, perhaps only once or twice.

Giovanni Gabrieli (CA. 1555–1612)

Canzon septimi toni a 8, from *Sacrae symphoniae*

Ensemble canzona

CA. 1597

Primus Chorus. Cantus

Primus Chorus. Altus

Primus Chorus. Tenor

Primus Chorus. Sextus

Sec. Cho. Septimus

Sec. Chorus. Quintus

Sec. Choro. Octavus

Sec. Chorus. Bassus

Basso per l'organo

From Giovanni Gabrieli, *Opera Omnia*, vol. 10, *Instrumental Ensemble Works in "Sacrae symphoniae" (Venice, 1597),
Printed Anthologies and Manuscript Sources*, ed. Richard Charteris, Corpus Mensurabilis Musicae 12 (American
Institute of Musicology, Hänssler-Verlag, 1998), 11–21. © American Institute of Musicology. Used with permission.

Giovanni Gabrieli's *Sacrae symphoniae* (Sacred Symphonies), published in 1597, was a collection of ensemble works ("symphonies" in the sense of "sounding together") that he had composed over the previous decade or so as part of his work as organist and composer at St. Mark's Church in Venice and at the Scuola Grande di San Rocco. The collection contained works for singers with instruments (forty motets, three mass movements, and two Magnificats) and for instruments alone (fourteen canzonas and two sonatas). Both vocal and instrumental works were conceived for divided choirs (called *cori spezzati*), ensembles divided into subgroups that engaged in dialogue and joined together for glorious climaxes.

The *Canzon septimi toni a 8* (Canzona in the Seventh Tone for Eight Parts) exemplifies Gabrieli's style and use of divided choirs. The "eight parts" are divided into two groups called first choir (*primus chorus*) and second choir (*secundus chorus*), each with four players in cantus, altus, tenor, and bassus range. Each choir is accompanied by an organ, as explained below. The "seventh tone" is the authentic mode on G, the Mixolydian mode, clearly defined in this piece by the opening and closing sonorities, the frequent cadences on G, and the ranges of the cantus and tenor parts. As is typical in this mode (but quite untypical in the key of G major), sonorities on C are about as prominent as those on D, and F is almost as common a note as F♯.

The first instrumental canzonas were transcriptions of French chansons (both the Italian *canzona* and the French *chanson* mean "song"). One legacy from that heritage is the opening rhythm of this and many other canzonas composed in the late sixteenth century—a half note followed by two quarter notes—which echoes the opening rhythm of many chansons (see *Tant que vivray*, NAWM 60). Also like the chanson, the canzona unfolds in a series of sections, some imitative and some largely homophonic. Typically, each section is based on different melodic material, but variation or repetition of material may also occur. The textures are relatively transparent, the music moves quickly, and the motives are strongly rhythmic.

This canzona features a refrain that appears three times, creating the following formal plan:

Measure	Section	Musical Description
1	A	Choir 1 alone, then choir 2 alone
18	B	Refrain: dialogue in triple meter, then together in duple
26	C	Choir 1 alone, then short dialogue, then choir 2 alone
39	B	Refrain
47	D	Choir 2 and choir 1 in dialogue, then together
60	B	Refrain
69	E	Choirs together with some imitation between them

Most of the piece is in duple meter, but the refrain begins in triple meter, setting it apart. The refrain is the same at each appearance: short phrases in homophony are presented in one choir and immediately echoed in the other, then the two choirs join in a mostly homophonic passage with a running scale figure in imitation between the two bass parts.

The sections before and after the refrains differ from each other in musical material, but together they create a sense of direction from complete separation to integration of the two choirs. In the opening section, choir 1 plays a point of imitation, and choir 2 then presents its own completely different material (measure 11). The section after the first refrain has a similar shape, but the two choirs engage briefly in dialogue, as if tossing ideas back and forth, before choir 2 takes over (measures 30–32). The next time (at measure 47), choir 2 begins, but its subject is soon taken up by choir 1, and after a brief dialogue they join together in a passage that mixes homophony with imitation between the upper lines of the two choirs (measures 56–60). After the last refrain, the choirs continue playing together with brief imitation between them. Metaphorically, what began as two people on opposite sides of the room speaking in monologues concludes with them engaged in eager conversation, echoing each other's ideas. Such a logical series of events, framed by the refrains, exemplifies the newfound freedom of instrumental music in the late sixteenth century. No longer bound by the forms and rhythms of dance (as in NAWM 66 and 67) or song (as in NAWM 68a and b), composers were free to create entirely new forms based on abstract ideas.

Gabrieli did not specify the instrumentation for this piece, although he did for the *Sonata pian' e forte* (Soft and Loud Sonata) in the same collection. One likely instrumentation, used on the accompanying recording, features violins on the top two lines in choir 1, cornetts (wooden instruments blown like a brass instrument but fingered like a recorder) on the top two lines in choir 2, and sackbuts (early trombones) on the bottom two lines in each choir. The original clef for each line, shown at the beginning of the score, indicated the range for which a suitable instrument would be found. The editor has marked the specific range for each part at the beginning of the piece. Today Gabrieli's canzonas and sonatas are often played by ensembles of modern brass instruments.

The staves marked "basso per l'organo" (bass for the organ) are for the two organs—one associated with each choir of instruments. Each organ plays a bass line derived from the lowest notes sounded in that choir by any instrument; thus, at the beginning, the organ for choir 1 (the upper of the two organ staves) plays with the cantus line for one measure, then with the altus, then with the tenor, and finally with the sextus starting in measure 6. The organ for choir 2 (the bottom staff) enters at measure 11 with its choir. The organist was expected to fill in the harmony above the notated bass line, guided at times by figures below the staff. The practice of writing out the bass line and leaving the player to add the appropriate chords became very common in the seventeenth and eighteenth centuries and was known as *basso continuo* (continuous bass). This particular type of bass line, following the lowest note sounded in the ensemble, became known as a *basso seguente* (following bass, or uninterrupted bass). The piece can be played without the organs, as it usually is today.

Claudio Monteverdi (1567–1643)

Cruda Amarilli

Madrigal

LATE 1590S

First published in Claudio Monteverdi, *Il quinto libro de madrigali a cinque voci* (Venice, 1605). This edition from Claudio Monteverdi, *Opera omnia*, vol. 6, *Madrigali a 5 voci: Libro quinto*, ed. Maria Caraci (Cremona: Fondazione Claudio Monteverdi, 1984), 107–10. Used by permission.

Cruda Amarilli che col nome ancora
D'amar, ahi lasso, amaramente insegni.
Amarilli del candido ligustro,
Più candida e più bella,
Ma dell'aspido sordo
E più sorda e più fera e più fugace.
Poi che col dir t'offendo
I mi morò tacendo.

— GIOVANNI BATTISTA GUARINI

Cruel Amaryllis, who with your very name
teach bitterly of love, alas!
Amaryllis, than the white privet flower
paler and more beautiful,
but deafer than the asp
and fiercer and more elusive.
Since by speaking I offend you,
I shall die in silence.

This madrigal is one of eleven in Claudio Monteverdi's fifth book of madrigals (1605) whose texts are drawn from Giovanni Battista Guarini's pastoral verse play *Il pastor fido*. Here, in the second scene from the first act, Mirtillo complains that Amarilli is spurning his love. His speech begins with a pun on the name Amarilli, whose stem "amar" can be a contraction either of "amare" (to love) or "amaro" (bitter). With her name, Mirtillo protests, Amarilli teaches bitterly of how to love (or, in other possible translations, teaches how to love bitterly or teaches that *she* loves bitterly).

Monteverdi expresses the bitter mood of the opening words "Cruda Amarilli" with striking dissonances that break the rules of normal counterpoint. For example, in the second measure the bass skips down to E, creating a seventh against the canto; the rules of proper counterpoint require the suspended dissonance in the canto to resolve before the bass moves again, but it does not. By the time the suspension in the canto resolves down to C, the bass has already moved on to B, creating an even more biting dissonance of a minor ninth plus a minor seventh with the alto. This sonority includes all the first five notes of the Mixolydian scale (G—A—B—C—D). The rules of counterpoint call for passing tones to fall on weak beats, so here the canto and alto notes should appear one quarter note earlier to create consonances on the third beat over the bass note B. The same phrase is repeated a fourth higher, and then Monteverdi echoes the text's sardonic humor by setting the next half line in a dancelike dotted rhythm that continues without a pause into the following line, which mixes the jeering laughter of sixteenth notes with the crudest dissonances in the piece.

This madrigal was already in circulation in 1598, the date of an imaginary dialogue in which these violations of the rules of counterpoint for the treatment of dissonance were discussed in Giovanni Maria Artusi's *L'Artusi overo delle imperfettioni della moderna musica* (The Artusi, or Of the Imperfections of Modern Music), published in 1600. In the dialogue, one speaker particularly objects to the dissonance in measures 12–14, pointing out that the soprano part in measure 13 fails to agree with the bass. The A in the soprano line, a ninth above the bass, seems to appear out of nowhere and leaps to a seventh, F. The other speaker defends the passage, arguing that if one imagines a G on the first beat of the soprano part, the figure is like an *accento*, an improvised embellishment common at this time, with the stepwise motion G—F—E embellished as G—A—F—E. Such written-out embellishments, or *passagi*, as they were called, also season the harmony with runs in measure 12 that include an augmented octave between F in the bass and F♯ in the quinto part.

Although some of Monteverdi's dissonances may thus be rationalized as embellishments, his real motivation for including them was to convey through harmony, rather than through the graphic melodic images of some earlier madrigals, the meaning and feeling of the poet's message. In his preface to the fifth book of madrigals, Monteverdi described his approach as that of a second practice (*seconda pratica*) by which, for the sake of expressing a text, composers were free to violate some of the strict rules of the first practice taught in the manuals on counterpoint. Indeed, asserting the dominance of the words and their meaning over the music virtually required doing violence to the traditional rules of music in order to convey the strength of the emotions and images. A listener who recognized the violations of the rules in the music had to search for explanations in the text, just as one might react to a friend's sudden outburst by trying to understand the emotions that motivated it.

Several other passages show the same use of rule-breaking as a rhetorical device, including the settings of "amaramente" (bitterly) in measures 19–23 and "l'aspido" (the asp) in measures 36–38. Throughout, *Cruda Amarilli* typifies the flexible, animated, evocative, and variegated style of Monteverdi's polyphonic madrigals.

By the time this madrigal was published in 1605, a new fashion had emerged for solo or ensemble madrigals to be accompanied by basso continuo. Thus, although it was conceived for five solo voices without accompaniment, *Cruda Amarilli* was published with a basso continuo part, marked "B.S." for basso seguente (see explanation in NAWM 70). This arrangement made the piece more flexible, for with the basso continuo it could be performed with one singer alone (on the top line) or with any number of the other voices added. However, the basso continuo remained only an option, not a necessary part of the music, and this madrigal was no doubt often sung unaccompanied, as on the recording for this anthology.

Giulio Caccini (CA. 1550–1618)

Vedrò 'l mio sol

Solo madrigal

CA. 1590

First published in *Le nuove musiche* (Florence, 1602). This edition from *Giulio Caccini: Le nuove musiche*, ed. H. Wiley Hitchcock, Recent Researches in the Music of the Baroque Era 9 (Madison, Wisc.: A-R Editions, 1970), 81–85. Reprinted by permission. Abbreviations used in the score: *senza mis.* (*senza misura*), freely, without beating the measure; *escl.* (*esclamazione*), a decrescendo after attacking a note, followed by a sforzando. Solid barlines appear in the original publication (see Figure 13.10 on page 302 of *A History of Western Music* for a partial facsimile), and dashed barlines are provided by the editor.

Vedrò 'l mio sol, vedrò prima ch'io muoia
Quel sospirato giorno
Che faccia 'l vostro raggio à me ritorno.

O mia luce, o mia gioia,
Ben più m'è dolc' il tormentar per vui
Che 'l gioir per altrui.

Ma senza morte io non potrò soffrire
Un sì lungo martire;

E s'io morrò, morrà mia speme ancora
Di veder mai d'un sì bel dì l'aurora.

— GIOVANNI BATTISTA GUARINI OR ALESSANDRO GUARINI

I'll see my sun; I'll see before I die
that wished-for day
when your ray returns to me.

O my light, O my joy,
much sweeter is my torment for you
than delight in others.

But without death I cannot suffer
such a long martyrdom.

And if I die, will die my hope
to see ever again the dawn of such a beautiful day.

Vedrò 'l mio sol is one of over two dozen songs for solo voice with basso continuo that Giulio Caccini wrote in the 1580s or 1590s and published in his collection *Le nuove musiche* (The New Music, 1602). In his foreword, he boasted that this madrigal was among those received "with loving applause" when performed in the late 1580s for the Camerata ("the club"), the group of gentlemen, scholars, and musicians who met in Count Giovanni de' Bardi's palace in Florence to discuss literature, science, and the arts and to hear new music.

This song is classified as a madrigal rather than an aria or other form because the text setting is through-composed rather than strophic, although both the words and the music of measures 14–42 are repeated in measures 43–75, with some changes in figuration. Solo madrigals set texts similar to those of polyphonic madrigals, but afforded solo singers greater opportunity to display emotion and virtuosity.

Each poetic line is set as a separate phrase, ending with a cadence, sustained note, or pair of notes. This convention was common in airs improvised on melodic formulas throughout the sixteenth century, as well as in polyphonic madrigals. The many repeated notes in speech rhythm are typical of solo airs, but can also be found in some polyphonic madrigals that were composed late in the century, as the declamatory style of text setting became more common. Thus, this piece draws on two long-standing traditions: madrigal settings and solo singing.

For emotional effect, Caccini borrowed from oratory the device of heightened repetition, as in measures 14–19, 35–37, 43–48, and 64–75. Such varied repetitions of text and music were customary in the polyphonic madrigal. However, he abandoned contrapuntal part-writing for a simple chordal accompaniment so that the words and melody would strike the listener with greater force.

At a number of the cadences, Caccini wrote out the embellishments that singers customarily would have added—for example, at the words "muoia" (measure 7) and "aurora" (measures 66 and 70–72). Caccini, himself a singer, notated the ornaments because he did not trust others to improvise appropriately. Other refinements that Caccini considered essential to performance—although not always indicated in the score—were crescendos and decrescendos, trills and turns (called *gruppi* or *groppi*), rapid repetitions of the same pitch (called *trilli*), *esclamazioni* ("exclamations," performed with a decrescendo after attacking a note, followed by a sforzando), and departures from strict observance of the printed note values (now called *tempo rubato* or "stolen time"). He described these refinements and gave examples of some of them in his foreword to *Le nuove musiche*. The editor of this edition of *Vedrò 'l mio sol* has suggested the placement of some of these effects in brackets. On the accompanying recording, the singer follows all of Caccini's ornaments, performs some but not all of those suggested by the editor, and adds several others as well.

The accompaniment is a basso continuo, specifically a *figured bass*, in which the composer has added numbers and flat or sharp signs below the bass notes to indicate what notes are to be played. Caccini claimed to have invented the practice of figuring the basso continuo, and indeed *Le nuove musiche* contains some of the earliest examples of scores with specific figuration. The editor has supplied one possible *realization* of the figured bass in smaller notes in the treble staff just above the bass. If there is no figure, the presumption is that the third and fifth above the bass note should be played (as in the first measure), although passing and other ornamental tones are allowed. Caccini's 11—♯10 figures in the second measure indicate that a G and F♯ are to be sounded in succession, exactly an eleventh and tenth above the D in the bass; later composers would simply have written 4—♯3 in the same circumstance, leaving it to the player to determine the correct octave for the G—F♯ suspension. A sharp without a number indicates that the third of the chord should be major, as in measure 25; a flat indicates that the third is minor, as in measures 32–33. The continuo player is welcome to introduce figuration as long as it does not overwhelm the singer. For example, the editor suggests imitating the singer's figure in measures 33 and 37, and playing a scale leading up to the singer's next note in measures 16 and 45.

The basso continuo can be played by one or more instruments. The most likely accompaniment would have been a lute or a *theorbo*, a large lute with extra bass strings. Caccini intended for the singer to accompany himself or herself (an indication of the high level of training required to perform his songs), but in recent times very few performers are trained both as singers and as lutenists. On the accompanying recording, a theorbo player improvises an introduction over the opening bass line of the song (measures 1–7 and 12–13) and then accompanies throughout, later joined by harp and viola da gamba.

Jacopo Peri (1561–1633)

Le musiche sopra l'Euridice: Excerpts

Opera
1600

(a) Aria: *Nel pur ardor*

Nel pur ar - dor del - la più bel - la stel - la Au - rea fa - cel - la
Lie - to I - me - neo d'al - ta dol - cez-za un nem - bo Tra - boc-ca in grem - bo a

Edited from Jacopo Peri, *Le musiche sopra l'Euridice* (Florence, 1601), 11–12 and 14–17. Note values reduced by half. Original barring retained. Time signatures added by the editor are in brackets; editorial accidentals are above the staff.

442

TIRSI

Nel pur ardor della più bella stella	With the pure flame of the brightest star
Aurea facella di bel foc'accendi,	light the golden torch with beautiful fire
E qui discendi su l'aurate piume,	and here descend on golden wings,
Giocondo Nume, e di celeste fiamma	O happy god, and with celestial fire
L'anime infiamma.	the souls inflame.
Lieto Imeneo d'alta dolcezza un nembo	Happy Hymen, let your shower of lofty sweetness
Trabocca in grembo a' fortunati amanti	overflow into the breasts of the fortunate lovers
E tra bei canti di soavi amori	and, amidst pretty songs of delightful loves,
Sveglia nei cori una dolce aura, un riso	stir in their hearts a gentle breeze, a smile
Di Paradiso.	of Paradise.

(b) Dialogue in recitative: *Per quel vago boschetto*

DAFNE

0:00	Per quel vago boschetto,	In the beautiful thicket,
	Ove, rigando i fiori,	where, watering the flowers,
	Lento trascorre il fonte degl'allori,	slowly courses the spring of the laurel,
	Prendea dolce diletto	she took sweet delight
	Con le compagne sue la bella sposa,	with her companions—the beautiful bride—
	Chi violetta o rosa	as some picked violets, others roses,
	Per far ghirland' al crine	to make garlands for their hair,
	Togliea dal prato o dall'acute spine,	in the meadow or among the sharp thorns.
	E qual posand' il fianco	Others lying on their sides
	Su la fiorita sponda	on the flowered bank,
	Dolce cantava al mormorar dell' onda;	sang sweetly to the murmur of the waves.
1:16	Ma la bella Euridice	But the lovely Eurydice
	Movea danzando il piè sul verde prato	dancingly moved her feet on the green grass
	Quand'ahi ria sorte acerba,	when—O bitter, angry fate!—
	Angue crudo e spietato	a snake, cruel and merciless,
	Che celato giacea tra fiori e l'erba	that lay hidden among flowers and grass
	Punsele il piè con si maligno dente,	bit her foot with such an evil tooth
	Ch'impalidì repente	that she suddenly became pale
	Come raggio di sol che nube adombri.	like a ray of sunshine that a cloud darkens.
2:16	El dal profondo core,	And from the depths of her heart,
	Con un sospir mortale,	a mortal sigh,
	Si spaventoso ohimè sospinse fuore,	so frightful, alas, flew forth,
	Che, quasi avesse l'ale,	that, almost as if they had wings,
	Giunse ogni Ninfa al doloroso suono.	every nymph rushed to the painful sound.
	Et ella in abbandono	And she, fainting,
	Tutta lasciossi all'or nell'altrui braccia.	let herself fall in another's arms.
3:06	Spargea il bel volto e le dorate chiome	Then spread over her beautiful face and her golden tresses
	Un sudor viè più fredd'assai che giaccio.	a sweat colder by far than ice.
	Indi s'udio 'l tuo nome	And then was heard your name, sounding
	Tra le labbra sonar fredd'e' tremanti	between her lips, cold and trembling,
	E volti gl'occhi al cielo,	and her eyes turned to heaven,
	Scolorito il bel volto e' bei sembianti,	her beautiful face and appearance discolored,
	Restò tanta bellezza immobil gielo.	this great beauty was transformed to motionless ice.

ARCETRO

4:25	Che narri, ohimè, che sento?	What do you relate, alas, what do I hear?
	Misera Ninfa, e più misero amante,	Wretched nymph, and more unhappy lover,
	Spettacol di miseria e di tormento!	spectacle of sorrow and of torment!

ORFEO

5:00	Non piango e non sospiro,	I do not weep, nor do I sigh,
	O mia cara Euridice,	O my dear Eurydice,
	Ché sospirar, ché lacrimar non posso.	for I am unable to sigh, to weep.
	Cadavero infelice,	Unhappy corpse,
	O mio core, o mia speme, o pace, o vita!	O my heart, O my hope, O peace, O life!
	Ohimè, chi mi t'ha tolto,	Alas, who has taken you from me?
	Chi mi t'ha tolto, ohimè! dove sei gita?	Who has taken you away, alas? Where have you gone?
6:16	Tosto vedrai ch'in vano	Soon you will see that not in vain
	Non chiamasti morendo il tuo consorte.	did you, dying, call your spouse.
	Non son, non son lontano:	I am not far away;
	Io vengo, o cara vita, o cara morte.	I come, O dear life, O dear death.

— OTTAVIO RINUCCINI

Le musiche sopra l'Euridice (The Music on The Euridice, or simply *Euridice*) is the earliest opera to survive in a complete score. Ottavio Rinuccini wrote the text (called the *libretto*), and Jacopo Peri set it to music. The opera was produced in Florence on October 6, 1600 for the wedding of King Henry IV of France and Maria de' Medici, niece of the grand duke of Tuscany. As important as the opera seems in retrospect, *Euridice* was only a small part of the wedding entertainment, overshadowed by other events that reached a wider audience and were better received. In that first performance, some of the music was replaced by Giulio Caccini's setting of the same libretto. Peri himself sang the role of Orfeo (Orpheus), and a boy soprano sang the part of Dafne, the messenger in the second excerpt given here. Caccini rushed his version into print that December, and Peri's was published the following February.

The plot of *Euridice* centers on the powers of music—an ideal topic for the first operas. According to the story, on the wedding day of the half-god musician Orpheus and his beloved Eurydice, the bride-to-be dies from a snakebite. Orpheus goes down to the underworld and wins her back through the beauty of his singing and playing on the lyre. The original story had a tragic ending, but Rinuccini altered the plot to end happily since the opera was to be performed in celebration of a wedding.

The two excerpts reprinted here from Peri's *Euridice* illustrate two styles of *monody*, or solo singing, found in this work: *aria* and *recitative*.

Tirsi's song (a) to Hymen, god of marriage, is an aria (Italian for "air"), a term that at the time simply designated a strophic song. Some arias, including the Prologue to this opera, were set to relatively simple melodic outlines like those used in the sixteenth century for singing poetry, with each line set to recitation on a repeated pitch followed by a cadential pattern. But Tirsi's song features a tuneful and rhythmically marked melody similar to that of a canzonetta.

There are two strophes of five lines, the first four with eleven syllables and the last with five. Most opera libretti primarily use lines of eleven and seven syllables, which were standard in Italian poetry (compare the poems for NAWM 30–32 and 56–59). But here, in the middle lines of each strophe, Rinuccini adds internal rhymes that rhyme with the previous line, creating an effect of five-syllable lines alternating with longer ones:

> Nei pur ardor della più bella stella
> Aurea facella
>   di bel foc' accendi,
> E qui discendi
>   su l'aurate piume,
> Giocondo Nume,
>   e di celeste fiamma
> L'anime infiamma.

Peri emphasizes each rhyming word with a similar figure: a rhythm of two quarter notes (or quarter and eighth), usually on a repeated note. The resulting melody is both simple and charming, perfectly reflecting the idealized shepherd who sings it.

This aria is introduced by music that was referred to as a *sinfonia*, a term that then simply meant a piece for instrumental ensemble. Despite its brevity, this sinfonia is the longest purely instrumental interlude in Peri's score. A shortened version of the sinfonia appears as a *ritornello*, or instrumental refrain, after each stanza. The undulating parallel thirds above a drone indicate the pastoral setting for the drama, a rural landscape populated by shepherds. Instruments are not specified, but the pastoral associations strongly suggest the use of two flutes or recorders, as in the performance on the accompanying recording.

By contrast to Tirsi's aria, Dafne's speech and the reactions to it of Arcetro and Orfeo (b) are examples of the new style of *recitar cantando* (literally, "to recite while singing"), later known as *recitative*, which Peri claimed to have pioneered and which was fundamental to the new genre of opera. In this style, the voice imitates the inflections and rhythms of speech, and the chords specified by the basso continuo simply provide support, having no rhythmic profile or formal plan of their own. The voice returns frequently to pitches consonant with the harmony on the main accents of the poetic line. But, in order to imitate the gliding contours of the natural speaking voice, the melody wanders from the chordal tones of the accompaniment on syllables that would not be sustained in a spoken recitation (for example, see measures 3 and 21–22). In order to highlight the meaning of the text, some dissonances are emphasized, particularly to convey strongly negative emotions, as at "Angue crudo e spietato" (cruel and merciless snake, measures 23–24) and "maligno dente" (evil tooth, measures 26–27). The poetry is laid out in lines of seven and eleven syllables in a free rhyme scheme. Only some line endings are marked by cadences; many are elided, which again suggests a naturalistic depiction of speech.

The dramatic style of recitative is especially appropriate for the text of this scene. In the midst of preparations for the wedding of the famed musician Orfeo and the nymph Euridice, Dafne reports that Euridice, while picking flowers to make a garland for her hair, was bitten by a snake and died. There is a natural progression in Dafne's speech. At first, it is emotionally neutral, consonant, and with slow-changing harmonies. As she tells of Euridice's fatal snakebite, it becomes more excited, with more dissonances, sudden changes of harmony, fewer cadences, and more rapid movement in the bass.

The responses to the news by the shepherd Arcetro and by Orfeo are also in the new recitative style. Peri made these melodies more lyrical and tuneful through varied repetitions and sequences. But the dissonances are even stronger than those in Daphne's speech, expressive of their grief, as at "Misera Ninfa" (wretched nymph, measures 58–59) and "Che sospirar" (to sigh, measure 67). Peri used melodic chromaticism to heighten emphasis on the words "miseria" and "tormento" (sorrow and torment, measures 62–63), and used chromatically contrasting chords to intensify the harmony, as at the change from an E-major triad on "o pace, o vita!" (oh peace, oh life!) to G minor on "Ohimè" (alas, at measures 72–73). When Orfeo vows to go down to the underworld to retrieve Euridice from the land of the dead (measures 80–87), the music returns to diatonicism, with several successive cadences that symbolize his resolve.

Claudio Monteverdi (1567–1643)

L'Orfeo: Excerpt from Act II

Opera

1607

74

(a) Aria/canzonetta: *Vi ricorda o boschi ombrosi*

From *Tutte le opere di Claudio Monteverdi*, ed. G. Francesco Malipiero, vol. 11, *L'Orfeo, favola in musica; Lamento d'Arianna* (Vienna: Universal Edition, 1929), 48–65. Used with kind permission of European American Music Distributors Company, U.S. and Canadian agent for Universal Edition A.G., Vienna.

Vissi già mesto e do_len_te, vis_si già mesto e do_lente Hor gio_i_sco e quegli af_

(Più tranquillo)

_fan _ ni che sof_fer_ti ho per tan _ t'an_ni   fan più ca _ ro il ben pre_

_sen _ te. Vis_si già me_sto e do_len_te, vis_si già   mesto e do_

(b) Song: *Mira, deh mira Orfeo*

(c) Dialogue in recitative: *Ahi, caso acerbo*

1) The character's name is missing, but it is a shepherd.

(d) Recitative: *Tu se' morta*

(e) Choral madrigal: *Ahi, caso acerbo*

CHORO

[Aria/canzonetta]

Orfeo

0:00	Vi ricorda, o boschi ombrosi,	Do you remember, O shady woods,
	de' miei lungh' aspri tormenti,	my long, bitter torments,
	quando i sassi ai miei lamenti	when the stones to my laments
	rispondean, fatti pietosi?	replied, being moved to pity?

0:37	Dite, all'hor non vi sembrai	Say, then did I not appear to you
	più d'ogn'altro sconsolato?	to be more disconsolate than any other?
	Hor fortuna ha stil cangiato	Now Fortune has changed her tune
	et ha volto in festa i guai.	and has turned to joys my troubles.

1:15	Vissi già mesto e dolente.	I once lived sad and sorrowful.
	Hor gioisco e quegli affanni	Now I rejoice, and those difficulties
	che sofferti ho per tant'anni	that I suffered for so many years
	fan più caro il ben presente.	make more dear my present blessings.

1:53	Sol per te, bella Euridice,	Only because of you, beautiful Eurydice,
	benedico il mio tormento;	do I bless my torment;
	dopo il duol vi è più contento,	after grief, one is more content,
	dopo il mal vi è più felice.	after misfortune, one is more happy.

[Song]

Shepherd

0:00	Mira, deh mira, Orfeo, che d'ogni intorno	Behold, ah, behold, Orpheus, how all around
	ride il bosco e ride il prato.	the woods laugh and the meadows laugh.
	Segui pur col pletr' aurato	Continue then, with golden plectrum
	d'addolcir l'aria in si beato giorno.	to sweeten the air on such a blessed day.

[Dialogue in recitative]

Messenger

0:00	Ahi, caso acerbo, ahi, fato empio e crudele!	Ah, bitter event, ah, fate wicked and cruel!
	Ahi, stelle ingiuriose, ahi, cielo avaro!	Ah, malicious stars, ah stingy heavens!

Shepherd

Qual suon dolente il lieto di perturba?	What mournful sound disturbs the happy day?

Messenger

Lassa, dunque debb'io,	Alas, therefore must I,
mentre Orfeo con sue note il ciel consola,	while Orpheus with his notes delights heaven,
con le parole mie passargli il core?	with my words pierce his heart?

Shepherd

1:01	Questa è Silvia gentile,	This is gentle Sylvia,
	dolcissima compagna	sweetest companion
	della bell' Euridice. O quanto è in vista	of the beautiful Euridice. O how her face looks
	dolorosa! Hor che fia? Deh, sommi Dei,	sorrowful! Now what has happened? Ah, great Gods,
	non torcete da noi benigno il guardo.	do not turn from us your benign gaze.

Messenger

Pastor, lasciate il canto,	Shepherd, leave off your song,
ch'ogni nostra allegrezza in doglia è volta.	for all our mirth is turned to grief.

ORFEO

1:47 D'onde vieni? Ove vai? Ninfa, che porti?	Whence do you come? Where do you go? Nymph, what news do you bring?

MESSENGER

A te ne vengo Orfeo,	To you I come, Orpheus,
messaggera infelice	unhappy messenger
di caso più infelice e più funesto.	of tidings yet more unhappy and more tragic.
2:11 La tua bella Euridice . . .	Your beautiful Eurydice . . .

ORFEO

Ohimè, che odo?	Alas, what do I hear?

MESSENGER

La tua diletta sposa è morta.	Your beloved wife is dead.

ORFEO

Ohimè.	Alas!

MESSENGER

2:50 In un fiorito prato	In a flowered meadow
Con l'altre sue compagne	with her companions
Giva cogliendo fiori	she was going about gathering flowers
Per farne una ghirlanda a le sue chiome,	to make a garland for her hair,
Quand'angue insidioso,	when a treacherous serpent
Ch'era fra l'erbe ascoso,	that was hidden in the grass
Le punse un piè con velenoso dente:	bit her foot with venomous tooth:
Ed ecco immantinente	then at once
Scolorirsi il bel viso e nei suoi lumi	her face became pale, and in her eyes
Sparir que lampi, ond'ella al sol fea scorno.	those fires that vied with the sun grew dim.
All'hor noi tutte sbigottite e meste	Then we all, frightened and sad,
Le fummo intorno, richiamar tentando	gathered around calling, tempting
Li spirti in lei smarriti	the spirits that were smothered in her
Con l'onda fresca e con possenti carmi;	with fresh water and powerful charms.
4:14 Ma nulla valse, ahi lassa!	But nothing helped, alas,
Ch'ella i languidi lumi alquanto aprendo,	for she, opening her languid eyes slightly,
E te chiamando Orfeo,	called to you, Orpheus,
Dopo un grave sospiro	and, after a deep sigh,
Spirò fra queste braccia, ed io rimasi	expired in these arms, and I remained
Piena il cor di pietade e di spavento.	with heart full of pity and terror.

SHEPHERD

5:32 Ahi caso acerbo, ahi fato empio e crudele!	Ah, bitter event, ah, fate wicked and cruel!
Ahi stelle ingiuriose, ahi cielo avaro!	Ah, malicious stars, ah, stingy heavens!

SHEPHERD

5:55 A l'amara novella	The bitter news
rassembra l'infelice un muto sasso,	has turned the unfortunate one into a mute stone;
che per troppo dolor non può dolersi.	from too much pain, he can feel no pain.

Shepherd

Ahi ben havrebbe un cor di Tigre o d'Orsa	Ah, he must have the heart of a tiger or a bear
Chi non sentisse del tuo mal pietate,	who did not feel pity for your loss,
Privo d'ogni tuo ben, misero amante!	as you are bereft of your dear one, wretched lover.

[Recitative]

Orfeo

0:00

Tu se' morta, mia vita, ed io respiro?	You are dead, my life, and I still breathe?
Tu se' da me partita	You have departed from me,
Per mai più non tornare, ed io rimango?	never to return, and I remain?

0:56

No, che se i versi alcuna cosa ponno,	No, for if verses have any power,
N'andrò sicuro a' più profondi abissi,	I shall go safely to the most profound abyss,
E intenerito il cor del Re de l'Ombre	and having softened the heart of the King of the Shades
Meco trarrotti a riveder le stelle,	I shall bring you back to see the stars once again,
O se ciò negherammi empio destino	and if this is denied me by wicked fate,
Rimarrò teco in compagnia di morte,	I shall remain with you in the company of death.

2:02

| A dio terra, a dio cielo, e sole, a dio. | Farewell earth, farewell sky and sun, farewell. |

[Choral madrigal]

Chorus

0:00

| Ahi caso acerbo, ahi fato empio e crudele! | Ah, bitter event, ah, fate wicked and cruel! |
| Ahi stelle ingiuriose, ahi cielo avaro! | Ah, malicious stars, ah stingy heavens! |

0:28

Non si fidi huom mortale	Trust not, mortal man,
Di ben caduco e frale	in goods fleeting and frail,
Che tosto fugge, e spesso	for they easily slip away, and often
A gran salita il precipizio è presso.	after a steep ascent the precipice is near.

—Alessandro Striggio

Monteverdi's *L'Orfeo* was first performed in 1607 for the Accademia degli Invaghiti in Mantua, where Monteverdi was maestro di cappella for Duke Vincenzo I. The academy was an aristocratic arts club (*invaghirsi* means to take a fancy to something) whose members included Francesco Gonzaga of the ducal family and Alessandro Striggio (ca. 1573–1630), who wrote the libretto. Striggio, the son of a Florentine musician and composer, expanded the story of Rinuccini's *Euridice* into a five-act play. Likewise, Monteverdi built on Peri's achievement, but used his own experience as a madrigal composer to create a musically and dramatically more satisfying form. The score was published in Venice in 1609, two years after the premiere in Mantua.

This extended excerpt from the middle of Act II exhibits Monteverdi's use of varied forms and styles for dramatic purposes. After a series of celebratory arias and ensembles at the beginning of the act, Orfeo sings a strophic aria in the style of a canzonetta, *Vi ricorda o boschi ombrosi* (a). In spirit, it resembles Peri's aria for Tirsi (NAWM 73a), but the ritornello is in five-part counterpoint. A note in the score explains that the ritornello should be played from behind the scene by five *viole da braccio* (viols played like violins), a contrabass, two harpsichords, and three *chitaroni* (theorbos) on the basso continuo. In this song, Orfeo recalls his earlier unhappiness, which has turned to joy now that he has won Euridice to be his bride. Orfeo's current happiness, conveyed by the light-hearted canzonetta style and bouncy rhythm of the music, makes the coming tragedy all the more poignant.

A shepherd then sings a brief, tuneful song (b) in which he claims that even the woods and fields are laughing on this blessed day. But ironically he is interrupted when the Messenger arrives with her cry, *Ahi, caso acerbo* (Ah, bitter event) (c). Here the basso continuo accompaniment changes character through a change in orchestration from strings to an organ with wooden pipes and a theorbo, evoking a much more somber mood. The tonal center changes too, from the happy tones of the shepherd's Hypoionian (the plagal mode on C), similar to C major, to Hypoaeolian (the plagal mode on A), which sounds to modern ears like A minor. In the ensuing dramatic dialogue, Monteverdi imitated the recitative style developed by Peri, but he introduced a greater variety of melodic styles and used the harmony as a dramatic and formal device. Throughout the dialogue, the Messenger maintains her mournful mode and instrumentation, while the shepherds remain in their same more cheerful tonal and timbral realm, illustrating their lack of understanding of her grief. When Orfeo asks from where she comes and what news she brings (measures 39–41), he quickly moves up the circle of fifths from their tonal region to hers, adopting her tone of concern. When the messenger tells him that Euridice is dead, there is a stark contrast between the E-major triad in her tonal realm and the G- and C-minor triads in Orfeo's interjection, "Alas, what do I hear?" (measures 46–47). This use of chromaticism resembles that of the madrigal tradition and suggests the deep emotional impact of her words.

The Messenger then relates the events leading to Euridice's death, varying her style from simple narration on repeated notes (as at "In un fiorito prato," measure 50) to highly emotive speech (as at the leaps on "ahi lassa," measure 68, and "Orfeo," measure 72). The tonal center wanders in this section, allowing more expressive uses of chromaticism and striking harmonic juxtapositions to convey the strong feelings and images of the text. A shepherd then repeats the Messenger's opening cry of despair (at measure 77), which returns several more times as a kind of ritornello framing the rest of the act.

In Orfeo's lament (d), Monteverdi attained a new lyricism that far surpassed that of the first monodic experiments. In the passage that begins "Tu se' morta," each phrase builds greater intensity through rising pitches, chromatic alterations, and rhythmic changes. When necessary, Monteverdi repeated words and phrases from the libretto to further exploit these musical techniques. By this process and by harmonic means, he linked the fragments of recitative into coherent arches of melody. Particularly notable is the setting of the last line, "a dio terra" (measures 110–113). Here the rhythmic parallelism, the chromaticism, the rising pitch to the climax on "e sole," and the leap down to a note sounding a seventh against the bass convey the depth of Orfeo's grief.

Monteverdi composed the first section of the chorus with the melody of the Messenger's opening cry in the bass (with slight rhythmic modifications) and with the other four parts built above it. In essence, Monteverdi merged the expressive recitative style of Peri with the expressive polyphony of the madrigal tradition. As in the *kommos* of ancient Greek tragedy, which was a lament by the chorus in dialogue with one or more characters on stage, here the chorus joins Orfeo and the shepherds in bemoaning Euridice's death. Then, in the second section (after the double bar), the chorus assumes its traditional function of offering moralizing reflections on the stage action. Humankind, it sings, should not trust in the goods and pleasures of the world, for they are elusive and pass quickly. Monteverdi here adopted the methods of word-painting that were commonly used in polyphonic madrigals: all voices speed up for the idea of flight at "che tosto fugge" (that soon fly away), rise at "gran salita" (steep ascent, rendered in some versions as "gran fatica," great effort), and leap down at "il precipizio" (the precipice).

Most of Monteverdi's score is explicit about which instruments are to play in each section, a specificity that was still rare at the time *L'Orfeo* was composed. The great number and variety of instruments was no doubt made possible by the opera's aristocratic sponsors, and may have been made explicit in the printed score to lend prestige to their musical connoisseurship. The score and libretto are less clear about which passages are to be sung by which shepherd; the ranges vary, and on the accompanying recording the parts marked "Pastore" (Shepherd) are distributed among three singers. The editor of this edition has added tempo and dynamic markings, which do not appear in the original score. On the recording, the changes of instrumentation that reflect changes of mood are readily heard. The singers add ornamentation in the manner customary at the time.

Claudio Monteverdi (1567–1643)

L'incoronazione di Poppea: Act I, Scene 3

Opera

1642

75

(a) Dialogue in recitative: *Signor, deh non partire*

From Claudio Monteverdi, *L'incoronazione di Poppea*. Music by Claudio Monteverdi. Libretto by Giovanni Busenello. Edited by Alan Curtis. Copyright © 1989 Novello & Company, Limited. International copyright secured. All rights reserved. Reprinted with permission of G. Schirmer, Inc. (ASCAP). English singing version by Arthur Jacobs. For the original Venice libretto in a more literal translation, see pages 483–85 below.

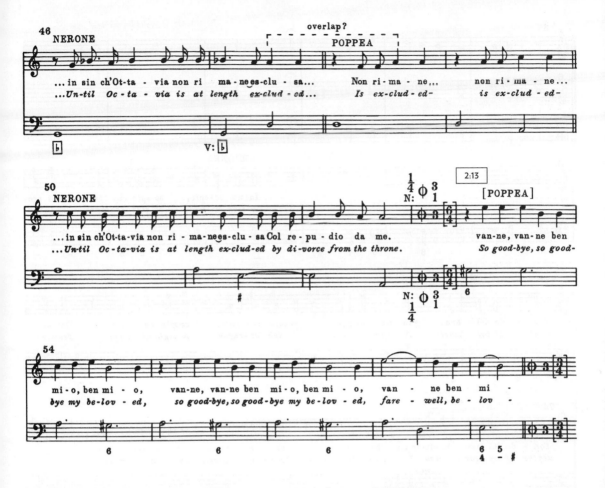

(b) Aria: *In un sospir*

(c) Aria: *Signor, sempre mi vedi*

(d) Dialogue in mixed styles: *Adorati miei rai*

1) Copied up a 3rd (surely by mistake!) in both MSS.

POPPEA

Signor deh non partire,	My lord, please don't go.
Sostien, che queste braccia	Allow these arms
Ti circondino il collo,	to encircle your neck,
Come le tue bellezze	as your beauties
Circondano il cor mio;	encircle my heart.
Apena spunta l'alba, et tu che sei	The dawn is barely breaking, and you, who are
L'incarnato mio Sole,	my sun made flesh,
La mia palpabil luce,	my light made palpable,
E l'amoroso dì della mia vita,	and the loving day of my life,
Vuoi sì repente far da me partita?	want to part from me so quickly?
Deh non dir	Please don't say
Di partir,	that you're leaving.
Che di voce sì amara a un solo accento,	It is such a bitter word that from one hint of it,
Ahi perir, ahi spirar quest' alma io sento.	ah, dying, ah, I feel my soul expiring.

NERONE

Poppea, lascia ch'io parta;	Poppea, let me leave.
La nobiltà de' nascimenti tuoi	The nobility of your birth
Non permette, che Roma	does not permit that Rome
Sappia, che siamo uniti,	should know that we are together,
In sin che Ottavia non rimane esclusa	until Ottavia is set aside,
Col repudio da me. Vanne ben mio;	repudiated by me. Go, my dear.
In un sospir, che vien	Within a sigh that rises
Dal profondo del sen,	from the depths of my breast
Includo un bacio, o cara, ed un addio:	I enclose a kiss, dearest, and a farewell.
Si rivedrem ben tosto, Idolo mio.	We shall see each other soon, my idol.

POPPEA

Signor, sempre mi vedi,	My lord, you see me constantly;
Anzi mai non mi vedi.	or better still, you never see me.
Perchè s'è ver, che nel tuo cor io sia	Because, if it's true that I am in your heart,
Entro al tuo sen celata,	hidden in your breast,
Non posso da' tuoi lumi esser mirata.	I cannot by your eyes be viewed.
Deh non dir	Please don't say
Di partir,	that you're leaving.
Che di voce sì amara a un solo accento,	It is such a bitter word that from one hint of it,
Ahi perir, ahi spirar quest' alma io sento.	ah, dying, ah, I feel my soul expiring.

NERONE

Adorati miei rai,	My adored rays,
Deh restatevi omai.	please stay, then;
Rimanti, o mia Poppea,	remain, O my Poppea,
Cor, vezzo, luce mia,	my heart, my charm, my light.
Non temer, tu stai meco a tutte l'ore,	Do not fear; you stay with me at all times,
Splendor negl'occhi, e deità nel core.	splendor of my eyes, and goddess of my heart.
Se ben io vò	Even if I go,
Pur teco io stò,	yet with you I stay.
Il cor dalle tue stelle	My heart from your stars [eyes]
Mai mai non si divelle;	never, never can tear away;
Io non posso da te viver disgiunto	I can no more live separated from you
Se non si smembra l' unità del punto.	than the unity of a point can be divided.

POPPEA

Tornerai?	Will you return?

NERONE

Tornerò.	I'll return.

POPPEA

Quando?	When?

NERONE

Ben tosto.	Very soon.

POPPEA

Me'l prometti?	You promise me?

NERONE

Te'l giuro.   I swear it.

POPPEA

E me l'osserverai?   And you'll keep your promise?

NERONE

E s'a te non verrò, tu a me verrai.   And if I do not come to you, you will come to me.

POPPEA

A Dio, Nerone, a Dio.   Goodbye, Nero, goodbye.

NERONE

A Dio, Poppea, ben mio.   Goodbye, Poppea, my darling.

   — GIOVANNI FRANCESCO BUSENELLO

In his seventy-fourth year, Monteverdi wrote this opera based on a libretto by Giovanni Francesco Busenello (1598–1659) for performances during Venice's carnival season in 1642–43. The opera was not published at the time, although the libretto was; indeed, throughout the seventeenth and early eighteenth centuries, an opera's librettist was generally considered more important than the composer. Two manuscript copies of *L'incoronazione di Poppea* survive, one apparently used for the Venice performances and the other associated with a revival of the opera in Naples in 1651. The editor of the edition included here has collated the two versions and has labeled variants found in only one manuscript with *N* for Naples or *V* for Venice. Modern scholars have argued that the last scene and perhaps other parts of the music were composed by others. Perhaps the opera was a collaboration to which Monteverdi contributed name recognition and music in older styles for which he was famous, while younger composers added music in a more modern style that also appealed to the public. In any case, the scene included here shows all the hallmarks of Monteverdi, such as his use of the older expressive recitative style and his rapid alternation between styles.

    Act I, Scene 3 marks the first time in the opera that we meet Nerone (Nero), emperor of Rome, and his mistress Poppea. But we have already heard much about them from Poppea's cuckolded husband Ottone and from two soldiers whom Nerone left as guards while he spent the night with Poppea. In this scene the lovers emerge from Poppea's house as she begs Nerone not to leave, showing the combination of seduction and flattery that has already won her the emperor's devotion.

    Monteverdi freely repeated or reordered the text to heighten the drama, as can be seen by comparing his setting with Busenello's original libretto (shown with translation on pages 483–85). In the libretto, the scene opens with a long, flowery speech for Poppea begging Nerone not to leave, followed by Nerone's reply that he must leave but will see her again soon. But Monteverdi relocates the first line of Nerone's speech much earlier, so that he interrupts Poppea after her first five lines, impatiently telling her to let him go (measures 12–14); Monteverdi underscores Nerone's imperious attitude with a dramatic pause and crisp cadence. Poppea reiterates the first line of *her* speech more pleadingly, adding repetitions for emphasis ("Don't go, don't go, my lord, please don't go") and echoing her previous melody a fourth higher (compare measures 16–17 to measures 2–4). She then continues where she left off, and in context the greater intensity of feeling already present in Busenello's poetry now seems motivated by Nerone's impatience to leave. Again, she repeats words and melody to heighten her pleas, asking if he really intends to depart "from me, from me, from me, from me" on a rising stepwise figure ("da me, da me, da me, da me," measures 26–28).

When Nerone responds (measure 38), he seems gentler, patiently explaining why he must leave before they are discovered together. When he speaks of his wife Ottavia, Poppea interrupts, repeating his words and egging him on until he says that he will repudiate Ottavia to be with Poppea (measures 42–52). On hearing this, Poppea finally says he may go ("Vanne ben mio," measures 53–59). In Busenello's libretto, these words are all Nerone's, but Monteverdi makes it into a dialogue. The editor has marked two places where the singers might overlap, so that Poppea literally interrupts Nerone (measures 43–44 and 47–48). In the next pair of speeches, Monteverdi moves Nerone's first four lines (set in measures 120–28) before Poppea's last four lines (measures 129–35), to sustain the sense of a dialogue. And in the rest of Nerone's speech, instead of waiting until he is finished as the librettist intended, Poppea keeps interrupting to ask "Will you return?" ("Tornerai?," measures 150, 153, and 157), until Nerone finally promises he will return soon. These interruptions show Poppea as a much stronger character than Nerone and reveal her as the driving force in their relationship, who pushes him until she gets she wants. That he is totally in her thrall is made clear at the end of the scene, as she stretches out their goodbyes—a perfunctory two lines in the libretto—to an extended threefold exchange in which he echoes her words and her music.

Their dialogue progresses through many moods that are reflected in Monteverdi's setting by a variety of styles, including several types of recitative, *arioso*, and aria. Aria style is characterized by a clear meter, a steadily moving bass line, and a tuneful melody in the voice, as in Nerone's "In un sospir" (measures 59–77) and Poppea's "Signor, sempre mi vedi" (measures 90–119). Recitative has a slower, freely moving bass and speechlike rhythms in the voice, as in the beginning of the scene (measures 1–52). Arioso is characterized by a mixture of elements from the other two styles, whether because the rhythmic profile falls between the regular rhythms of aria and the freer rhythms of recitative (as at measures 151–52), or because aria and recitative style alternate rapidly (as at measures 162–69). A short passage in aria style (such as measures 120–24) is also sometimes termed an arioso.

By the time Monteverdi composed *Poppea*, there was an emerging tradition of separating recitatives and arias into longer sections, often with a recitative leading to an aria. Recitative texts were usually in unrhymed lines known as blank verse (*versi sciolti*), sometimes ending in a rhymed couplet, and aria texts were in rhymed verse, often in strophic or other closed forms. But Monteverdi dealt freely with these expectations, as we have seen him do with the libretto's formal structure.

Content rather than poetic form, and the urge to heighten emotional expression rather than the desire to charm and dazzle, determined the shifts between recitative style and aria style, and from one level of speech-song to another.

For example, the librettist wrote the beginning of this scene in blank verse, and accordingly Monteverdi set it in speechlike recitative, with a slightly more active bass for Nerone's words "let me go" (measures 13–14) to convey his impatience to leave. But when Poppea's text changes to rhymed couplets at "Doh non dir/ DI partir" (measure 30), which might suggest an aria, Monteverdi instead uses a highly expressive recitative style that recalls Orfeo's lament (NAWM 74d). The insistent repeated B♭ against an A in the bass, the chromatic motion between B♭ and B♮, and the uncanny alternation of half and whole steps in the vocal descent to the cadence (measures 34–37) perfectly express Poppea's mournful, pleading tone. Indeed, this style of recitative more clearly conveys her mood than any aria melody could do. Conversely, Poppea's speech at "Signor, sempre mi vedi" (measure 90), though written in blank verse by Busenello, is set by Monteverdi in aria style, complete with an opening ritornello, quickly moving bass, melodic sequences, and repeating phrases. Monteverdi composed it as such because the aria style more effectively conveys the appropriate emotion of coy flirting. Similarly, Poppea bursts into aria style (or a short arioso in triple meter) at "Vanne ben mio" (measures 53–58), conveying her happiness at hearing the words she had been hoping to hear from Nerone, and letting the audience see that her real goal is not to love Nerone but to be empress. As would have been expected, Nerone then sings an aria to the rhymed couplets at "In un sospir" (measure 59), but he switches briefly to impassioned recitative for the emotional words "a kiss, dearest, and a farewell" and "my idol" (measures 78–80 and 85–89).

Because *Poppea* was written for a public opera house, a money-making operation, Monteverdi used a much smaller and less varied group of instruments than he used for *Orfeo*, which was written for and funded by aristocratic patrons. The instrumental parts other than the basso continuo are found only in the Naples manuscript, but it seems likely the ritornellos were played by an ensemble in Venice as well. The musicians on the accompanying recording add additional instrumental parts, as in Poppea's aria (measures 94–119) and Nerone's "Splendor negl'occhi" (measures 143–49).

The focus in Venetian opera was always on the singers. Monteverdi provided several opportunities for vocal display, but the singers also likely added expressive ornaments and decorative embellishments, especially at cadences, as on the accompanying recording. The part of Nerone was written for a *castrato*, a male singer castrated before puberty to preserve his high vocal range. By the mid-seventeenth century, the leading male roles in many operas were sung by castratos, who were prized for their brilliant sound and powerful voices. In modern performances these roles are performed by mezzo-sopranos (as on the accompanying recording); are sung by countertenors or male contraltos; or are pitched down an octave and performed by tenors or baritones.

Antonio Cesti (1623–1669)

Orontea: Excerpt from Act II

Opera

1656

76

(a) Scene 16: Recitative, *E che si fa?*

From Antonio Cesti, *Orontea*, ed. William Holmes, Wellesley Edition 11 (Wellesley, Mass.: Wellesley College, 1973), 156–62.

(b) Scene 17: Opening aria: *Intorno all' idol mio*

-la —— te – li per me —— , lar ——————————————— ve d'a – mo —— re ————— .

[Scene 16: Recitative]

Orontea

E che si fa?   What are you doing?

Gelone

Ohimè.   Oh!
Io sfibbiavo costui per carità.   I unbuckled him for charity's sake.

Orontea

Ove fosti fin ora?   Where were you until now?

Gelone

All'altro mondo.   In the other world [i.e., dead drunk].

Orontea

S'obbedisce così?   Is this how you obey me?

Gelone

Se delle mie dimore   If of my delays
Bacco fu la cagione,   Bacchus was the cause,
La botte ch'il versò   the bottle that he poured for me
Si punisca, O Signora, e non Gelone.   should be punished, O Lady, and not Gelone.

ORONTEA

Parti, fuggi di quà.   Leave, get out of here.

GELONE

Parto, fuggo, sparisco, e che sarà?   I leave, I flee, I disappear, and then what?

[Scene 17: Opening aria]

ORONTEA

Intorno all' idol mio	Around my idol
Spirate, pur spirate	breathe, just breathe,
Aure soave e grate	breezes sweet and pleasant,
E nelle guance elette	and on the favored cheeks
Baciatelo per me, cortesi aurette.	kiss him for me, gentle breezes.
Al mio ben che riposa	To my darling, who sleeps
Su l'ali della quiete	on the wings of calm,
Grati sogni assistete,	happy dreams induce;
E 'l mio racchiuso ardore	and my hidden ardor
Svelateli per me, larve d'amore.	unveil to him, phantoms of love.

— GIACINTO ANDREA CICOGNINI

Antonio Cesti established himself as an opera composer by writing for the public opera houses in Venice. Beginning in 1652 he was employed by the archduke of Tyrol (a region in Austria), who was a great fan of Italian opera. Cesti's *Orontea*, with a libretto by Giacinto Andrea Cicognini, was first performed in 1656 at the archduke's newly built Venetian-style opera house in Innsbruck, and it became one of the most frequently staged operas of the mid-1600s both in Italy and abroad.

The opera tells the story of Orontea, an unmarried queen of Egypt who is reluctant to acknowledge her love for a painter named Alidoro until she discovers him painting a portrait of a rival lady of the court. Upon this discovery, Orontea realizes that she is about to lose Alidoro and resolves to marry him despite their difference in social status. In Act II, Scene 16, she encounters Alidoro asleep and the drunken servant Gelone, a comic figure in the opera, picking through Alidoro's pockets in search of money. The style of recitative in this scene is far different from the style common earlier in the century, which could serve a range of purposes from narration to intense emotional expression. The newer style of recitative, which became standard for the next hundred years, is simply a vehicle for rapid dialogue, and the vocal line usually includes many repeated notes on chord tones. The harmony maintains interest and suggests the progress of a conversation through frequent secondary dominant chords and changes of key. Singers sometimes altered the written notes and rhythms for expressive reasons, as on the accompanying recording.

After Orontea sends Gelone packing, she watches Alidoro sleeping, and in the first aria of Scene 17 she confesses her love for him. This aria is more elaborate than those in the early operas. The two violins play throughout, not merely in ritornellos before and after the singer's strophes. Moving away from the strict monody common in earlier operas, Cesti used a new texture of voice with instruments over basso continuo. He and his contemporaries reestablished counterpoint in the upper parts as a standard practice in opera by blending elements of older polyphonic music with the new style. The form is strophic, as in earlier arias, but the music is adjusted to fit the text of the second strophe. There are only two strophes, compared to four or more in some earlier arias (such as NAWM 74a), and the music for each strophe is longer, with many repetitions of words and whole phrases of text to accommodate this greater length.

This aria exhibits a new style of vocal music that was cultivated in Venice and is characterized by tuneful, mostly stepwise, mainly diatonic, and rhythmically simple melodic lines. The smooth contours of the vocal line contrast with and thereby throw into relief the more markedly expressive melodic and harmonic gestures, such as the leap down of a diminished seventh in measure 23 and the unprepared harmonic seventh in the following measure. This passage is heard in the opening ritornello and returns several times. After this aria, the scene continues with a monologue in recitative and another aria in which Orontea further expresses the complexity of her feelings through contrasting sentiments and styles.

Barbara Strozzi (1619–1677)

Lagrime mie

Cantata

1650s

Published in Barbara Strozzi, *Diporti di Euterpe overo Cantate & ariette a voce sola*, Op. 7 (Venice: Alessandro Magni, 1659). Cantata *Lagrime me* by Barbara Strozzi, from Carol MacClintock, ed., *The Solo Song 1580–1730* (New York: W. W. Norton & Company, 1973), 81–88, corrected by reference to the 1659 edition. Copyright © 1973 by W. W. Norton & Company, Inc. Used by permission of W. W. Norton & Company, Inc. Half-brackets indicate colored notation for hemiola.

-mè,_____ mi___ do-nò, Il pa-ter-no ri-gor,_____ il pa-ter-no ri-

-gor _____ l'im-prig-gio-nò.   Tra due mu-ra rin-chiu-sa   stà la bel-la   in-no-

-cen - te   Do-ve giun-ger non può   rag-gio di so - le,   E quel che più mi

duo - le   ed ac-cresc' il mio mal,   tor-men - ti e pe - ne,   È

che per mia ca - gio-ne, per mia ca - gio-ne pro-va ma - le il _____ mi - o be -

- ne. _____ E voi lu - mi do - len - ti, do -

-len - ti, e voi lu - mi do - len - ti, do - len - ti, non pian -

-ge - - - - - - - - - -

80

spi - ro, per cui spi - ro E pur _____ non mo - - ro. Stà co - lei tra du - ri
pre - go, ve ne pre - go) a - spre mi e po - - ne. Dhè to - glie - te - mi la

mar - mi, per cui spi - ro, per cui spi - ro E pur _____ non mo - - ro.
vi - ta, (ve ne pre - go, ve ne pre - go) a - spre mie pe - - ne. _____

85

1.   85   2.

6:11   Adagio   90

Ma ben m'ac - cor - go,   che per tor - men - tar - - mi mag - gior - men -

-te, La sor - te mi nie-ga an-co la mor - te, mi nie-ga an - co,   mi

95

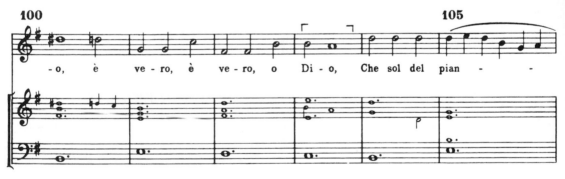

6:49/7:41

nie-ga an-co la mor - te.   Se dun - qu'è ve - ro, o____ Di -

100   **105**

-o,   è ve - ro, è ve - ro, o Di - o,   Che sol del pian - -

110

- to, del pian - - - to, del pian - - - to____ mi -

0:00	Lagrime mie, à che vi trattenete,	Tears of mine, what holds you back,
	Perchè non isfogate il fier' dolore,	why don't you give vent to the fierce pain
	Chi mi toglie 'l respiro e opprime il core?	that takes away my breath and weighs on my heart?
1:38	Lidia, che tant' adoro,	Lidia, whom I adore so much,
	Perchè un guardo pietoso, ahimè, mi donò,	because of a pitying glance, alas, that she gave me,
	Il paterno rigor l'impriggionò.	paternal severity has imprisoned her.
	Tra due mura rinchiusa	Locked up between two walls,
	Stà la bella innocente,	remains the innocent beauty,
	Dove giunger non può raggio di sole,	where no ray of sun can reach,
	E quel che più mi duole	and what most pains me
	Ed accresc'il mio mal, tormenti e pene,	and increases my discomfort, torments, and anguish,
	È che per mia cagione	is that because of me
	Prova male il mio bene.	my beloved suffers.
3:12	E voi lumi dolenti, non piangete!	And you, pained eyes, do not weep!
3:47	Lagrime mie, à che vi trattenete?	Tears of mine, what holds you back?
4:27	Lidia, ahimè, veggo mancarmi.	Lidia, alas, I feel myself failing.
	L'idol mio, che tanto adoro,	My idol, whom I adore so much,
	Stà colei tra duri marmi	remains between hard marble walls,
	Per cui spiro e pur non moro.	her for whom I sigh and yet I don't die.
5:18	Se la morte m'è gradita,	If death suits me,
	Or che son privo di spene,	now that I am deprived of hope,
	Dhè, toglietemi la vita	Oh, take away my life—
	(Ve ne prego) aspre mie pene.	I beg you—my bitter sufferings.

6:11	Ma ben m'accorgo, che per tormentarmi	Still I realize that to torment me
	Maggiormente, la sorte	the more, destiny
	Mi niega anco la morte.	even denies me death.
6:49	Se dunqu'è vero, o Dio,	If it is true then, O God,
	Che sol del pianto mio,	that only for my tears
	Il rio destino ha sete,	does cruel fate thirst,
8:34	[Lagrime mie, à che vi trattenete?]	[tears of mine, what holds you back?]

Barbara Strozzi was one of the most important women composers of the seventeenth century and was especially well known as a composer of cantatas. In 1659 *Lagrime mie* appeared in her third published collection of cantatas and arias, *Diporti di Euterpe* (Pleasures of Euterpe, the muse of music and lyric poetry). The poet may have been her adoptive (and perhaps biological) father Giulio Strozzi, who came from a Florentine noble family but resided in Venice. Partly to give her an outlet for her performances and compositions, he founded a society called the Academy of the Unisoni, and she undoubtedly composed and sang this cantata for that group.

The cantata's form is similar to that of most solo cantatas composed during the mid-seventeenth century, with sections in recitative, arioso, and aria styles that alternate corresponding to changes between narrative and lyric poetry in the text. Except for two lyric stanzas of four eight-syllable lines each, which Strozzi set as a strophic aria (measures 71–87), the text is in madrigal-type verse with seven- and eleven-syllable lines that do not follow a regular rhyme scheme.

Strozzi divided this free-form verse into sections according to content. In the first three lines, the poet addresses his tears; she composed this section as a lament in impassioned recitative style, with long, expressive melismas. The next ten lines are a narration about Lidia, the object of the poet's love; Strozzi set this section as an *arioso*, which combines recitative with some elements of aria style, including passages that feature florid runs, a quickly moving bass, or rhythmic regularity. As the poet recalls the weeping eyes at "E voi lumi dolenti" ("And you, pained eyes," beginning at measure 49), Strozzi invokes the conventional emblem of the lament—the descending bass in triple meter. With the return of the opening line, "Lagrime mie, a che vi trattenete?" ("Tears of mine, what holds you back?," at measure 63), Strozzi repeats the opening musical passage as a kind of refrain. After the Aria (so marked in the original publication), a short recitative leads to a triple-time section built on a descending-fourth bass. The final line receives two parallel settings, the first cadencing on G (measure 116) and the second on the tonal center E, on which most of the earlier sections also closed. Although the music ends here, the poetry strongly implies a return to the opening line, which rhymes with the closing line ("sete" and "trattenete") and completes the thought (beginning at "Se dunqu'è vero," "If it is indeed true"). The performers on the accompanying recording reprise the entire first section of the cantata (measures 1–22); an alternative would be to sing the refrain at measures 63–70, which repeats only the first line but closes on the tonal center E.

The dry declamatory style of theatrical dialogue did not suit such intimate poetic texts, so composers softened, sweetened, and intensified the style of their recitatives in these cantatas, which were meant for chamber performance. In the opening recitative, Strozzi very artfully exploited many of the rhetorical devices that the Roman composers Luigi Rossi (1597–1653) and Giacomo Carissimi (1605–1674) had introduced into cantata recitative. For example, the hesitations on the dissonant D♯, A, and F♯ over the opening E-minor harmony, together with the C♮ of the harmonic-minor scale, create a moving and vivid projection of the lamenting lover's weeping and sobbing. In the Arioso, the tasteful word-inspired runs at "adoro" (adore, measure 25), "pietoso" (pitying, measure 27), and "rigor" (severity, measures 30 and 32); the delicate chromaticism at "tormenti" (torments, measure 42); and the compelling seventh chords and suspensions—particularly over the descending basses—demonstrate Strozzi's mastery in applying music to express the affective vocabulary of this genre.

The cantata is scored for solo voice with continuo, played on a harpsichord on the accompanying recording. In accordance with the performing practice of Strozzi's time, both the singer and the continuo player add improvised embellishments.

Giovanni Gabrieli (CA. 1557–1612)

In ecclesiis

Sacred concerto (motet)

CA. 1610

From Giovanni Gabrieli, *Symphoniae sacrae* (Venice, 1615). Edition from Gabrieli, *Opera omnia*, vol. 5, ed. Denis Arnold (N.p.: American Institute of Musicology, 1969), 32–55. © American Institute of Musicology. Used with permission.

In ecclesiis benedicite Domino, Alleluia.	In churches bless the Lord, Alleluia.
In omni loco dominationis benedic	In every place of government, bless the
anima mea Dominum, Alleluia.	Lord, O my soul, Alleluia.
In Deo salutari meo et gloria mea,	In God is my salvation and my glory,
Deus auxilium meum et spes mea in Deo est,	God is my help, and my hope is in God,
Alleluia.	Alleluia.
Deus noster, te invocamus, te laudamus,	Our God, we implore you, we praise you,
te adoramus;	we worship you;
libera nos, salva nos, vivifica nos, Alleluia.	free us, save us, enliven us, Alleluia.
Deus adiutor noster in aeternum, Alleluia.	God, our helper in eternity, Alleluia.

In ecclesiis is a spectacular example of the large-scale sacred concerto, combining solo singers with vocal and instrumental ensembles and including a wide variety of strongly contrasting textures and styles. Composed in the last few years of Gabrieli's life, it was published in 1615, three years after his death, in a collection titled *Symphoniae sacrae* (Sacred symphonies). The text is not liturgical, but combines phrases from the Office of Holy Trinity, celebrated on the first Sunday after Pentecost (and thus eight weeks after Easter). This motet has also been linked to a mass celebrated each year on the third Sunday of July at the Church of the Redeemer in Venice, with the doge (the city's elected leader) in attendance, giving thanks for the end of an epidemic of plague that hit the city in the 1570s. The words suit the occasion, invoking both church and government and combining pleas for help with praise. There are five sentences in the text, each closing with the word "Alleluia."

We saw in his earlier instrumental canzona (NAWM 70) that Gabrieli was a master of the medium of *cori spezzati* (divided choirs). In that canzona, two groups of instruments play in alternation, engage in dialogue, and then combine in refrains and in a closing climactic section. Here the alternations and combinations are more complex, because Gabrieli draws brilliant sonorities from three distinctive groups: four solo voices (marked voce, meaning "voice"); a four-part chorus (marked *capella*), probably sung with two to four singers on each part; and an ensemble of six instruments. At a time when parts were usually issued without designating the instruments, Gabrieli carefully specified the instrumentation: three cornetts, an alto violin (analogous to the modern viola), and two sackbuts. The organ plays continuo throughout, providing accompaniment for the vocal soloists and following the lowest notes sounded by the vocal and instrumental choirs when they are playing.

Gabrieli has carefully structured the alternating forces to provide variety while gradually building to a climax. The vocal soloists sing at first one by one, then in pairs (starting at measure 39), and finally as a group for the last sentence of the text (measure 102). The vocal choir sings the Alleluias as a refrain with the same music each time, together with whichever soloist or ensemble has preceded them, and then joins with the soloists for the final sentence. After the first two sentences of the text, the instrumental ensemble plays a sinfonia (in the sense of instrumental interlude) on its own and then undergirds the next sentence, dropping out again for the fourth sentence and joining everyone else for the final section. The resulting formal plan is unique but easy for a listener to follow:

Measure	Text	Musical Description
1	First sentence	soprano soloist
6	Alleluia	Refrain: chorus with soprano soloist
13	Second sentence	bass soloist
25	Alleluia	Refrain: chorus with bass soloist
31		Sinfonia: instrumental ensemble
39	Third sentence	alto and tenor in duet, with instrumental ensemble
62	Alleluia	Refrain: chorus, alto and tenor, instrumental ensemble
68	Fourth sentence	soprano and bass in dialogue and duet
95	Alleluia	Refrain: chorus with soprano and bass
102	Fifth sentence	all four soloists, chorus, and instrumental ensemble
119	Alleluia	Refrain: all four soloists, chorus, and instrumental ensemble

Gabrieli uses this variety of forces to introduce a variety of styles and textures. The vocal solos alternate slow passages that sometimes suggest Renaissance polyphony (as in the imitation between voice and organ bass line at measures 12–16) with faster phrases in modern aria-like style, marked by a repeating bass figure (measures 3–5) or sequences (measures 17–19). The refrains begin with chordal homophony in triple meter and continue in duple with a bit of imitation between two parts. The sinfonia is canzona-like, beginning with the standard opening rhythm of a half note followed by two quarter notes (see discussion of NAWM 70), then alternating that with other figures such as dotted rhythms and descending sixteenth-note scales that echo between instruments. The third sentence is like a late-sixteenth-century motet, with frequent imitation or near-imitation between voices and instruments, building from slow to more rapidly moving figuration. The duet between soprano and bass combines Renaissance imitation between the parts with modern touches such as soloistic vocal embellishment (measures 68–69) and a leap of a tritone (measures 72–73), and it changes to a dancelike triple meter for "libera nos" (free us) and "vivifica nos" (enliven us). The final section alternates the entire group with smaller combinations, moving from slow homophony (measure 102) to an increasingly imitative texture with rapid virtuosic embellishment by the instruments and vocal soloists (measures 115–17).

In ecclesiis has a clearly defined tonal center on A, established at the outset and confirmed by the cadences on A at the end of every section. Gabrieli conceived his music in relation to the twelve-mode system put forth by Glareanus in his *Dodekachordon*, as evident in such works as Gabrieli's *Intonationi d'organo* (1593), a collection of intonations (preludes) for organ in all twelve modes. Given the plagal ranges of the soprano and tenor in this motet, spanning from about a fourth below to about a fifth above the modal final, *In ecclesiis* is in mode 10 (Hypoaeolian), the plagal mode on A. There are some striking harmonic touches, such as the juxtaposition at the beginning of each Alleluia between the opening chord of F major and the preceding A-major triad, and the top cornetto's strident F over an A-major triad in the sinfonia (measure 31). The final section begins with startling harmonic motion between major triads related by thirds, from A to F to D, from G to E, and from D to B♭ to G to E (see measures 101–3 and 107–9), emphasizing the word "Deus" (God).

The music was issued in partbooks, with the traditional four partbooks for Cantus, Alto, Tenor, and Bass (assigned to the top and bottom instrumental parts and the middle two vocal soloists) supplemented by ten additional partbooks numbered 5 through 14 plus the "basso per l'organo" for the continuo. In this edition, the original part names are indicated at the beginning of the score, along with the first notes of the original notation. As the latter shows, the musicians were reading from parts without barlines, as in Renaissance notation; the editor shows this in the score by placing barlines between the staves but not through them and by leaving notes that are sustained across barlines in whole values rather than using ties, as in the solo voices in measures 123–28.

On the accompanying recording, the vocal parts are all sung by men, as was the custom in Catholic churches at the time. The solo voices are accompanied by an organ and two theorbos playing continuo; the capella features about four men on each part, two violins doubling two of the parts, and two organs; and the instrumental ensemble is accompanied by yet another organ on continuo. When all three choirs—soloists, capella, and instruments—join together, the sound is truly magnificent.

Alessandro Grandi (1586–1630)

O quam tu pulchra es

Solo motet (sacred concerto)

CA. 1625

79

O quam tu pulchra es,
amica mea, columba mea, formosa mea.
Oculi tui columbarum,
capilli tui sicut greges caprarum
et dentes tui sicut greges tonsarum.
Veni de Libano, amica mea,
columba mea, formosa mea,
veni, coronaberis.
Surge, propera, sponsa mea,
dilecta mea, immaculata mea.
Surge, veni, quia amore langueo.

    —Adapted from Song of Songs,
      4:1–2, 4:8, 2:10, 5:2, and 2:5

O how beautiful you are,
my love, my dove, my beauty.
Your eyes are like doves,
your hair like a flock of goats,
and your teeth like a flock of ewes newly shorn.
Come with me from Lebanon, my love,
my dove, my beauty,
come, make a garland.
Arise, hasten, my bride,
my delight, my spotless one.
Arise, come, for I grow weak with love.

Alessandro Grandi was serving as deputy choirmaster under Monteverdi at St. Mark's Basilica in Venice when he wrote this motet, published in an anthology in 1625. He drew the text from various verses of the Song of Songs, an ancient love poem that was included in the Bible because its erotic imagery was understood to represent the love between God and those who worship him. It was a popular source for musical settings in the seventeenth century, in part because the words invited a rich and varied musical treatment. This setting for solo voice with continuo was considered a motet because it served the same function as Renaissance motets; like them, it was a setting of a Latin text other than the Mass Ordinary that was appropriate for use during a Mass or Office service. But, like Caccini's solo madrigal in NAWM 72, this work uses the new styles of monody to realize a text that in previous generations would have been set polyphonically.

Grandi's solo motet is a religious composition that incorporates elements from dramatic recitative, solo madrigal, and aria. The sections alternate between styles in the same manner as in a cantata (such as Strozzi's *Lagrime mie* in NAWM 77) or in an operatic scene (like the scene from Monteverdi's *L'incoronazione di Poppea* in NAWM 75), demonstrating that the structure of the motet had changed fundamentally from that of its polyphonic predecessors. The first twenty-one measures are recitative, but in a more melodious, rhythmic style than that of recitative used in the theater. The composer and writer Marco Scacchi (ca. 1600–1662) coined the term "hybrid recitative" (*recitativo imbastardito*) to describe this mixed style, which he found more appropriate for church music. The opening phrase, "O quam tu pulchra es" (O how beautiful you are) recurs several times as a kind of refrain. In the following passage, triple-time aria style (measures 22–34) represents greater activity at the words "Veni, veni de Libano" (Come, come from Lebanon). Next follow five measures of recitative that recall the opening section. The triple-time aria style then returns (measures 40–51), again symbolizing activity at "Surge, propera" (Arise, hasten). The rest of the motet features a new refrain on "Surge, veni" (Arise, come) in duple-time aria style that suggests motion through quickly moving bass and vocal lines. This refrain alternates with languid, drawn-out recitative settings for the words "Quia amore langueo" (For I grow weak with love). Pieces composed during this period in the concertato medium (voices with obligatory instrumental accompaniment) often had refrains, so Grandi's use of textual repetition to create two refrains reflects a practice that was common among his contemporaries.

By this period, representing words through music in motets was a century-old tradition. However, Grandi's use of the new monodic styles pioneered in opera and vocal chamber music to express text in motets was novel. It is interesting to note that many more listeners were likely to have encountered these new styles in sacred music than in operas or cantatas, whose audiences were relatively small and elite.

This motet could have been performed in church services or in devotions at the confraternities that were an important part of social life in Venice. The continuo part could be performed on an organ, but theorbo, lute, and harpsichord were also used for playing continuo in churches at this time. On the accompanying recording the continuo is performed on a theorbo, supported by a lirone (a bowed string instrument) that sustains the bass notes. The singer adds appropriate embellishments, especially at cadences.

Giacomo Carissimi (1605–1674)

Historia di Jephte: Conclusion

Oratorio

CA. 1648

80

(a) Recitative: *Plorate colles*

Edited by Gottfried Wolters, figured bass realized by Mathias Siedel (Wolfenbüttel: Möseler Verlag, 1969), 29–39.

Is - ra - el et glo - ri - a pa - tris me - i,   e - go si - ne

fi - li - is vir - go,   e - go fi - li - a u - ni - ge - ni - ta

mo - ri - ar et _____ non vi - - -

vam.   Ex-hor - re - sci - te ru - pes,   ob-stu - pe - sci - te col - les,

val - les et ca - ver - nae in so - ni - tu hor - ri - bi - li re - - so -

me - am   et   Jeph - te   fi - li-am u - ni - ge - ni-tam in car - mi-ne do -

lo - - ris   la - men - ta - - - mi - ni,   et

Jeph - te   fi - li-am u - ni - ge - ni-tam   in   car - mi - ne do -

lo - - ris   la - men - ta - - - mi - ni.

(b) Chorus: *Plorate filii Israel*

[Recitative]

DAUGHTER

0:00	Plorate colles, dolete montes	Weep, hills; grieve, mountains;
	et in afflictione cordis mei ululate!	and in the affliction of my heart, wail!

ECHO

Ululate!	Wail!

DAUGHTER

0:59	Ecce moriar virgo	See, I shall die a virgin
	et non potero morte mea	and I shall not be able at my death
	meis filiis consolari,	to be consoled by my children.
	ingemiscite silvae,	Groan, forests;
	fontes et flumina,	springs and rivers,
	in interitu virginis lachrimate!	for the death of a virgin, weep!

ECHO

Lachrimate!	Weep!

DAUGHTER

2:00	Heu me dolentem	Woe is me, sorrowful,
	in laetitia populi,	amidst the people's joy
	in victoria Israel	in Israel's victory
	et gloria patris mei,	and my father's glory.
	ego sine filiis virgo,	I, without children, a virgin,
	ego filia unigenita	I, an only daughter,
	moriar et non vivam.	will die and not live.
	Exhorrescite rupes, obstupescite colles,	Shudder, crags; be stupefied, hills;
	valles et cavernae	valleys and caves,
	in sonitu horribili resonate!	with the horrible sound resound!

ECHO

Resonate!	Resound!

DAUGHTER

3:14	Plorate filii Israel,	Weep, sons of Israel,
	plorate virginitatem meam	bewail my virginity
	et Jephte filiam unigenitam	and Jephtha's only daughter
	in carmine doloris lamentamini.	lament in songs of sorrow.

[Chorus]

CHORUS

0:00/1:56	Plorate filii Israel,	Weep, sons of Israel;
	plorate omnes virgines	weep, all virgins,
	et filiam Jephte unigenitam	and Jephtha's only daughter
0:45/2:41	in carmine doloris lamentamini.	lament in songs of sorrow.

The *oratorio* is a genre that first developed in Rome during the seventeenth century as a musical setting of a sacred narrative or dialogue in either Latin or Italian. Such works were not used in church services, but were performed in church halls known as oratories, from which the new genre got its name. Oratorios resembled operas without staging, costumes, or action, and they used similar forms of monody, such as recitative and aria. But oratorios differed from operas by sometimes including a narrator and by giving a greater role to the chorus, which had associations both with Greek tragedy and with liturgical polyphony. Oratorios were performed during Lent, the period of penitence before Easter, and they emphasized subjects appropriate to that season.

This excerpt from Giacomo Carissimi's *Jephte* exhibits some of the common characteristics of oratorios. The biblical story, drawn from Judges 11:29–40, emphasizes the Lenten themes of suffering and obedience to God. Jephtha, the military leader of the Israelites, is victorious in battle and owes the victory to a promise he made to the Lord. He vowed that if allowed to defeat the Ammonites, on his return home he would sacrifice the first person to come out of his house. It is his daughter, his only child, who first runs out to meet him with timbrels and dances. Despite his grief, he must keep his vow, but he allows her two months to wander the mountains and bewail her fate.

A contemporary writer, perhaps a priest at the Jesuit college in Rome where Carissimi was maestro di cappella, expanded the brief biblical narrative with additional text, including the closing scene reprinted here. The daughter's lament is a long, sorrowful recitative that is sweetened with arioso passages. Carissimi repeated words and phrases of the text for rhetorical effect, as at "Plorate" (Weep) in measures 287–88 and "et in afflictione cordis mei ululate!" (and in the affliction of my heart, wail!) in measures 291–98. He intensified the effect of text repetition by repeating the melodic gesture a step higher (at "Plorate") or by repeating an entire phrase up a fourth, in what would now be considered a sequence (measures 287–91 and 291–98). The frequent flatting of melodic notes (as at measures 297, 299, and 296) conveys pathos. Two other singers, who echo some of the daughter's cadential phrases, represent her companions.

Carissimi's recitative uses expressive dissonances in a way that recalls early Florentine opera, but they exist in a more chordally conceived environment. For example, the A in measure 292 is not simply a free dissonance, but a member of a chord, and the F♯ in measure 302 is part of a D chord over a G pedal point. Similarly, the skip to the seventh over the bass in measures 308–9 and the Neapolitan sixth chord in measure 310 and elsewhere (featuring a lowered note a minor sixth above the bass and a semitone above the subsequent cadential note) are harmonic rather than purely melodic effects. These passages demonstrate how much the emotional intensity of this scene is expressed through harmonic as well as melodic means.

The oratorio closes with a magnificent six-voice chorus of lamentation. In what became an emblem of lament during the seventeenth century, the bass line descends repeatedly by step through a fourth (measures 358–63 and 367–70); a chromatic variant of the same figure appears in Dido's lament at the end of Purcell's

Dido and Aeneas (NAWM 89b). Especially striking is how Carissimi conveys the intensification of grief by building from single suspensions (measures 377–78) to double suspensions (measures 380ff) and even a triple suspension (measure 381), combining powerful dissonances with a mournful descending gesture.

On the accompanying recording, the continuo is played on theorbo, and the chorus is sung by six solo voices, as was probably the performance practice of the time. As suggested by the editor (with the mark "*Vi- -de*"), measures 413–24 are omitted from the performance on the recording.

Heinrich Schütz (1585–1672)

Saul, was verfolgst du mich, SWV 415, from *Symphoniae sacrae III*

Sacred concerto

CA. 1650

81

First published in *Symphoniarum sacrarum tertia pars, worinnen zubefinden sind deutsche Concerten*, Op. 12 (Dresden, 1650), No. 18. This edition of Heinrich Schütz, *Saul, was verfolgst du mich*, edited by Werner Breig, *Neue Ausgabe sämtlicher Werke*, vol. 21, *Symphoniae Sacrae III* (1650) (Kassel: Bärentreiter, 2002), 95–110.
© 2002 Bärenreiter-Verlag. All rights reserved. Used by permission of European American Music Distributors Company, U.S. and Canadian agent for Bärenreiter-Verlag.

*)The dynamic markings in Violin I and Cantus I apply to both violins and the six solo voices.

*)From here on the dynamic markings in Tenor I are independent from the echo-dynamics of the other voices.

Saul, Saul, was verfolgst du mich?	Saul, Saul, why do you persecute me?
Es wird dir schwer werden,	It will be hard for you
wider den Stachel zu löcken.	to kick against the thorns.

— Acts 26:14

The financial strain and economic privations brought about by the Thirty Years' War (1618–1648) drastically reduced the forces of the court chapel at Dresden, where Heinrich Schütz was chapel master. During that time, he produced mostly pieces for a few singers and instrumentalists, published in his collections of *Kleine geistliche Konzerte*. After the end of the war in 1648, he once again had the full resources of the Dresden chapel at his disposal, and he returned to writing large-scale works. *Saul, was verfolgst du mich* is in the grand polychoral style of Gabrieli (see NAWM 78), with whom Schütz had studied decades earlier. The text is from one of the most dramatic episodes in the New Testament, Paul's description of how he was converted to Christianity:

> Thus I journeyed to Damascus with the authority and commission of the chief priests. At midday, O king, I saw on the way a light from heaven, brighter than the sun, shining round me and those who journeyed with me. And when we had all fallen to the ground, I heard a voice saying to me in the Hebrew language, "Saul, Saul, why do you persecute me? It hurts you to kick against the goads." (Acts 26:12–14, Revised Standard Version)

According to the Bible, Saul, a Jew, had been sent to Damascus to fetch Christian prisoners, and the voice he heard in the desert was that of Christ. The experience led to Saul's conversion and to his career (under the name Paul) as an advocate for Christianity.

The concerto is set for six solo voices (the ensemble Schütz called *favoriti*, or favored ones), two violins, two four-voice choirs (possibly with one to three singers per part), and continuo. Other instruments may have doubled the choral parts. At the opening of the piece, two-note chords from the D-minor triad rise from the depths of the solo basses through the tenors. The same music is then heard shifting to an A-minor triad in the sopranos, and finally the violins present an F-major triad before returning to cadence on D. Christ's question "Was verfolgst du mich?" (Why do you persecute me?) is set to grinding, dissonant anticipations and suspensions that break the rules of traditional counterpoint in order to highlight the harshness of the text. Through all this, the repetition of the very brief text reinforces its intensity.

Thus far in the piece, the texture has been that of a concerto for few voices. Now the polychoral medium conveys the same musical material on a bright D-major triad (measure 17), and the choruses and soloists together reverberate with echoes, suggesting the effect of Christ's voice bouncing off rocky projections in the desert. The dynamic markings—*forte* when the choruses enter, *mezzopiano* for the first echo, and *pianissimo* for the second—are printed in the original publication, showing Schütz's attention to detail for the sake of creating an impressive effect. The slight metric shift in measures 21–23 and the wavering between major and minor triads on G reinforce the effect by creating the sense of the echoing sound being distorted as it ricochets off nearby cliffs.

The following section (beginning at measure 24) is in a contrasting style, a recitative on the words "Es wird dir schwer werden, wider den Stachel zu löcken" (It will be hard for you to kick against the thorns). Here, Schütz demonstrates his skill at text depiction with a large melodic leap downward and a circling melisma on "löcken" (kick), suggesting a flailing, ultimately fruitless gesture of resistance. After a varied reprise of the choral "Saul, Saul" as a refrain (measure 34), the recitative material is developed in duets, imitation, and dialogue (beginning at measure 39), and then the polychoral and recitative ideas are combined (measure 60). At the final return of the "Saul, Saul" chorus, one tenor voice, perhaps representing Christ's clarion call, sounds out "Saul, Saul, Saul" in long notes (measure 66), gradually rising in pitch as the chorus repeats its cry and is echoed by the other soloists, until with a last echo the piece ends quietly.

Original performance practice likely called for all the parts to be sung by men and boys, but on the accompanying recording women sing the upper parts. They are joined by organ and cello performing the continuo, with theorbo added to highlight the contrast in style for the sections on "Es wird dir schwer warden."

Girolamo Frescobaldi (1583–1643)

Toccata No. 3

Toccata

CA. 1615, REV. 1637

82

First published in Girolamo Frescobaldi, *Toccate e partite d' intavolatura di cimbalo . . . Libro primo* (Rome, 1615); printed in this revised form in *Toccate d'intavolatura di cimbalo et organo libro 1* (Rome, 1637). This edition of Girolamo Frescobaldi, Toccata No. 3, from Frescobaldi, *Orgel- und Klavierwerke*, ed. Pierre Pidoux, vol. 3, *Das erste Buch der Toccaten, Partien usw. (1637)* (Kassel: Bärenreiter-Verlag, 1954), 11–13. © 1954 Bärenreiter-Verlag.

Although Girolamo Frescobaldi wrote music in a variety of genres, he made his international reputation with his keyboard music. His 1615 collection entitled *Toccate e partite d' intavolatura di cimbalo . . . Libro primo* (Toccatas and Partitas Intabulated for Harpsichord . . . Book I) was the first that he conceived exclusively for keyboard. The pieces in it, including an early version of this toccata, are idiomatically suited to the harpsichord; the music fits easily under two hands at the keyboard, and Frescobaldi avoided the long sustained notes common in his organ music because they decay too quickly on the plucked strings of the harpsichord. The revised toccata shown here was published in a later collection, *Toccate d'intavolatura di cimbalo et organo libro 1* (Toccatas Intabulated for Harpsichord and Organ Book 1), printed in 1637.

A toccata is a piece in improvisatory style, in which the player explores a range of harmonies and figurations. *Toccata* means "touched" in Italian, referring to the act of touching the keys, as if improvising. (The term may also come from the

Spanish *tocar*, "to play an instrument," since one of the earliest toccata traditions arose in Naples, then ruled by Spain.) Toccatas were often played as preludes to other pieces, and one function of a toccata was to clearly define the mode of the piece that it preceded. This toccata is centered on G with a signature of one flat, suggesting the transposed Dorian or Hypodorian mode on G, identified by most theorists of the time as mode 2. The music is constantly approaching a cadence on either G or D, but in most cases the composer evades or weakens the sense of a cadence through harmonic or rhythmic effects, or through continued motion in one or more part. As a result, the music maintains forward momentum until the final cadence on G.

Like most of Frescobaldi's toccatas, this one unfolds as a series of brief phrases or sections, each closed with a cadence or similar punctuation. Each section treats a distinctive figure that is passed between voices, as in measures 1–2, or varied in some other way, like the sequence in measures 5–6. The style shifts frequently, further distinguishing the sections. At the outset, the toccata breathes the spirit of recitative, with jagged lines and nervous rhythms. At measure 5 there is a short arioso passage with chains of suspensions over a walking bass. A rapid run in the bass in measure 7 leads to an imitative section in measures 8–11. Figurations and textures continue to change every two or three measures throughout the rest of the piece, which gradually builds in intensity as sixteenth-note rhythms come to predominate. According to his preface, Frescobaldi considered that the affection, or feelings, conveyed by the music would also change with the figuration and texture, so that the piece presents a series of contrasting moods. The sectional quality of a toccata derives from its purpose as a prelude or as music to play on the harpsichord for one's own enjoyment, for as Frescobaldi observed, the performer may stop at any cadence that seems appropriate, tailoring the length of the piece to suit the situation.

In accordance with the improvisatory spirit of the toccata, Frescobaldi noted in the preface to this collection that the harpsichordist need not play in strict time, but may accelerate or retard the tempo as prompted by the mood or character of the music, and particularly should play more slowly at cadences. The performer on the accompanying recording, Gustav Leonhardt, follows this suggestion. He also freely arpeggiates chords and adds ornaments, in accordance with the performance practice of Frescobaldi's time.

Girolamo Frescobaldi (1583–1643)

Ricercare after the Credo from *Mass for the Madonna*, in *Fiori musicali*

Ricercare

CA. 1635

From Girolamo Frescobaldi, *Fiori musicali*, ed. Christopher Stembridge (Padua: Armelin Musica, 1997), 68–69. Used by permission.

41

* The sharp indicates that the last chord is major, with B natural (not G sharp).

Girolamo Frescobaldi spent most of his career as organist at St. Peter's Cathedral in Rome, but *Fiori musicali* (Musical Flowers, 1635) was his only published collection that consisted solely of music intended specifically for church services. The collection consists of three *organ masses*, each of which comprises all the music that an organist would need to play for the celebration of Mass in a major church or cathedral. This included a toccata before the Mass, settings of parts of the Kyrie played in alternation with the choir, a canzona after the Epistle, a ricercare after the Credo, a toccata at the Elevation of the Host, and a few other pieces. Included here is the Ricercare after the Credo from the Mass for the Madonna, used for feasts of the Blessed Virgin Mary.

By the early seventeenth century, a *ricercare* was an imitative composition based on the continuous development of a single subject, sometimes with a countersubject. The subject of this ricercare is easy to pick out of the texture because of its distinctive shape, with a rising minor sixth, dotted rhythm, downward leap, and rising chromatic line in deliberate half notes. It appears several times in the first half of the piece, in all four voices, and usually in counterpoint with the lively countersubject that first appears in measure 4. After a cadence in measure 24, the subject appears in augmentation, and a variant of the countersubject in original and inverted form weaves around it. The ricercare is in what most theorists of the time identified as mode 2, the Hypodorian mode transposed up a fourth to center on G. This is confirmed by the strong cadences on G and by the subject, which most often either enters on G and rises chromatically to D (as in measures 1–4) or enters on D and rises to G (as in the bass at measures 5–7). The player has the option to end the piece at the fermata in measure 24 if a shorter ricercare is desired.

Although Frescobaldi conceived *Fiori musicali* for organ, he published the compositions in score rather than organ tablature, and the edition included here maintains that appearance. Such scores were common for organ music around this time in both the Italian and the German traditions, and Frescobaldi commented in his preface to *Fiori musicali* that any accomplished organist should be able to play from a score. The symbol after the barline at the end of each staff indicates the next note that part is to play.

The performance on the accompanying recording is on an organ that was built during the mid-sixteenth century at a convent in Milan, Italy. The organ has been preserved almost intact, allowing us to hear the piece on a type of instrument that Frescobaldi would have known.

This organ is tuned in mean-tone temperament, the most common tuning system for keyboard instruments during the sixteenth and seventeenth centuries. It differs from equal temperament in that the most common intervals and chords are much closer to pure tuning, and the thirds especially are sweeter. However, the half steps are not all the same size, as they would be in equal temperament. Rather, in mean-tone temperament the diatonic semitones (such as B to C and C♯ to D) are larger than the chromatic semitones (such as B♭ to B♮ and C to C♯)— about 50 percent larger. As a result, modern listeners may find the chromatic lines particularly bracing, even unsettling. If the organ seems "out of tune," that is evidence of how accustomed we have become to equal temperament.

84

Biagio Marini (1594–1663)

Sonata IV per il violino per sonar con due corde

Sonata for violin and continuo

CA. 1626

From Biagio Marini, *String Sonatas from Opus 1 and Opus 8*. Transcribed and edited by Thomas D. Dunn; continuo realization by William Gudger. Collegium Musicum: Yale University, Second Series, vol. 10 (Madison, Wisc.: A-R Editions, Inc., 1981), 115–21. Used with permission. All rights reserved.

4:51

115

120

5:14/6:07

125

groppo al alta

130

The sonata for one or two instruments with basso continuo became an important genre in the seventeenth century, signifying a shift in instrumental music that paralleled the increased focus on solo singing in the new vocal genres of the time. Among the first significant sonatas for violin and continuo are the four Biagio Marini included in his Op. 8 (1629), a compendium of his instrumental works in various genres that was published while he was serving as violinist and composer for the ducal court of Neuburg in southern Germany. Marini's sonatas are notable for taking advantage of the idiomatic possibilities of the violin and for borrowing expressive gestures and figuration from vocal monody.

Sonata IV per il violino per sonar con due corde (Sonata IV for the violin to play on two strings) takes its name from its use of double stops (playing on two strings simultaneously, as in measures 31–50). The first published work to make use of this effect was Marini's Op. 2 (1618), published while he was working with Monteverdi at St. Mark's in Venice. Like a canzona (see NAWM 70), the sonata presents a series of contrasting sections, each distinguished by a particular figuration and sometimes by different moods, meters, or tempos. Changes of style between recitative-like and aria-like sections recall similar stylistic alternations in the vocal music of Monteverdi (NAWM 75), Strozzi (NAWM 77), and Grandi (NAWM 79). In sonatas composed later in the century, these contrasting sections would be separated to form individual movements (see NAWM 94).

The first section, marked *Tardo* (slow), begins with an expressive melody in the style of a solo madrigal or recitative above a slowly moving bass. At measure 6, the texture changes to rapid figures that are idiomatic for the violin, and then the two styles alternate. In measures 20–26, the range of the melody expands beyond two octaves, and there are leaps of a seventh, ninth, twelfth, and even larger. The extensive range and large leaps would be difficult or impossible for a singer to perform, so the use of these effects helped to distinguish the new violin idiom from the vocal monody that inspired it.

The second section begins at measure 31 and moves at a more regular pace, like an aria. It presents material in double stops, first moving mostly in parallel thirds or sixths, and then in imitation between two voices (measure 40). In the next section, beginning at measure 51, the violin plays scale figures, trills, and large leaps, as the tempo alternates between *Tardo* (Slow) and *Presto* (Quickly). The *affetti* marking at measure 70 indicates that the player should draw the most intense possible emotion from the passage by using unusual playing techniques or adding highly expressive ornamentation; the violinist on the accompanying recording does so with pulsations on the written notes.

The brief section at measure 83 is distinguished by a change to triple meter and fast tempo, as the violin executes jagged leaps that extend to a range of two and a half octaves. A return to a slow recitative-like melody in quadruple meter at measure 95 leads to an aria-like passage at measure 102, in which the bass moves steadily while the violin spins out a short phrase through transposition and variation. There follows another rhapsodic section at measure 116, marked by scalar figures. The final section, comprising an aria in triple meter (measure

127) and a slow arioso-like conclusion (measure 148), is marked to be repeated, providing the listener with some welcome repetition after the many varied styles and figurations in the sonata, and giving the performers the opportunity to embellish the repetition.

The sonata has a clear tonal center on A. Each section fits into an overall structure of tonal areas: the first section opens and closes on A, the second on G, and the rest of the sections alternate closing on C and on A. Modern listeners may hear this piece in the key of A minor, but the new system of common-practice tonality and of major and minor keys was not widely adopted until a generation later. (Indeed, starting with NAWM 85, all of the remaining selections in this volume are tonal.) That this piece is modal rather than tonal is evident in the chordal progressions. In common-practice tonal music from the second half of the seventeenth century on, root motion is directional, normally moving down by a fifth or third and up by a fourth or second. This is true of some passages in Marini's sonata, such as measures 77–82, but there are at least as many passages in which the opposite is true, such as the Presto in measures 83–94, in which the bass primarily moves up by a fifth or third or down by a fourth or second. The lack of a strong directional pull, and the tendency to move around the circle of fifths in both directions in roughly equal proportions, link this piece to the modally conceived music of the Renaissance and differentiate it from the strongly directional tonal music in the sonatas of Arcangelo Corelli (see NAWM 94).

In the performance on the accompanying recording, the violinist emphasizes the contrast between the recitative-like and aria-like sections by playing with much greater rhythmic freedom in the former. Both soloist and harpsichordist add embellishments, especially at cadences, as was customary performance practice during the period.

Jean-Baptiste Lully (1632–1687)

Armide: Excerpts

Opera (tragédie en musique or tragédie lyrique)

1686

85

(a) Overture `concise ))`

From Jean-Baptiste Lully, *Oeuvres Complètes*, series 3, vol. 14, Armide, ed. Lois Rosow, text edited by Jean-Noël Laurenti (Hildesheim: Georg Olms, 2003), 31–33, 165–66, and 173–82.

(b) Conclusion of divertissement from Act II, Scene 4: *Laissons au tendre amour*

Premier Air

2:09

* On the recording, the chorus is preceded by this Prelude, which introduced the same chorus when it was
sung earlier, near the beginning of the divertissement.

(c) Act II, Scene 5: *Enfin il est en ma puissance*

concise

Prélude

'Armide tenant un dard à la main'

'Armide va pour fraper Renaud, et ne peut executer le dessein qu'elle a de luy oster la vie.'

* On the recording, the music returns to measure 71, continues through measure 90, and again repeats measures 86–90.

[Conclusion of Act II, Scene 4]

SHEPHERDESS

2:09	Laissons au tendre amour la Jeunesse en partage,	Let us leave Youth to tender love,
	La Sagesse a son temps, il ne vient que trop tost:	Wisdom in his time comes too soon:
	Ce n'est pas estre sage	it is not wise
	D'estre plus sage qu'il ne faut.	to be more wise than necessary.

CHORUS OF HEROIC SHEPHERDS AND SHEPHERDESSES

3:21	Ah! quelle erreur! quelle folie!	Ah! what an error! what madness!
	De ne pas joüir de la vie!	to not rejoice in life!
	C'est aux Jeux, c'est aux Amours	To games, to loves
	Qu'il faut donner les beaux jours.	one must give one's best days.

[Scene 5]

ARMIDE
(holding a dagger in her hand)

0:00	Enfin il est en ma puissance,	Finally he is in my power,
	Ce fatal Ennemy, ce superbe Vainqueur.	this mortal enemy, this superb conqueror.
	Le charme du sommeil le livre à ma vengeance;	The charm of sleep delivers him to my vengeance;
	Je vais percer son invincible coeur.	I will pierce his invincible heart.
	Par luy tous mes captifs sont sortis d'esclavage;	Through him all my captives have escaped from slavery.
	Qu'il éprouve toute ma rage.	Let him feel all my anger.

(Armide goes to strike Renaud, but cannot carry through her plan to take his life.)

1:26 Quel trouble me saisit? qui me fait hésiter?	What confusion grips me? What makes me hesitate?
Qu'est-ce qu'en sa faveur la pitié me veut dire?	What in his favor does pity want to tell me?
Frapons . . . Ciel! qui peut m'arrester?	Let us strike . . . Heavens! Who can stop me?
Achevons . . . je frémis! vengeons-nous . . .	Let us get on with it . . . I tremble! Let us avenge . . .
je soûpire!	I sigh!
2:08 Est-ce ainsi que je doy me venger aujourd'huy?	Is it thus that I must avenge myself today?
Ma colère s'éteint quand j'approche de luy.	My rage is extinguished when I approach him.
Plus je le voy, plus ma vengeance est vaine;	The more I see of him, the more my vengeance is
	ineffectual.
Mon bras tremblant se refuse à ma haine.	My trembling arm denies my hate.
2:41 Ah! quelle cruauté de luy ravir le jour!	Ah! What cruelty, to rob him of the light of day!
A ce jeune Héros tout cède sur la Terre.	To this young hero everything on earth surrenders.
Qui croiroit qu'il fut né seulement pour la	Who would believe that he was born only for war?
Guerre?	He seems to be made for love.
Il semble estre fait pour l'Amour.	
3:12 Ne puis-je me venger à moins qu'il ne périsse?	Could I not avenge myself unless he dies?
Hé! ne suffit-il pas que l'Amour le punisse?	Oh, is it not enough that Love should punish him?
Puisqu'il n'a pû trouver mes yeux assez charmants,	Since he could not find my eyes charming enough,
Qu'il m'aime au moins par mes enchantements,	let him love me at least through my sorcery,
Que, s'il se peut, je le haïsse.	so that, if it's possible, I may hate him.
3:43 Venez, venez, seconder mes désirs,	Come, come support my desires,
Démons, transformez-vous en d'aimables	demons, transform yourselves into friendly
zéphirs.	zephyrs.
Je cède à ce vainqueur, la pitié me surmonte.	I give in to this conqueror; pity overwhelms me.
Cachez ma foiblesse et ma honte	Conceal my weakness and my shame
Dans les plus reculez déserts.	in the most remote desert.
Volez, volez, conduisez-nous au bout de l'Univers.	Fly, fly, lead us to the end of the universe.

— PHILIPPE QUINAULT

Armide was one of Jean-Baptiste Lully's last operas and the last with a libretto by his longtime collaborator, the playwright Philippe Quinault. In the early 1670s, the two had developed a new French form of opera known as *tragédie en musique* (tragedy in music), later called *tragédie lyrique* (lyric tragedy), by combining elements of classical French drama with ballet, the French song tradition, and a new form of recitative. The orchestra consists of strings divided into five parts rather than the four that later became standard; some of the parts may have been doubled by winds in some performances.

   Armide was first produced in February 1686 at the Académie Royale in Paris, and it was regarded from the day of its premiere as the greatest work Lully and Quinault created. Quinault based the story on an episode from Torquato Tasso's epic poem *Gerusalemme liberata* (Jerusalem Delivered, 1575), about the first Crusade. The title character, Armide, is a sorceress who captures knights of the Crusades, casts a spell over them, and holds them for her pleasure in her palace. The knight Renaud incites her anger by freeing her captives, yet against her will she falls in love with him. He returns her love only because of a magic spell. When the spell is broken, he leaves, and in a fury of despair she destroys her own palace.

Like a court ballet, a tragédie en musique begins with an ouverture, or overture, in the form and genre known as the *French overture*. The overture to *Armide*, included here (a), is exemplary of the genre. There are two sections, each marked with a repeat. The first part is in a relatively slow duple meter and is mostly homophonic. It has a majesty suitable for the king of France, whose entrance into the theater the overture usually accompanied when he was in attendance. Dotted rhythms pervade the texture, some notated and others played in accordance with a French performance convention of the time called *notes inégales* (unequal notes), whereby even eighth notes in slow or moderate tempos were performed as unequal, with the first somewhat longer than the second. Most modern performers interpret this as dotted-eighth-sixteenth figures, though there is reason to believe that contemporary performers kept a fluid ratio between longer and shorter notes. A related convention encouraged "over-dotting," the playing of singly dotted quarter notes as somewhat longer than notated, which modern performers tend to interpret as double-dotted. In this section of the overture, applying both conventions causes the short notes in the bass to align with those in the upper voices. The second section of the overture (measure 11) begins in a faster tempo and in compound triple meter, with imitative entrances leading to development of the opening motive. The duple meter and slower tempo return in the latter part of the second section (measure 27), recalling the mood and figuration of the first section.

Each act of Lully's tragédies en musique includes a *divertissement*, an extended interlude featuring solo *airs*, homophonic choruses, and instrumental dances, performed with visually pleasing costumes and choreography. Although *air* is the French cognate for the Italian word *aria*, French airs were relatively simple, mostly syllabic songs with regular meter and phrasing, quite distinct from Italian arias. The divertissements continue the tradition of court ballets, but are woven into the plot of the tragédie en musique. The divertissement excerpted here (b) occurs in Act II of *Armide*, after Armide, furious that Renaud has freed the captive Crusaders, has ordered the infernal spirits she commands to deliver Renaud to her so that she can take revenge by killing him. Renaud arrives, lured by the beauty of her garden and then lulled to sleep by their bewitching music. The divertissement then presents a series of airs, choruses, and dances performed by demons disguised as nymphs, shepherds, and shepherdesses while Renaud sleeps. They sing of the pleasures of love, cast a spell on him, and encircle him with garlands of flowers.

Perhaps to represent the encircling of Renaud in flowers, songs, and spells, Lully arranged the divertissement in an archlike form, with a solo air; a chorus; first and second instrumental airs for dancing; a central solo air; the second and first instrumental airs, now in reversed order; another solo air; and a repetition of the earlier chorus. The excerpt given here (b) includes the last three elements, illustrating the three kinds of music typically included in divertissements. The Premier Air (first instrumental air) moves in an almost uninterrupted flow of quarter notes, neatly conveying the act of entwining Renaud in garlands. A shepherdess then sings an air in a simple AABB' form with full orchestral accompaniment, advising the young to love and leave wisdom for later. The divertissement concludes with a chorus declaiming together in homophony that it is folly not to spend one's youth in games, love, and rejoicing—advice aimed at the sleeping Renaud but no doubt intended to be heard as unwise by those in the audience who know that it is demons who offer it. The vocal numbers as well as the instrumental interludes were likely danced. Remarkably, only the shepherdess's air is in even four-measure phrases; in the other numbers, uneven and changing phrase lengths are part of the charm.

Immediately after the divertissement, the demons depart, leaving Armide alone with the sleeping Renaud. Her monologue (c) includes one of the most impressive recitatives in all of Lully's operas. In this scene, she intends to slay Renaud as he sleeps. Her dagger is ready, but because of her love, Armide cannot bring herself to kill him.

The orchestra introduces this scene with a tense prelude that has some characteristics similar to those of the slow section of a French overture. Beginning with the upbeat to the prelude, the textures is suffused with *tirades*, fast runs that lead from one long note to another, usually filling in the interval between two notes (as in measures 11 and 18) but sometimes decorating the melodic motion in other ways (as in measures 1–3). The use of *tirades* with overture style in French opera was associated with powerful or supernatural characters, making this prelude suitable entrance music for the sorceress. Armide, accompanied only by continuo, then sings in a style of recitative that Lully created to suit the declamation of French drama, which was written in rhymed poetry with variable line lengths. In this style, the music alternates freely between measures of two, three, and four beats to create a natural declamation for the text, with the two main accents found in each poetic line falling on downbeats. The changing meters can be compared to those of *musique mesurée* (see NAWM 62), though recitative tends to be much more irregular. All the line endings and some caesuras within the lines are marked by rests. Lully also uses rests dramatically, as in the passages where Armide hesitates, her revenge interrupted by warm feelings for Renaud (for example, "Let us get on with it . . . I tremble! Let us avenge . . . I sigh!" at measures 38–42). Finally, she decides to use her magic to make him love her (measures 65–71). Suggesting her new resolve, the style here changes to a more regular, metrical style of recitative with a more active bass. Like most of Lully's recitatives, this one is more melodious than its Italian counterparts, with melodic lines driven by a more active harmonic background.

The recitative leads directly to an air, a full-fledged song with regular meter and phrasing. In it, Armide calls on her demons to transform themselves into zephyrs and transport her and Renaud to some remote desert, where her shame and weakness will not be observed. The meter, rhythm, and tempo are those of the minuet, a dance that during Lully's time was associated with surrendering to love and thus was perfectly suited to the dramatic situation. The orchestra introduces the entire melody, and then Armide sings the air accompanied by continuo alone, repeating the first period and the final phrase. The text-setting is syllabic, and overall the air is simpler in style than the contemporary Italian arias, which feature more florid passages and more repetition of text. Yet Armide's changing emotions are aptly conveyed by Lully's simple yet rhetorically powerful style and by the structure of the scene—a combination of orchestral preludes and two types of recitative, culminating in a dance-like air.

In the score, Lully labels the five orchestral parts using the traditional terms borrowed from vocal music (see NAWM 62): *dessus* (top line or soprano), *haute-contre* (contratenor altus or alto), *taille* (tenor), *quinte* (quintus or fifth voice), and *basse* (bass). The *dessus* was played by violins, the bass by bass violins (the bass of the violin family before the invention of the violoncello), and the middle parts by alto and tenor violins tuned like the modern viola. The top line was typically doubled by oboes (*hautbois*), and the bass line by bassoons (*bassons*) and continuo.

On the accompanying recording, drums announce the overture, and flutes double the top violin line. Trills and other ornaments, called *agréments*, are added where appropriate, whether notated or not (on these, see NAWM 88). In this edition, trills are indicated by the letter t over a note. During the orchestral introduction to Armide's monologue, a wind machine is used to suggest the swirling winds aroused by her magic. The rhythm of Lully's recitatives is meant to be flexible. It follows a notational convention whereby measures of two beats (such as measure 35) are in cut time, with the half note receiving one beat, but in measures of three or four beats, the quarter note receives one beat. On the recording, the orchestral introduction to Armide's air (measures 71–90 of the scene) is repeated after the air, with an added repetition of the last phrase for finality.

Jean-Baptiste Lully (1632–1687)

Te Deum: Conclusion

Grand motet

1677

86

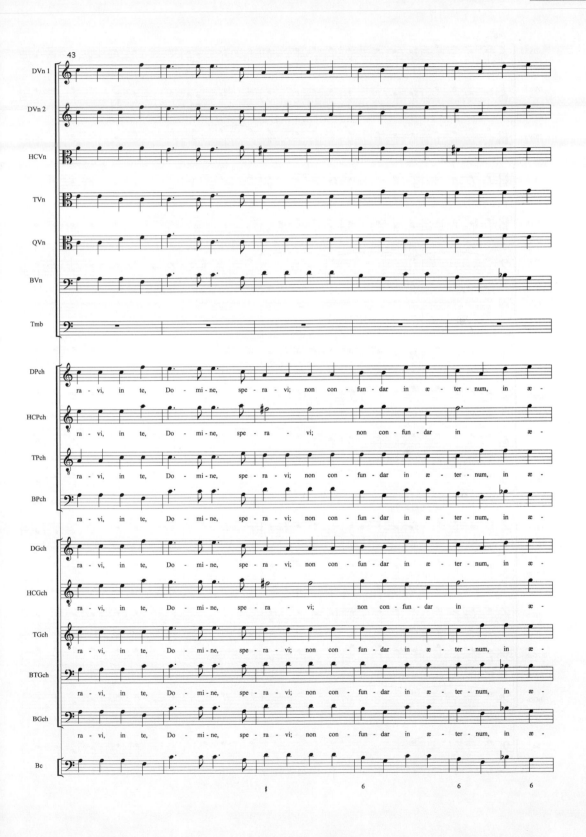

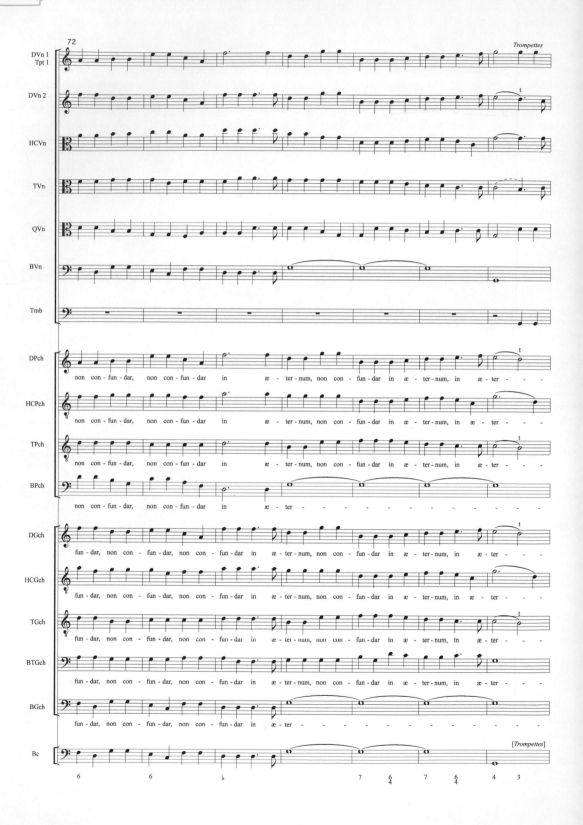

In te, Domine, speravi;	In you, Lord, I have trusted;
non confundar in aeternum.	do not ever let me be confounded.

Lully's *Te Deum* is his longest and most splendid *grand motet*, scored for five-part *grand choeur* (large choir), four-part *petit choeur* (small choir), soloists drawn from the *petit choeur*, six-part string orchestra augmented with trumpets and timpani, and basso continuo. The use of soloists, two choirs, and orchestra is typical of the grand motet, but this is the first such work to incorporate timpani and is unusual in specifying more than one voice per part in the *petit choeur*. When a soloist sings, the line is marked *récit*, as at the beginning of this excerpt; when all the singers on the same voice part join in, it is marked *tous* (all).

The text is a Latin hymn of praise and thanksgiving to God dating back to the fourth century. In the Catholic liturgy, a *Te Deum* was sung at the end of Matins on most Sundays and feast days. Festive settings of the text were also frequently performed at religious services on special occasions.

Lully's setting was first performed at Fontainebleau on September 9, 1677, for the baptism of his son Louis, named after King Louis XIV, who served as godfather. The performance combined the singers and organist of the Royal Chapel with the violin orchestra of the king's chamber and trumpeters and drummers from the outdoor band, known as the Music of the Great Stable. The scale of the work, the most grandiose motet that had ever been composed in France, may have been suggested by the king to show his attachment to Lully, his favorite musician. The Paris journal *Mercure galant* reported that "the king found it so beautiful that he wanted to hear it more than one time." It was performed again in 1679 at Versailles, this time with 120 musicians, for the marriage of Louis XIV's niece Marie-Louise d'Orléans to Charles II of Spain. The forces were even larger, about 150 musicians, for the third known performance, given in Paris in January 1687 to celebrate the king's recovery from surgery. But during rehearsal, Lully was beating time with a staff and hit his foot; the injury was so severe that gangrene set in, and he died two months later.

The motet, which takes about thirty minutes to perform, is divided into eight large sections, demarcated by changes of key and meter and by an opening *symphonie* (instrumental prelude or interlude). The excerpt given here is the final section, on the last sentence of text.

This section begins with a brief solo for alto (*haute-contre*) that states the entire text and the most important musical ideas for the section. The words "In te, Domine, speravi" (In you, Lord, I have trusted) are set to an energetic motive that outlines the tonic triad, emphasizes "Domine" (Lord) with dotted rhythms that suit its natural spoken rhythm, and leaps up a fifth on "speravi" (I have trusted), matching the optimism of the text. The opening text repeats with the same rhythm but a varied melody ending with a downward leap of a fifth. At the words "non confundar" (do not let me be confounded), a rapid descending chain of thirds, repeated in sequence over quickly changing harmony, suggests the confusion and terror the supplicants hope to avoid. The solo ends with a confident cadence on "in aeternum" (in eternity).

The ideas introduced by the alto solo are then taken up by the other forces, but are constantly varied. A brief *symphonie* for string orchestra paraphrases the first and last phrases of the alto melody. The choruses join the instruments to sing the alto's first phrase in homophony, with the melody appearing first in the basses (measures 17–20) and then in inversion in the sopranos (*dessus*, measures 20–23). Variants of the "non confundar" motive echo back and forth between the choruses, leading to a cadence in the dominant. A bass soloist (measure 27) sings another variation of the alto solo with interjections from the chorus, leading back to the tonic and a brief instrumental interlude featuring the trumpets and timpani (measure 39). Here the descending thirds of the "non confundar" motive are transformed into cascading lines in the trumpets and violas over a sustained C-major harmony, which may symbolize God's power to turn confusion into certainty and danger into victory.

Three more choral statements follow, featuring homophonic declamation alternating with dialogue between the choirs, and punctuated by expanded instrumental interludes with trumpets and timpani. In the first of these choral statements, development of the "non confundar" motive leads to D minor and G minor, with cadences prepared by long pedal points on "aeternum." After the instruments restore the tonic C major, the next choral statement moves from dialogue to homophony, and the final statement is almost wholly homophonic, closing the work with a powerful unity of sound. Throughout, the dotted rhythms on "Domine" lend an air of majesty, recalling Lully's French overtures (see NAWM 85a). The even rhythms, disjunct lines, and rapidly changing harmonies on "non confundar" provide a strong contrast, and their gradual transformation into the trumpet cascades and unified choral declamation conveys a strong message of triumph and celebration.

The score uses the French names for the voice parts: *dessus* (soprano), *haute-contre* (alto), *taille* (tenor), *basse-taille* (between bass and tenor), and *basse* (bass). Similar names are used for the string parts, with the upper parts performed on violins, the middle parts on alto and tenor violins (tuned like modern violas), and the bass line on bass violin, used in France until it was replaced by the violoncello in the early eighteenth century. On the accompanying recording, the basso continuo is played by lutes, as was the frequent practice in seventeenth-century France.

Denis Gaultier (CA. 1603–1672)

La Coquette virtuose

Courante

CA. 1650

87

(1)

From Denis Gaultier, *Oeuvres de Denis Gautier*, ed. Monique Rollin and François-Pierre Goy (Paris: CNRS-Éditions, 1996), 112–13. We have made diligent efforts to contact the copyright holder to obtain permission to reprint this selection. If you have information that would help us, please write to Permissions Department, W. W. Norton & Company, Inc., 500 Fifth Avenue, New York, NY 10110.

Denis Gaultier (or Gautier) was the most important lutenist and composer for lute in mid-seventeenth-century France. Widely renowned in his lifetime, he was active in Paris as a performer in salons but had no known court appointment. Most of his pieces for lute are stylized dances, such as this *courante* from a manuscript titled *La Rhétorique des dieux* (The Rhetoric of the Gods), prepared between 1648 and 1652 for a wealthy patron, Anne de Chambré. Whether Gaultier had any role in its compilation is unknown. The preface explains that the collection's purpose was to assemble Gaultier's most beautiful lute pieces and explained the title by noting that "human understanding cannot imagine a more eloquent language" than Gaultier's music.

The manuscript is laid out in twelve sections or suites labeled with the names of the twelve Greek modes as described by Zarlino (Dorian, Hypodorian, and so on), although the music has no relation to those modes and is closer to the tonal system of major and minor keys that gradually emerged over the seventeenth century. *La Coquette virtuose* appears as the second courante in a suite in A major, consisting of a prelude, allemande, two courantes, two gigues, and sarabande (see the discussion of the dance suite and of these types of dance in NAWM 88).

Many dances of the time were given fanciful titles, including about half of the dances in *La Rhétorique des dieux*. We do not know whether these titles were bestowed by Gaultier or by the manuscript's compilers, but the title of this courante appears in none of the eight other manuscripts in which the dance itself appears, suggesting that it was added later and is not intrinsic to the work's meaning. The title *La Coquette virtuose* (The Virtuous Coquette) offers a paradox, because a coquette is a flirt who seeks to attract men simply to gratify her vanity and without really caring about them. A brief note below the music explains: "This beauty, who makes for herself as many lovers as there are men who hear her, shows through her precious discourse the sweetness that she finds in the love of virtue, the attention she pays to those who worship it, and that she will belong to him who first acquires the title of Magnanimous."

Like most seventeenth-century dances, this one is in *binary form*, with two sections, each repeated, the first moving from the tonic A major to a cadence on the dominant E major, and the second returning to close on the tonic. As is typical of Gaultier's lute style, the number of contrapuntal voices seems to change from moment to moment. The melody and bass are present throughout, but one or more middle voices appear (as in measures 4–5 or 10–11), disappear, and reappear again at will. This flexibility is a natural response to the quick decay of notes plucked on the lute. On a sustaining instrument such as the organ, the end of a note is almost as evident as its beginning, making it obvious when a voice exits; but on a lute, a long note may fade rapidly to nothing, making it difficult to keep track of each individual voice.

This rapid decay of notes prompted lutenists to animate each voice and the entire texture with almost constant motion, reserving longer notes and chords to mark the ends of phrases. Although Gaultier sometimes notates all the notes of a chord as simultaneous (as in the second half of measure 10), more often he breaks them up in various ways. At the ends of phrases, he typically sounds the cadential melody note first, then arpeggiates the chord up from the bass (measures 7, 12, and 16), though at some internal cadences he sounds the bass note last (measures 3 and 10). Some chords are arpeggiated from the bottom up (as in the middle of measure 3 and the last two beats of measure 6), while others start with the outer voices and fill in an inner voice (second half of measure 9, last two beats of measure 14). Often neighbor notes decorate the chord (as in measures 5–6), and sometimes notes of the chord simply repeat (measure 14). Frequently Gaultier delays notes in the melody, presenting them just after the accompanying chord or bass note changes, in what François Couperin termed a *suspension* (measures 4–6). Throughout, the effect is of an ever-varying, unpredictable pattern that engages the listener's attention and keeps the music interesting. Toward the end of each half of the dance, some note is played on almost every eighth note of the measure, producing a rhythmic intensification that leads to a satisfying close. The broken chords, delayed melody notes, and constantly varying texture were aspects of the *style luthé* (lute style) or *style brisé* (broken style) that characterized lute music and were borrowed by harpsichordists as well.

This dance was notated in French lute tablature, shown here below the transcription. To play it requires a lute with eleven courses. The top six courses (each with a pair of strings) are tuned *A–d–f–a–d′–f′*. For these courses, letters indicate what pitch to play: the letter a above the line indicates an open string, b a finger on the first fret for a pitch a half step higher, c another half step higher, and so on. Below these six courses are five added bass strings that are not stopped with the fingers to change pitch; each note from *G♯* (in measure 1) down to *C♯* (measure 9) must be played on one of these strings. The tablature indicates when a note is to be plucked but not how long it is to last (unless it is immediately succeeded by another note on the same string), leaving it to the player to determine which notes to sustain. In doing so, the performer also decides how many contrapuntal voices will be present. For example, if the low *E* in measure 2 is sustained through the entire measure, the *a*, *f♯*, and *g♯* that follow will be heard as belonging to a middle voice between bass and melody.

Barlines in the tablature indicate $\frac{3}{4}$ meter, but the editors have transcribed the dance in $\frac{6}{4}$ to accommodate the occasional suggestion of $\frac{3}{2}$ or hemiola (as in measures 2, 4, and 15). Gaultier did not indicate the ornaments, so the lutenist on the accompanying recording adds several in the appropriate style, using them to emphasize the opening of each section, cadences, and other important melody notes. The performer also uses *notes inégales* throughout, so that the first eighth note of each beat is about twice as long as the second (see explanation in NAWM 85), giving the dance a lilt that would be missing if it were played as notated.

Elisabeth-Claude Jacquet de la Guerre
(1665–1729)

Suite No. 3 in A Minor, from *Pièces de clavecin*

Keyboard suite

CA. 1687

88

(a) Prelude

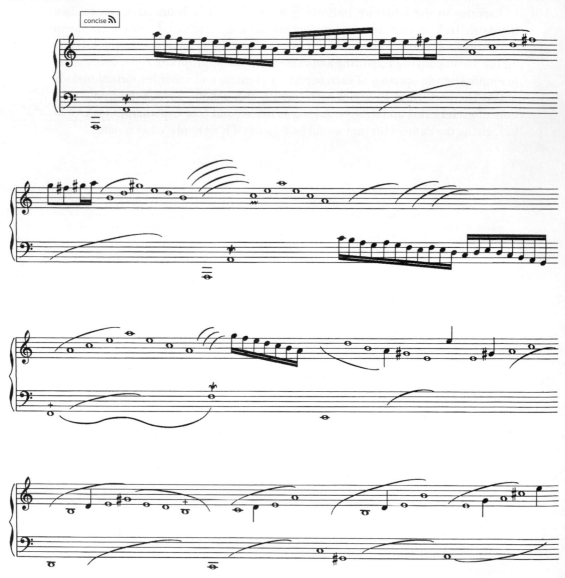

From Elisabeth-Claude Jacquet de la Guerre, *Pièces de Clavecin*, ed. Carol Henry Bates (Paris: Heugel, 1982), 28–39. Used with permission. The second courante is not included on the recording.

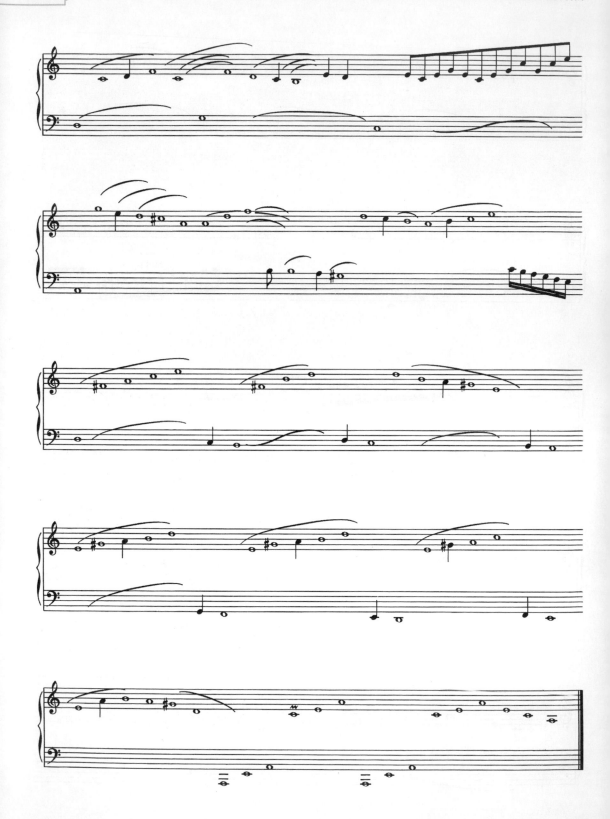

(b) Allemande

(c) Courante I and II

[2ᵉ] **Courante**

(d) Sarabande

(e) Gigue

(f) Chaconne

(g) Gavotte

(h) Menuet

Elisabeth-Claude Jacquet de la Guerre was a child prodigy in music and a favorite of King Louis XIV, to whom she dedicated almost all of her works. Her first publication, issued when she was twenty-two, was a collection called *Pièces de clavecin* that included four suites for harpsichord. Keyboard suites of the time were intended for amateurs to play for their own enjoyment or for family and friends. They consisted primarily of stylized dances, most of which were in binary form (see commentary for NAWM 87). Jacquet de la Guerre's Suite No. 3 in A Minor is typical of the genre and includes all of the most common types of dance.

As in most French harpsichord music of the time, the composer used figuration borrowed from the style that musicians used for playing the lute, known as the *style luthé* (lute style) or *style brisé* (broken style). Rather than plucking all the notes at once, lutenists usually picked out one or two notes at a time, arpeggiating chords and alternating between melody and harmony (see NAWM 87). A similar texture is evident throughout this harpsichord suite—for example, in the arpeggiated closing chords of each section (see allemande, measures 8 and 17) and in the frequent alternation between voices (see allemande, measures 10–16, where three or four voices are present but rarely are more than two notes struck simultaneously).

Many notes are marked with ornaments, called *agréments*, of which the most important are these:

Agréments compensate for the quick decay of plucked string tones on a harpsichord and draw attention to notes that deserve emphasis, including active tones that propel a melody forward and cadential notes that draw a phrase to a close. The player is also free to add appropriate ornaments, within the limits of taste. The performer on the accompanying recording does so especially when repeating a section, and also plays notes *notes inégales* when appropriate (see NAWM 85).

Like many suites, the Suite in A Minor begins with a prelude in an improvisational style similar to that of a toccata. Here, Jacquet de la Guerre follows the French tradition of the *unmeasured prelude*, in which a special notation without meter is used to allow greater rhythmic freedom. Arpeggiated chords are written in whole notes with occasional quarter notes interspersed to indicate notes that are played but not held, such as passing tones or appoggiaturas. Most melodic passages are notated in eighths and sixteenths, although the rhythm remains somewhat free. Perhaps most striking to the eye are the slurs, used to show sustained notes or phrase groupings. Typical of preludes, there are no repetitions or notable melodies. Instead, the player explores the key and its available harmonies, moving to the dominant and gradually returning to the tonic. This exploration of the key recalls the original function of the prelude as a means of establishing the keynote before a song or of testing and adjusting a lute's tuning before playing a dance.

The first four dances—allemande, courante, sarabande, and gigue—are those most frequently used in suites. Indeed, in Germany (though not in France), the standard suite contained these four dances in this order, often preceded by a prelude and with some other dances added near the end. Each of the four dances has a different meter, character, and national origin, providing a great deal of variety.

The *allemande* (meaning "German"), presumably of German origin, developed from a fast couple dance based on a repeating pattern of walking three steps and then lifting the free foot in the air. By the seventeenth century, the allemande was no longer danced, and the music became slower and highly stylized—far from the dance that was its source. Allemandes are in a moderate $\frac{4}{4}$ meter, always begin with an upbeat, and progress almost continuously in eighth and sixteenth notes. Within these parameters, Jacquet de la Guerre created a striking variety of rhythms and textures. In some passages, the contrapuntal voices contract or expand in contrary motion (as in measures 1–2), and in other passages, the voices rise or fall together (as in measures 10–11). As a result of these variations in texture, the sonorities are constantly changing.

The *courante* ("running" or "flowing") was a French dance whose choreography included bending the knee on the upbeat or offbeat and rising on the beat, often followed by a step or glide. The music is in moderate triple or compound meter and always begins with an upbeat. In many courantes, including the two in this suite, the meter shifts back and forth between $\frac{3}{2}$ and $\frac{6}{4}$, sometimes with different voices simultaneously implying different meters. Although the composer included two courantes in this suite, only the first is performed on the accompanying recording—a reminder that the performer had the discretion to omit dances if he or she so desired. This first courante features some interesting chromaticism, including an unexpectedly dissonant chord in the next-to-last measure of each section: a dominant seventh chord in the right hand over the third of the chord to which it will resolve in the bass (B7 over G in measure 8, E7 over C in measure 19).

The *sarabande* originated in Central America as a fast dance-song with ribald lyrics, then in the late sixteenth century crossed the Atlantic to Spain, where it was the most popular dance for a generation. When it spread into France in the seventeenth century, French musicians modified the dance to be slow and dignified in triple meter with a stress on the second beat. The rhythmic figure in the first measure of the sarabande from this suite (a dotted quarter note on beat two and an eighth leading into the downbeat) is particularly characteristic. In the second half of the dance, Jacquet de la Guerre shifts this figure forward one beat (to the first two beats of the measure). However, since the harmony tends to resolve on the third beat of the measure, as if that were the downbeat, the characteristic sarabande rhythm can still be heard. This device creates an intriguing dissonance between notated and perceived meter.

The *gigue* ("jig") originated in England and Ireland as a solo dance distinguished by rapid footwork. Introduced into France in the mid-seventeenth century, it was stylized as a dance in fast compound meter. The wide leaps and fugal imitation at the beginning of both sections of this gigue are typical, as is the almost constant motion.

The remaining three dances are also common in suites. The *chaconne* originated in the New World as a triple-time dance-song, then in the early seventeenth century traveled to Spain, where it displaced the sarabande as the most popular dance and soon spread across Europe. In Italy, it evolved into a form for variations over an ostinato bass, while in France it developed into a stately dance that was often shaped by repetition rather than variation. Like many French chaconnes, this one is in *rondeau form*, with a four-measure chaconne theme (repeated each time it is played) that alternates with contrasting eight-measure periods called *couplets*, each with its own figuration and harmonic scheme. Each couplet is more active than the preceding one, and the progressive increase in activity gives a satisfying shape to the piece. Since the repetitions of the theme are exact, in the original score they were not written out in full. However, in the present edition, the editor has supplied the missing measures in brackets.

The *gavotte* was a vigorous dance in duple time with a characteristic rhythm of two quarter notes leading to a half note on the downbeat. The choreography of the dance included bending the knee prior to the beat, jumping on the downbeat, and then taking one or two steps. The music was often simpler and more repetitive than the heavily stylized allemande or courante, as seen in the varied repetition from phrase to phrase in this suite's gavotte.

Simplest of all dances in this suite was the *minuet*, an elegant couple-dance in moderate triple meter. Still danced through the early eighteenth century, the minuet was the one dance from the Baroque suite that became part of Classic-era genres such as the symphony and string quartet (see NAWM 118 and 119). Minuets were danced using various patterns of four steps within a basic rhythmic unit of two measures. As a result, the sense of two-measure units is stronger in the minuet than in any of the other dances in the suite. The last eight measures of the second section are a varied repetition of the first section, producing a *rounded binary form*, which became one of the most common forms in the eighteenth century and is the direct ancestor of sonata form.

This sequence of dances in contrasting meters, tempos, and textures offered a variety of moods and styles, as was valued in the seventeenth century. Furthermore, all were presented with the elegance and emotional restraint prized at Louis XIV's court and in French culture of the period.

In nearly all the dances of this suite, as in many publications of the time, the word *Reprise* (repetition) is printed at the beginning of the second half. This serves as a visual cue to help the performer locate the point to return to for the repetition of the second strain, after playing through it for the first time.

Henry Purcell (1659–1695)

Dido and Aeneas: Conclusion

Opera
1689

89

(a) Recitative: *Thy hand, Belinda*

From *The Works of Henry Purcell*, vol. 3, *Dido and Aeneas*, rev. ed. Margaret Laurie (Sevenoaks, Kent: Novello, 1979), 94–99. Libretto by Nahum Tate. Music by Henry Purcell. Edited under the supervision of The Purcell Society by Margaret Laurie and Thurston Dart. © Copyright 1961 by Novello & Company, Limited, 14–15 Berners Street, London WIT 3LJ, United Kingdom. © Copyright renewed 1989. All rights reserved. International copyright secured. Reprinted by permission of G. Schirmer, Inc. (ASCAP).

(b) Lament (ground bass aria): *When I am laid in earth*

(c) Chorus: *With drooping wings*

The first known performance of Henry Purcell's *Dido and Aeneas* was given in 1689 by pupils at Josias Priest's boarding school for young gentlewomen in Chelsea, a suburb of London. Priest's school offered training in the arts to the daughters of London's rich and powerful. Students there had previously performed *Venus and Adonis*, a masque by John Blow that had been written for the king and premiered at the royal court. Purcell had several royal appointments, including as organist at the Chapel Royal, and his librettist, Nahum Tate, was soon to be appointed as poet laureate (court poet). These connections between its creators, its performers, and the royal court suggest that *Dido and Aeneas* may have been written for performance at court, perhaps for the coronation of William and Mary that year. It has been suggested that the opera's prologue refers allegorically to the Glorious Revolution of 1688, when the new rulers deposed Mary's brother James II. The music for the prologue is lost, but the libretto describes how Phoebus, the Sun, crossed the sea and was then joined by Venus, just as William invaded from the Continent, followed by Mary. Yet there is no record of any performance of *Dido and Aeneas* at court, or even plans for one, leaving the reasons Purcell and Tate wrote their opera a matter for speculation.

The plot of *Dido and Aeneas* is derived from the fourth book of Virgil's *Aeneid*, but with some added twists. Dido, queen of Carthage, loves the visiting hero Aeneas, who is fleeing the destruction of Troy and is destined to found Rome. Although he returns her affection, a sorceress plots to destroy the romance by sending an elf disguised as Mercury to remind Aeneas of his destiny. He is persuaded and agrees to depart. When Aeneas appears at court to say farewell, Dido condemns him for his weakness and deception, and she orders him away even after he has a last-minute change of heart. Then, in the scene included here, Dido realizes she cannot live without him. She sings a lament before dying broken-hearted, and the chorus mourns as cupids appear and scatter roses on her tomb.

Dido's recitative that begins the scene, addressed to her confidante Belinda, conveys her despair through an evocative melisma on "darkness" and sighing figures on "bosom," "would," "Death," and "now." Purcell used a distinctively English style of recitative that he had helped to develop. It resembles the expressive recitatives of Monteverdi (see NAWM 74d and 75) and Strozzi (NAWM 77), and is quite unlike the rapid Italian recitative of the time (NAWM 76a and 92a) or the wholly syllabic French style of Lully (NAWM 85b). Through its slow, stepwise descent of a seventh, the melody portrays the dying Dido and prepares listeners for the lament.

Dido's lament is one of the landmarks of seventeenth-century music, a justly famous adaptation of technique to expression. Purcell followed an Italian tradition of setting laments over a basso ostinato, or ground bass. The bass grows out of the descending fourth common to laments, but changes the usual diatonic pattern (G—F—Eb—D) to chromatic (G—F♯—F♮—E♮—Eb—D) and adds a cadential extension (Bb—C—D—G) to create a five-measure pattern that is heard eleven times. Over these inexorable repetitions, symbolizing her inevitable fate, Dido's melody conveys great tension by following an independent course. Purcell intensifies the dissonances by re-attacking suspended notes on strong beats, as in measures 7, 10, 12, and 13. We feel a further jolt when, several times, dissonances are resolved by skip instead of step, as on the word "trouble" in measures 12 and 13. When Dido hammers out a relentless D against the changing harmonies on the words "Remember me!" (measures 17–20 and 28–31), we gain a sense of her obstinacy and pride. The violins augment the grieving effect with added suspensions, sighing figures, and other dissonances, and close with a chromatic descent through an octave.

As was customary in the early Italian operas and many French operas, the act and the opera end with a chorus, in emulation of the choruses of ancient Greek tragedy. Here, the slowly sinking lines of the preceding recitative and aria reach their culmination in the repeated descending minor-scale figures on "drooping wings" and the sighs on "soft" (measures 14–20). Text-painting is notable throughout, including eighth-note undulations on "scatter roses" (measures 11–13) and dramatic rests to mark "Keep here your watch, and never part" (measures 22–30). But it is the recurring stepwise descending motions that link the elements of this entire scene and convey the mournful mood so powerfully.

The edition reprinted here includes both the original basso continuo and, for the recitative and closing chorus, a realization by the editor. In the aria, possible rhythmic variants through double-dotting are indicated by stems and flags above those notes that could be delayed and shortened. Accidentals, ornaments, and dynamics suggested by the editor are printed in small type, and slurs added by the editor are marked through with a vertical line.

Tomás de Torrejón y Velasco (1644–1728)

La púrpura de la rosa: Excerpt

Opera

1701

(a) Dialogue in strophic song: *Y bien, ¿qué es lo que adviertes?*

0:30	del monte, en tu coturno,	1:02	de suerte que dejando
	todo el bello matiz,		sin ti el sol sin lucir,
	que en cintas de esmeralda		la aura sin respirar,
	son lazos de rubí;		el monte sin vestir,
	del abril, en tu seno,		y el abril, en efecto,
	o blanco, o carmesí,		sin lograr y pulir
	todo el candor, y nácar		las flores ciento a ciento,
	del clavel, y el jazmín:		las rosas mil a mil,

Score excerpt from Tomás de Torrejón y Velasco and Juan Hidalgo, *La púrpura de la rosa*, ed. Louise K. Stein, Musica Hispana, ser. A, vol. 25 (Madrid: Instituto Complutense de Ciencias Musicales, 1999), 74–80. Reprinted with permission. Edition and English translation by Louise K. Stein, from the CD booklet for Tomás de Torrejón y Velasco, *La púrpura de la rosa*, The Harp Consort directed by Andrew Lawrence-King (Deutsche Harmonia Mundi 05472 77355 2, 1999), pp. 70–72.

que ya desde esta parte
le deja descubrir
de atalaya un laurel
que abraza amante vid,

2:20 todo es amor, por señas
que dél a recibir
a su deidad, las ninfas
en alegre festín

salen al paso; y tú,
para llegar aquí,
no temes las fierezas,
y las bellezas sí.

2:49 Adonis ¡Ay!, que no sé qué afecto . . .
Venus No has de pasar de aquí.
Adonis . . . Me hace no obedecer.
Venus Y agradecer a mí.

(b) Chorus: *Corred, corred, cristales*

Múdase el teatro en el de jardín, y por las puertas salen cantando y bailando las Ninfas, y Celfa y Chato

[The set changes to that of the garden, and the nymphs enter singing and dancing, and Celfa and Chato]

Co-rred,   co-rred,   cris-ta - les;   plan-tas, vi - vid, vi-vid;   a-ves, can - tad, can-tad;

Co-rred,   co-rred,   cris-ta - les;   plan-tas, vi - vid, vi-vid;   a-ves, can - tad, can-tad;

Co-rred,   co-rred,   cris-ta - les;   plan-tas, vi - vid, vi-vid;   a-ves, can - tad, can-tad;

Co-rred,   co-rred,   cris-ta - les;   plan-tas, vi - vid, vi-vid;   a-ves, can - tad, can-tad;

flo-res, lu - cid, lu - cid;   pues que vuel - ve Ve - nus, her - mo-sa y gen - til,   tra - yen-do   des-

flo-res, lu - cid, lu - cid;   pues que vuel - ve Ve - nus, her - mo-sa y gen - til,   tra - yen-do   des-

flo-res, lu - cid, lu - cid;   pues que vuel - ve Ve - nus, her - mo-sa y gen - til,   tra - yen-do   des-

flo-res, lu - cid, lu - cid;   pues que vuel - ve Ve - nus, her - mo-sa y gen - til,   tra - yen-do des -

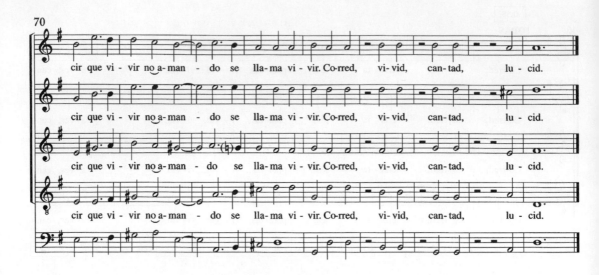

cir que vi - vir no a-man - do se lla-ma vi - vir. Co-rred, vi-vid, can-tad, lu - cid.

cir que vi - vir no a-man - do se lla-ma vi - vir. Co-rred, vi-vid, can-tad, lu - cid.

cir que vi - vir no a-man - do se lla-ma vi - vir. Co-rred, vi-vid, can-tad, lu - cid.

cir que vi - vir no a-man - do se lla-ma vi - vir. Co-rred, vi-vid, can-tad, lu - cid.

[Dialogue in strophic song]

VENUS

| 0:00 | Y bien, ¿qué es lo que adviertes? | And so, what do you notice? |

ADONIS

Que te llevas tras ti,	That you carry behind you,
en tus rizos, del sol	in the curls of your hair,
todo el nevado [dorado] Ofir;	all the golden sun of Ophir;
del aura, en tus alientos,	and in your breath,
todo el humor [humo] sutil,	all the subtle vapor of the dawn
que en destiladas gomas	that, distilled in drops,
cualquiera es ámbar gris;	any one of them is ambergris;

0:30	del monte, en tu coturno,	all the beautiful hues of the mountain
todo el bello matiz,	reflect you,
que en cintas de esmeralda	so that in emerald ribbons
son lazos de rubí;	there are ruby knots;
del abril, en tu seno,	and in your breast,
o blanco, o carmesí,	whether white or crimson,
todo el candor, y nácar	is all the freshness and the dew of April's
del clavel, y el jazmín;	carnations and jasmine;

1:02	de suerte que dejando	so that to be
sin ti el sol sin lucir,	without you leaves the sun unable to shine,
la aura sin respirar,	the dawn breathless,
el monte sin vestir,	the mountain bare,
y el abril, en efecto,	and Spring, in effect,
sin lograr y pulir	unable to grow and adorn itself with
las flores ciento a ciento,	hundreds of flowers,
las rosas mil a mil,	thousands of roses.

| 1:37 | quedan mustios sin ti el sol, | Without you all remain lifeless: the sun, |
| | el aura, el monte y el abril. | the dawn, the mountain, and Spring. |

VENUS

| 1:50 | ¡Qué atrasadas lisonjas! | What old-fashioned flattery! |

ADONIS

Perdona, que he de ir   Pardon me, but I have to go forth
siguiendo tu hermosura.   following your beauty.

VENUS

¿A qué? si en mi jardín,   To what end? in my garden,

que ya desde esta parte   that now from this side
le deja descubrir   shows just
de atalaya un laurel   the watchtower of a laurel tree
que abraza amante vid,   embraced by a loving vine,

2:20	todo es amor, por señas	there are signs that all is love,
	que dél a recibir	and from there, to receive
	a su deidad, las ninfas	their deity, the nymphs
	en alegre festín	in happy celebration

salen al paso; y tú,   come forth; and you,
para llegar aquí,   in coming here,
no temes las fierezas,   need not fear the fierce,
y las bellezas sí.   but only the beautiful.

ADONIS

| 2:49 | ¡Ay!, que no sé qué afecto . . . | Oh! I don't know what emotion . . . |

VENUS

No has de pasar de aquí.   You must not come any closer than this.

ADONIS

. . . Me hace no obedecer.   . . . forces me to disobey you.

VENUS

Y agradecer a mí.   And thus gratify me.

[Chorus]

[*The set changes to that of the garden, and the nymphs
enter singing and dancing, and Celfa and Chato.*]

ALL

0:00	Corred, corred, cristales;	Flow, flow, crystal fountains;
	plantas, vivid, vivid;	grow, plants, grow;
	aves, cantad, cantad;	sing, birds, sing;
	flores, lucid, lucid;	bloom, flowers, bloom;
	pues que vuelve Venus,	now that Venus returns,
	hermosa y gentil,	beautiful and graceful,
	trayendo depojos	bringing the spoils

del amore tras sí,	of love with her,
porque nadie puede	because nobody can
exento decir	claim, in truth,
que el vivir no amando	that to live without loving
se llama vivir.	is really to live.
Corred, vivid, cantad, lucid.	Flow, grow, sing, bloom.

VENUS

0:43 | ¿Que aún no te vuelves? You are not leaving yet?

ADONIS

No.   No.

VENUS

¿Y a entrar te atreves? And do you dare to enter?

ADONIS

Sí.   Yes.

VENUS

Entra, pues; y vosotras Enter, then; and you nymphs
alegres proseguid. proceed with the celebration.

ALL

0:55 | Corred, corred, cristales . . . Flow, flow, crystal fountains . . .

— PEDRO CALDERÓN DE LA BARCA — TRANS. LOUISE K. STEIN

La púrpura de la rosa was the first opera composed and produced in the New World. It was commissioned by the viceroy of Peru and performed at his palace in Lima, Peru on October 19, 1701, to celebrate Philip V's eighteenth birthday and his first year as king of Spain. The libretto, by the Spanish playwright Pedro Calderón de la Barca, was originally set by Juan Hildalgo for an opera performed in Madrid, Spain, in 1660 on the occasion of the marriage of Philip V's grandparents, Louis XIV of France and the Spanish princess Maria Teresa. The plot, about the erotic love of Venus and Adonis, was appropriate for a royal wedding and also appealing for a colonial audience. An unknown poet adapted the libretto to suit the celebration for Philip V. The composer of the Lima version was Tomás de Torrejón y Velasco, who had come to Peru as a young man, served as chapelmaster at the Lima Cathedral, and became the most famous composer in the New World.

Patron, librettist, and composer were all thoroughly familiar with the conventions of Spanish opera, which were quite different from those of Italy, France, or England. In the Spanish opera tradition, almost all the roles, male and female, were sung by women, excepting only the role of the male member of a peasant couple, who offered comic relief. The sound of the accompaniment in Spanish operas was distinctive as well, for the continuo was usually realized by harps, guitars, and viols rather than by lute or keyboard. But the greatest difference was in the dominance of lyrical song. Rather than setting dialogue in recitative and emotional moments in arias, Spanish composers set both in strophic songs.

In the excerpt included here, Adonis praises Venus's beauty and then follows her into her garden, where they are welcomed by a chorus of nymphs and the peasant couple Chato and Celfa. Adonis begins his song in response to a question from Venus, then sings five short stanzas to a melody that is only five measures long (measures 5–9). The second stanza would start in measure 10, but since the music simply repeats, the composer included only a few notes and a *dal segno* sign to indicate the repetition to be used for the later stanzas. To orient modern musicians unaccustomed to these performing conventions, the editor included some repeated music in brackets, and the measures in the excerpt are numbered as if all of the music were written out.

Adonis closes his song with a couplet that introduces a new melodic idea (measures 31–37), which is expanded into a twelve-measure melody (measures 38–49) that becomes the basis of the next song. The middle stanzas are a solo for Venus, but the first and fifth stanzas present a dialogue between Venus and Adonis, who sing phrases in alternation. Here, there is no musical distinction between dialogue and monologue or between recitative and aria. Rather, the music flows in unbroken song, accommodating the libretto's mostly unrhymed poetry. This is characteristic of the Spanish style, as are the lilting syncopations in the melody. The effect of the frequently repeating short melodies is hypnotic and, in the context of this scene, erotic, offering a pleasure unlike that of other operatic traditions.

The closing chorus is simple and almost entirely homophonic, as are many choruses in French opera. But the rhythms here are borrowed from the syncopated dances and songs of Spain. Any of the three beats in triple meter may receive a text accent or long note, creating a vibrant and unpredictable flow. Between two statements of the chorus, Venus and Adonis engage in a last, brief dialogue, set to the same melody as before, and then they enter Venus's garden together.

Juan de Araujo (1646–1712)

Los coflades de la estleya

Villancico

LATE SEVENTEENTH CENTURY

91

Original parts written a fourth higher.

Edited by Robert Stevenson in *Inter-American Music Review* 6, no. 2 (Spring–Summer 1985): 37–45. Used by permission of Robert Stevenson. Translation by Jules Whicker, from liner notes to *New World Symphonies: Baroque Music from Latin America*, performed by Ex Cathedra, conducted by Jeffrey Skidmore (London: Hyperion Records CDA67380, 2003).

Estribillo:

`0:00`	a	Los coflades de la estleya	Fellow brothers of the Star

Los coflades de la estleya
vamo turus a Beleya
y velemo a ziola
beya con ziolo en lo poltal.
Vamo, vamo currendo ayá.
Oylemo un viyansico
que lo compondlá Flasico
ziendo gayta su fosico
y luego lo cantalá Blasico,
Pellico, Zuanico i Tomá,
y lo estliviyo dilá:

Fellow brothers of the Star
let us all go to Bethlehem,
and we shall see Our beautiful Lady,
with Our Lord in the manger.
Let's go, let's run there.
We shall hear a villancico
that Francisco will compose,
piping in his little voice,
and then Blasico will sing it
with Perico, Juanico, and Tomás,
and the estribillo [refrain] will go:

`0:35` B Gulumbé gulumbé gulumbá
        Guache moleniyo de Safala.

Gulumbé, gulumbé, gulumbá,
Poor boys, black boys from Safala.

`0:50` c Bamo abel que traen de Angola

a ziolo y a ziola
Baltasale con Melchola
y mi plimo Gasipar.
Vamo, vamo currendo ayá.

Let us go and see what they have
        brought from Angola
for Our Lord and Our Lady,
Balthasar and Melchior
and my cousin Caspar.
Let's go, let's run there!

`1:06` B Gulumbé gulumbé gulumbá
        Guache moleniyo de Safala.

Gulumbé, gulumbé, gulumbá,
Poor boys, black boys from Safala.

Copla 1:

`1:25` d Vamo siguiendo la estleya   *eya*   Let us follow the star,   *Come on!*
           lo negliyo coltezano   *vamo*   we black courtiers,   *Let's go!*
           pus lo Rey e cun tesuro   *turo*   since the Three Kings   *All of us!*
           de calmino los tlesban   *ayá.*   are coming with treasure.   *That way!*

Blasico, Pellico, Zuanico i Tomá,
eyá! vamo turo ayá.

Blasico, Perico, Juanico, and Tomás,
come on! let's all go there!

`1:44` B Gulumbé gulumbé gulumbá
        Guache moleniyo de Safala.

Gulumbé, gulumbé, gulumbá,
Poor boys, black boys from Safala.

`2:00` d' Vamo turuz los Neglios   *plimos*   Let's go, all the black boys,   *my cousins!*
            pues nos yeba nostla estleya   *beya*   since our Star is leading us,   *beautiful!*
            que sin tantuz neglos folmen   *noche*   even though we're all as black   *as night,*
            mucha lus en lo poltal   *ablá.*   on the manger, plenty of light   *there'll be.*

Blasico, Pellico, Zuanico i Tomá,
plimos beya noche ablá.

Blasico, Perico, Juanico, and Tomás,
cousins, it will be a beautiful night!

`2:20` B Gulumbé gulumbé gulumbá
        Guache moleniyo de Safala.

Gulumbé, gulumbé, gulumbá,
Poor boys, black boys from Safala.

Copla 2:

2:38   d   Vaya nuestra cofladia   *linda*   Let's go, all our brotherhood   *fine!*
            Pues que nos yeba la eztleia   *nueztla*   Since the star leads us,   *ours!*
            tlas lo Rey e pulque aya   *danza*   after the kings, and since   *a dance*
            que pala al niño aleglan   *yra.*   to cheer the child there   *will be.*

            Blasico, Pellico, Zuanico i Tomá,   Blasico, Perico, Juanico, and Tomás,
            linda nuestla danza yra.   Our dance will be so fine!

2:57   B   Gulumbé gulumbé gulumbá   Gulumbé, gulumbé, gulumbá,
            Guache moleniyo de Safala.   Poor boys, black boys from Safala.

3:13   d' Vamo alegle al poltariyo   *plimo*   Let's go merrily to the stable   *cousins.*
            velemo junto al peseble   *bueye*   We'll see next to the manger   *oxen.*
            que sin tantuz neglos folmen   *neglo*   Even though we're all jet   *black,*
            mucha lus en lo poltal   *ezá.*   on the manger, plenty of light   *there is!*

            Blasico, Pellico, Zuanico i Tomá,   Blasico, Perico, Juanico, and Tomás,
            plimo neglo buey e ezá.   black cousins, here are the oxen.

3:32   B   Gulumbé gulumbé gulumbá   Gulumbé, gulumbé, gulumbá,
            Guache moleniyo de Safala.   Poor boys, black boys from Safala

3:51   *(Repeat Estribillo)*

                        —ANONYMOUS   —TRANS. JULES WHICKER

The villancico began its career in fifteenth-century Spain as a courtly secular song in mock-peasant style (see NAWM 54), but by the seventeenth century it had become a vernacular sacred genre cultivated by the Roman Catholic Church throughout the Spanish-speaking world. Performed by professional church musicians during Matins and other religious services, villancicos added splendor and festivity to Christmas and other important feasts. While their works preserved distinctly Spanish elements, villancico composers in both Spain and the Americas incorporated the new techniques of the Baroque era, including the concertato medium, continuo accompaniment, monody, polychoral or other antiphonal effects, rhetorical approaches to text setting, and, in some works, instrumental ritornellos.

One of the most important composers of villancicos in the New World was Juan de Araujo, born in Spain but trained in Peru and active as chapelmaster at the cathedrals of Lima and La Plata (now Sucre, Bolivia). At least 263 pieces by Araujo survive, mostly villancicos. They exemplify the Spanish theater style of the seventeenth century, characterized by lyric song and syncopated rhythms (see also NAWM 90).

In *Los coflades de la estleya*, Araujo uses syncopation within triple meter to joyously evoke the journey of one of the three Magi and his retinue from Africa to Bethlehem. Like their courtly predecessors, sacred villancicos follow Spanish literary traditions of addressing elite audiences through stories of shepherds, slaves, foreigners, and others outside the elite. The depiction here of African boys preparing to sing and dance before the newborn Jesus and his mother Mary parallels Renaissance and Baroque paintings of the Adoration of the Magi, which portray the three kings as representative of Europe, Asia, and Africa, the three continents known to the ancient world. The inclusion of Africa allegorically reinforces the Roman Catholic Church's claim to be a universal church, and the references to the boys' poverty allude to the humbleness of Christ's birth, as do the popular literary and musical styles in the villancico.

The text uses a stereotyped literary dialect that satirizes how Africans were perceived to speak Spanish. One aspect of this dialect involves switching the letters "r" and "l"; thus "cofrades" (fellow members of a religious brotherhood) and "estrella" (star) become "coflades" and "estleya." The racism inherent in this dialect is offensive today, as is the text's association of blackness with the lowness of the manger. On the other hand, the poet's intent seems to have been to evoke Africans positively, by means of endearing diminutives (the "-iyo" word endings) and an internal refrain on "gulumbé, gulumbé" that refers to the *guineo*, a popular Spanish dance of the period that emulated West African dancing within European conventions.

The rhythmic pattern at the beginning of the piece (long-long, short-long, short-long, short-short) also signifies the *guineo*. This syncopated rhythm and others derived from it recur frequently, creating a wonderful musical evocation of boys running eagerly, almost stumbling over each other in their impatience to see the newborn child. But both this rhythm and the literary dialect were products of Spain, however much they may have symbolized Africa to the Spanish. Although it might be tempting to find in this villancico elements of African or Latin American rhythm, representing the presence in colonial Peru of native Americans, free and enslaved Africans, and people of mixed race, the syncopations are drawn primarily from Spanish traditions.

The form of *Los coflades de la estleya* resembles that of Renaissance villancicos, with a refrain, called an *estribillo*, that precedes and follows one or more stanzas, called *coplas*, which typically end with the same music as the refrain. But seventeenth-century villancicos are often much longer and therefore more complex than earlier ones. Here the *estribillo* is sixty measures long and is subdivided into two parts by its own brief internal refrain, creating the form aBcB (as marked next to the text above, with B beginning in measures 27 and 50). The same internal refrain recurs in the *coplas* (at measures 75 and 101), dividing them in a similar manner, to produce the following form for the entire piece: aBcB dBd'B dBd'B aBcB.

Araujo scored the piece for two treble soloists (on the upper two staves), choir (on the next two staves), and continuo. Antiphonal exchanges between soloists and choir energize the music, especially in the *coplas*, where the choir interjects single words—taken from the last line before the internal refrain—between phrases sung by the soloists, creating new meanings through the juxtaposition (see for instance measures 61–71, and compare the words sung in measures 73–75). These interjections, often rhyming or punning with the soloists' words, dramatize the group's interactions on the way to Bethlehem.

The edition presented here and used on the accompanying recording takes into consideration modern performance conventions. The music is transposed down a fourth to fit the standard vocal ranges of modern choirs. The note values are reduced by a factor of four—a half note in the original notation appears here as an eighth note—so the performers do not have to contend with half, whole, and dotted whole notes racing by at a brisk tempo. But the edition also makes the rhythm seem more complex than it already is by grouping two measures of the original triple meter into one measure of $\frac{6}{8}$ meter; for example, the melody in measures 5–9 features the same *guineo* rhythm as the melody in measures 1–5, but seems more syncopated and complicated because the ties cross the barline instead of coming in the middle of a measure.

On the accompanying recording, the treble soloists are women, although in the original context boys trained at the cathedral school would have sung the high parts. In accord with Spanish tradition, the continuo group includes guitar and harp. Latin American percussion instruments such as maracas and small drums are added, especially during the internal refrains, making the music sound more exotic but reflecting today's performance customs rather than seventeenth-century cathedral practice.

Alessandro Scarlatti (1660–1725)

Clori vezzosa, e bella: Conclusion

Cantata

CA. 1690–1710

(a) Recitative; *Vivo penando*

From Alessandro Scarlatti, *Three Cantatas for Voice and Cello with Keyboard*, ed. Peter Foster, Nona Pyron, and Timothy Roberts (Fullerton, Calif.: Grancino Editions, 1982), 16–19.

(b) Aria: *Sì, sì ben mio*

[Recitative]

Vivo penando, è ver; ma son contento	I live suffering, it is true; but I am content
dell'istesso tormento,	with that same torment,
perchè se penso che	because if I think that
tu sola sei cagion	you alone are the cause
di tanti affanni miei,	of so many of my troubles,
diventa mio gioire	it becomes my joy,
la pena ed il martire,	that suffering and that torture,
e più penar vorrei	and I would like to suffer more
per palesarti più, gl'affetti miei.	to reveal to you more of my feelings.

[Aria]

Sì, sì ben mio, sì, sì	Yes, yes, my love, yes, yes,
ancor vorrei per te più pene al core.	I would like, through you, still more torments for my heart.
Pietosa al mio dolore,	Feeling pity at my pain,
forse diresti un dì:	perhaps you will say one day:
"Chi vidde maggior fè, più fido amore?"	"Who ever saw greater faith, or a more devoted love?"

Alessandro Scarlatti was the most prolific composer of cantatas, with over six hundred to his credit. Typical of the cantatas that Scarlatti composed after about 1690, *Clori vezzosa, e bella* has two recitative-aria pairs and is scored for voice and continuo. The poetry freely alternates lines of six, seven, and eleven syllables with an irregular rhyme scheme.

As in most cantatas of the time, the text is a pastoral love poem in the form of a monologue, written as though it were a portion of a drama in which one character is speaking to another, with each section conveying a different reflection on the central theme. Here, the protagonist is a shepherd addressing the nymph Clori. In the first recitative, he swears that he loves only her, and in the following aria, he declares that he suffers from a burning passion. In the second recitative-aria pair, included here, he claims that he is glad for his pain since Clori is the cause, and he then asks for more suffering, hoping that perhaps some day she will see how faithful he is to her.

Scarlatti used a wide range of harmonic vocabulary in the recitative to portray the lover's torments. The key modulates quickly from A minor to G minor and F minor (measure 43), and then a chromatically rising bass line leads to cadences in A minor and finally F major. At several of the cadences, the local dominant is preceded by a diminished seventh chord (measures 39, 46, and 49), a type of dissonance that was still unusual for the time but that Scarlatti used frequently to add harmonic intensity and suggest strong emotions. The rhythms in the vocal line imitate natural speech, but emotionally charged words are highlighted with melodic effects such as a short melisma on "pena" (suffering) and an emphasis on semitone motion at "penando" (suffering), "dell'istesso tormento" (with that same torment), "gioire" (rejoice), and "affetti" (feelings).

Both arias in this cantata follow the *da capo* form that became standard around 1690 and remained the most common aria form for almost a century. The term derives from the words "Da capo" ("from the head," meaning "over again"), which are written in the music at the end of the second section (measure 87) to indicate that the performers should return to the beginning and repeat the first section, creating an overall form of ABA. The text for a da capo aria is typically in two stanzas that express related but different thoughts. In the A section of this aria, the shepherd welcomes more torments of love, and in the B section (at measure 74), he expresses the hope that Clori may someday feel pity and recognize his devotion. In both sections, words and phrases are repeated many times as the composer spins out the musical material with variations, extensions, and sequences.

As in most da capo arias, the A section is itself a small two-part form: the text is set twice, preceded each time by an instrumental ritornello. In the first vocal statement (measure 54), the voice repeats and develops a motive from the ritornello and then cadences in the subdominant. The continuo repeats a segment of the ritornello in the new key (measure 59), and then in the second vocal statement, the voice develops the material further, eventually modulating back to the tonic, D minor.

Section	A					B	A repeats
	Ritornello	A1		Ritornello	A2	B	
Key	Dm i	Dm → Gm i → iv		Gm iv	Gm → Dm iv → i	FM → Am III → v	Dm i
Measure	51	54		59	60	74	51

The B section offers contrasts of key and mood, beginning in F major and modulating to several new keys, including G minor, C major, and A minor. The bass continues to vary the ritornello theme while the voice introduces several new but related ideas.

As in the recitative, chromatic harmonies suggest strong and poignant emotions. In the A section, the word "pene" (torments) is set once over a diminished seventh chord (measure 58) and later over a Neapolitan sixth chord (measure 64), a first-inversion triad on the flatted second degree of the scale. Both types of chord recur in the B section (see measures 78 and 86–87). But throughout, the quick gigue rhythm and bouncy melodic gestures produce a witty irony by suggesting that the lover's feelings are at least as pleasurable as they are painful.

On the accompanying recording, this cantata is sung by a *countertenor*, a high male voice, and the continuo is played by cello, archlute, and harpsichord. As was customary in Scarlatti's time, the singer embellishes many of the cadences in the recitative with added appoggiaturas and varies some phrases during the reprise of the aria's A section.

Alessandro Scarlatti (1660–1725)

La Griselda: Excerpt from Act I, Scene 2

Opera

1720–21

Da capo

0:00/1:53	In voler ciò che tu brami,	In wanting that which you desire,
in bramar ciò che a te piace,	in desiring that which pleases you,
la mia gioia e la mia pace	my joy and my peace
sempre o caro io troverò.	always, O dear one, I will find.

0:59	Non mi chieder che io non t'ami,	Do not ask of me that I not love you,
non vietarmi che io t'adori.	do not forbid me to adore you.
Dimmi poi: "Griselda mori,"	But say to me: "Griselda, die,"
che io contenta morirò.	and I will die content.

La Griselda was Scarlatti's last opera, premiered in January 1721 at the Teatro Capranica in Rome under the sponsorship of Prince Francesco Maria Ruspoli, one of the leading patrons in Rome. The libretto, perhaps by the prince himself, was adapted from one by Apostolo Zeno that had been set by fifteen other composers over the previous two decades. Zeno, the leading librettist of his generation, based the plot on the last story in Boccacio's *Decameron*, written almost four centuries earlier. The libretto was so popular because it addressed one of the constant themes in opera of the time—virtue triumphing over adversity—while highlighting in particularly stark terms issues of class, gender roles, and stoic acceptance of suffering.

Years before the opera begins, Gualtiero, king of Sicily, married the peasant Griselda, but because of her low birth she has not been accepted by his subjects. In order to prove to them that she has the patience, virtue, and constancy to be their queen, he pretends to accede to their wishes, publicly renouncing her and saying that he plans to take a new bride of royal blood. Ever loyal and loving, she gives him back her crown and scepter, then sings this aria, the first in the opera. Over the opera's three acts, she endures further tests with humility and dignity, acceding to Gualtiero's every demand except his last, that she marry another man. When she refuses, pleading that she will always love and be faithful only to him, Gualtiero embraces her again as his wife. The people hail her, and he tells them that it is her virtue and noble conduct, not her blood, that makes her worthy to be their queen.

Griselda's aria *In voler ciò che tu brami* follows the conventions of the da capo aria: a first section with two vocal statements of the first stanza of text, framed by ritornellos; a second section to the second stanza, with contrasting music; and a reprise of the first section.

Section	A					B	A repeats
	Ritornello	A1	Ritornello	A2	Ritornello	B	
Key	B♭ I	B♭ → Cm i → ii	Cm ii	Cm → B♭ ii → I	B♭ I	Gm → Dm vi → iii	B♭ I
Measure	1	3	12	14	24	26	1

As usual, the first vocal statement modulates to a new key that is confirmed by the second ritornello. The second vocal statement then modulates back to the tonic, confirmed by the third ritornello, and the B section introduces contrasting keys and lacks any ritornellos or interludes. In this aria, both the second and third ritornellos are abbreviated variants of the first, with the second ritornello drawing on the middle portion and the closing ritornello using the first and final segments. The four-part orchestra with continuo plays throughout, coming to the fore in the ritornellos, then dropping back to *piano* while the voice sings, with frequent orchestral punctuation between phrases.

This aria illustrates the effectiveness of the da capo form, which became so widely used and lasted so long because it was so well suited to capturing a moment of conflicting emotions.

In the A section, Griselda declares to Gualtiero that she finds her own joy and peace in desiring what pleases him, showing that she is a noble and obedient wife. Her dignity and resolve are evident in the music. The tempo marking *Allegro e sciolto* (fast and staccato) and the loud, rapid sixteenth notes in the opening orchestral ritornello establish a character that is the opposite of lyricism, conveying instead determination and strength. The orchestra occasionally interjects elements from the ritornello even after the voice enters (for example at measures 5 and 7). When Griselda refers to herself (at "in voler," "in bramar," and "la mia gioia e la mia piace"), the vocal line is disjunct, with wide leaps that again suggest strength and resolve. By contrast, her references to Gualtiero's desires are mostly stepwise with small turning figures, suggesting the tenderness and love she feels for him. Her love and devotion to him are especially emphasized in the second vocal statement through curling triplet figures (measures 14–15 and 18–19) and repeated rising half steps on the word "caro" (dear one, measure 22).

The mood and the music change in the middle section (measures 26–45). Here Griselda states her limits: she will do as Gualtiero wishes, but she will not stop loving him, and she commands him not to make such a request. The opening figure of repeated notes rising to a peak suggests that she is immovable, every inch the queen, in contrast to the deferential wife of the A section. Of course there is no change for her; these are two sides of her character, a duality that the da capo aria is perfectly designed to capture. When she repeats the same text, the figure is different but repeats with equal insistence (measures 35–36). She goes on to say that she would die content if Gualtiero demanded it of her. Again this gets two different settings: the second (measures 37–40) imitates military fanfares, appropriate to the imperiousness of such a demand, but the first subtly refers back to the tenderness of the A section, echoing at the word "mori" (die) in measures 31–32 the rising half steps (in the voice) and curling figures (in violin I) that earlier framed the word "caro."

The repetition of the A section reinforces the combination of dignity, strength, and tenderness in Griselda, now deepened by the aspects of her character and feelings explored in the B section. The repetition also provides an opportunity for the singer to vary and decorate the material, as on the accompanying recording. This embellishment, including a brief cadenza before the final vocal cadence, not only shows off the singer's voice but ideally is also expressive, adding to our sense of the character and her feelings.

Although the music is tonal and in the key of B♭ major, there is only one flat in the key signature. It was often true in the late seventeenth and early eighteenth centuries that pieces were notated with a key signature missing one flat, so that major-mode pieces look as if they are in the Lydian mode, and minor-mode pieces as if they are in the Dorian mode. This shows the continuing strength of the modes as a concept and was also a matter of convenience, since the fourth degree in a major key and the sixth degree in a minor key are so often raised a semitone, as when moving to the dominant chord or key.

Arcangelo Corelli (1653–1713)

Trio Sonata in D Major, Op. 3, No. 2

Trio sonata

1680s

94

(a) Grave (first movement)

Arcangelo Corelli, *Historisch-kritische Gesamtausgabe der musikalischen Werke*, vol. 1, *Sonate da chiesa, Opus I und III*, ed. Max Lütolf (Laaber: Laaber-Verlag, 1987), 123–29.

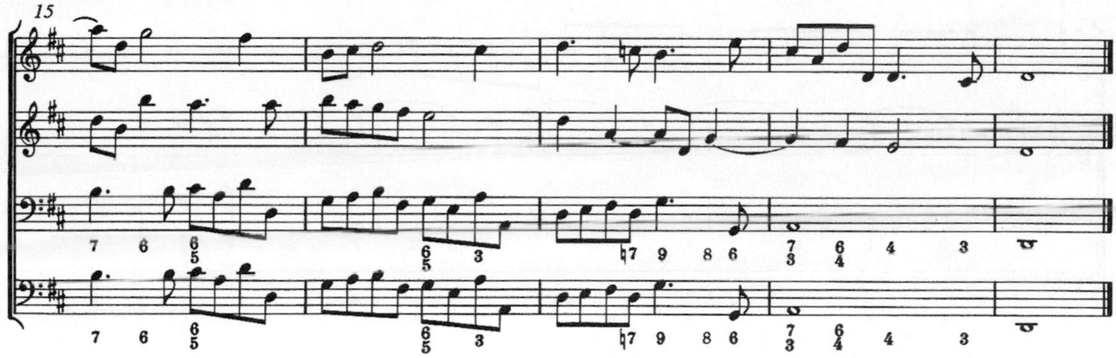

(b) Allegro (second movement)

concise

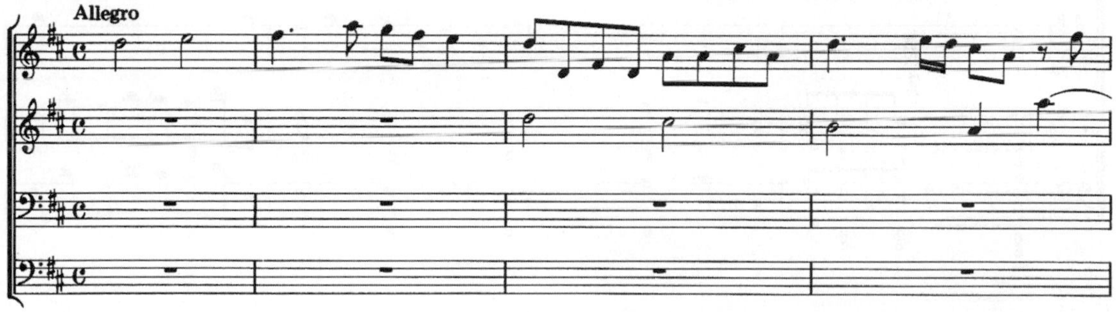

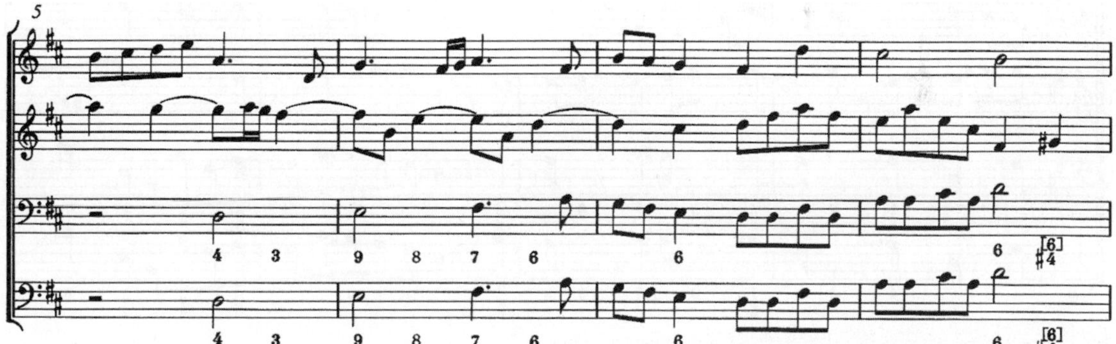

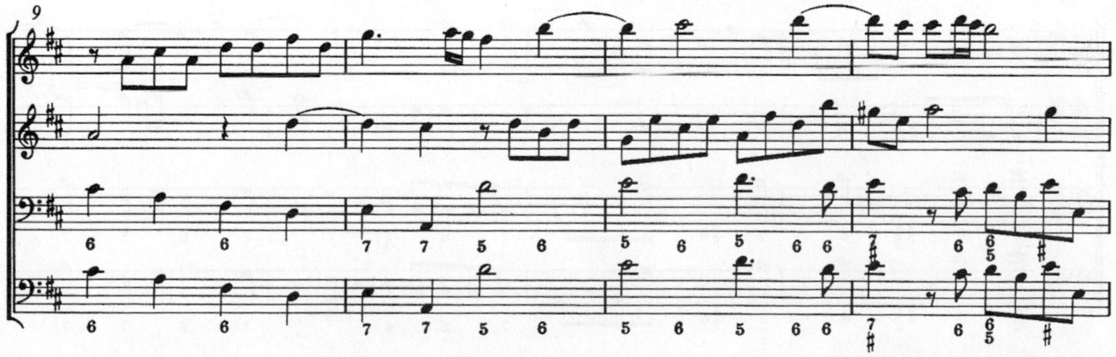

(c) Adagio (third movement)

(d) Allegro (fourth movement)

concise 🔊

Arcangelo Corelli published his *Sonate a tre*, Op. 3, while he was employed by Cardinal Pamphili in Rome as music master, composer of instrumental music, and orchestra director. A set of twelve trio sonatas, the collection was published in Rome in 1689. Corelli dedicated it to another of his patrons, Francesco II, duke of Modena.

Biagio Marini's Sonata IV (NAWM 84) featured a series of sections contrasting in tempo, figuration, and mood. In Corelli's sonatas, the sections have been expanded to form separate movements. The sonatas in Op. 3 are in *sonata da chiesa* (church sonata) format, and No. 2 in D major features the slow-fast-slow-fast succession of movements typical of church sonatas. Although Corelli avoided obvious secular connotations, this sonata bears a similarity to the stylized dance suite: the last movement resembles a gigue, and the third hints at the rhythm of the sarabande. All the movements are in D major except for the third, which is in the relative minor, B minor. Although the movements all feature different themes, there is a subtle motivic connection among them: the first movement opens with D—E—F♯—E—D—C♯ in the first violin, and each subsequent movement begins with a variant or elaboration of the same idea. The variant at the opening of the third movement is easier to hear than to see, moving from the first note of violin 1 (D) to the first note of violin 2 (E) and on to F♯ in violin 1 (measure 4), then back down.

Grave, the marking at the beginning of the first movement, does not merely designate the tempo but also indicates that the character of the music is serious, intense, and profound. The intensity is expressed by the determined march of the walking bass and the suspended dissonances on most downbeats. By Corelli's time, suspensions, passing tones, neighbor tones, and similar dissonances were understood as nonchord tones sounding against a chordal background, rather than as part of a contrapuntal web regulated by the rules of sixteenth-century counterpoint. As a result, voices in the texture were free to leap between the chord tones against the dissonances (as the bass does in measure 2) or even to leap from a suspension down to a chord tone and then up to the note of resolution (as in measures 15 and 17, and also in measures 24 and 46–48 of the second movement). Typical of Corelli's music are the chains of suspensions created by the two violins when their lines meet, cross, and separate, accompanied by a series of sequences created by the steadily walking bass. The forward momentum of suspensions and sequences contributes to the strong sense of harmonic direction that Corelli is known for. Marini's Sonata IV reveals elements of Renaissance modality, but Corelli's sonata is tonal. The first movement moves from the tonic to cadences on V (A major), V of V (E major), and vi (B minor, the relative minor) before returning to close on the tonic.

The first Allegro is fugal, as in most of Corelli's church sonatas, and the basso continuo participates fully in the imitation. Indeed, the bass is the first to answer the subject in exact imitation, the second violin having answered with an inverted, incomplete variant of the subject. This movement is remarkable in its nearly complete exclusion of nonthematic material. After the subject, its inversion, and its counterpoints are introduced, they return in numerous permutations and variations. The harmony explores the same harmonic regions as in the first movement, cadencing on A major, B minor, and E major before returning to D.

The Adagio resembles a passionate vocal duet in which two singers alternately imitate each other and proceed in parallel thirds. Syncopations and suspensions on the first and second beats of the triple-time measures emphasize the second beat, as in a sarabande rhythm, through both resolution and dissonance. The dance character is reinforced by hemiola passages at cadences (measures 19–21 and 36–39). A half cadence at the end of the Adagio causes listeners to expect B minor, but instead the finale returns to D major.

The final movement is labeled Allegro, but it shares many characteristics with movements marked by Corelli as gigues. It involves all three instrumental parts in fugal imitation, as was customary for gigues from this era and later (especially those of Johann Sebastian Bach), and it is in the binary form of a dance. The subject of the second half is an inversion of that in the first half, a technique typical of many later gigues. Additionally, there are two sequential episodes of the kind found in later fugues (measures 8–10 and 28–32). The extensive use of contrapuntal devices such as inversion, stretto (imitating the subject in close succession, as in measures 32–35), and pedal point (measures 15–18) demonstrates the influence of the Bologna school, in which such techniques were cultivated and where Corelli was trained.

Trio sonatas (especially in the *da chiesa* tradition) were normally performed by at least four players: one on each violin line; a cello or bass viola da gamba to play the bass line; and a lute or keyboard instrument to play continuo, doubling the bass line and filling in the harmonies. Either an organ or harpsichord could be used to play continuo, but the organ was more typical for church performances. On the accompanying recording, both organ and theorbo play continuo, together with a cello. Corelli published his church sonatas with two mostly identical bass parts, one designated for organ and the other for cello or archlute; occasionally the parts diverge, as in the last movement, where Corelli apparently considered the sixteenth notes in the subject too fast for the organ (see measures 7 and 22). Throughout all four movements, the two violin parts are almost equally active and avoid the embellishments and virtuosic display common in solo sonatas such as Marini's. Trio sonatas such as this were also occasionally played by orchestras, with more than one player on each string part. This practice shows the close relationship between the trio sonata and the new genres of the *orchestral concerto* and the *concerto grosso*.

Dieterich Buxtehude (CA. 1637–1707)

Praeludium in E Major, BuxWV 141

Organ prelude

LATE SEVENTEENTH CENTURY

95

For almost forty years, Dieterich Buxtehude served as organist at St. Mary's Church in Lübeck, in northern Germany. As in most Lutheran churches, services there began with a substantial prelude for organ, and several later portions of the service were also introduced with preludes. Buxtehude likely played his Praeludium in E Major as an opening prelude, and he may also have used it as a challenging assignment for his organ students. Unlike some of his contemporaries, he did not seek to publish his organ music, and none of his original manuscripts survive. The earliest source for this piece dates from after his death.

Although this piece is called a Praeludium (Latin for "prelude"), it is in the style of a toccata, in which free and fugal sections alternate. Here, there are five free sections, of which the first two are the most substantial, the next two are shorter transitions, and the last is a climactic coda on a motive from the final fugue. The fugal sections differ from each other in subject, meter, tempo, character, style, and treatment. The contrasts between free and fugal textures and between different sections of the same type create tremendous variety within the piece. But it is unified by the key of E major and by the sense of continuity from one section to the next; each of the fugues blends into the following free section without a cadence, and only the first and last sections close on the tonic.

The piece begins with a three-measure flourish in the right hand that serves as a grand upbeat to the first E-major chord. The next eight measures explore a number of figurations while the harmony moves slowly to the dominant and back to the tonic. This and the other free sections sound improvisatory because of frequent and unpredictable changes in rhythm, melodic direction, harmony, phrasing, and texture.

The next section exhibits all the typical characteristics of a seventeenth-century fugue. The fugue subject (measure 13) is imitated in all four voices in turn, in Buxtehude's favorite order of soprano—alto—tenor—bass. A series of entries like this is called an *exposition*. As usual, the second entrance, called the *answer*, is altered intervallically to fit the key, and later voices alternate subject and answer. If the subject begins on the dominant note (as here), the answer begins on the tonic, and vice versa. In Buxtehude's Praeludium, a second four-voice exposition (measures 24–32) is followed by a brief episode (measures 32–36) that is built on the end of the subject and modulates to the dominant. Then a final series of entrances (measure 36) ends with an embellished variant in the tenor (measures 44–46). Throughout the fugue, the part for pedal keyboard is a full participant in the counterpoint, and the sixteenth-note passages demonstrate that Buxtehude was a virtuoso with his feet as well as his hands.

Before the fugue reaches a final cadence, a free toccata section begins (measure 47), full of exuberant runs that take the pitch to the highest point in the piece. After the tonic chord finally arrives, there are two "long trills" (so marked in the score) in the pedal part (measures 51 and 53) that create new energy.

The second fugal section, marked *Presto* (measure 60), breaks up into imitations of a short figure after only two entries of the subject. A brief, suspenseful transition reestablishes the tonic for the third fugal section (measures 75–86), a three-voice fugue in gigue rhythm and tempo on a subject that is derived from the subject of the first fugue. Neither of these middle fugues includes the pedal. A transitional Adagio (measure 87) leads to the final fugue (measure 91), which returns to a four-voice texture that includes the pedals and features another subject derived from the first. In the coda (measure 104), the opening motive of the final fugue alternates between the pedal and the other voices, bringing the prelude to a rousing close.

Antonio Vivaldi (1678–1741)

Concerto for Violin and Orchestra in A Minor, Op. 3, No. 6

Violin concerto

CA. 1710

96

(a) Allegro (first movement)

From Antonio Vivaldi, *L'estro armonico*, Op. 3, ed. Eleanor Selfridge-Field with Edmund Correia Jr. (Mineola, N.Y.: Dover, 1999), 100–113.

(b) Largo (second movement)

(c) Presto (third movement)

Antonio Vivaldi's *L'estro armonico* (Harmonic Inspiration, Op. 3) was published in Amsterdam in 1711 with a dedication to Grand Prince Ferdinand III de' Medici of Florence, a patron of the concerts led by Vivaldi at the Pio Ospedale della Pietà in Venice. The first set of Vivaldi's concertos to be printed, it established the composer's European reputation and became the most influential collection of music published during the early eighteenth century, reprinted over two dozen times. The twelve concertos it contains are written for a variety of soloists with orchestra: four feature solo violin, and the others feature combinations of two to five instruments (two concertos each for two violins, two violins with cello, four violins, and four violins with cello). The solo violin concertos and most of the others have three movements in the order fast–slow–fast, which became the most common structure for concertos, but a few begin with one or two added slow movements. Concerto No. 6 for Violin and Orchestra in A Minor was among the first of Vivaldi's concertos to become popular, circulating through reprintings and manuscript copies. In recent decades it has become popular again, in concerts and recordings and as a teaching piece in the Suzuki training program for young violinists, a modern reflection of its original role as a piece for Vivaldi's students at the Pietà. It exhibits many of the characteristics that are typical of his concerto style.

For the fast movements of his concertos, Vivaldi used *ritornello form*, in which ritornellos played by the full orchestra alternate with episodes that feature the soloist or soloists. The opening ritornello statement is made up of several small units. The subsequent ritornellos may repeat this entire opening statement, but most repeat only one or some of its smaller units, often varied. In Vivaldi's concertos, the ritornellos form the pillars of the movement's tonal structure: the first and last ritornellos are in the tonic, at least one ritornello (usually the first to be in a new key) is in the dominant, and others are usually in closely related keys. The episodes feature virtuosic, idiomatic passages for the soloists, either developing material drawn from the ritornello or presenting new ideas. A solo episode typically drives the music forward by modulating to a new key that is then confirmed by the next ritornello. Within these general guidelines, Vivaldi's ritornello forms show almost limitless invention.

In the first movement, the opening ritornello presents three ideas: A, the opening phrase; B, a related motive treated in sequence (measures 3–7); and C, an arpeggiated figure (measures 7–9) that is immediately varied (measures 10–12). The second ritornello varies A, and then the third states A, B, and a variant of A in the key of the minor dominant. All the later ritornellos are in the tonic, presenting phrases A or C. Over a light accompaniment played by the orchestra, the episodes spin out material that focuses either on elements from the ritornellos (A in the first ritornello, B in the last) or on new figuration. Motives are often treated in sequence over changing harmonies, with motion around the circle of fifths frequently used for modulations (as at measures 51–55). In the last quarter of the movement, the complete material of the opening ritornello reappears in the tonic, but spread out through three ritornellos and an episode. The form of the movement can be diagrammed as follows:

Measure	Forces	Section	Motives	Key	Tonal plan
1	Tutti	Ritornello	A B C C'	a	i
13	Solo	Episode	A, A'	mod to C	
21	Tutti	Ritornello	A"	a	
24	Solo	Episode	new, A'	mod to e	
35	Tutti	Ritornello	A B A'''	e	v
45	Solo	Episode	new	mod to a	
58	Tutti	Ritornello	A	a	i
60	Solo	Episode	new	mod	
68	Tutti	Ritornello	C'	a	
71	Solo	Episode	B'	a	
75	Tutti	Ritornello	C C'	a	

The finale differs from the first movement in that its opening ritornello (measures 1–30) has more segments, the subsequent ritornellos are more varied in the material they repeat, and the key structure is somewhat different:

Measure	Forces	Section	Motives	Key	Tonal plan
1	Tutti	Ritornello	ABABCDEF	a	i
30	Solo	Episode	AB', new	mod	
50	Tutti	Ritornello	AA	e	v
55	Solo	Episode	C'	e	
62	Tutti	Ritornello	DEF'	a	i
71	Solo	Episode	F', new	mod to C	
91	Tutti	Ritornello	AAC'F'AAC	C, e, a	III, v, i
109	Solo	Episode	new	a	
115	Tutti	Ritornello	AB	a	i
122	Solo		C'	a	
127	Tutti		D	a	
130	Solo, Tutti		E	a	
134	Solo, Tutti		F"	a	
138	Solo	Episode	new	a	
143	Tutti	Cadence	end of F"	a	

Typically, modulation is common in episodes, and ritornellos are stable in key, but the fourth ritornello in this finale actually modulates through three keys, from the relative major through the minor dominant and back to the tonic (measures 91–109). The last ritornello (measures 115–38) repeats all the material of the opening ritornello in order, but several short segments are presented by the soloist rather than by the orchestra, further confusing the distinction between ritornellos and episodes. The freedom with which Vivaldi deploys the ritornello principle in this finale and the differences between the finale and first movement only begin to suggest the variety of formal structures he achieved in his ritornello-form movements.

Both the ritornellos and the episodes feature almost constant motion in eighth and sixteenth notes. This driving, motoric rhythm is characteristic of Vivaldi's fast movements and of much music from the late Baroque period, but very different from the rhythmically varied, constantly changing music by composers of the early Baroque period, such as Monteverdi or Frescobaldi.

The slow middle movement is a rhapsodic interlude for solo violin over sustained chords in the orchestral violins and violas, with the cellos, basses, and continuo silent. The effect is dreamlike, with the soloist's smoothly flowing figures treated in sequence over chromatic progressions in the other instruments. Although the omission of continuo is unusual, light scoring and emphasis on the soloist are typical of Vivaldi's slow movements, offering a strong contrast to the outer movements. Also typical of his middle movements is the use of a different but closely related key—here, D minor, the subdominant of A minor.

The original print of *L'estro armonico* consisted of eight partbooks: four for violins, numbered 1 through 4; two for violas 1 and 2; one for violoncello; and the continuo part for cembalo (harpsichord) and violone (bass viol). In the present edition of this concerto, the violin 1 partbook is transcribed in the top staff, with markings for solo and tutti to indicate where the soloist should play alone if more than one player is reading from this part. The partbooks for violins 2–4 all contain the same music in the first and last movements, shown on the second staff down, but diverge in the slow middle movement. Violas 1 and 2 play in unison throughout, and the cello and continuo parts are the same except for the figured bass in the continuo. Vivaldi intended it to be possible to play this piece with only eight performers, one reading from each partbook (as might a group of amateurs playing for their own enjoyment), or with a small string orchestra of about twenty to twenty-five players like the one at the Pio Ospedale della Pietà and on the accompanying recording.

Vivaldi wrote his concertos for string players performing on instruments with gut strings in small ensembles directed by the leader of the violins. They can be and often are played by larger orchestras on modern instruments with metal strings and led by a conductor. However, in the last several decades it has become common for performers to attempt to recreate the sound, performing forces, and performance practices that would have been familiar to Vivaldi, as on the accompanying recording.

As can be heard on that recording, string players of Vivaldi's time typically played in a nonlegato style, articulating each note with a separate stroke of the bow, and with a strong emphasis on the main beats of the meter. The slurred groupings in solo passages, as in the solo episode in measures 24–31 of the first movement and in the slow movement, are a special effect; each slur indicates a group of notes to be played with a single bowstroke. On the bow of the time, the bow strings were pulled less taut, allowing greater agility and facilitating the articulations but producing a less penetrating sound than the modern bow. The soloist was expected to add ornamentation in the slow movement, already richly embellished by Vivaldi in the manner of a slow aria.

François Couperin (1668–1733)

Vingt-cinquième ordre: Excerpts

Keyboard suite

CA. 1730

(a) *La visionaire*

(b) *La muse victorieuse*

(c) *Les ombres errantes*

François Couperin published twenty-seven *ordres*, or suites, for harpsichord between 1713 and 1730. They were intended for amateurs to play for their own entertainment. The three movements reprinted here are from Couperin's twenty-fifth ordre, which was included along with seven others in his fourth book of harpsichord suites, published in 1730. The ordres were made up mostly of dances in binary form, like earlier keyboard suites, but the dances did not follow any particular sequence. As in earlier suites, these movements represent a process of abstraction, from the relatively simple and straightforward music used for dancing, to music in dance rhythms and forms that composers made more challenging and rhythmically intricate for the entertainment of the player or listeners.

Couperin gave suggestive titles to most movements in his ordres. Those in his twenty-fifth ordre include *La visionaire* (The Visionary or The Seer), *La misterieuse* (The Mysterious One, an allemande), *La monflambert* (a gigue, probably named after Anne Darboulin, who married the king's wine merchant Monflambert in 1726), *La muse victorieuse* (The Victorious Muse), and *Les ombres errantes* (The Errant Shades or The Lost Souls). These titles evoke images that are realized in the music, so that each movement is a *pièce de caractère* or *character piece*. This is a fashion Couperin himself had helped to create in the early 1700s, going beyond the fanciful titles attached to some pieces in the seventeenth century, such as *La Coquette virtuose* (NAWM 87), which did not necessarily have anything to do with the character of the music. Of these five movements, the first, fourth, and fifth are included here. Unlike Jacquet de la Guerre's Suite in A Minor (NAWM 88), in which every dance is in the same key, Couperin's ordre includes movements in three different keys: E♭ major for the opening movement (despite the key signature with two flats), C major for the second and fourth, and C minor for the third and last (again with two flats in the key signature).

La visionaire, the first movement of this ordre, is a whimsical take on the conventions of the French overture. In the slow opening section, labeled *Grave et marqué* (solemn and marked), Couperin embellished the traditional dotted rhythms of the overture style by replacing many of the short notes with fast runs called *tirades*; the combination of overture style with *tirades* was associated with powerful or supernatural characters in French opera (as in Armide's entrance music in NAWM 85c) and thus fits the title "The Visionary." After modulating to the dominant in measure 14, the music confirms the new key with a momentary turn to the dominant minor, adding a mysterious cast to the music. The second half, marked *Viste* (fast), begins with imitation between the hands, a tribute to the traditional imitative fast second section of the French overture. This section becomes a bit too exuberant, suggesting that the visionary of the title has a witty or comic side as well as a serious, mysterious aspect. The movement then lapses into an allemande style, haunted by memories of the majestic first half and suffused with *tirades*. This movement exemplifies the later Baroque keyboard style that differentiates Couperin's later ordres from earlier suites (compare NAWM 88), featuring thick chords, leaping figures, scalar passages, dense but expressive ornamentation, and a dissonant harmonic style drawn from Italy, with many suspensions and seventh chords (see for example measures 3–6). Typical of Couperin, it combines traditional French elements, such as the French overture form, short phrases, dotted figures, and *tirades*, with Italian elements, including longer phrases composed of short ideas spun out by sequence, driving, regular harmonic rhythm, and the more chromatic and dissonant harmonic language.

La muse victorieuse, marked *Audacieusement* (audaciously or boldly), offers a witty take on both its title and tempo marking. The audacity lies in the quick tempo, nearly continuous sixteenth-note motion, leaping figures, and changes of register. The "victorious muse" depicted in the quick dance is also the player: most amateur harpsichordists were women, as were the muses, and here the player audaciously triumphs over technical adversities generally considered unladylike. The dance is in the meter, rhythm, and phrasing of a *passepied*, a faster relative of the minuet that is typically written in $\frac{3}{8}$ meter with an upbeat, four-measure phrases, and cadences marked by hemiola rhythms. As is typical of dances for harpsichord, the dance characteristics are abstracted and manipulated for the enjoyment of the player (and any listeners). Here the expected four-measure units are extended by sequential motion, unlike in most passepieds, so that the phrasing sounds less regular than it actually is. The hemiolas at cadences appear in measures 26–28 and especially measures 30 and 74, where the hemiola is written out as a measure in $\frac{3}{4}$ meter. The last eleven measures of the first half of the movement are paralleled at the end of the second half, transposed down a fifth to create a final cadence in the tonic C major rather than in the dominant. Such a musical rhyme creates a close relationship between the two halves and produces a variant of binary form known as *balanced binary form*. This formal device was common in binary movements by Couperin and Domenico Scarlatti (see NAWM 113).

In *Les ombres errantes*, Couperin reimagines the old *style brisé* (see NAWM 87 and 88) in a new harmonic and more consistently linear contrapuntal context. By sustaining the first note of the eighth-note figures in measures 1–8, he creates a texture of three voices rather than two, then expands this to a four-voice texture at measure 9, with the offbeat eighths now creating a syncopated inner voice. "The Lost Souls" of the title are depicted through a sad mood, the tempo marking *Languissamment* ("listlessly" or "sluggishly"), slurred sighing figures of a falling step or half step, affective dissonances, and chromaticism, including a chromatic descending line in an inner voice in measures 16–17. Many of these features, including the sigh figures, chains of suspensions, and chromaticism, are drawn from Italian opera, reflecting Couperin's interest in blending the French and Italian styles.

Throughout the ordre, Couperin uses agréments and other forms of ornamentation to stress important notes, maintain forward momentum, and achieve an elegant line. Refined elegance, vibrant energy, and logical clarity in harmony, melody, and form made Couperin's suites very appealing to the courtiers and amateurs of his time. So did Couperin's ability to work on different emotional levels at the same time. On the surface, he presents witty, elegant plays on familiar genres and styles, but the chromatic harmony, expressive dissonances, sigh figures, and dense textures suggest deeper emotions. The two levels balance each other and appeal to different kinds of listeners. As an experienced harpsichord teacher, Couperin recognized the need to entertain while challenging his students, so that they would engage in the music without noticing (or resenting) the work involved. This is especially useful if the student is of higher social rank than the teacher, as was true for Couperin; his students, mostly upper-class girls and young women, might be more likely to appreciate the witty than the soulful when young, but come to appreciate the soulful as they grew up.

In all the dances of this ordre, as in Jacquet de la Guerre's suite (NAWM 88), the word *Reprise* is printed at the beginning of the second strain as a visual aid to the performer, highlighting the point to which the eye must return for the repetition of the second half. However, all the marked repetitions are omitted from the accompanying recording.

Jean-Philippe Rameau (1683–1764)

Hippolyte et Aricie, Act IV: Conclusion

98

Opera

1733

(a) Conclusion of Scene 3

From Jean Philippe Rameau, *Oeuvres complètes*, vol. 6, *Hippolyte et Aricie*, ed. Vincent d'Indy (Paris: Durand, 1900), 306–27.

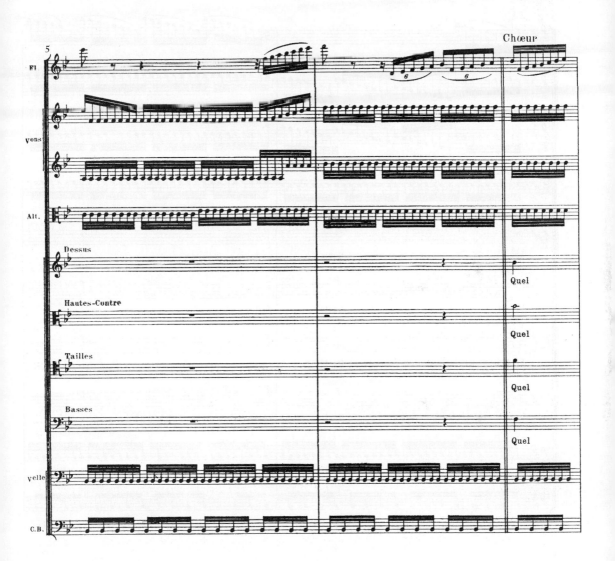

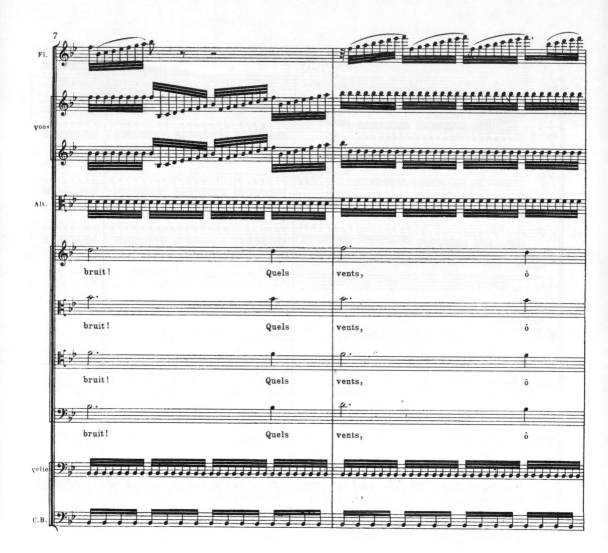

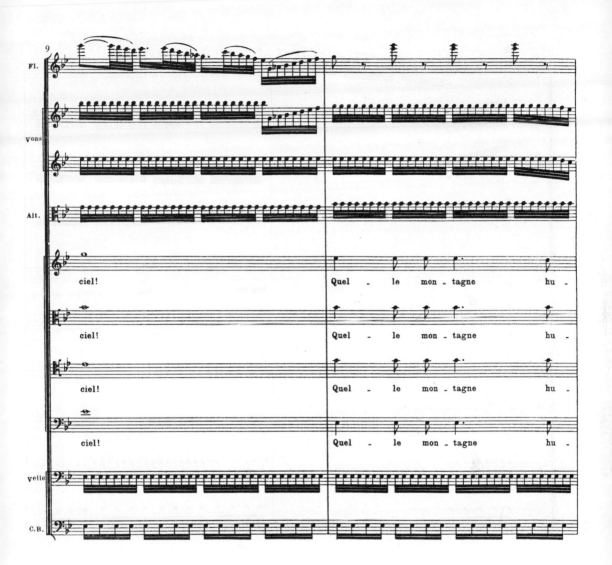

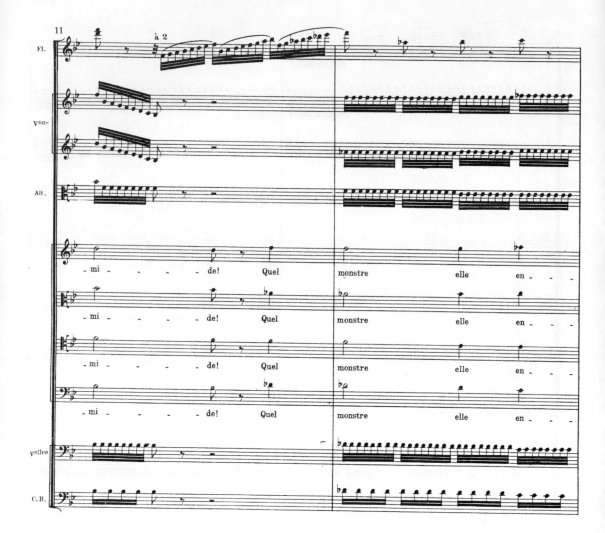

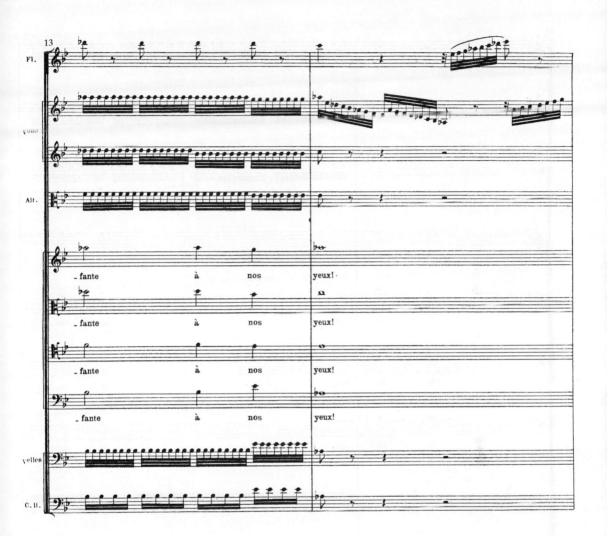

(b) Scene 4

concise

Scène IV _ PHÈDRE, troupe de chasseurs et chasseresses
Chœur
Hb
1o
2o
Bons
Vons
Alt.
(doux)
(plus fort)
PHÈDRE
Quelle plainte en ces lieux m'ap_pel_le?
Il n'est plus! ô douleur mor_tel_le!
Quel
Hip_po_ly_te n'est plus.
O re_grets super_
(Clavecin avec un pupitre de Velles)
(TOUS)
B.C.

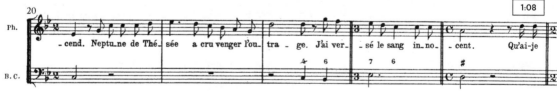

[Conclusion of Scene 3]

(Noise of sea and winds. The sea becomes agitated, and out of it comes a horrible monster.)

Chorus

Quel bruit! Quels vents, ô ciel! Quelle montagne humide!	What noise! What winds, O heavens! What a mountain of water!
Quel monstre elle enfante à nos yeux!	What a monster it bears to our eyes!
O Diane, accourez! Volez du haut des cieux!	O Diana, hasten [to help us]! Fly down from the top of the heavens!

Hippolyte

(going toward the monster)

Venez! qu'a son défaut je vous serve de guide. | Come! in her absence I will serve you as guide.

ARICIE

Arrête, Hippolyte, où cours-tu?	Stop, Hippolyte, where are you going?
Que va t il devenir! Je frémis, je frissonne.	What will happen! I tremble, I shudder.
Est-ce ainsi que les Dieux protègent la vertu?	Is this how the gods protect virtue?
Diane même l'abandonne.	Even Diana deserts him.

CHORUS

Dioux! Quelle flamme l'environne!	Gods! What a flame envelops him!

ARICIE

Quels nuages épais!	What thick clouds!
1:05 Tout se dissipe . . .	All is clearing . . .
Hélas! Hippolyte ne parait pas . . .	Alas! Hippolyte does not appear . . .
Je meurs . . .	I am dying . . .

CHORUS

1:33 O disgrâce cruelle,	O cruel disfavor,
Hippolyte n'est plus . . .	Hippolyte is no more . . .

[Scene 4]
(Phèdre enters)

PHÈDRE

0:00 Quelle plainte en ces lieux m'appelle?	What lament calls me to this place?

CHORUS

Hippolyte n'est plus.	Hippolyte is no more.

PHÈDRE

Il n'est plus! ô douleur mortelle!	He is dead! O mortal grief!

CHORUS

O regrets superflus!	O useless regrets!

PHÈDRE

Quel sort l'a fait tomber dans la nuit éternelle?	What fate cast him into eternal darkness?

CHORUS

Un monstre furieux, sorti du sein des flots,	A raging monster, which came out from the bosom of the deep,
Vient de nous ravir ce héros.	Just now snatched this hero from us.

PHÈDRE

0:38 Non, sa mort est mon seul ouvrage.	No, his death is my handiwork alone.
Dans les Enfers c'est par moi qu'il descend.	It is because of me that he descends into the underworld.
Neptune de Thésée a cru venger l'outrage.	Neptune thought to avenge the affront to Thésée.
J'ai versé le sang innocent.	I have shed innocent blood.
1:08 Qu'ai-je fait? Quel remords! Ciel! J'entends le tonnerre.	What have I done? What remorse! Heavens! I hear the thunder.
Quel bruit . . . Quels terribles éclats!	What a noise . . . What terrible flashes!

Fuyons! Où me cacher? Je sens trembler la terre.	Flee! Where shall I hide? I feel the earth quaking.
Les Enfers s'ouvrent sous mes pas.	Hades opens under my feet.
Tous les Dieux, conjurés pour me livrer la guerre,	All the gods, conspiring to wage war against me,
Arment leurs redoutables bras.	take up their formidable armaments.
Dieux cruels, vengeurs implacables!	Cruel gods, implacable avengers!
Suspendez un courroux qui me glace d'effroi!	Cease your wrath that freezes me with dread!
Ah! si vous êtes équitables,	Ah! if you are fair-minded,
Ne tonnez pas encor sur moi!	do not thunder any more at me!
La gloire d'un héros que l'injustice opprime,	The glory of a hero whom injustice oppresses
Vous demande un juste secours.	demands your rightful aid.
Laissez-moi révéler à l'auteur de ses jours	Let me reveal to the author of his days [his father]
Et son innocence et mon crime!	Both his innocence and my crime!

[1:51]

CHORUS

[3:19]

O remords superflus!	O useless remorse!
Hippolyte n'est plus.	Hippolyte is no more.

— SIMON-JOSEPH PELLEGRIN

❧

Hippolyte et Aricie was Jean-Philippe Rameau's first opera. It premiered in Paris in 1733 and provoked a stormy debate between Rameau's admirers, who became known as Ramistes, and supporters of the older French style of Lully, known as Lullistes. The libretto had a distinguished pedigree: its author Abbé Simon-Joseph Pellegrin drew heavily on the drama *Phèdre* (1677), by Jean Racine, the leading author of tragedies in seventeenth-century France, and Racine in turn had drawn on ancient plays by Euripides and Seneca.

According to the story, Phèdre (Phaedra) is attracted to Hippolyte (Hippolytus), son of her husband Thésée (Theseus), King of Athens. But when she approaches Hippolyte, he refuses her advances and raises his sword to protect himself. Theseus discovers the two in the midst of this encounter, and when neither will explain what was going on, Theseus assumes that Hippolyte was trying to force himself on Phèdre. Left alone, Theseus calls on his own father, Neptune, god of the sea, to avenge the wrong by killing Hippolyte. Shamed by the encounter with Phèdre, Hippolyte resolves to flee with his beloved Aricie. They encounter hunters and huntresses who celebrate Diana, goddess of the hunt, in a *divertissement*, an interlude for dances, songs, and choruses that was a standard part of each act of French operas in the Lully mold (see NAWM 85b).

At the beginning of the excerpt included here, the revels for Diana are interrupted by a raging sea, from which emerges a great fire-breathing monster. Rameau uses the descriptive orchestral writing style that French audiences prized, depicting the wind and waves with rapid pulsations and scales in the strings and flute. The soloistic wind writing is typical of Rameau. The harmony is equally dramatic, reflecting Rameau's use of his theories of harmony in his own compositions; when the chorus sees the monster ("Quel monstre," measures 11–12), the harmony suddenly lurches from the tonic B♭ to a D♭-major chord, leading to a cadence in A♭. When Hippolyte rushes to fight the monster and Aricie begs him to stop, the orchestral effects continue in a texture of accompanied recitative adapted from that of Italian opera. Hippolyte is engulfed by flames, again depicted by the orchestra, and when the smoke clears, he is gone. He is mourned in a moving, brief statement by the chorus that is highlighted by appoggiaturas and by one of the most eloquent silences in all of opera.

In an exchange marked by heart-breaking simplicity, Phèdre enters the scene and the chorus tells her what happened. Once again there is a chromatic shudder in the harmony, including a diminished seventh chord (measure 10 of scene 4), when the chorus tells her that it was a monster who caused Hippolyte's death. Phèdre realizes that she alone caused the disaster, since the monster must have been sent by Neptune, and she resolves to reveal to Theseus her guilt and Hippolyte's innocence. Her monologue begins in recitative accompanied by continuo alone as she admits her guilt (measure 16); changes to accompanied recitative in a faster tempo and measured declamation when she senses thunder, lightning, and an earthquake, all imitated by the orchestra (measure 25); and closes with dignified resolve in a slower accompanied recitative (measure 47), capped by a final comment from the chorus (measure 70). This scene has long been recognized as one of the most moving and remarkable in all of eighteenth-century opera.

Rameau conveys the anguish of Aricie, Phèdre, and the chorus through harmony highly charged with dissonances that propel it forward. Many chords feature sevenths, ninths, diminished fifths, and augmented fourths (evident in the figured bass, where a line through a figure indicates a diminished fifth, augmented fourth, or chromatically altered interval), and dissonant appoggiaturas are common. Particularly plangent are the accented appoggiaturas on the cadential melody note each time the chorus sings "Hippolyte n'est plus" (Hippolyte is no more). The prominence of dissonant harmonies, borrowed from Italian opera, is characteristic of Rameau and quite distinct from the much more consonant language of Lully (compare NAWM 85).

As striking as the harmony is Rameau's integration of musical genres, mixing and juxtaposing types that in earlier operas would have remained separate. Here the descriptive orchestral music depicting a storm is joined by a chorus in homophonic declamation, two textures that in Lully's operas are typically kept separate. Later, the chorus alternates with recitative, including accompanied recitative; this close juxtaposition of textures is rare in previous French or Italian opera (compare the later "reform opera" of Gluck in NAWM 110). Rameau uses recitative accompanied by the orchestra for the same purpose as in Italian opera, to dramatize a monologue where a character's mood constantly shifts, using the orchestral effects and interjections to portray these strong swings of emotion.

This edition was prepared by the prominent nineteenth-century composer Vincent d'Indy, who looked to Rameau, Couperin, and other early French composers as the embodiment of a distinctively French tradition. The edition preserves some of the old C clefs, notably the alto clef (which marks the middle line as middle C) for Hippolyte and the choral altos, and the tenor clef (which marks the second line from the top as middle C) for the choral tenors. In other ways, d'Indy modernized the score, changing the bass violins to cellos, reinforcing the flute with parallel octaves in oboes and bassoons (omitted here) to balance the larger Romantic string section, and making other alterations. He also added tempo and dynamic markings in parentheses. The performers on the accompanying recording add a few expressive embellishments, especially appoggiaturas on cadential notes, which heighten the tragic tone.

Georg Philipp Telemann (1681–1767)

Paris Quartet No. 1 in G Major (*Concerto primo*),
TWV 43:G1: Movements 3–5

Quartet for flute, violin, viola da gamba or cello, and continuo

1730

99

(a) Presto

From Georg Philipp Telemann, *1. Pariser Quartett in G-dur für Flöte, Violine, Viola da gamba oder Violoncello und Basso continuo*, ed. Manfredo Zimmermann (Winterthur: Amadeus, 1997), 10–28. Continuo realization by Manfredo Zimmermann.

(b) Largo

(c) Allegro

99 Georg Philipp Telemann · *Paris* Quartet No. 1 in G Major (*Concerto primo*)

Telemann was a master of the mixed taste, blending elements of Italian, French, and German styles to create attractive music with wide appeal to performers and listeners. Among his most iconic examples are the so-called *Paris* Quartets, two sets of six pieces scored for flute, violin, viola da gamba or cello, and basso continuo. What differentiates a quartet texture from that of a trio sonata (see NAWM 94) is that the part played by the viola da gamba or cello is largely independent from the basso continuo, so there are three equally important soloists over the continuo accompaniment. In addition, the use of a flute for one of the two treble parts (rather than two violins) gives these quartets a distinctive scoring with a variety of contrasting timbres.

The first set (Nos. 1–6) was published as *Quadri* (Quartets) by Telemann himself in Hamburg in 1730 and republished as *Six Quatuors* (Six Quartets) by Le Clerc in Paris in 1736. In 1737, Telemann went to Paris for eight months, and while there he had a second set (Nos. 7–12) published by Le Clerc with the title *Nouvelles Quatuors en Six Suites* (New Quartets in Six Suites, 1738). Telemann reported in his 1739 autobiography that performances of the new quartets "were listened to extraordinarily attentively at court and in the city, and earned me, in a brief time, an almost universal honor, which was accompanied by a multitude of compliments." Because of their association with Paris, all twelve have become known as the *Paris* Quartets, and they are among Telemann's best-known chamber works, in his time and in ours.

Telemann called all the pieces in the second collection "suites," but used three different generic titles in his first collection, with two concertos, two sonatas, and two suites. The piece excerpted here is the first labeled "concerto" (hence the title *Concerto primo*) and the opening piece in the set. This label invokes the genre of the concerto for soloists with orchestra, even though Telemann scored the work for a chamber ensemble of soloists accompanied only by continuo, for which the usual term would be "sonata." The piece blends elements of the concerto, especially ritornello form and soloistic display, with the smaller performing forces, imitative textures, and equal partnership typical of the sonata. Such mixing of genres was a way for composers in the early eighteenth century to play on the expectations of audiences and performers, giving them intellectual puzzles to solve as they listened to or played through the music and tried to make sense of its genre, form, and gestures. There were so many sonatas that invoke concerto style in this way, by Telemann, J. S. Bach, and other composers, that one writer, Johann Adolph Scheibe, coined the term *Sonata auf Concertenart* (sonata in concerto style) in 1740 to describe this type of piece.

Concerto primo is in five movements, of which the last three are included here. The first movement begins with a brief slow introduction marked Grave and proceeds with a fast contrapuntal Allegro that modulates from the tonic G major to the dominant D major; the second half repeats the Grave and Allegro in transposition, with the instruments interchanging the music they play, and with the harmony leading back to the tonic. The second movement is a brief Largo in E minor. There follow the three movements given here: the third movement Presto in E minor, an exact repetition of the Largo, and the closing Allegro. The resulting overall form is somewhat like an arch or palindrome, with two Allegros in G major framing the two transitional Largos and the central E minor Presto.

The most concerto-like movement is the third. It is in ritornello form, alternating ritornello statements by the whole ensemble with episodes that feature each instrument in turn:

Measure	Forces	Section	Key	Tonal plan
1	Tutti	Ritornello	e	i
12	Solo (flute)	Episode	mod	
42	Tutti	Ritornello	b	v
59	Solo (violin)	Episode	mod	
84	Tutti	Ritornello	G, then a	III, then iv
97	Solo (viola da gamba)	Episode	mod	
122	Tutti	Ritornello	e	i

Instead of dividing the ritornello into units, as Vivaldi would have done (see NAWM 96), Telemann sets it up as three distinct ideas that sound simultaneously:

a. a theme in relatively long notes syncopated across the barline;
b. an undulating figure in eighth notes interspersed with trilled half notes; and
c. a figure that begins with repeated quarter notes and continues with scalar eighth-note figures in sequence.

In the opening ritornello, these ideas are presented simultaneously by the viola da gamba, violin, and flute respectively. At the second ritornello (measure 42), the viola da gamba and violin trade off elements from a and b, then all three settle in with the violin playing a, the flute on b, and the viola da gamba on c (measures 49–59). At the third ritornello (measure 84), after a brief stretto on the opening motive of a, each instrument takes up whichever idea it has not yet played; thus a is in the flute, b in the viola da gamba, and c in the violin. The final ritornello (measure 122) has yet another combination: a in the flute, b in the violin, and c in the viola da gamba. The invertible counterpoint (in which contrapuntal lines work equally well when arranged in any order from top to bottom) is a typically German tour de force, and, given the very different timbres of the three instruments, Telemann's redistribution of melodic ideas among them provides the variety Vivaldi achieved by recombining the phrases of his ritornellos. The succession of keys for the ritornellos follows a plan typical for concertos, beginning and ending in the tonic, moving to the dominant for the first change of key, then visiting closely related keys. One interesting touch is in the third ritornello, which begins as if in G (the relative major) but quickly moves to the subdominant A minor for the full statement of the three contrapuntal ideas; thus Telemann hints at but never offers a major-mode form of the ritornello.

Each of the three episodes begins with the same motto, stated twice, as if to introduce that episode's soloist, then continues with new material. Such motto openings are found in many Italian concertos, making this one of the clearest markers of concerto style in the movement. Amusingly, the viola da gamba states the first motto before the violin's solo turn in the second episode, and vice versa in the third episode, as if jesting with the audience's expectations. After the shared motto, the material in each episode is like that in a concerto episode, idiomatic for the particular instrument.

The Largo that follows is transitional, beginning on a diminished seventh chord and concluding with a half cadence on the dominant of E minor. The Phrygian cadence here is characteristically Italianate, used by Italian composers such as Corelli (see the final cadence in NAWM 94c). This movement recalls certain triple-meter slow movements of Vivaldi concertos, which alternate repeated chords with florid solo interjections. Here each instrument in turn is briefly featured as the soloist.

The Allegro finale is a *gigue en rondeau*, combining the fast compound meter of a gigue with rondeau form, in which the theme (called the refrain) alternates with contrasting episodes called *couplets*. In comparison with the *chaconne en rondeau* in Jacquet de la Guerre's suite (NAWM 88f), here the theme is much longer (sixteen measures rather than four), and the repetition is written out to allow some variation and a stronger close on the tonic the second time through (measures 17–32). The couplets are likewise much longer, and there are only two of them (measures 33–70 and 103–39), resulting in the form ABACA. While the theme is solidly in the tonic G major and repeats exactly at each appearance, the couplets modulate to closely related keys. In this and other respects they resemble episodes in concertos, drawing on ideas from the theme and featuring considerable soloistic display, as in the flute and violin at measures 45–55. The second couplet ends with all four parts in unison (measures 135–39), a gesture borrowed from concertos. But there are also elements of the new *galant* style that was beginning to compete with older Baroque styles; one example is the passage in parallel thirds over a throbbing bass in measures 10–13, a texture we will see in numerous works of the Classic era.

The combination of Italian concerto form and soloistic gestures, German contrapuntal ingenuity, French dance meter and rondeau form, and Baroque and galant styles exemplifies the mixed taste. All five movements play the three soloists against each other as they trade roles, themes, motives, and counterpoints, in chamber music that can be regarded as a conversation among equals. This made it very gratifying to play and thus appealing to amateur performers, while also engaging for listeners. Such double appeal to players and audiences helped to make Telemann one of Europe's most famous composers.

The parts for viola da gamba (written in alto clef) and for violoncello (written in bass clef and tenor clef) are mostly identical, except for a few passages where the cello lies an octave lower, as at measures 3–6 in the Presto, or where each part reflects what is more idiomatic for the instrument, as at measures 108–11 of the Presto. Only one of the two instruments is to be used; Telemann labeled the cello part "Violoncello, in place of Viola [da gamba]," suggesting that he preferred the sound of the viola da gamba, and that instrument is used on the accompanying recording.

Johann Sebastian Bach (1685–1750)

Prelude and Fugue in A Minor, BWV 543

Organ prelude and fugue

CA. 1715

100

(a) Prelude

(b) Fugue

Johann Sebastian Bach is believed to have composed the organ Prelude and Fugue in A Minor while at Weimar (1708–17), where he served as court organist and later as concertmaster. During these years, he became fascinated with the new style of concerto developed by Vivaldi and other Italian composers. Bach copied many of their concertos by hand, a traditional method for thoroughly learning a piece, and he arranged several for organ or harpsichord solo. As a result, his own style began to change. In his toccatas (or preludes) and fugues, he blended elements of the Italian concerto with the tradition he had inherited from Buxtehude and other north German organists, as is evident in this piece.

Buxtehude's Praeludium in E Major (NAWM 95) contained a series of alternating toccata-like and fugal sections. In contrast, Bach's standard practice was to compose only two main sections, a prelude and a fugue, each much longer than a similar section in a Buxtehude work. Like the first section of Buxtehude's prelude, but on a greatly enlarged scale, Bach's prelude begins with virtuosic passagework, confirms the tonic, and then ranges through the harmonies in the key before returning to the tonic at the end. There are pedal points (as at measures 10–23), pedal solos (measures 25–28 and 46–47), dialogues between the pedals and the upper voices (measure 40–44), and even some passages of fugal imitation (measures 36–37 and 47–48), all reminiscent of Buxtehude. But much of the figuration is violinistic, modeled on the solo episodes in Vivaldi concertos. For instance, the opening figure imitates a common pattern that violinists perform by moving rapidly back and forth between the strings. The figure sinks chromatically in a manner that is typical neither of Buxtehude nor of Vivaldi, but rather of Bach's own rich harmonic style. Vivaldi's influence is also evident in the many sequences, circle-of-fifths progressions, and repetitions of the opening material in contrasting keys.

Like the prelude, the fugue (marked *Fuga*) features violinistic figuration. The surprisingly long fugue subject (measures 1–5 of the fugue) includes a motive, treated in sequence, that jumps between a repeated high note and a moving lower line. This type of figuration is idiomatic for the violin, on which it would be played by alternating between strings. The form of the fugue is analogous to that of a fast movement in a Vivaldi concerto, with the subject serving the function of a ritornello. In the opening exposition, each of the four fugal voices states the subject on either the tonic or the dominant minor, in the order soprano–alto–tenor–bass. The following episode (measure 31–43) and others later in the fugue are similar to the solo episodes in a concerto movement, moving rapidly through sequences or around the circle of fifths while elaborating motives from the subject and new material.

Later entrances of the subject—some of them disguised by embellishments to the opening figure—establish the tonal structure of the piece. The subject appears on the tonic A minor (measure 44), dominant E minor (measure 51), and other closely related keys, including C major (measure 62), G major (measure 71), and D minor (measure 78). Near the end of the fugue, the subject returns on A minor (measure 96), E minor (measure 113, echoing the opening motive in other voices before continuing), and A minor again (measure 131). Between these statements are additional episodes that each develop the material in a different way, and most of which modulate to a new key that is confirmed by the next entrance of the subject.

Bach's adaptation of ritornello form to the fugue allowed him to write fugues that maintained coherence but were much longer and more varied than those by earlier composers. This ritornello-like structure, alternating expositions of the subject with extended episodes, became typical of Bach's fugues, and because of Bach's prominence as a model composer of fugal works, it soon became a standard characteristic of fugue. After the last statement of the subject, this fugue breaks off at a moment of high dissonance (measure 139), followed by a toccata-like coda. Such a return to toccata style at the end of an organ fugue is reminiscent of Buxtehude (see NAWM 95).

Johann Sebastian Bach (1685–1750)

Chorale Prelude on *Durch Adams Fall*, BWV 637

Chorale prelude

CA. 1716

From *Johann Sebastian Bach's Werke*, vol. 25/2, *Orgelwerke*, vol. 2 (Leipzig: Bach-Gesellschaft, 1875), 53. Chorale edited from Joseph Klug, *Geistliche Lieder auffs new gebessert* (Wittemberg, 1535), after Johannes Zahn, *Die Melodien der deutschen evangelischen Kirchenlieder* (Gütersloh, 1892), vol. 4, No. 7549.

In his last years at Weimar (1716–17), Bach began to compile a collection he called *Orgelbüchlein* (Little Organ Book) that contained short chorale preludes for organ. Chorale preludes were designed to be played during church services as a way to introduce the tune of a chorale before the congregation sang it. This prelude is on the chorale *Durch Adams Fall*, first published in 1524:

Durch Adams Fall ist ganz verderbt	Through Adam's fall are utterly corrupted
Menschlich Natur und Wesen;	human nature and essence;
Dasselb Gift ist auf uns geerbt,	this same poison [original sin] is inherited in us,
Daß wir nicht mochten g'nesen	such that we could not recover
Ohn Gottes Trost, der uns erlöst	without God's confidence, which has redeemed us
Hat von dem grossen Schaden,	from the great damage,
Darein die Schlang' Evam bezwang	wherein the Serpent subdued Eve
Gotts Zorn auf sich zu laden.	to bear the wrath of God upon herself.

— LAZARUS SPENGLER

The chorale text refers to the Christian doctrine of original sin, which holds that every human shares in the first sin—Adam and Eve's disobedience in the Garden of Eden—and thus inherits what St. Augustine called a corrupted essence. References in the text to the serpent who tempted Eve, to God's wrath, to the first couple's fall from grace and expulsion from Eden, and to God's redemption of humanity through Christ would have been clear to everyone in the congregation.

Like many chorales, the tune is in bar form (AAB), consisting of a repeated section (two *Stollen*, each with two lines of text) and a closing section (*Abgesang* of four lines). In Bach's day, chorale melodies that originally included long and short notes in irregular patterns with rests between phrases, like this one, were often sung in even quarter notes with fermatas marking the ends of phrases. It is this smoother rhythmic version of the tune that Bach uses in this prelude, in which the fermatas are not intended to be observed as pauses, but simply indicate cadential notes.

As in the other chorale preludes in the *Orgelbüchlein*, the melody is heard once in complete, continuous, and readily recognizable form. It appears in the top line with only a few brief embellishments. The other voices portray the images in the poem through some of Bach's most graphic representations. Large, dissonant leaps in the pedals depict the idea of Adam's fall; several of them depart from a consonant chord and fall into a dissonant one, as if from innocence into sin. The twisting, chromatic line in the alto suggests the slithering of the serpent. The tenor repeatedly slides downward and then struggles upward again, perhaps representing the pull of temptation, the sorrow of sin, and the struggle to overcome them. As the congregation prepared to sing, each member holding up the text of the first verse, such musical imagery must have seemed particularly vivid. Like a short musical sermon, the prelude would bring the minds of the worshipers to the meaning and import of the words they were about to sing.

The chorale tune is modal: not in A minor, as might be suggested by the key signature, but in the Dorian mode, with a final cadence on A rather than on the modal final D. The chorale's cadential notes largely determine the harmonic structure of the piece. This accounts for the prominent cadences on D minor and F major in the first part of the piece, and for the turn toward G major and A minor for the last two cadences.

Johann Sebastian Bach (1685–1750)

The Well-Tempered Clavier, Book I: Prelude No. 8 in E♭ Minor and Fugue No. 8 in D♯ Minor, BWV 853

Prelude and fugue

1722

102

(a) Prelude No. 8 in E♭ Minor

Reengraved by David Botwinik from *Johann Sebastian Bach's Werke*, vol. 14, *Das wohltemperierte Clavier* (Leipzig: Bach-Gesellschatt, 1866), 32–35.

(b) Fugue No. 8 in D♯ Minor

The Well-Tempered Clavier (in the original German, *Das wohltemperierte Clavier*) is one of Bach's most familiar collections of pieces. Beyond regular appearances on concert programs and recordings, selections from *The Well-Tempered Clavier* are encountered by almost everyone who takes piano lessons past the beginning stages and by music students when learning fugue, for its fugues have become the very model of what a fugue should be. There are two books, the first completed in 1722 while Bach was in Cöthen, and the second around 1740 when he was in Leipzig. Each book consists of twenty-four pairs of preludes and fugues, in all twenty-four major and minor keys, arranged in order up the chromatic scale from C to B, with each major key before its parallel minor.

One purpose of the collection was to show that it was possible to compose and perform pieces in all twenty-four keys. This required a tuning for the harpsichord in which every possible major and minor triad sounds good, which was not true of the mean-tone temperaments then typically used for keyboard instruments; for example, the fifth from G♯ to E♭ was far out of tune, making A♭-major and G♯-minor triads impossible to use. The organ builder Andreas Werckmeister (1645–1706) coined the term "wohltemperirte" (well-tempered) for tunings in which all triads and keys were usable, and Bach appears to have borrowed the term from him. Equal temperament, in which every semitone is identical, was one possibility, but there were numerous shadings with slight differences and compromises that allowed the various keys to keep some of the special character each one had in mean-tone temperament. Writers of the time debated which tuning was best, and the debate continues today.

The eighth pair in Book I, the prelude in E♭ minor and fugue in D♯ minor, illustrates the extremes of the new tuning system. The key signatures of six flats and six sharps are as far away as one can get from the white-note collection of C major or A minor, and both keys include triads that would have been hopelessly out of tune in mean-tone temperament. This is the only pair in Book I in which the key signature of the prelude changes to its enharmonic equivalent for the fugue.

There was a practical reason for this: Bach adapted the prelude from an earlier prelude in E♭ minor and the fugue from an earlier fugue in D minor, and in the latter case it proved easier to change the key signature and adjust the accidentals than to renotate the entire piece. But the change of key signature from prelude to fugue also means that together these two pieces explore the entire spectrum of notated pitches Bach used in *The Well-Tempered Clavier*, from B♭♭ up the circle of fifths to G𝄪 (B♭♭–F♭–C♭–G♭–D♭–A♭–E♭–B♭–F–C–G–D–A in the prelude and E–B–F♯–C♯–G♯–D♯–A♯–E♯–B♯–F𝄪–C𝄪–G𝄪 in the fugue, for twenty-five different notes in all!).

As in his other didactic works, Bach aimed in *The Well-Tempered Clavier* to represent the widest range of possibilities, so each of the preludes is different from the others. Many represent or allude to types of music familiar at the time, and this prelude evokes several at once. Although Bach did not mark tempos in *The Well-Tempered Clavier*, the tempo of this movement must be relatively slow if the performer is to have time to play the runs of sixteenth and thirty-second notes within a 𝟑/𝟐 meter. Some commentators have suggested that the slow tempo and triple meter indicate a sarabande, but a more likely model for this movement lies in triple-meter slow movements of some Vivaldi concertos, where repeated chords underlie or alternate with a florid melody, as in the Largo of Telemann's *Paris* Quartet No. 1 (NAWM 99b), which imitates that style. In this prelude, the repeated chords sound on almost every beat, very untypical of sarabandes (compare NAWM 88d). Similarly untypical of sarabandes are the rapid runs interspersed throughout, which recall the scalar figures in Italian or German toccatas (see NAWM 82 and 95) and French unmeasured preludes (compare NAWM 88a). Also more typical of Italian or German styles than of French music are the dramatic large melodic leaps, such as the diminished seventh, major sixth, and minor tenth in measures 2–4; the imitation between the hands at measures 20–21; and the chromatic harmonies, including a surprising Neapolitan sixth chord (measure 26) and numerous diminished seventh chords, some of which remain unresolved for several measures (as in measures 32–35). On the other hand, the surface has several French features: the ornaments resemble French *agréments* (see NAWM 88); the chords preceded by wavy vertical lines are arpeggiated, which together with the arpeggiating melodic figures throughout the prelude suggest the French *style brisé* (see NAWM 87 and 88); the melody resembles in some respects a French air; and the dotted rhythms and *tirades* (as in measure 5) also hint at a French style, evoking the stately atmosphere of the French overture (compare NAWM 86a, 86c, and 97a) or of the *tombeau*, an instrumental lament. The effect is a cosmopolitan mixture of traditions and thus is quintessentially Bach.

Bach's fugues in *The Well-Tempered Clavier* also represent a wide variety of approaches and styles. The fugue in D♯ minor lies near one end of the spectrum. It is relatively old-fashioned in treatment and style in comparison with Bach's A minor fugue for organ (NAWM 100). Rather than feature long episodes within a formal plan adapted from ritornello form, as that fugue does, this fugue concentrates almost entirely on the opening subject (measures 1–3); only 23 of its 87 measures lack the theme (including the coda in measures 83–87), and only two episodes (measures 15–18 and 33–35) are longer than a measure or two. In its singular focus on the subject it resembles a fugue by Buxtehude, such as the first fugal section in his Praeludium in E Major (NAWM 95), or a ricercare by Frescobaldi (NAWM 83). Also typical of the older style is the constant variation of the subject, not just in the initial tonal answer, in which the upward leap of a fifth is changed to a fourth to project the key of D♯ minor (measure 3), but through numerous other intervallic and rhythmic changes over the course of the piece. Even the subject itself is old-fashioned, with leaps of a fifth or fourth that define the key by emphasizing the tonic and dominant (D♯ and A♯), balanced by stepwise motion in the opposite direction, all within a narrow range of a sixth and relatively narrow spectrum of note values (just eighth, quarter, and dotted quarter notes).

As part of its treatment of the subject, this fugue offers a compendium of contrapuntal devices, including stretto, inversion, and augmentation. After the initial entrances of the three voices in the order alto, soprano (measure 3), and bass (measure 8), the subject returns in the bass (measure 12), followed by a short episode. At measure 19, after a cadence on the dominant A♯ minor, the subject is treated in stretto—with closely overlapping entrances—in the alto and soprano. A second stretto at measure 24 in soprano and bass frames a new elongated variant of the subject in the alto, with a distinctive dotted rhythm (measures 24–26). After a third stretto (measures 27–29) and a cadence in the relative major F♯, the subject appears in inversion in the soprano (measures 30–32), followed by inverted statements in the alto (measures 36–38) and bass (measure 39–41, with the opening leap filled in by stepwise sixteenth notes).

Having introduced the idea of stretto and the elongated and inverted forms of the subject, Bach now combines these ideas, presenting a stretto in inversion between bass and soprano (measures 44–47); the inverted form in the alto in counterpoint with the elongated variant in inversion in the soprano (measures 47–50); and strettos in all three voices of the original subject (measures 52–53) and of the inverted form (measures 54–55). Having quickly moved through several keys, Bach returns briefly to the tonic D♯ minor for another statement of the subject in the soprano (measures 57–59), then introduces another twist; the subject now appears in augmentation, in doubled note values, in the bass (measure 62) and then in the alto (measure 67). Both augmented statements are accompanied by the subject in original or inverted form in both other voices in succession, and in each case the augmented form is immediately followed by the original form in the same voice. Now comes the contrapuntal climax: the three different versions of the subject are presented in counterpoint in the tonic at measure 77, the original form in the bass, the elongated variant in the alto, and the augmented form in the soprano, its latter half accompanied by one final statement of the original subject in the alto (measures 80–83). After a swerve toward the subdominant in that final statement, the coda confirms the tonic.

In addition to illustrating the possibilities of well-tempered tuning and evoking a range of genres and compositional approaches, the preludes and fugues in *The Well-Tempered Clavier* also serve as études or studies, each one offering the player a particular set of technical challenges. In this prelude, the challenges include balancing the steady rhythm of the rolled chords with the songlike melody and improvisatory runs; in the fugue, articulating the entrances and transformations of the fugue subject and creating a sense of progression that leads up to the contrapuntal climax.

Johann Sebastian Bach (1685–1750)

Nun komm, der Heiden Heiland, BWV 62

Cantata

1724

(a) No. 1, Chorus: *Nun komm, der Heiden Heiland*

Johann Sebastian Bach, *Nun komm, der Heiden Heiland*, BWV 62, from *Neue Ausgabe sämtlicher Werke*, series 1, vol. 1, *Adventskantaten*, ed. Alfred Dürr and Werner Neumann (Kassel: Bärenreiter-Verlag, 1954), 77–98.

Nun komm, der Heiden Heiland,
Der Jungfrauen Kind erkannt,
Des sich wundert alle Welt:
Gott solch Geburt ihm bestellt.

Now come, Savior of the gentiles,
known as Child of the Virgin,
at which all the world marvels
that God such a birth for him ordains.

— MARTIN LUTHER

(b) No. 2, Aria (tenor): *Bewundert, o Menschen*

Bewundert, o Menschen, dies große Geheimnis:
Der höchste Beherrscher erscheinet der Welt.

Hier werden die Schätze des Himmels entdecket,
Hier wird uns ein göttliches Manna bestellt,
O Wunder! die Keuschheit wird gar nicht beflecket.

Admire, O humankind, this great mystery:
the supreme ruler appears to the world.

Here are the treasures of Heaven revealed,
here is a divine manna prepared for us,
O wonder! Virginity is not at all blemished.

(c) No. 3, Recitative (bass): *So geht aus Gottes Herrlichkeit und Thron*

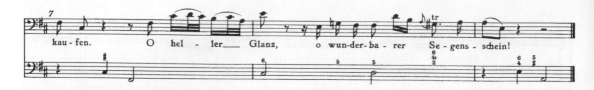

So geht aus Gottes Herrlichkeit und Thron	Thus goes out from God's glory and throne
Sein eingeborner Sohn.	His only-begotten Son.
Der Held aus Juda bricht herein,	The hero from Judah appears,
Den Weg mit Freudigkeit zu laufen	to run the course with joy
Und uns Gefallne zu erkaufen.	and to redeem us fallen creatures.
O heller Glanz, o wunderbarer Segensschein!	O brilliant radiance, O marvelous light of blessing!

(d) No. 4, Aria (bass): *Streite, siege, starker Held!*

Da Capo

Streite, siege, starker Held,
Sei vor uns im Fleische kräftig!

Struggle, triumph, mighty hero!
Be strong for us in the flesh.

Sei geschäftig,
Das Vermögen in uns Schwachen
Stark zu machen!

Be active,
that the abilities of us weak creatures
will be made strong!

(e) No. 5, Accompanied recitative (soprano and alto): *Wir ehren diese Herrlichkeit*

Wir ehren diese Herrlichkeit	We honor this glory
Und nahen nun zu deiner Krippen	and now approach your manger
Und preisen mit erfreuten Lippen,	and praise with joyful lips
Was du uns zubereit;	what you have prepared for us;
Die Dunkelheit verstört uns nicht	the darkness does not trouble us,
Und sahen dein unendlich Licht.	and we have seen your endless light.

(f)   No. 6, Chorale: *Lob sei Gott, dem Vater, ton*

Lob sei Gott, dem Vater, ton,	Praise be made to God the Father,
Lob sei Gott, sein'm ein'gen Sohn,	praise be to God his only Son,
Lob sei Gott, dem Heilgen Geist,	praise be to God the Holy Spirit
Immer und in Ewigkeit!	forever and in eternity!

One of Bach's duties as cantor and music director in Leipzig (1723–50) was to provide a large vocal composition each week to be performed between the Gospel reading and the sermon during the main Sunday morning service at either St. Thomas's or St. Nicholas's, the two largest churches. Following the general pattern introduced by Lutheran theologian and poet Erdmann Neumeister in 1700, Bach composed each sacred work in several movements, to a text that combined verses from chorales or the Bible with poetic texts set as recitatives and arias. Neumeister adopted the Italian term *cantata* for such pieces, although Bach typically referred to them by other terms, such as "the principal composition" or simply "the music." Such works share with the Italian secular cantata (see NAWM 92) the use of recitatives and arias, but include choral movements and chorales as well.

During his first years in Leipzig, Bach wrote three (or perhaps four) complete cycles that each included cantatas for the entire church year. For his second cycle, composed in 1724–25, he based each cantata on a chorale. *Nun komm, der Heiden Heiland*, BWV 62, is the cantata from that cycle for the first Sunday in Advent. First performed on December 3, 1724, this cantata was based on Martin Luther's Advent chorale *Nun komm, der Heiden Heiland* (NAWM 46b).

The anonymous author of the cantata's text preserved the first and last of Luther's eight stanzas for the opening and closing movements, both sung by the chorus, as was customary in Bach's church cantatas. The poet paraphrased the remaining stanzas in poetry that was suitable for arias (with regular meter and rhymes) and recitatives (somewhat more irregular), which Bach used for the four middle movements. The cantata thus took this form:

Measure	Movement and voices	Movement type	Key
1	1. Chorus	Chorale motet	b
2–3	2. Tenor soloist	Da capo aria, with orchestra	G
4–5	3. Bass soloist	Recitative with continuo	mod
6	4. Bass soloist	Da capo aria, continuo with unison orchestra	D
7	5. Soprano and alto soloists	Accompanied recitative	mod
8	6. Chorus	Chorale harmonization	b

Within this structure, Bach included maximum variety. Each of the four vocal soloists is featured in a type of movement that is borrowed from Italian opera. The two recitatives—one with continuo alone and one accompanied by the orchestra—encompass the two standard types of the time. One aria features the full orchestra, and the other is essentially a continuo aria (for voice and continuo alone) in which the upper strings play in octave unison with the basso continuo. Only the third and fourth movements adopt the recitative-aria pairing for the same soloist that was typical in Italian operas and cantatas; the tenor aria and soprano-alto recitative are free-standing. The two choral movements are the only sections that incorporate the tune of the chorale, but Bach also made them as different from each other as possible. One is an elaborate chorale motet and the other is a simple harmonization in four parts. The choral movements retain the minor mode of the chorale, so the cantata opens and closes in the same key. The other movements are in closely related keys, with major mode in the rejoicing, active arias and rapid modulations in the recitatives.

The opening chorus is always the aesthetically weightiest movement in Bach's chorale cantatas, and in them Bach often combines traditional genres in ingenious ways. Here, the movement blends the ritornello structure and instrumental writing of a concerto with the cantus-firmus counterpoint of a chorale motet. The sopranos, reinforced by the horn, sing the chorale in long notes in the style of a cantus firmus (see measures 22, 33, 43, and 63). The other voices weave imitative counterpoint beneath the soprano line. The first and last phrases of the chorale are introduced by a point of imitation based on the chorale melody (measures 17 and 56). The four phrases of the chorale are framed by an instrumental ritornello whose sequences, idiomatic string figuration, and vigor recall Vivaldi and whose rising motives suggest the optimism and anticipation of Advent. The opening ritornello (measures 1–16) remains in the tonic B minor, but later ritornellos change keys to follow the tonal progress of the chorale. After the last phrase of the chorale, the opening ritornello is repeated (marked with a da capo). The ritornello and chorale are not kept separate, but are linked through counterpoint. The first phrase of the chorale appears in most of the ritornellos (for instance, in the first ritornello at measures 3–5 and 15–17), and the orchestra develops ideas from the ritornello as accompaniment to each segment of the chorale.

The tenor aria follows the traditional structure of a da capo aria. The A section begins and ends with a substantial ritornello that frames two vocal statements (at measures 24 and 56) separated by an abbreviated ritornello (measure 52). The first statement modulates to the dominant D major, and the second wends its way back to the tonic G major. The B section, which also features two vocal statements punctuated by the orchestra, explores closely related tonal realms, including E minor, B minor, and C major. The meter and phrasing resemble a minuet or passepied (see NAWM 97b), with two- and four-measure units in triple time. This secular dance rhythm and its associations with bodily movement reinforce the text's focus on the mystery of the Incarnation (God's embodiment in human form). Long melismas and melodic high points call attention to the important words "höchste Beherrscher" (supreme ruler).

The bass recitative is typical of Bach in its angular melody, large intervals, and text-painting, which includes a quickly rising scale on "laufen" (run), a falling seventh on "Gefallne" (the fallen), and rapid motion on "heller" (brilliant). The following aria adopts a heroic, martial style that is well suited to its text, with many arpeggiations, brilliant runs, large leaps, and the orchestra playing in octaves throughout. The form is similar to that of the tenor aria.

In the final recitative, the soprano and alto soloists sing mostly in parallel thirds and sixths that combine with the soft, slowly changing chords in the strings to create an aura of reverence and mystery appropriate to the words and to the season of Advent.

The closing chorale is set in four-part harmony, though Bach energizes the harmonization with eighth notes that appear almost continuously in at least one part. The entire orchestra plays *colla parte*, doubling the vocal parts, with all the winds reinforcing the chorale melody. By beginning with the most elaborate movement and ending with a simple chorale, Bach's church cantatas tend to move from complexity to simplicity, closing with a musical thought that is like an aphorism, a brief statement that sums up what has come before. Here, the text of the final verse of the chorale is the German translation of the Lesser Doxology (see NAWM 3a and 4a), a centuries-old formula of praise for the Trinity.

Bach drew on a wide range of styles and genres for this cantata, including Lutheran chorale and chorale motet, Italian opera, cantata, and concerto, and French dance. The variety evident here demonstrates Bach's tendency to assimilate all the types of music he knew, blend them together, and elaborate on them.

At the beginning of each movement in this edition of the score, the editor shows the first note of each part in the original notation. In Bach's time, the singers sang from individual parts, not from a choral score as is the custom today, and Bach used soprano, alto, tenor, and bass clefs rather than the mix of treble and bass clefs that singers are accustomed to today. We know from Bach's records and from the surviving parts that the chorus was small, with only four to twelve singers, although modern performances often use more.

Johann Sebastian Bach (1685–1750)

St. Matthew Passion, BWV 244: Excerpt

Passion

1727, REVISED 1736

104

(a) No. 36, Biblical narrative: *Und der Hohepriester antwortete*

From Johann Sebastian Bach, *Neue Ausgabe Sämtliche Werke*, ser. 2, *Messen, Passionen, oratorische Werke*, vol. 5, *Matthäus-Passion* BWV 244, ed. Alfred Dürr with Max Schneiders (Kassel: Bärenreiter, 1972), 169–85. ©1972 Bärenreiter-Verlag. © Renewed. All rights reserved. Used by permssion of European American Music Distributors Company, U.S. and Canadian agent for Bärenreiter-Verlag. English translation of Johann Sebastian Bach, *St. Matthew Passion*, Nos. 36a–40, from Michael Marissen, *Bach's Oratorios: The Parallel German-English Texts with Annotations* (New York: Oxford University Press, 2008), 50–53. By permission of Oxford University Press.

(b) No. 37, Chorale: *Wer hat dich so geschlagen*

(c) No. 38, Biblical narrative: *Petrus aber saß draußen im Palast*

*) Instrumentalvarianten

(d) No. 39, Aria: *Erbarme dich*

39. Aria

mei - - ner Zäh-ren wil - len.

(e) No. 40, Chorale: *Bin ich gleich von dir gewichen*

[No. 36, Biblical narrative]
[36A] EVANGELIST

Und der Hohepriester antwortete und sprach zu ihm:	And the high priest answered, saying to him:

HICH PRIEST

Ich beschwöre dich bei dem lebendigen Gott, daß du uns sagest, ob du seiest Christus, der Sohn Gottes?	I ajdure you by the living God that you tell us whether you are Christ, the Son of God?

EVANGELIST

Jesus sprach zu ihm:	Jesus said to him:

JESUS

Du sagests. Doch sage ich euch: Von nun an wirds geschehen, daß ihr sehen werdet des Menschen Sohn sitzen zur Rechten der Kraft und kommen in den Wolken des Himmels.	You are saying so. Yet I say to you all: From now on it will take place that you all will see the Son of Man sitting at the right [hand] of the Power [God] and coming on the clouds of Heaven.

EVANGELIST

Da zerriß der Hohepriester seine Kleider und sprach:	And the high priest rent his clothing and said:

HIGH PRIEST

Er hat Gott gelästert; was dürfen wir weiter Zeugnis? Siehe, itzt habt ihr seine Gotteslästerung gehöret. Was dünket euch?	He has blasphemed God; what further need do we have of testimony? Look, now you have heard his blasphemy of God. What does it seem to you?

EVANGELIST

Sie antworteten und sprachen:	They answered, saying:

[36B] CHORUS

Er ist des Todes schuldig!	He is deserving of death!

[36C] EVANGELIST

Da speieten sie aus in sein Angesicht und schlugen ihn mit Fäusten. Etliche aber schlugen ihn ins Angesicht und sprachen:	Then they spat out in his face and struck him with fists. But some struck him in the face and said:

[36D] CHORUS

Weissage uns, Christe, wer ists, der dich schlug?	Prophesy to us, Christ: who is the one that struck you?

[No. 37, Chorale]
CHORUS

Wer hat dich so geschlagen,	Who has struck you so,
Mein Heil, und dich mit Plagen	my Salvation, and beat you up
So übel zugericht'?	so badly, causing plague-spots?
Du bist ja nicht ein Sünder	You are by no means a sinner,
Wie wir und uns're Kinder,	like we and our children [are];
Von Missetaten weißt du nicht.	you do not know of any misdeeds.

0:00
0:21
1:15
1:28
1:42

[No. 38, Biblical narrative]

[38a] Evangelist

`0:00` Petrus aber saß draußen im Palast; und es trat zu ihm eine Magd und sprach:

But Peter sat outside, in the [courtyard of the] palace; and a maid approached him and said:

First Maid

Und du warest auch mit dem Jesu aus Galiläa.

And you, too, were with that Jesus from Galilee.

Evangelist

Er leugnete aber vor ihnen allen und sprach:

But he denied it before them all, saying:

Peter

Ich weiß nicht, was du sagest.

I do not know what you're talking about.

Evangelist

Als er aber zur Tür hinausging, sahe ihn eine andere und sprach zu denen, die da waren:

But when he went out to the door, another [maid] saw him and said to those who were there:

Second Maid

Dieser war auch mit dem Jesu von Nazareth.

This one, too, was with that Jesus from Nazareth.

Evangelist

Und er leugnete abermal und schwur dazu:

And he denied it once more, taking an oath to it:

Peter

Ich kenne des Menschen nicht.

I do not know the man.

Evangelist

Und über eine kleine Weile traten hinzu, die da stunden, und sprachen zu Petro:

And after a little while, those who were standing there stepped forward and said to Peter:

[38b] Chorus

`0:54` Wahrlich, du bist auch einer von denen; denn deine Sprache verrät dich.

Truly, you are also one of them; for your way of speaking betrays you.

[38c] Evangelist

`1:05` Da hub er an, sich zu verfluchen und zu schwören:

Then he started to curse at himself and to take an oath:

Peter

Ich kenne des Menschen nicht.

I do not know the man.

Evangelist

Und alsbald krähete der Hahn. Da dachte Petrus an die Worte Jesu, da er zu ihm sagte: "Ehe der Hahn krähen wird, wirst du mich dreimal verleugnen." Und ging heraus und weinete bitterlich.

And immediately the cock crowed. Then Peter remembered the words of Jesus, when he said to him: "Before the cock has crowed, you will disavow me three times." And [Peter] went out and wept bitterly.

[No. 39, Aria]

ALTO

Erbarme dich,
Mein Gott, um meiner Zähren willen!
  Schaue hier,
  Herz und Auge weint vor dir
  Bitterlich.

Have mercy,
my God, for the sake of my tears!
  Look here—
  [my] heart and eyes weep before you
  bitterly.

[No. 40, Chorale]

CHORUS

Bin ich gleich von dir gewichen,
Stell ich mich doch wieder ein;
Hat uns doch dein Sohn verglichen
Durch sein Angst und Todespein.
Ich verleugne nicht die Schuld;
Aber deine Gnad und Huld
Ist viel größer als die Sünde,
Die ich stets in mir befinde.

Though I have turned aside from You,
I do, indeed, come back;
Your Son has indeed reconciled [the ledger] for us
by his fear and [his] death pains.
I do not disavow my debt;
but Your grace and favor
is much greater than the sin
that I find ever within myself.

— PICANDER (CHRISTIAN FRIEDRICH HENRICI)

— TRANS. MICHAEL MARISSEN

Bach composed his *St. Matthew Passion* in early 1727 in Leipzig, where he was civic music director. It was most likely first performed during the Good Friday Vespers (commemorating Jesus' crucifixion) in St. Thomas Church on April 11 of that year and repeated in 1729. A revised version debuted at the same service nine years later on March 30, 1736, and Bach further revised it in the 1740s. After his death, portions were performed in Hamburg, where his son Carl Philipp Emanuel Bach was music director. Then it lay unperformed for decades until 1829, when the young Felix Mendelssohn conducted a performance in Berlin that helped to launch the Bach revival.

A Lutheran Passion of Bach's time set the story of Jesus' last days, trial, crucifixion, and entombment as recounted by one of the four Gospels (Matthew, Mark, Luke, and John), using the biblical text in Martin Luther's translation, interspersed with commentary. The libretto for the *St. Matthew Passion* was created by Picander (the pen name of Christian Friedrich Henrici), who also collaborated with Bach on numerous cantatas. The text interweaves the story as told in Matthew chapters 26–27 with Picander's new poetic texts and with chorale verses reflecting on the meaning of the events just described. The work is in two parts, presented before and after the sermon in a long Good Friday afternoon Vespers service, and each half begins and ends with an elaborate choral movement. By weaving together the old Gospel story, the Lutheran chorale tradition, and newly written poetry, the *St. Matthew Passion* makes events from long ago contemporary again, invites the listener to experience and reflect on them anew, and links both the events and the listeners to the Lutheran church.

In Bach's Passions, the Gospel narrative is assigned to the Evangelist, sung by a high tenor in the style of recitative. Individual characters in the story are portrayed by individual singers, again in recitative style, and words of a group, such as the crowd witnessing Jesus' trial, are sung by the chorus. In the *St. Matthew Passion*, there are two choirs, each with its own continuo group (in the 1736 version) and instrumental ensemble. Although since the nineteenth century the Passion has typically been performed by large choral groups with many singers on each part and with large orchestras, Bach's original performing parts show that Coro I (Choir I) consisted of four singers who sang the main characters' lines and the solo interpolations and joined together to form the chorus for choral movements and chorales. Coro II likewise had only one singer on each part, variously singing solo parts, arias, and choruses as needed. In this arrangement the same singers alternate between playing roles in the biblical drama and offering responses to it. In this regard a Passion setting, while it told a story, was not dramatic and representational in the manner of opera, even though it drew on poetic and musical types (arias and recitatives) from stage music.

The excerpt given here, from Matthew 26:63–75, comes early in Part II and includes some of the most dramatic moments in the Passion story. Jesus has been arrested and brought before the religious authorities, but he has remained silent as false witnesses have testified against him. As this excerpt begins (36a), the high priest challenges Jesus to say whether he is Christ, the Son of God. Jesus does not answer directly, but his prophecy of the Son of Man (an allusion to the prophecy in Daniel 7:13–14) is taken as blasphemy. Here and throughout the Passion, Bach's recitative is full of leaps, emphasizing the notes of the underlying harmony and allowing a dramatic expression of the text. All the recitative is undergirded just by continuo except for that sung by Jesus, whose words are accompanied by sustained strings; here, the violins anticipate and repeat in sequence a sixteenth-note figure Jesus sings on "Wolken" ("clouds"), as if depicting the clouds of Heaven.

The priests, scribes, and elders judge Jesus as blaspheming and therefore deserving of death. The brief choral setting of their words (36b) conveys the many overlapping voices of a crowd through a bouncy motive treated in rapid imitative entrances and taken through fast changes of key. They spit on Jesus and strike him, taunting him to prophesy who is hitting him; in this chorus (36d), the rapid alternation of leaping figures and runs between the two choirs suggests remarkable violence.

After this shocking outburst, the text swiftly changes to contemplative reflection in a chorale (37) sung and played by the two choirs and ensembles together, with instruments doubling the voices. The tune is the old song *Innsbruck, ich muss dich lassen* (set by Henricus Isaac in NAWM 41), which in the sixteenth century had been retexted as a chorale, *O Welt, ich muss dich lassen* ("O world, I must leave you"). The words sung here, however, come from a seventeenth-century Passion hymn sung to this same tune. They speak directly to Jesus, expressing the feelings of the congregation who know that Jesus did not deserve such treatment.

The focus then shifts to Peter, one of Jesus' closest disciples, who had fled with the others when Jesus was arrested but followed at a distance to see what would happen to him. First one maid, then another, then a group of bystanders come up to him and say they recognize him as a friend of Jesus (38a–b), and he denies it each time—as Jesus predicted he would do three times before the cock crowed to signal dawn. Just then the cock crows, and Peter realizes what he has done, and weeps bitterly (38c). The chorus of bystanders (38b) is agitated, with constant motion over a descending sequence of suspensions. The recitative is in Bach's typical angular style, except for a masterly depiction of Peter's weeping in a chromatically tinged melisma marked by drooping lines and an anguished wail of a rising diminished seventh (38c, measures 31–32).

There follows one of the most beautiful arias Bach ever wrote (39), his contribution to a Lutheran tradition of reflection on this moment in the Passion story. Peter's remorse provided a direct path for librettist and composer toward their chief goal: getting the contemporary believing listener to identify with the narrative and experience it emotionally. Peter's tears become the listener's own through Picander's text, addressed directly to God in the first person (my God, my tears). Bach's musical response is an *obbligato* aria, one scored for voice with one solo instrument, basso continuo, and strings. His choice of solo violin for the obbligato marks this as a moment of particular expressivity.

Throughout, the solo violin is the main carrier of the expression, presenting the principal melodic material both alone and alongside the voice. The opening ritornello (measures 1–8) invokes familiar emblems of weeping and lament—the minor mode, a stepwise descending bass line, and numerous appoggiaturas and sighing figures—but the sheer profusion of sighing gestures, joined with chromaticism, irregular rhythms including ties over the beat, and descending sequences, all woven into a continuous melody that seems never to rest, conveys a sense of overwhelming grief, from which the voice's pleas for mercy emerge like a prayer from the depths. The voice enters with the violin's opening motive, but then the subject switches back to the solo violin, leaving the voice to sing freely expressive material in counterpoint with it.

Picander's text, in two brief stanzas, suggests a da capo setting in line with the operatic model for this sort of aria (see NAWM 93) and with Bach's typical cantata arias (see NAWM 103b and d). Bach's aria at first conforms to expectations, with an opening ritornello in the tonic B minor (measures 1–8); a first vocal statement based on the first stanza of text that modulates to a new key, the dominant F♯ minor (measures 9–22, closing with a transposed variant of the ritornello material); and an abbreviated statement of the ritornello that confirms the new key (measures 23–26). A typical da capo aria would continue with a second vocal statement on the first stanza that modulates back to the tonic, a repetition of the ritornello in the tonic to close the first section, then a contrasting middle section setting the second stanza, and a reprise of the first section. But given the length of the ritornello and first vocal statement, this would result in a very long aria, over twelve minutes; moreover, any departure in the middle section from the weeping ritornello theme would undercut the sense of overwhelming grief. Bach's solution is ingenious: he introduces the text of the second stanza at this point (measures 26–31), while continuing to spin out motives from the ritornello theme. The opening words "Erbarme dich" (Have mercy) soon return (measures 31–32), then the entire first vocal statement returns in varied form (measures 33–46), this time moving back to the tonic, and the aria concludes with the ritornello in the tonic (measures 47–54). In effect, Bach creates a continuous unfolding of his expressive and musical ideas by combining the musical form of the first section of a da capo aria with the textual alternation of a full da capo aria.

Uniquely in the *St. Matthew Passion*, this is a moment of double interpolation, with two commentary movements inserted into the Gospel narrative after the description of Peter's remorse: this aria and the following chorale harmonization (40). The chorale, *Werde munter, mein Gemüte* (tune by Johann Schop, text by Johann Rist), dates from the seventeenth century. Picander specified the fifth of eight original stanzas, choosing one whose opening words ("Though I have turned aside from You, I do, indeed, come back") can be heard to bring the contemporary listener directly into the situation of the remorseful Peter.

The performance on the accompanying recording is staffed instrumentally and vocally the way Bach is known to have performed the *St. Matthew Passion*, with relatively small instrumental ensembles (four violins and one viola, cello, and bass in each orchestra) and with exactly four principal singers in each chorus who also serve as aria soloists and play roles in the Gospel narrative. Some of the small roles are taken, as in Bach's performances, by additional singers who do not participate in other movements.

George Frideric Handel (1685–1759)

Giulio Cesare: Act II, Scenes 1–2

Opera

1724

(a) Recitative: *Eseguisti, oh Niren*

From *George Friedrich Händels Werke: Ausgabe der Deutschen Händelgesellschaft*, ed. Friedrich W. Chrysander, vol. 68, 51–58. Bärenreiter Music Corporation.

(b) Aria: *V'adoro, pupille*

[Recitative]

Scene 1

CLEOPATRA

Eseguisti, oh Niren, quanto t'imposi?   Did you carry out, Nireno, what I commanded?

NIRENO

Adempito è il commando.   The order has been executed.

CLEOPATRA

Giunto è Cesare in corte?   Has Caesar arrived in the court?

NIRENO

Io vel condussi, ed ei   I led him here, and he
Già a queste soglie il piè rivolge.   is already directing his steps toward this threshold.

CLEOPATRA

Ma dimmi: è in pronto   But tell me, is the
La meditata scena?   projected stage-set ready?

NIRENO

Infra le nubi l'alta regia sfavilla;   Among the clouds the lofty kingdom sparkles;
Ma che far pensi?   but what are you thinking of doing?

CLEOPATRA

Amore   Cupid
Già suggerì all'idea   gave me the idea—
Stravagante pensier; ho già risolto   an extravagant thought; I have resolved
Sotto finte apparenze   in disguise
Far prigionier d'amor chi 'l cor m'ha tolto.   to make prisoner of love him who has stolen my heart.

NIRENO

A lui ti scoprirai?   Will you reveal yourself to him?

CLEOPATRA

Non è ancor tempo.   It's not time yet.

NIRENO

Io che far deggio?   What must I do?

CLEOPATRA

Attendi   Wait for
Cesare in disparte: indi lo guida   Caesar aside, then lead him
In questi alberghi, e poi lo guida ancora   to these quarters, and afterwards show him
Colà nelle mie stanze, e a lui dirai   to my chambers, and I will tell him
Che, per dargli contezza   that—to give him an account
Di quanto dal suo Rè gli si contende,   of the nature of the dispute with his king—
Pria che tramonti il sol Lidia l'attende.   before the sun sets Lidia will be waiting for him.

(Cleopatra exits.)

SCENE 2

NIRENO

`1:20` Da Cleopatra apprenda chi è seguace
D'amor l'astuzie e frodi.

From Cleopatra, let those who follow Love
learn [his] tricks and deception.

CESARE

Dov'è, Niren, dov'è l'anima mia?

Where is she, Nireno, where is my soul?

NIRENO

In questo loco in breve
verrà Lidia, Signor.

Here in this place shortly
will come Lidia, my Lord.

(A Sinfonia of various instruments is faintly heard.)

CESARE

Cieli! E qual delle sfere
Scende armonico suon, che mi rapisce?

Heavens! What harmonious sound
descends from the spheres and enchants me?

NIRENO

Avrà di selce il cor chi non languisce.

He has a heart of stone who does not surrender.

`2:11`   *(Parnassus opens and we see Virtue in her throne, accompanied by the nine Muses.)*

CESARE

`3:00` Giulio, che miri?
E quando con abisso di luce
scesero i Numi in terra?

Julius, what do you see?
When, in a blaze of light,
did the gods descend to earth?

[Aria]
CLEOPATRA
(in costume as Virtue)

`0:00` V'adoro pupille,
Saette d'Amore,
Le vostre faville
Son grate nel sen;

I adore you, pupils,
Cupid's darts.
Your sparks
are welcome to the heart.

`1:57` Pietose vi brama
Il mesto mio core,
Ch'ogn'ora vi chiama
L'amato suo ben.

Pitiable, for you longs
my gloomy heart,
which every hour calls you,
its beloved treasure.

CESARE

Non ha in cielo il Tonante melodia,
Che pareggi un si bel canto.

Jupiter in heaven has no melody
that matches such beautiful song.

CLEOPATRA

`2:56` V'adoro pupille, etc.

I adore you, pupils, etc.

— NICOLA HAYM

Between 1711 and 1741, George Frideric Handel composed about forty operas for performance in London. His *Giulio Cesare*, produced in 1724, was one of his greatest successes and has become probably his best known opera. The libretto is by Nicola Haym (1679–1729), a cellist and composer as well as a producer and poet.

The opera begins with the arrival of Giulio Cesare (Julius Caesar) in Egypt. Cleopatra, in her official capacity as co-ruler of Egypt (with her brother Ptolemy), welcomes Cesare, and she quickly falls in love with him. Not wishing to reveal her weakness, she tries to seduce him disguised as her handmaiden Lidia. In this scene, Cleopatra's confidant Nireno leads Cesare to a grove where a woman is singing to the accompaniment of an orchestra. It is Cleopatra in costume as Virtue, surrounded by the nine Muses.

The standard elements of an operatic scene from this period are present: dialogue in simple recitative accompanied by continuo, followed by a da capo aria introduced by the orchestra. But these elements are slightly rearranged to create greater realism and enhance the drama. Instead of presenting a static orchestral introduction and aria, Handel intersperses the recitative with the sections of the aria so that the plot advances continuously throughout the scene.

According to the stage directions, the orchestral sinfonia is faintly heard during the preceding recitative, as if Cesare (and the audience) were hearing from a distance a performance already in progress. As the scene is revealed and Cesare beholds Virtue on her throne in Parnassas, the sinfonia is played in full. It anticipates the main figure of the aria to follow, as if it is an opening ritornello. But Cesare breaks in after the sinfonia with his reaction in recitative: "Julius, what do you see? When, in a blaze of light, did the gods descend to earth?" By breaking the conventional link between orchestral prelude and aria, Cesare surprises the audience and thus conveys his own surprise and awe. Then Cleopatra begins her aria, drawing on material from the orchestral sinfonia. The A section includes the usual two vocal statements of the text (the second begins at measure 18), but there is no ritornello between them, as if we are so charmed by Cleopatra that we could not stand to have her stop singing.

After the brief closing ritornello, the B section modulates through several minor keys (D minor, G minor, and A minor) and introduces contrasting material suited to the more wistful text of this section. We expect the repetition of the A section to follow immediately, but instead Cleopatra simply stops. We are transfixed. Cesare comments in recitative, "Jupiter in heaven has no melody that matches such beautiful song." Cesare's interjection brings us to a new level of realization; our recognition of his total enchantment with Cleopatra makes the reprise of the A section not only a conventional formal device but a deepening of the dramatic situation.

Both the opening sinfonia and the accompaniment to Cleopatra's aria are scored like a concerto with multiple soloists, contrasting a small ensemble of oboe, two muted violins, viola, viola da gamba, harp, theorbo, bassoon, and cello with the full orchestra of strings and oboes. The sinfonia begins with the solo ensemble alone, and then the orchestra joins in varying the four-note motive that will open Cleopatra's aria. In the aria, the small ensemble continually accompanies the voice, and the orchestra punctuates and complements this accompaniment during the A section and remains silent during the B section. Handel rarely used such a division of soloists contrasted with the orchestra; here it achieves a magical, ethereal effect.

The vocal line grows from a four-note motive into paired antecedent-consequent four-measure phrases, as in a dance. The word "saetta" (Cupid's arrow) probably inspired the flirting, darting motive. The sinfonia and the A section of the aria have the rhythmic character of a sarabande, with emphasis on the second of the three beats in each measure, suggesting associations of dignity and of allure. The combination of French and Italian influences—a French dance style in a da capo aria form with concerto-like texture—is typical of many German composers. It is especially characteristic of Handel, whose upper-class English audience appreciated both the grand French style (associated with the monarchy in England as well as France) and the newer, more dramatic Italian style. The B section contrasts markedly in rhythm, featuring almost constant eighth-note motion in the accompaniment. As was customary, the singer on the accompanying recording embellishes the vocal line in the aria, especially during the repetition of the A section.

George Frideric Handel (1685–1759)

Saul: Act II, Scene 10

Oratorio

1738

106

(a) No. 66, Accompanied recitative: *The Time at length is come*

(b) No. 67, Recitative: *Where is the Son of Jesse?*

(c) No. 68, Chorus: *O fatal Consequence of Rage*

End of the Second Act

Handel composed *Saul* from July to September 1738, and it premiered at the King's Theatre in the Haymarket on January 16, 1739. It was one of Handel's first English oratorios, preceded only by *Esther* in 1732, and *Deborah* and *Athalia* in 1733. The success of *Saul* encouraged Handel to shift the focus of his efforts from opera to oratorio. Charles Jennens, who also wrote librettos for *Messiah* and other oratorios, here dramatized the Bible's First Book of Samuel, Chapters 16 to 20, 24, 28, and 31, and Chapters 1 and 2 of the Second Book.

David, who played the harp to calm Saul during his fits of anger, became a military hero by defending the Israelites against Goliath and other enemies. In Act I, at a victory celebration for David, a chorus of women praises him for having slain "ten thousands," compared with Saul's "thousands." This and similar incidents arouse Saul's jealousy. The scene included here is set at a banquet during which Saul plans to take his revenge. When David wisely does not attend, Saul becomes so angry that he throws the javelin meant for his rival at his own son Jonathan, David's beloved friend.

In Saul's accompanied recitative (No. 66), he expresses his resolve to have David killed. Between the lines of rhymed poetry, the violins and violas simulate bellicose trumpet fanfares.

The continuo recitative (No. 67) is set to unrhymed verse, mostly in ten-syllable lines. Saul's fury intensifies as he listens to the excuses Jonathan makes for David's absence. The accompaniment, en route from the initial D minor to its dominant, passes through alien chords of G# major, C# minor and major, F# minor, and E major. In the many seventh chords, the seventh of the chord is often in the bass, so that the resolution is to a first-inversion chord and the harmonic tension is maintained. Finally, Saul orders Jonathan to capture David, to face his death. But when Jonathan again pleads David's innocence, Saul threatens: "Dar'st thou oppose my Will? Die then thy self." He throws the javelin at Jonathan, who manages to dodge it and escape. In this score, the editor has indicated the traditional appoggiaturas that singers customarily add to the cadential note at the end of each sentence.

The chorus, "O fatal Consequence of Rage" (No. 68), which Jennens modeled on choruses from Greek tragedy, reflects on the morality of the situation and closes the act. The chorus comprises a succession of three fugues, each of which ends with majestic homorhythmic passages. Such systematic use of homophony, stemming from the English choral tradition, distinguishes Handel's choral writing from the complex polyphonic web that Bach spins in his choral movements (compare NAWM 103a).

The first fugue in the chorus is based on "Quos pretioso sanguine," from the *Te Deum* by Antonio Francesco Urio (ca. 1631–ca. 1719), and is one of six passages in *Saul* that feature material borrowed from Urio's *Te Deum*. Such borrowing was a frequent practice for Handel, as for other Baroque composers, but he usually repaid with interest, developing the existing material in new ways. Like Urio's fugue, Handel's begins with a stretto, in which the voices enter in quick succession rather than after the entire subject has been heard. This is a device that composers usually saved for the final climactic effect rather than using it in the first entries. Handel undoubtedly chose to borrow from Urio's fugue because the downward leap of a tritone or sixth, combined with the stretto, is an apt fit for the words, suggesting anger, agitation, and grief. The similarity between Handel's and Urio's fugues ends at the first exposition (measures 1–6). Handel then treats the subject in another point of imitation in which he explores new ways to combine the subject with itself in counterpoint. Next, he alternates fugal expositions with homophonic declamation.

The second fugue aptly illustrates the furious assailant, who goes blindly "from Crime to Crime," with a subject that, after a rising second, leaps down a minor seventh (measure 56), and an episode that meanders over a chromatic bass (measures 73–78). The last fugue (measure 94) portrays Saul's headstrong drive to self-destruction. A partial return of the previous fugue (measure 111) and full repetition of the last one (measure 137) lead to the final denouement, as the chorus pronounces the moral of the tale in forceful homophony (measure 155).

INSTRUMENT NAMES AND ABBREVIATIONS

The following tables set forth the English, Italian, German, and French names used for the various musical instruments in these scores, and their respective abbreviations.

WOODWINDS

English	Italian	German	French
Piccolo (Picc.)	Flauto piccolo (Fl. Picc.); Ottavino (Ott.)	Kleine Flöte (kl. Fl.)	Petite flûte
Flute (Fl.)	Flauto (Fl.), pl. Flauti; Flauto grande (Fl. gr.)	Flöte (Fl.), pl. Flöten; Große Flöte (gr. Fl.)	Flûte (Fl.)
Alto flute	Flauto alto (Fl. alto); Flauto contralto (fl.c-alto)	Altflöte	Flûte en sol
Oboe (Ob.)	Oboe (Ob.), pl. Oboi	Hoboe (Hb., Hob.), pl. Hoboen; Oboe (Ob.), pl. Oboen	Hautbois (Hb., Hautb.)
English horn (E.H.)	Corno inglese (C. ing., C. ingl., Cor. ingl., C.i.)	Englisches Horn, Englisch Horn (engl. Horn, Egl. H., Englh.)	Cor anglais (C.A., Cor ang.)
Heckelphone		Heckelphon	
Sopranino clarinet	Clarinetto piccolo (clar. picc.)		
Clarinet (C., Cl., Clt., Clar.)	Clarinetto (Cl., Clar.), pl. Clarinetti (Cltti.)	Klarinette (Kl., Klar.), pl. Klarinetten; Clarinette (Cl., Clar.)	Clarinette (Cl.)
Alto clarinet (A. Cl.)			
Bass clarinet (B. Cl.)	Clarinetto basso (Cl. b., Cl. bas., Cl. basso, Clar. basso); Clarone (Clne.)	Bass Klarinette, Bassklarinette (Bkl., B.-Kl., Basskl.), Bassclarinette (Basscl., B.-Cl.)	Clarinette basse (Cl. bs.)
Contrabass clarinet (Cb. Cl.)			
Saxophone (Sax.) [soprano, alto (A. Sax.), tenor (T. Sax.), baritone (Bari. Sax.), bass]	Sassofone	Saxophon [Sopransaxophon (Ssax.), Altsaxophon (Asax.), Tenor-saxophon (Tsax.)]	Saxophone
Bassoon (Bn., Bsn., Bssn.)	Fagotto (Fag., Fg.), pl. Fagotti	Fagott (Fag., Fg.), pl. Fagotte	Basson (Bn., Bssn., Bon.)
Contrabassoon (C. Bn., C. Bsn.); Double bassoon (D. Bsn.)	Contrafagotto (Cfg., C. Fag., Cont. F.)	Kontrafagott (K.-Fag., Kfg.); Contrafagott (Contrafag.)	Contrebasson (C. bssn.)
Cornett	Cornetto	Zink	Cornet-à-bouquin

BRASS

English	Italian	German	French
Horn, French horn (Hr., Hn.)	Corno (Cor., C., Cr.), pl. Corni	Horn (Hr.), pl. Hörner (Hörn., Hrn.)	Cor; Cor à pistons
Trumpet (Tpt., Trpt., Trp., Tr.)	Tromba (Tr., Trb.), pl. Trombe (Trbe., Tbe.); Clarino, pl. Clarini	Trompete (Tr., Trp., Trpt., Tromp.), pl. Trompeten	Trompette (Tr., Trp.)
Piccolo trumpet	Tromba piccola (Tr. picc.)		
Bass trumpet	Tromba bassa (Tr. bas.)		
Cornet	Cornetta, pl. Cornetti	Kornett	Cornet à pistons (C. à p., Pist.)
Trombone (Tr., Tbe., Tbn., Trb., Trm., Trbe.) [alto, tenor]	Trombone (Trbn., Tromb.), pl. Tromboni (Tbni., Trbni., Trni.) [alto, tenore]	Posaune (Ps., Pos.), pl. Posaunen [alt, tenor]	Trombone (Tr., Trb.)
Bass trombone (B. Tbn.)	Trombone basso (Trne. B.)	Bass Posaune	
Contrabass trombone	Cimbasso (Cimb.)		
Baritone horn (Baritone, Bar.)			
Euphonium (Euph.)			
Tenor tuba		Tenortuba	
Tuba (Tb., Tba.)	Tuba (Tb., Tba.), pl. Tube	Tuba (Tb.); Basstuba (Btb.)	Tuba (Tb.)
Ophicleide	Oficleide	Ophikleide	Ophicléide

STRINGS

English	Italian	German	French
Violin (V., Vl., Vn., Vln., Vi.)	Violino (V., Vl., Vn., Vln., Viol.), pl. Violini (Vni.); Viola da braccio	Violine (V., Vl., Vln., Viol.), pl. Violinen; Geige (Gg.), pl. Geigen	Violon (V., Vl., Vln., Vn., Von.)
Viola (Va., Vl., pl. Vas.)	Viola (Va., Vla., Vl.), pl. Viole (Vle.)	Bratsche (Br.), pl. Bratschen	Alto (A., Alt.)
Violoncello (Vcl., Vc.); Cello, pl. Celli	Violoncello (Vc., Vcl., Vcll., Vcllo., Vlc.), pl. Violoncelli	Violoncell (Vc., Vcl., Violinc.), pl. Violoncelli (Vcll.); Cell.	Violoncelle (Vc., Velle., Vlle., Vcelle.)
Contrabass (Cb.); Double bass (D. B., D. Bs.); String bass; Bass viol	Contrabasso (Cb., C. B.), Basso, pl. Contrabassi or Bassi (C. Bassi, Bi.); Violon, violone [may also designate or include cello or bass viola da gamba]	Kontrabass (Kb., K.-B.), pl. Kontrabässe; Contrabass (Contrab., C.-B., C. B.); Bass, pl. Bässe	Contrebasse (C. B.)
Viola da gamba; Viol; Gamba	Viola da gamba	Gambe	Viole
Bass violin			Basse de violon

PERCUSSION

English	Italian	German	French
Percussion (Perc.)	Percussione	Schlagzeug (Schlag., Szg.)	Batterie (Batt.)
Timpani (Timp.); Kettledrums (K. D.)	Timpani (Timp., Tp.)	Pauken (Pk.)	Timbales (Timb.)
Snare drum (S. D., Sn. Dr.) [soprano, alto, tenor]; Side drum	Tamburo piccolo (Tamb. picc.); Tamburo militare (Tamb. milit.); Tamburo (Tro.)	Kleine Trommel (Kl. Tr.)	Caisse claire (C. cl.); Tambour militaire (Tamb. milit.)
Tenor drum (Ten. Dr., T. D.)	Cassa rullante	Rührtrommel	Caisse roulante
Indian drum			
Tom-tom		Tomtom (Tom.)	
Tumba; Conga drum; Quinto		Tumba	
Bongos			
Caja			
Cuica			
Bass drum (B. drum, Bass dr., Bs. Dr., B. D.)	Gran cassa (Gr. Cassa, Gr. C., G. C.); Cassa (C.); Gran tamburo (Gr. Tamb.)	Große Trommel (Gr. Trommel, Gr. Tr.)	Grosse caisse (Gr. c., G. C.)
Tambourine (Tamb.)	Tamburino (Tamb.)	Schellentrommel, Tamburin	Tambour de Basque (T. de Basq., T. de B., Tamb. de Basque), Tambourin (Tambin., Tin.)
Lion's roar			
Cymbals (Cym., Cymb.)	Piatti (P., Ptti., Piat.); Cinelli	Becken (Beck.)	Cymbales (Cym., Cymb.)
Traps			
Suspended cymbal (Sus. cym., Susp. cymb.)		Becken-freihängend	
Sizzle cymbal (Sizz. cym.)			
Hi-Hat (HH)			
Tam-Tam (Tam-T.); Gong	Tam-Tam (Tam-T., T-tam)	Tam-Tam, Tamtam	Tam-Tam
Triangle (Trgl., Tri.)	Triangolo (Trgl.)	Triangel (Trgl.)	Triangle (Triang.)
Anvil			
Glockenspiel (Glocken.)	Campanelli (Cmp., Campli.)	Glockenspiel (Glsp.)	Carillon
Bells; Tubular bells (Tub. bells); Chimes	Campane (Cam., Camp., Cmp.); sing. Campana (Cna.)	Glocken	Cloches
Agogó			

PERCUSSION (continued)

English	Italian	German	French
Japanese bells	Campanelli giapponesi (Camp. giapp.)		
Cowbells	Cencerro	Kuhglocken	Sonnailles
Sleighbells	Sonagli	Schellen	Grelots
Crotales (Crot.); Antique Cymbals	Crotali; Piatti antichi	Antiken Zimbeln	Cymbales antiques (Cym. ant.)
Xylophone (Xyl., Xylo.)	Xilofono, Silofono	Xylophon (Xyl.)	Xylophone (Xyl.)
Xylorimba			Xylorimba
Vibraphone (Vibr.)			Vibraphone (Vibr.)
Marimba			
Woodblock (Wd. Blk.)	Cassa di legno	Holzblock, Holztrommel (HzTr.)	Bloc de bois
Chinese blocks			
Slap stick			
Rattle			
Claves			
Raspador			
Gourd			
Maracas; Maraca			Maracas (Mrc.)
Shaker			
Gua gua			
Siren			
Whistle			

OTHER INSTRUMENTS

English	Italian	German	French
Harp (Hp., Hrp.)	Arpa (A., Arp.); Harpa	Harfe (Hfe., Hrf.), pl. Harfen	Harpe (Hp.)
Piano (Pno., Pa.)	Pianoforte (P.-f., Pft., Pfte.); Piano	Klavier (Klav.)	Piano
Celesta (Cel.)	Celesta (Cel.)	Celesta (Cel.)	Céleste
Harpsichord	Cembalo (Cemb.); Clavicembalo	Cembalo	Clavecin
Organ (Org.)	Organo (Org.) [Organo di legno is an organ with wooden pipes]	Orgel	Orgue
Harmonium		Harmonium (Harm.)	
Synthesizer			
Guitar (Gtr.)	Chitarra	Gitarre (Git.)	Guitare (Guit.)
Electric Guitar (Elec. Guit.)			
Lute	Lauto, leuto, liuto	Laute	Luth
Theorbo	Teorba; Chitarrone	Theorb; Chitarron	Téorbe
Archlute	Arcileuto	Erzlaute	Archiluth
Banjo		Banjo (Bjo.)	

Transposing instruments and timpani tunings are indicated using the following pitch names:

English	C	Db	D	Eb	E	F	G	Ab	A	Bb	B
Italian	Do	Reb	Re	Mib	Mi	Fa	Sol	Lab	La	Sib	Si
French	Ut	Réb	Ré	Mib	Mi	Fa	Sol	Lab	La	Sib	Si
German	C	Des	D	Es	E	F	G	As	A	B	H

For transposing instruments, if the music is written in C major, it will sound in the designated key; thus "in A" means that a notated C will sound as A, and every notated pitch will sound a minor third lower than written. Horns, clarinets in Bb and A, and trumpets in Bb sound lower than written; clarinets in D and Eb and trumpets in D and F sound higher than written. English horns are in F, sounding a fifth lower than written; alto flutes are in G, sounding a fourth lower.

GLOSSARY OF SCORE AND PERFORMANCE INDICATIONS

For a glossary of general music terms, including terms used in the commentaries, see *A History of Western Music*, 9th ed.

a, à The phrases a 2 (à 2), a 3 (à 3), and so on, indicate that the music is to be played or sung by 2, 3, or more players or singers.

A Alto or altus.

à deux cordes On two strings; double stop, playing on two strings simultaneously.

a tempo At the (basic) tempo; marks a return to the main tempo, usually after a ritardando or other temporary change.

a tempo giusto At a moderate tempo.

accompagnato (accomp.) In a continuo part, this indicates that the chord-playing instrument resumes (cf. tasto solo).

adagio Slow, leisurely.

ad libitum (ad lib.) An indication giving the performer liberty; for example, to vary from strict tempo or to include or omit the part of some voice or instrument.

affetti Add expressive ornamentation.

allegretto A moderately fast tempo (between allegro and andante).

allegro A rapid tempo (between allegretto and presto).

alto, altus (A.) The deeper of the two main divisions of women's (or boys') voices; in vocal music in four or more parts, a part above the tenor and below the highest voice.

andante A moderately slow tempo (between adagio and allegretto).

andare Go. In Landini's ballata *Non avrà ma' pietà* (p. 173), "andare" marks the beginning of the piedi (b sections) in the untexted parts, indicating where to return for the repetition of the b section with new text.

animé Animated.

assai, assez Very.

audacieusement Audaciously.

avec With.

B Bass, basso, bassus, basse, or basse-contre.

bass, basso, bassus, basse, basse-contre (B.) The lowest part in a vocal or instrumental work, or a low male voice.

basse-continue, basso continuo (B.C., Bc) See *continuo*.

basso See *bass*.

basso per l'organo Basso seguente played on the organ.

basso seguente (B.S.) Continuo part, usually optional, that follows the lowest note sounding in the ensemble.

bassus See *bass*.

B.S. Basso seguente.

burden In English polyphony, a refrain.

C Cantus or canto.

cantabile (cant.) In a singing style.

cantate Sung. In Gabrieli's *In ecclesiis* (p. 521), "cantate" marks the first time the *capella* (chorus) sings outside the refrain Alleluia.

cantus, canto (C.) In Renaissance and seventeenth-century music, the highest part in a vocal work.

capella Choir or group of singers.

chant In French vocal music, a verse, used in alternation with *rechant* (refrain).

chiuso Closed ending; see *open and closed endings*.

choeur Chorus.

choro (pl. chori) Chorus.

chorus (1) Group of singers, normally several on each part. (2) In Renaissance and Baroque music, a group of instrumentalists, each playing a separate part, or a group of singers, with one or more singers on each part.

cinquiesme Fifth part in a polyphonic vocal work.

con With.

con discrezione With discretion, or ad libitum.

continuo (Con., Cont.) An instrumental accompaniment consisting of a bass line, usually together with figures designating the chords to be played above them. In general practice, the chords are played on a lute, theorbo, harpsichord, or organ, and often a viola da gamba or cello doubles the bass notes.

contra Contratenor.

contratenor (Co., Ct., CT) In medieval and Renaissance music, the name given to the third voice part that was added to the basic two-voice texture of cantus and tenor, often having the same range as the tenor, which it frequently crosses.

contratenor altus, contratenor bassus In Renaissance polyphony, contratenor parts that lie relatively high (altus) or low (bassus) in comparison to the tenor; also simply called *altus* and *bassus*.

corda, corde String on a string instrument.

coro Chorus.

couplet In a rondeau, a passage heard between statements of the refrain.

crescendo (cresc.) Increasing in volume.

Ct., CT Contratenor.

D Duplum, discantus, or dessus.

da capo (D.C., D.C. al Fine) Repeat from the beginning, usually up to the indication *Fine* (end).

dal segno (D.S.) Repeat from the sign, usually up to the indication *Fine* (end).

de Of.

déclamation mesurée Measured declamation, in tempo.

decrescendo (decresc., decr.) Decreasing in volume.

dessus (D) Treble.

discantus (D) In Renaissance polyphony, the highest part in a vocal work; cantus.

doux Gentle, soft.

du Of the.

due chori Both choruses.

duplum (D., Du.) In medieval polyphonic music, the first voice composed over the tenor.

e And.

ergänzt Restored or completed by the editor.

esclamazione (escl.) An embellishment consisting of a decrescendo on a note, followed by a sforzando.

espressivo Expressively.

et And.

f. Folio.

fauxbourdon (faulx bourdon) Three-voice texture in the Renaissance in which two voices are written, moving mostly in parallel sixths and ending each phrase on an octave, while a third unwritten voice is sung in parallel perfect fourths below the upper voice. Also used for the unwritten voice in such a texture.

ff. Folios.

fine End, close; marks the end of a piece in which the first section repeats after a later section is heard.

folio (fol., f.) A leaf of a bound manuscript; "fol. 10" means the front side of the tenth leaf of the manuscript, and "fol. 10v" (v for *verso*) is the back side of the same leaf.

forte, fort (f) Loud.

fortissimo (ff) Very loud.

giusto Moderate.

grand choeur Large chorus; used in contrast to *petit choeur*, indicates at least three singers per part.

grave Slow, solemn.

gravement Gravely, solemnly.

groppo, groppo al alta Trill on the upper note.

haute-contre (HC) Contratenor altus or alto part in vocal music; in instrumental music, second-highest part.

Instrumentalvarianten Variant readings in the parts for instruments that diverge from the vocal parts.

languissamment Languidly.

larghetto Slightly faster than largo.

largo A very slow tempo.

lentement Slowly.

lento A slow tempo (between andante and largo).

ma But.

ma non troppo But not too much.

marqué Marked, with emphasis.

meno mosso Less fast.
mezzo forte (*mf*) Moderately loud.
mezzo piano (*mp*) Moderately soft.
motetus In medieval polyphonic music, especially in motets, the texted voice part just above the tenor.
M.S. Manuscript.

non Not.

octavus Eighth part in a polyphonic vocal or instrumental work.
open and closed endings In medieval music, two different endings for a repeated section, the first (open, ouvert, verto) ending on a pitch above the final of the mode, the second (closed, clos, chiuso) ending with a full cadence on the final.
orchestra Ensemble of strings with more than one player on each string part, often with other instruments as well.
organal voice (vox organalis) In an organum, the voice that is added above or below the original chant melody.

pedal On an organ, the pedals are a keyboard played with the feet.
pes In English medieval polyphony, a tenor, not from chant, usually with a short repeating melody.
petit choeur Small chorus, probably with one singer per part.
pianissimo (*pp*) Very soft.
piano (*p*) Soft.
più More.
più mosso, più vivace Faster.
pizzicato On a string instrument, plucked with the finger instead of played with the bow.
plus More.
poco (un poco) Little, a little.
presto A very quick tempo, faster than allegro.
prima, primus, primum First.
prima pars First part of a piece in two or more large sections.
principal voice (vox principalis) In an organum, the voice that carries the original chant melody.
principale (pr.) Principal, solo.
pupitre Music stand; in an orchestra, "un pupitre" (one stand) is two players of a string instrument.

Q Quadruplum, quintus, quinto, or quinte.
quadruplum (Q.) In medieval polyphony, the fourth voice, added to tenor, duplum, and triplum.
quintus, quinto, quinte, quintus pars (Q.) Fifth part in a polyphonic vocal or instrumental work.

R Ritornello.
rechant Refrain.
récit (1) A passage for solo voice. (2) Recitative.
recitando Sing in the manner of a recitative.
recitative, récitatif (recit.) A vocal style designed to imitate and emphasize the natural inflections of speech; or a passage in that style.
refrain Recurring line(s) of text set to a recurring melody or passage.
reprise (Rep.) A repetition. In French Baroque dances, "Reprise" is used to highlight the point to which the player must return to begin the repetition of the second half of the dance.
ritardando (rit., ritard.) Gradually slackening in speed.
ritenuto Held back; implies a more sudden slowing than ritardando.
ritornello (R., ritor.) (1) In a fourteenth-century madrigal or caccia, the closing section. (2) In sixteenth- and seventeenth-century vocal music, instrumental introduction or interlude between sung stanzas. (3) In an aria or similar piece, an instrumental passage at the beginning that recurs several times, like a refrain. (4) In a concerto fast movement, the recurring thematic material played at the beginning by the full orchestra and repeated in shortened or varied form throughout and at the end of the movement.

S Soprano or superius.
sciolto Staccato; to be played detached.
secondus, secundum Second, as in the second violin part.
secunda pars Second part of a piece in two or more large sections.
segno Sign in form of 𝄋 indicating the beginning and end of a section to be repeated.
sempre Always, continually.
senza Without.

senza misura (senza mis.) Free of regular meter.

septimus Seventh part in a polyphonic vocal or instrumental work.

sextus Sixth part in a polyphonic vocal or instrumental work.

sforzando, sforzato (*sfz*, *sf*) With sudden emphasis.

sinfonia, symphonie Instrumental introduction to or interlude in a vocal piece.

solo, solus Part for one singer or instrumentalist; also used to alert the accompanying part, such as the continuo, of a solo passage.

soprano (Sop., S.) The uppermost part, or the voice with the highest range.

sordino, sordini (sord.) Mute.

sourdines With mutes.

superius The uppermost part in a polyphonic vocal or instrumental work.

symphonie See *sinfonia*.

T Tenor, tenore, or taille.

tacet Be silent; rest throughout a passage.

taille In French vocal or instrumental music, the tenor part.

Takt Measure.

tardo Slow.

tasto solo In a continuo part, this indicates that only the string instrument plays; the chord-playing instrument is silent.

tempo The speed or relative pace of the music.

tempo primo (tempo Io) At the original tempo.

tenor (T., ten.) (1) In medieval and some Renaissance polyphony, the main structural voice, usually the lowest voice, carrying the chant or other borrowed melody if there is one, and serving as the foundation for the other voices. (2) In later polyphony and choral music, the second

voice from the bottom of the texture. (3) Relatively high male voice or part.

tenor bassus The lower of two tenor parts in a polyphonic work.

tenore Italian for tenor (2) or tenor (3).

tiple Spanish for treble.

todas All, tutti.

tous All, tutti.

tranquillo Quiet, calm.

treble (Tr.) (1) The highest part in a polyphonic vocal or instrumental work. (2) A high voice, especially a soprano, or a part written for high voice or soprano.

très Very.

trill (trillo, tr., t.) The rapid alternation of a given note with the note above it.

trillo (tr.) In Italian vocal music of the late sixteenth and very early seventeenth centuries, a vocal ornament consisting of rapid repetition on a single note.

trillo longo Long trill.

triplum In medieval polyphonic music, a voice part above the tenor and duplum.

troppo Too much.

tutti Literally, "all"; usually means all the instruments or singers in a given category as distinct from a solo part.

V Verse, as in a psalm verse in Gregorian chant.

verse (1) In Gregorian chant, setting of a psalm verse or similar text. (2) Stanza of a hymn or strophic song, whether or not the song has a refrain.

verso The back side of a leaf in a bound manuscript. See *folio*.

verto Open ending; see *open and closed endings*.

vite, viste Fast.

vivace Quick, lively.

voce Voice, usually implying a single voice.

INDEX OF COMPOSERS

INDEX OF TITLES

INDEX OF FORMS AND GENRES